# A Change Is Gonna Come

## MUSIC, RACE & THE SOUL OF AMERICA

### Craig Werner

CANONGATE

Published in the US by Plume, a member of Penguin Putnam Inc.

First published in Great Britain in 2000 by
Canongate Books Ltd, 14 High Street,
Edinburgh, EH1 1TE

This edition published in 2002

10 9 8 7 6 5 4 3 2 1

*British Library Cataloguing-in-Publication Data*
A catalogue record for this book is available upon request from the
British Library.

ISBN 1 84195 296 6

Printed and bound by Creative Print and Design, Ebbw Vale, Wales.

**CRAIG WERNER** is a professor of Afro-American Studies at the University of Wisconsin, where he teaches courses on Black Music and American Cultural History. He is the recipient of the Chancellor's Award for Excellence in Teaching. He lives in Madison, Wisconsin.

*For Geoff, Tim and
the Students of Afro 156*

# Contents

## Section Four: "And That's the Way That It Is": The Reagan Rules, Hip-hop, and the Megastars

## Section Five: "Holler If Ya Hear Me": In the Nineties Mix

# Introduction: "What's Going On"

"When would the war stop? That's what I wanted to know . . . the war inside my soul." That was the question that inspired Marvin Gaye to create the great 1971 album that provides the title of this section. He could have been speaking for the country. On the cover of *What's Going On*, Gaye gazed out over a nation torn by conflicts: the war in Vietnam and a racial war raging sometimes in the streets, but always in our hearts. Nearly three decades later, we're still looking for answers to Gaye's question. Voices of despair sometimes seem to have carried the day. Difference is real, they say; there's no point in trying to change human nature. War, like the poor, will be with us always. That's just the way it is.

They're wrong.

*A Change Is Gonna Come* is my attempt to help renew a process of racial healing that at times seems to have stopped dead. Like Marvin Gaye, I believe that black music provides a clear vision of how we might begin to come to terms with the burdens of our shared history. During nearly two decades of conversations with students desperately seeking ways to make sense of their lives, I have found that black music and the not-quite-white music that responds to its calls can provide many with insight that allows healing to begin. It's a wisdom grounded in process; it can't be reduced to "Aretha's Little Book of Life," "The Wit and Wisdom of Miles Davis," or "Ten Ways to Beat the Blues." The best way to get a sense of what black music offers is to follow its story through the decades that have shaped the world we live in today.

History never happens in straight lines. The lines connecting events extend across space and time in tangled, irreducible patterns. All forms of storytelling oversimplify the patterns, but music simplifies less than most. Structurally, music mirrors the complications of history. Moving forward through time, music immerses us in a narrative flow, gives us a sense of how what happened yesterday shapes what's happening now. But the simultaneous quality of music—its ability to make us aware of the many voices sounding at a single moment—adds another dimension to our sense of the world. When a jazz trumpeter incorporates a Louis Armstrong riff into her solo or a hip-hop DJ samples James Brown, music transcends time. When a London remix of a Jamaican version of a Curtis Mayfield classic plays in a Tokyo dance club, music conquers space. When "glory hallelujah" is the line that follows "Nobody knows the trouble I see," and no one finds that confusing, music captures the paradoxes of the human heart.

*A Change Is Gonna Come* makes no attempt to tell a definitive story. Rather, I look at what's happened in America since the fifties from as many angles as possible. At times, I stick close to the chronological sequence of events; at others, I deliberately create dialogues between songs released years apart. In all cases, my underlying intention is to suggest useful ways of thinking about the problems that keep America from realizing its own democratic ideals. There are no more compelling statements of human potential than the Declaration of Independence and the Constitution. But, perhaps because the ideals are so visionary, there's probably never been a nation that more consistently failed to live in accord with what it imagined itself to be.

Nowhere has that been clearer than in America's experience with race. From the moment the first slave ship landed at Jamestown in 1619, America has struggled—sometimes heroically, sometimes evasively—with the reality of a multicultural society. The attempt to express the inner meaning of that struggle gives American art its unique power. You can feel it in the novels of Mark Twain and Ralph Ellison, Herman Melville and William Faulkner, Toni Morrison and Leslie Silko, in the collages of Romare Beardon and the photographs of Dorothea Lange. But its strongest expression comes in music. Since the barriers imposed by legal segregation began to come down after World War II, music has provided a unique forum for dialogue—sometimes harmonious, sometimes angry—between black and white voices.

The primary goal of *A Change Is Gonna Come* is to tell the story of that beautiful and complicated dialogue. It's a story of how music radiates healing energies, how gospel and soul and reggae help us imagine a world where we can get along without turning off our minds. But it's also a story about how history erodes hope, how the lures of money and power tempt us to betray our best selves. And how often we give in.

The music of the last four decades refuses to forget either part of the story. If we forget where we've come from, we have no chance of knowing who we really are, what we can become. Frequently the music tells a truer story than the ones recorded in the newspapers or broadcast on TV. Rapper Chuck D's claim that "rap music is black America's CNN" applies equally well to the gospel music that powered the freedom movement, the soul music that carried the message of love through the sixties, the funk, reggae, and disco that testify to the confused crosscurrents of the seventies.

It's not just a black thing. *A Change Is Gonna Come* places black music at the center of the story for reasons that have a lot to do with history and nothing to do with the melanin content of an individual's skin. Most of the people taken into slavery came from West African cultures that understood how developing individual character contributed to the health of the community. When West Africans confronted the nightmare realities of slavery, they improvised ways of surviving that have come down to us through the voices of Mahalia Jackson and Sam Cooke, the instruments of Jimi Hendrix and John Coltrane, and the communal explorations of Sly and the Family Stone and the Wu-Tang Clan. While those strategies are grounded in the specific history of blacks in what Bob Marley called "Babylon," they're available to anyone who doesn't call Babylon home. Bruce Springsteen, Madonna, and Steve Cropper have their place in the story that, today, is being passed on by blacks and whites, Asians and Latins. The spirit doesn't check IDs.

In telling this story, *A Change Is Gonna Come* uses a conceptual framework derived from gospel, jazz, and the blues. Together, the musical "impulses"—the term originates with Ralph Ellison—provide a way of thinking through the most fundamental human problems. Readers who prefer to begin with the concepts can consult the definition sections (see pages 28, 68, and 132) before plunging into the story. The blues, jazz, and gospel impulses highlight black music's refusal to simplify reality or devalue emotion. Even when they force you to accept uncomfortable truths, the blues never explain away how things feel. They make you deal with the evil in the world and the evil in your head, help you find the strength to get up and face another blues-haunted day. Testifying to the power of love, gospel gives us the courage to keep on pushing for a redemption that is at once spiritual and political. Gospel reminds us we're all in it together, though the definition of "we" varies. Jazz is innovation; it refuses to accept the way things are, envisions ways of reaching a higher ground we're only beginning to be able to imagine.

Marvin Gaye's *What's Going On* gives voice to all of these currents. Introducing Gaye's main concerns, the title cut opens the album with the sounds of a party, the celebration of black family and community. But the three-song sequence that continues with "What's Happening Brother?" and "Flying High" collapses the distance between the gospel feeling of unity and the isolation experienced by a Vietnam veteran returning to a world of unemployment, political confusion, and drugs. As the story unfolds, Gaye moves back and forth between the visionary hopes of "Save the Children" and "God Is Love" and the hard-edged realism of "Mercy Mercy Me" and "Inner City Blues." Warning of a time "when the world won't be singing," he calls out in words that have echoed down the decades: "Makes me wanna holler / throw up both my hands." However bleak the prospect, the sound of the music holds out the hope that, someday, we'll arrive in that promised land where our actions correspond to our ideals.

Marvin Gaye didn't make it. The last years of his life disintegrated into a hell of self-doubt and withdrawal. When he was shot and killed by his father, it seemed all too emblematic of what had happened in black America since the sixties. Part of the story I'm telling has to do with lost hope, the death of the dream shared by Martin Luther King, Ella Baker, Malcolm X, and the hundreds of thousands who responded to their calls. When you look at the personal stories of the men and women who created the music, there's a temptation to sign on with the cynics.

Too many have died. Sam Cooke, Flo Ballard of the Supremes, Jimi Hendrix, Phyllis Hyman, John Coltrane, Janis Joplin, Elvis, Dinah Washington, Tupac Shakur, Kurt Cobain, Motown's brilliant bass player James Jamerson, Jim Morrison, Tammi Terrell, Peter Tosh, Memphis drummer Al Jackson, DJ Scott LaRock, Sylvester, John Lennon, Biggie Smalls, Otis Redding, Bob Marley, Donny Hathaway. The deaths of the stars sometimes obscure the many thousands gone whose names most of us don't know. The names lined up in military rows on the black marble walls of the Vietnam memorial, the names embroidered in the heartbreaking and celebratory squares of the AIDS quilt, the names of the young black men in the newspaper reports of drive-by shootings, the women whose lives are destroyed by rape and abuse. It doesn't detract from our sadness over Tupac or Donny Hathaway or Marvin Gaye, to understand their deaths as part of a larger tragedy.

But the music insists that tragedy isn't the whole story. *A Change Is Gonna Come* seeks out moments of resistance, celebration, joy. It's important to savor even the momentary victories, to remember what worked and why. To adapt the lessons to the changing world we'll encounter tomorrow and the day after. To understand that the struggle for love and justice will be a long one, but that, for anyone who resists the notion that humanity can be measured in dollars, it's what makes life worth living. Even as we mourn the dead, it's crucial that we honor the living, the elders who have shown us the path and the new voices who continue to explore how to keep it real: George Clinton, Aretha Franklin, Rakim, John Fogerty, Stevie Wonder, Cassandra Wilson, Prince, Dianne Reeves, Al Green, Dorothy Love Coates, KRS-One, Mavis Staples, Bruce Springsteen, Curtis Mayfield.

In the course of writing this book, I was privileged to speak with many of the musicians who have given the music its meaning. All of them insisted that music can help bring the world back into harmony. Charles Wright of the Watts 103rd Street Rhythm Band, best known for "Express Yourself," stated the shared feeling with unmistakable intensity: "Our purpose is to try to keep the healing process going. I want to make music of the nature of the healing heart. Music has to do with the heart and the bloodstream." Like many who have watched the changes in America since the sixties, Wright fears for the future: "I feel like we're missing out, like we're going in the wrong direction. Music has to turn it back in the right direction. If we don't then the world is on its way to doom."

When Mavis Staples echoes Wright, she's drawing on her long experience in the worlds of gospel, soul, and popular music. "It's healing, music is healing," testifies one of the few artists who can claim to have traveled the gospel highway during the sixties, had number one soul hits in the seventies, and recorded with Prince in the nineties. Mavis's belief that the key to realizing music's healing power lies in an understanding of history carries special weight: "We have a history that needs to be known. We have been through some stuff and the world needs to know about it. The stories need to be known to the young people so they can know what we've gone through to get them to where they are."

My deepest hope is that *A Change Is Gonna Come* spreads some of those stories in a way that helps the healing begin. My primary regret is that I simply don't have room to tell all the stories that have made a difference to me. *A Change Is Gonna Come* concentrates on the *public* dimension of the story. Whenever I've had to decide what to include and what to leave out, I've gone with the better-known music, in part because real dialogue requires a shared vocabulary. One of the costs of this approach is that I spend much less time writing about jazz than I spend listening to it. As I wrote this book, I frequently went to Charles Mingus's music, especially "Meditations on Integration" and "Haitian Fight Song," to renew my spiritual energy and intellectual focus. An intensely introspective man, Mingus knew that even the loneliest work takes its meaning from how it relates to the larger world. Capturing the complicated energy of the freedom movement, "Haitian Fight Song" provides a way of thinking about the relationship between intellectual work and social movements. Alone and confused, Mingus gathers his thoughts and begins to test his voice in the bass solo that opens the piece. Gradually other instruments enter, echoing phrases, helping Mingus figure out what works and what doesn't. A compelling rhythm takes shape and Mingus moves out into a public world, calling his community to join in the struggle. The rhythm changes, staggers, regains its focus, encounters resistance, but always moves ahead. As Mahalia Jackson sang in one of her most powerful songs, "Keep your hand on the plow." What it's all about is setting ourselves and our people in motion on what the Staple Singers called the "Freedom Highway."

It's a model and a vision that helped me through the difficult stages of writing *A Change Is Gonna Come*. Often people asked me why a white boy from the Rocky Mountains was spending so much energy, and felt so much passion, for music that wasn't, in any simple sense, his own. Sometimes I responded by quoting what John Fogerty said when I asked him a similar question, "I wasn't born on Tibet or Mars." This is the music I've heard all my life. Sometimes I talked about the fact that I grew up in a home where the freedom movement was taken seriously, where democratic values weren't just words. But the real answer is *A Change Is Gonna Come* itself. The answer isn't a stock phrase, it's a story, the kind of story Mingus tells in "Haitian Fight Song." It's a story about how individual voices find their truest tones when they commune with others, how we come to terms with our limits, share our insights, band together to try and change the world. In "Haitian Fight Song," Mingus creates a complicated soundworld where the voice he found in darkness undergoes changes as other voices enter and leave, in frustration and in triumph. His meaning is clear: We can never separate who we are from the people around us. Their fate is our own.

# Acknowledgments

*A Change Is Gonna Come* represents a momentary pause in a series of interlinking conversations about music that began on the streets of Colorado Springs with Brian Berry, Mike DeLong, Kent Lawyer, and Jim Allen. It's a conversation that has been enriched by the voices of Steve Schultz, Dan Schultz, Michael and Keisha Bowman, Shanna Greene, Donia Allen, David Wright, Gloria Abney, Brian Bischel, Mikki Harris, Yorel Lashley, Duer Sharp, Bill Van Deburg, Kevin Stewart, Mike Reese, Karah Stokes, Mike Allen, Steve Baker, Aja Brown, Sam Chaltain, Tess Scogans, Yasmin Cader, Barbara Ewell, Jerry Speir, Ben Fisher, Eli Goldblatt, Trudi Witonsky, Craig McConnell, Sue Christel, Richard Powers, Nellie McKay, Ron Radano, Sandy Adell, Anthony Stockdale, Malin Pereira, and many others, including the folks down at the Harmony Bar. Missy Kubitschek and Barbara Talmadge will know why this book closes a circle with a long circumference.

For the last decade, the most important part of the conversation for me has grown out of the classes I teach on black music at the University of Wisconsin. The students of Afro-American Studies 156 and 403 have taught me far more than they could possibly have learned. Special thanks to Eric Schumacher-Rasmussen, Ed Pavlic, Melvina Johnson Young, Glenn Berry, Gant Johnson, Scott Sherman, and Lori Leibovich, all of whom taught me to hear the beauty in what I'd sometimes thought was noise. As always, I have been blessed with a wonderful family: my father, my brothers, Brian and Blake, the Nelson clan that's somehow gotten used to me, and my nieces and nephews. My deepest love to my wife, Leslee Nelson, and our daughters, Riah and Kaylee.

I owe a lot to Dave Marsh for helping *A Change Is Gonna Come* become what it is. Among many other things, Dave put me in contact with Greil Marcus, Jon Landau, and Danny Alexander, who provided useful suggestions as the book developed. Howard Fields, Steve

Brown, Sarah Heal, Dave Lieben, and Nancy Humphreys aided in my research. Jeanne Comstock saw to it that words made it from computer to page without catastrophe. Irwin Soonachan of *Goldmine Magazine* generously got me in touch with many of the musicians whose voices carry the story along. Thanks to my agent, Dan Greenberg of James Levine Communications, and my editor, Deborah Brody, both of whom kept reminding me to get out of the way and let the story tell itself.

Finally, *A Change Is Gonna Come* is dedicated to Geoff King, who insisted that the best ideas not be left lying on the table around a pitcher of beer, and Tim Tyson, who, in addition to heroically finishing the pitcher, put the manuscript back on the right path so often he should probably be listed as co-author. It's your turn, guys.

# Section One

## "A Change Is Gonna Come": Mahalia Jackson, Motown, and the Movement

# 1
# The Dream

Everyone knows the image and the words. Standing on the steps of the Lincoln Memorial, Martin Luther King, Jr., wiped his brow in the August heat, challenged the salt-and-pepper crowd spread out before him to create a world where children will "not be judged by the color of their skin but by the content of their character." Beamed by television from the snowcapped Rockies of Colorado to Stone Mountain in Georgia, King's vision of interracial harmony called forth an unprecedented display of shared faith. For one day in 1963, America transcended its history and let freedom ring.

Like its defining snapshot at the March on Washington, the larger story of the freedom movement is familiar if not altogether accurate. Bearing its anthems of redemption down the streets of the civil rights–era South, the movement called out to America's conscience—and the country answered. Repudiating violence, King led the masses of the black South up from the shadows of slavery and segregation. Inspired by King's compelling moral vision, mainstream America heeded the call of King's allies, the Kennedys, and dismantled the barriers separating blacks from whites. Like Lincoln and JFK, King was rewarded for his struggle and his martyrdom with a hallowed place in the gallery of American heroes.

The images and the stories that go with them are so familiar they've lost their meaning. It's not that they're entirely false. King *was* an inspirational leader. For people of all colors committed to racial justice, the sixties *were* a time of hope. You could hear it in the music: in the freedom songs that soared high above and sunk deep within the hearts of the marchers at Selma and Montgomery; in the gospel inflections of Sam Cooke's teenage love songs; in Motown's self-proclaimed sound track for "young America"; in blue-eyed soul and English remakes of the Chicago blues; in Aretha Franklin's resounding call for respect; in Sly Stone's celebration of the everyday people and Jimi Hendrix's vision of an interracial tribe; in John Coltrane's celebration of a love supreme. For brief moments during the decade surrounding King's speech, many of us harbored real hopes that the racial nightmare might be coming to an end.

It didn't. It still hasn't. And there's a bitter irony in the fact that King has become as much a problem as an inspiration for those seeking to fulfill his vision. Reverberating for three decades, invoked by politicians of all races and parties, quoted by his enemies to bolster causes he condemned in life, King's words too often drown out the multitude of voices that made the freedom movement something more than a frozen image on a stamp. Representing the march and the movement requires a montage, not a close-up. When all we can hear are the words of the great man, we miss the deeper sources of the movement's energy.

The story was larger, deeper, more troubling than any one dream. The hope was more complicated, the inspiration more profound, than our public memory admits. To hear the real story, we need to listen carefully to the voices of those who were there, starting with the gospel music that gave the marchers the strength to go on. We can begin, simply enough, by pulling back from the close-up of King's sweat-streaked face and refocusing on a woman standing in the second row, in the shadow of the Great Emancipator. Mahalia Jackson.

# 2
# Mahalia and the Movement

If King gave the movement a vision, Mahalia Jackson gave it a voice. By 1963, she was nearly as well known as King among both whites and the blacks whose support had lifted her out of poverty and obscurity. During the mid-fifties, Mahalia's weekly CBS radio show brought gospel music into the homes of white Americans who would never have gone near the black churches of New Orleans and Chicago where she had learned to sing. Mahalia achieved the nearly impossible feat of becoming a major star without crossing over into the secular world. On occasion, she agreed to sing pop songs like "Danny Boy" and "The Green Leaves of Summer," but she steadfastly resisted the producers who wanted to cash in on her powerful voice in the new interracial market for rhythm and blues.

Like Ray Charles, who played a crucial role in opening that market, Mahalia modeled her style on the singing of the black sanctified churches. Often the poorest churches in poor communities, sanctified churches valued religious ecstasy more highly than polished phrasing or perfect pitch. At times, a sanctified church could erupt with a collective energy that transformed centuries of bitter hardship into moments of pure connection—with self, community, and the soul-deep presence of the Lord. Hinted at in Brother Ray's "I Got a Woman"—a secular remake of the gospel classic "There's a Man Going Round Taking Names"—such moments were the core of what the white audience was just beginning to hear in Little Richard's ecstatic whoops, lifted straight from gospel singer Marion Williams. Although Mahalia showed little interest in the spiritually suspect rock and roll, she understood the point: "I believe the blues and jazz and even the rock and roll stuff got their beat from the Sanctified Church. We Baptists sang sweet . . . but when those Holiness people tore into 'I'm So Glad Jesus Lifted Me Up!' they came out with real jubilation." Mahalia's resistance helped maintain her strong connection with the churchgoing black community—still a large majority in the early sixties—even as she gained the ear of whites ranging from my grandparents listening to her radio show in rural South Dakota, where I first heard her voice, to John Kennedy, who hosted her at the White House.

Mahalia's presence at the Lincoln Memorial on that blistering August afternoon in 1963 was no accident. During the early days of the Montgomery bus boycott, Mahalia met King and Ralph Abernathy at the 1955 National Baptist Convention meeting in Denver. When the two young ministers asked her to lend her voice to the struggle, she embraced the opportunity. In Montgomery, she stayed with the Abernathys and performed at one of the rallies that defined the movement. Looking back, it's difficult to imagine the pressures at work on each black person who found the courage to attend that rally. The threat of physical violence was real. Two days after Mahalia left Montgomery, a dynamite bomb went off outside the bedroom where she had slept. But beyond that, the black residents of Montgomery faced the constant threat of economic retaliation. In an economy controlled by whites, being branded a troublemaker meant being fired. And retribution could be extended to family members— elderly parents, children starting out in the world. It could mean a hasty midnight departure for the North—or a long, slow parade to the local cemetery.

Again and again, movement veterans testify to the central role gospel music played in helping them find the strength to overcome their fears. So it was crucial that Mahalia was physically present while the police and the Ku Klux Klan—not always two distinct groups in the Deep South—circled the church. That night in Montgomery, Mahalia sang "I've Heard of a City Called Heaven" and "Move On Up a Little Higher."

Her choices illuminate the political power of gospel music, which is obvious to most blacks and obscure to most whites. When Mahalia sings that she's going to make heaven her home, she's most certainly singing about saving her soul. When she moves on up, her destination is a place by the side of Jesus. But she's also, and without any sense of contradiction, singing about freedom, moving up to full participation in American society. Heaven is heaven, but it's also a seat at the front of the bus. When, in a classic gospel cut that rocks as hard as anything the Rolling Stones ever played, Mahalia promises that she's going to "walk in Jerusalem," none of the cooks and maids whose marching feet carried the movement misunderstood her.

The strategy of expressing dangerous political messages under the cover of, and in concert with, religious lyrics extends back to slavery times. For Southern black communities whose cultural traditions had been passed down through the generations, the ultimate goal was freedom. The use of double meanings, accessible only to those attuned to the cultural code, developed as a survival strategy. Any slave openly expressing dissatisfaction, much less calling for resistance or rebellion, risked beating, whipping, death. Still, slaves *did* resist—sometimes spectacularly, as with the Nat Turner rebellion of 1831, which resulted in the deaths of fifty-five whites in rural Virginia. But, in large part because hundreds of blacks were killed in retribution for Turner's revolt, resistance typically took less direct forms: work slowdowns, which whites attributed to black "laziness"; failure to follow simple directions, attributed to black "stupidity"; "lost" property, blamed on black propensity for theft. When slaves stood barefoot in a white church and sang to their masters that "everybody talkin' 'bout heaven ain't goin' there," the singers knew whose destination was in question.

Unable to communicate openly in public spaces, slaves developed ways of sharing information that remained invisible to their white masters. Aware that the Christianity they were taught by proslavery ministers counseled endurance on earth in exchange for a heavenly reward, "docile" slaves sang ostensibly passive lyrics like "swing low, sweet chariot, coming for to carry me home." Taking the black song as evidence of the slaves' "childlike" acceptance of their condition, few whites heard the political message. But the slaves knew that the "River Jordan" was also the Ohio River, that the chariot's destinations included Philadelphia, Buffalo, Boston, Canada. "Wade in the Water," one of the most common slave songs and still a gospel standard, provided literal escape instructions for slaves pursued by bloodhounds. When they heard a voice call out "Steal away to Jesus, I ain't got long to stay here," slaves knew that Harriet Tubman used the song as a summons to the Underground Railroad.

Schooled in the cultural traditions of the segregation-era South, Mahalia was deeply aware of the power of masking. Studs Terkel, whose Chicago radio show first introduced her to a large white audience in 1947, recalls: "She explained to me that the spiritual wasn't simply about Heaven over there, 'A City Called Heaven.' No, the city is here, on Earth. And so, as we know, slave songs were code songs. It was not a question of getting to Heaven, but rather to the free state of Canada or a safe city in the North—liberation here on Earth!"

While the songs Mahalia sang in Montgomery testify to the push for liberation, they highlight two very different aspects of that drive. "Move On Up a Little Higher," Mahalia's signature song, sold over two million copies, almost all of them to blacks, when it was released in 1947. Accompanied only by piano and organ, Mahalia carries her audience into a world impervious to the violence and poverty that have torn the black community apart, a world where "it's always howdy howdy and never goodbye," where the saints can lay down their burdens and put on their robes. The quiet confidence that allows Mahalia's voice to move just ahead of the beat, to lead the community, anticipates the more obvious assertive energies underlying the masked messages in "Walk in Jerusalem," "I'm On My Way," and "Walk All Over God's Heaven." The black community's overwhelming affirmation of Mahalia's voice expressed a shared determination grounded in the unshakable knowledge that, in the eyes of God, their struggle was righteous. When Mahalia assured them that his eyes were on the sparrow, that he *would* calm the raging sea, it helped black folks gather their energy. When Mahalia called on her people to keep their hands on the plow, her voice helped them hold the plow, and each other, tight.

Mahalia's powerful voice always carried undertones of something like despair, undertones that provide the emotional center of "I've Heard of a City Called Heaven." Reaching deep into the agonies of black history, the song testifies to losses that, from any earthly perspective, seem too much to bear: the four young girls who died in the Sunday morning bombing of a Birmingham church in 1963; the millions of Africans who died in the cramped holds of the slave ships and whose bones littered the Atlantic. The litany of horrors has been recited so often that it has lost its ability to shock. Almost no one stops to think what it means that during the search for the three murdered civil rights workers whose deaths gave the Freedom Summer of 1964 its symbolic meaning, workers pulled up body after body of black men who had simply been forgotten, whose deaths had never attracted any attention outside the black communities who knew only that they were gone, who could never be sure whether they had been killed or simply run away.

It gets to the point where none of it can be said in words. Yet it is the foundation of black life in America. Even as she dedicated herself to a future in glory, Mahalia refused to forget the past. In "I've Heard of a City Called Heaven," she voices that refusal as a moan. As theologian and social critic Cornel West observes in *The Future of the Race*, the moan lies at the core of black expression:

> . . . it is a guttural cry and a wrenching moan—a cry not so much for help as for home, a moan less out of complaint than for recognition. . . . The deep black meaning of this cry and moan goes back to the indescribable cries of Africans on the slave ships during the cruel transatlantic voyages to America and the indecipherable moans of enslaved Afro-Americans on Wednesday nights or Sunday mornings near god-forsaken creeks or on wooden benches at prayer meetings in makeshift black churches. This fragile existential arsenal—rooted in silent tears and weary lament—supports black endurance against madness and suicide.

When Mahalia sang "I've Heard of a City Called Heaven," she was reaching out for a home, trying to find a way to hold on to the belief that, someday, things would change. That night in Montgomery, as the community gathered in the church prepared to take the movement to a new level, it was crucial that Mahalia acknowledged both the reality of the moan and the determination to "move on up a little higher."

The people heard Mahalia at the same time they heard King. And they found the strength to march out and meet "the man." Often in the name of their ancestors, always for the sake of their children. Eventually, a lot of white folks found the strength to join them. Some of them began to understand the hope inside the moan. The paths of some of the black folks, some of the white folks, led to the steps of the Lincoln Memorial.

The setting for King's speech already resonated with a history that made Mahalia's contribution that shining August day particularly appropriate. In 1939, black concert singer Marian Anderson had presented one of the most politically important concerts of the century from almost exactly the same spot. When the Daughters of the American Revolution denied her permission to sing at still-segregated Constitution Hall, Anderson moved to the Lincoln Memorial, where numerous political figures including Eleanor Roosevelt watched and endorsed her dignified protest. Challenging the nation to live up to its betrayed ideals, Anderson sang "My Country 'Tis of Thee." When King introduced Anderson to sing "He's Got the Whole World in His Hands" twenty-four years later, he was acknowledging that he hadn't made it there entirely on his own. When Mahalia moved to the microphone to sing, she was carrying on a tradition that placed black women and their voices at the center of the freedom struggle.

Between Montgomery and Washington, Mahalia had frequently warmed up crowds for King. The two had developed a kind of ritual where King would gauge the specific energy of a crowd and suggest a song to Mahalia. Before the march, King and Mahalia had tentatively agreed that she would sing Thomas Dorsey's gospel classic "Take My Hand Precious Lord," which Mahalia would later sing at her martyred friend's funeral. But in Washington, just before she was to sing, King leaned over and asked for "I've Been 'Buked and I've Been Scorned." As deeply rooted in the moan as anything Mahalia ever sang, it reminded the crowd just what the price of the ticket had been and would continue to be. As Mahalia began to sing, a low-flying airplane threatened to drown out her voice. But, drawing the energy from her massive frame and from the history that surrounded her at the memorial, Mahalia's voice surmounted its mechanical competition and rose up singing.

No better symbolic moment could have been imagined. As Mahalia's triumph, the triumph of King and the march and the movement, became clear, the crowd began to wave white handkerchiefs. Although the plan had been for her to sing only one song, the crowd called out for more. Mahalia answered with a quietly joyous rendition of "How I Got Over." If "I've Been 'Buked" moans, "How I Got Over" shouts in celebration. The song has been performed by almost every major gospel artist, but it never sounds the same. Compare Mahalia's best-known recording, which resembles "Move On Up" in style and feel, with the equally well-known version by the Swan Silvertones. Lead vocalist Claude Jeter turns the song into a high-energy expression of how individual brilliance can merge with a highly structured, polished background; change a couple of lyrics and the Swan's version could have been a Motown hit. In contrast, Mahalia's version tells of a very different path to the promised land; the slower tempo, the give-and-take between her voice and Mildred Falls's piano, lets you know that movement doesn't have to be feverish, that what's important is to keep on moving. As in Montgomery, Mahalia grounded the experience in both the realities of the past and the belief in a better world to come.

There's a story that credits Mahalia with another role in the success of the March on Washington. The written text of King's speech did not include the "I Have a Dream" section. And, while the crowd was certainly with King throughout, it's clear that without the "dream" section, an improvised version of a set piece he had used several times previously, the speech wouldn't have gone down as a classic. A few days before the march, Mahalia had heard King invoke the "dream" in a speech at the Detroit church pastored by the Reverend C. L. Franklin, Aretha's father. The story goes that, feeling the energy starting to slip away, Mahalia leaned forward to King and whispered, "Tell them about the dream, Martin." At the moment when it seemed most likely that the movement just might get all of us over, it was about Martin *and* Mahalia, the politics *and* the music. Most important, it was about the movement as a whole.

# 3
## "The Soul of the Movement": Calls and Responses

It wasn't just Mahalia's voice, any more than it was just Martin's courage and determination, that gave the movement its strength. The power came from the community that responded so deeply to the songs that, as King wrote, "bind us together . . . help us march together." The songs Mahalia sang were both a call for renewal and a response to her people's courage. Like their ancestors who imagined themselves as Daniel in the lions' den, the black people who made the movement real in the small towns away from the cameras had been turning the moan into music long before Mahalia and Martin forged their gospel politics.

The core of gospel politics lies in the "call and response" principle of African-American culture. The basic structure of call and response is straightforward. An individual voice, frequently a preacher or singer, calls out in a way that asks for a response. The response can be verbal, musical, physical—anything that communicates with the leader or the rest of the group. The response can affirm, argue, redirect the dialogue, raise a new question. Any response that gains attention and elicits a response of its own becomes a new call. Usually the individual who issued the first call responds to the response, remains the focal point of the ongoing dialogue. But it doesn't have to be that way. During the movement, Charles Mingus, fascinated with the political and spiritual implications of call and response, explored ideas of community based on the constant redefinition of the relationship between group and leader in "Wednesday Night Prayer Meeting" and "Three or Four Shades of Blue."

Similar experiments took place in the ranks of the freedom movement, especially in the local communities where the activities organized by the Student Nonviolent Coordinating Committee (SNCC, pronounced "snick") often differed sharply from those planned by King's Southern Christian Leadership Conference (SCLC). Most of the leaders recognized by the media were men, but SNCC organizers were often women who remained in the communities long after the television cameras had moved on to the next event orchestrated by the SCLC leadership from its Atlanta offices. Like the music itself, the grassroots organizing that made the movement happen was rooted in the local culture of the rural black South. And that gave the women who carried that culture a unique sense of the relative value of leadership and community, the balance of call and response.

After several decades of work with leadership-oriented civil rights organizations like the NAACP and the SCLC, which she said had too much of the "pulpit mentality," Ella Baker committed herself to SNCC, saying, "Strong people don't need strong leaders." For Baker and Fannie Lou Hamer, the guiding spirit of the Mississippi Freedom Democratic Party, it was about the "beloved community" as a whole: the women, the poor, the young. Reverend King was magnificent, but if the movement was going to work, it had to work in Holly Springs, Mississippi, and Barnwell, South Carolina, not just in New York, Atlanta, and whatever small town the SCLC chose for its stage.

While the SCLC focused on issues of political strategy, SNCC demonstrated a deeper appreciation of the role of culture, especially music, in the movement. Somehow, communities had to find a way to break the old patterns, transform fear into resistance. SNCC field secretary Phyllis Martin pointed to music's crucial role: "The fear down here is tremendous. I didn't know whether I'd be shot at, or stoned, or what. But when the singing started, I forgot all that. I felt good within myself. We sang 'Oh Freedom' and 'We Shall Not Be Moved,' and after that you just don't want to sit around anymore. You want the world to hear you, to know what you're fighting for!"

One of the original members of the SNCC Freedom Singers, Cordell Reagon, put it even more directly: "Without these songs, you know we wouldn't be anywhere. We'd still be down on Mister Charley's plantation, chopping cotton for 30 cents a day." Bernice Johnson Reagon, then a member of the SNCC Freedom Singers, now presiding spirit of the black womanist group Sweet Honey in the Rock, recalls Ella Baker's influence on her sense of the connection between music and politics: "She urged us as organizers to understand how to create structures that allowed others in our group to also be leaders as well as followers. Her power was in her wanting to increase others' sense of their own power and their access to power." Reagon describes the courage the songs gave to the Freedom Riders jailed in Hinds County, Mississippi; the students participating in SNCC's voter education project in McComb, Mississippi; the marchers in Pine Bluff, Baton Rouge, Selma, Birmingham: "They sang as they were dragged into the streets. They sang in the paddy wagons and in the jails. And they sang when they returned to the Black community's churches for strategy rallies." One of those rallies took place in Dawson, Georgia, where, Reagon remembered, "I sat in a church and felt the chill that ran through a small gathering of Blacks when the sheriff and his deputies walked in. They stood at the door, making sure everyone knew they were there. Then a song began. And the song made sure that the sheriff and his deputies knew we were there. We became visible, our image was enlarged, when the sound of the freedom songs filled all the space in that church."

Mahalia testified to the music's power in her description of the Freedom Riders' arrival at the Montgomery bus depot in 1961. Remembering how "gospel music had given the people courage and spirit when they were in danger" during the early days of King's movement, Mahalia describes the community's fear as "cars were set on fire and bombs were set off, but the Negroes kept right on coming. They filled up the church and began singing hymns and gospel songs." Ultimately, music helped transform the burden into a movement. Mahalia describes Ralph Abernathy rising up and crying, "We don't have to sweat and gasp in here! Those U.S. marshals are supposed to protect us. Open the windows! Let the fresh air in! Let those outside hear us singing a little louder!" No wonder King called music the "soul of the movement."

As a man of the word, King attributed much of music's power to the lyrics, but the local people usually echoed Bernice Johnson Reagon's emphasis on the sound. The interlocking rhythms, the calls and responses, helped create a sense of the "beloved community." If they marched alone, they could be isolated, picked off, made into examples of the futility of resistance. If they found a way to move together, then walking in Jerusalem could be, would be, real.

The words did help focus attention and spread the message beyond the beloved community. Bernice Johnson Reagon's description of music's importance anticipates Chuck D's description of rap as "Black America's CNN": "With the need to gather supporters and disseminate information on the civil rights movement, the music gained increased importance as a means of conveying the nature and intensity of the struggle to audiences outside the geography of the movement."

No one did more to bring the power of the words together with the underlying power of the music than Fannie Lou Hamer, SNCC field secretary from 1963 to 1967 and cofounder of the Mississippi Freedom Democratic Party, which challenged the state's segregationist delegation to the 1964 party convention in Atlantic City. At rallies, demonstrations, and SNCC meetings, Hamer used songs to bring her audience to a sense of connection. One of her favorites was "This Little Light of Mine," another way of phrasing her best-known words: "I'm sick and tired of being sick and tired." One MFDP member described the political impact of her songs: "When Mrs. Hamer finishes singing a few freedom songs one is aware that he has truly heard a fine political speech, stripped of the usual rhetoric and filled with the anger and determination of the civil rights movement."

Both in its political contexts and its more strictly musical settings, call and response moves the emphasis from the individual to the group. For African American performance to work, the performer *must* receive a response, whether the rallying of the beloved community around the women who were redefining everyone as leaders, the chaotic participation of the crowd greeting the landing of George Clinton's P-Funk mothership, or the intense concentration—punctuated by cries of "Yes Lord!" and "Tell it!"—that the Washington audience gave Martin and Mahalia. At its core, call and response is the African American form of critical analysis, a process that draws on the experience and insights of the entire community. The individual maintains a crucial role; a carefully crafted call can lead to the best, most useful insights. But the individual does not necessarily, or ideally, maintain *control.*

Mahalia linked her style with that of the pulpit, emphasizing the way both responded to their people's moan: "It *is* the basic way that I sing today, from hearing the way the preacher would sort of sing in a—I mean, would preach in a cry, in a moan, would shout sort of, like in a chant way—a groaning sound which would penetrate to my heart." When the preacher or singer shapes a call, it is already a response to the shared suffering of the community. If the members of the congregation or audience recognize their own experiences in the call, they respond. The simplest response consists of an "amen," but responses can also call on the preacher to consider something he's overlooked—the role of the sisters, for example—or challenge the singer to take it deeper, make it real. In its pure form, call and response can exist only in the interaction between people present with one another in the real world. But the underlying dynamic can be re-created in various ways. On many of Mahalia's greatest records, Mildred Falls's piano models the response of an aware congregation, walking at her side in the valley of despair, urging her up toward the mountaintop, letting her know, in good times and bad, that she isn't alone. On record, background singers or choirs stand in for the community in the world. The best gospel records always sound *live,* because they capture the uncontainable energy unleashed by call and response, even if they were recorded in studios. The producers and musicians who turned gospel into Chicago soul and Motown never forgot the principle. The calls and responses between Curtis Mayfield and the Impressions came straight from the churches of Chicago's South Side; Smokey Robinson and the Miracles re-created the dialogue between Claude Jeter and the Swan Silvertones. And those sounds had their origins in the slave songs and coded spirituals crafted in the centuries-old struggle for freedom. I second that emotion.

# 4
# Motown:
# Money, Magic, and the Mask

The story of Motown is almost as familiar as the story of Martin Luther King, Jr.'s movement. And just about as trustworthy. The standard version goes something like this. A bunch of poor Detroit natives led by Berry Gordy, Jr., and Smokey Robinson decide it doesn't make any sense that black folks aren't making any money off their music. Paying careful attention to the most successful mainstream labels, they round up the local talent and put out about sixteen thousand number one singles. Motown helps realize the dreams of upward-bound black kids looking to get over like everyone else. White folks open their arms wide to embrace the Supremes, the Four Tops, the Temptations, Martha and the Vandellas, Marvin Gaye, Stevie Wonder, and the Jackson Five. Everybody gets rich and, having put an end to cultural segregation, moves to L.A. No one has to think too much about desolation row. Or, for that matter, look very far for a sound track for a nostalgic movie about the sixties. It's the most compelling version of the American dream ever released in blackface.

Like the standard version of King's movement, it's not entirely wrong. Berry Gordy was certainly trying to cash in on the popularity of black music; the company slogan—"the sound of young America"—told a good bit of the truth. Some of the main players got rich, and most of them made a hell of a lot more money than anyone growing up in black Detroit could have reasonably expected. But if the public image of the movement misrepresents the deeper sources of its strength, the Motown myth obscures some hard truths about how money can undercut gospel politics.

In different ways, gospel and Motown exemplify the underlying drive of black culture in the fifties and sixties. Literary critic Robert Stepto labels the drive "ascent," observing that ever since the days of folk tales and slave spirituals, black expression has placed a central emphasis on the interdependence of freedom and literacy. Black leaders from Frederick Douglass and Sojourner Truth to Malcolm X and Jesse Jackson have said it over and over: No literacy, no freedom.

But literacy is more complicated than the basic ability to read and write. Becoming literate means learning to play the game by the real rules. You can't believe what the white world *says* about how things work. You have to be smart enough to play the game within the game if you want to have any real chance of making it. Part of literacy involves knowing when to put up a good front, when to claim the moral high ground while you're busy greasing palms. Not that ascent counsels cynicism. Handled carefully, the financial part of ascent maintains its link to communal freedom. The trick is to get paid without selling your people.

Stepto sets up a "symbolic geography" of black life based on the movement from the slavery of the "symbolic South" to the relative—but never absolute—freedom of the "symbolic North." In slavery times, the movement was literal; Harriet Tubman and the Underground Railroad carried people up from the slave states to free soil. By the time Berry Gordy, Jr., and Martin Luther King, Jr., appeared on the scene, however, history had complicated the geography. Mississippi remained as far South as it had been a century before, but now it was clear that Harlem, Chicago's South Side, and Boston's Roxbury were North in name only. The cities that their parents had envisioned as "the promised land," second-generation immigrants now laughingly referred to as "up South." The North could be a seat in a classroom at Central High School in Little Rock or at the front of the bus in Montgomery. But it could also be a house in a redlined area of middle-class Chicago.

For Berry Gordy, the North was located in the Top 40 charts, just across the Jim Crow line from the "Race" or "R & B" charts. The North was where they kept the money. Describing the situation just before the founding of Motown, Gordy reflected on the record industry he was about to transform:

> In the music business there had long been the distinction between black and white music, the assumption being that R&B was black and Pop was white. But with Rock 'n' Roll and the explosion of Elvis those clear distinctions began to get fuzzy. Elvis was a white artist who sang black music. What was it? (a) R&B, (b) Country, (c) Pop, (d) Rock 'n' Roll or (e) none of the above.
>
> If you picked C you were right, that is, if the record sold a million copies. "Pop" means popular and if that ain't, I don't know what is. I never gave a damn what else it was called.

Although Gordy shared his awareness of money with numerous other black musicians, he had a unique ability to play the game as it's really played. The stories of Mahalia Jackson and James Brown serve as cautionary tales concerning the costs of failing to master the unwritten rules. Mahalia's obsession with money eventually alienated her from many of her closest friends. Throughout her career, she performed only after she'd been paid in cash. At times, she carried up to $15,000 in her bra, which led to some extremely tense moments when she was pulled over by Southern police. Her obsession with money was legendary among those who knew her, ultimately putting an end to her longtime collaboration with pianist Mildred Falls, whom Mahalia never paid more than a minimal fee. As Brother John Sellers, another of Mahalia's friends alienated by financial problems, remembers: "We didn't do right by [Mildred]. But you couldn't talk to Mahalia about Mildred's situation. She didn't want to hear about her. When Mahalia had money, nobody could talk to her."

James Brown dealt with the money problem by emphasizing the need for black economic self-determination. An ad Brown placed in New York City newspapers just before a 1969 appearance at Madison Square Garden proclaimed: "James Brown is totally committed to black power, the kind that is achieved not through the muzzle of a rifle but through education and economic leverage." Brown's embrace of "black capitalism" grew out of his experience on the "chitlin

circuit": the black theaters and clubs famed for presenting performers with the toughest audiences imaginable. Exercising total control
over his creative product and enforcing band discipline with mone-
tary fines for mistakes, Brown earned nearly universal recognition as
the "hardest-working man in show business" and "the Godfather of
Soul." Even after he'd performed at the inaugural ball for Richard
Nixon, another advocate of black capitalism, Brown steadfastly
maintained, "I'd rather play for my folks at the Apollo than play the
White House." But he definitely cashed Nixon's check.

Although Brown was delighted when his records crossed over
onto the pop charts, he never surrendered the profound suspicions
he'd acquired growing up in South Carolina, where it wasn't any too
clear the white folks had gotten word that slavery had come to an
end. Brown never established a workable relationship with the
mainstream economic system. For all his emphasis on black economic power, he simply didn't take good care of the books. The IRS
wasn't buying his lack of formal education as an adequate excuse, a
point it made absolutely clear in 1968 when it confiscated his files
and billed him for $1,870,000 in back taxes. As a result, he spent a
good part of the seventies struggling to clear his tax problems and
extricate himself from disastrous record contracts.

Berry Gordy wasn't about to make those sorts of mistakes, even if
it meant relying heavily on experienced white accountants to take
care of financial business. Motown's rise presents a perfect parable
of black capitalism in action. For Gordy, attention to economics was
a family tradition. As Motown chronicler Nelson George points out,
the Gordy family moved from Georgia to Detroit for the most unlikely of all reasons: Berry Gordy, Sr., "made too much money,"
thereby attracting the envy of local white merchants who set about
relieving him of the problem. The younger Gordy grew up in an atmosphere where capitalism's primary virtues—competitiveness and
a strong appreciation for the dollar bill—were articles of faith. It's
appropriate that Gordy's first real success in the music business
came when he wrote Barrett Strong's hit "Money (That's What I
Want)." Looking back on his breakthrough, Gordy said: "I was broke
until the time I wrote 'Money'; even though I had many hits, and
there were other writers who had many hits, we just didn't have profits. And coming from a business family, my father and mother always
talked about the bottom line, and simple things, and the bottom
line is profit. You know, are you making money or not?"

Like Booker T. Washington, whom the family's grocery business was named after, Gordy wore whatever mask suited his purposes. Where the masks of Mahalia's music covered a political agenda, Motown's masks were designed to bring the highest price on the open market. Gordy was aware that white folks wanted to get close to the aura of black sexuality, black danger, without putting their self-image at risk. He'd served his apprenticeship in the music world writing songs such as "Lonely Teardrops" and "To Be Loved" for Jackie Wilson, whose sexuality was just dangerous enough to keep him on the wrong side of the color line. At Motown, Gordy kept enough of the blackness—the churchy feel of David Ruffin's lead vocals or the label's signature tambourine—to set Motown apart from bland white pop. But he repressed the sexuality sufficiently to soothe the fears of uneasy parents. Motown worked hard to reassure America that the danger was safely under control, that the songs were about romance, not sex. Diana Ross and Tammi Terrell sounded like nice teenage girls; Eddie Kendricks, David Ruffin, and the young Marvin Gaye aspired to Las Vegas respectability. In a country conditioned to fear black females as Jezebels threatening the sanctity of white marriage, Motown promoted the Supremes as the quintessential "girl group."

Gordy owed much of Motown's success to the Artist Development Department. Under the guidance of etiquette expert Maxine Powers, choreographer Cholly Atkins, and musical director Maurice King, Artist Development transformed talented but unsophisticated teenagers into polished entertainers. If the opportunity to dine at the White House arose, Motown's acts would know which fork to use.

Artist Development had an equally profound impact on the records released on the Motown, Tamla, Gordy, and Anna labels. Singers attended elocution lessons to help them with the press and to make sure white listeners unaccustomed to the sound of black voices could understand the words. Otis Williams of the Temptations recalled: "A producer or a singer might love a great, elaborate vocal riff, but we rarely put them on our records because we knew that most people who bought the records wouldn't be able to sing along to those parts, especially not the white folks."

For all the awareness of the mainstream audience, Motown singles spoke deeply to almost everyone who heard them, black or white. The obvious key to the success was that the label featured some of the most distinctive voices in popular music history. David Ruffin of the Temptations accented syllables that most other singers would have treated as throwaways; Smokey Robinson's delicate lilt reconciled the choir loft and the malt shop; Levi Stubbs of the Four Tops expressed the darkest corners of the blues; Tammi Terrell radiated a girl-next-door sweetness; Martha Reeves added gospel depth to "Dancing in the Street" and "Nowhere to Run." On almost any other label, Marvin Gaye and Stevie Wonder wouldn't have had serious competition.

But great as the singers were, the house musicians informally known as the Funk Brothers contributed at least as much to Motown's success. The lineup varied somewhat, but the core consisted of Earl Van Dyke on keyboards; Robert White or Eddie Willis on guitar; Jack Ashford on vibes and tambourine; Eddie "Bongo" Brown on percussion; Benny Benjamin on drums; and James Jamerson, the least-recognized indisputable genius of soul music, on bass. Frequently playing off dramatic horn charts that established a compelling hook, the percussionists laid down a polyrhythmic foundation while Jamerson played bass lines that remain as stunning today as they were in the sixties. No one has ever matched his ability to improvise bass lines that define a song's spirit. He seemed equally at home with the deceptively simple solo that opens "My Girl"; the dramatic runs that reconcile the pop verses with the gospel chorus of "Nowhere to Run"; the bouncy pop of "Stop! In the Name of Love"; and the intricate funk of "I Was Made to Love Her" and "Ain't Too Proud to Beg." Jamerson attributed his style to influences that ranged from the arcane to the everyday call-and-response rituals of black Detroit:

> My feel was always an Eastern feel, a spiritual thing. Take "Standing in the Shadows of Love." The bass line has an Arabic feel. I've been around a whole lot of people from the East, from China and Japan. Then I studied the African, Cuban, and Indian scales. I brought all that with me to Motown. There were people from the East in my neighborhood. I'd run into Eastern musicians who liked the way I played and they'd keep in contact with me.
>
> I picked up things from listening to people speak, the intonations of their voices; I could capture a line. I look at people walking and get a beat from their movements. . . . There was one of them heavy, funky tunes the Temptations did. . . . I can't remember the name but there was this big, fat woman walking around. She couldn't keep still. I wrote it by watching her move.

The Funk Brothers aren't recognized by the general public in part because Motown's emphasis on marketing stars kept the musicians' names off the album covers. The label's production strategy, a variation on Phil Spector's "wall of sound," made it easy to overlook their individual brilliance. The major Motown producers—Gordy,

Smokey Robinson, the songwriting team of Holland-Dozier-Holland, Norman Whitfield—filled in all available sonic space. Instruments emerge from the mix briefly, but the richly orchestrated harmonies make it difficult to follow particular instruments or voices through entire songs. Yet almost every singer who worked with the Funk Brothers speaks of them in reverential tones. Seconding Otis Williams's claim that the Funk Brothers "must go down in history as one of the best groups of musicians anywhere," Martha Reeves writes: "These musicians were responsible for all of the success of the singers at Motown, because it was their music that inspired us to sing our best with excitement."

Based in the unassuming Gordy house identified only by a carved wooden sign with blue letters reading "HITSVILLE U.S.A.," the Motown production style expressed the communal dynamic that almost everyone who was there in the early years describes as "magic." Musicians hung out at Hitsville at all hours of the day and night. When a song was ready to be recorded, whoever happened to be around chipped in. No one minded being called out of bed to contribute a riff or lay down another take. Major stars sang backup and provided handclaps on each other's records. Disputes over billing, favoritism, and royalty payments eventually soured many of the original Motown artists, but at the start they cherished their own beloved community.

The best emblem of that community may have been the Motown Revue, which toured the South late in 1962, when memories of the vicious attacks on the Freedom Riders were fresh in everyone's minds. A lineup including Mary Wells, the Supremes, the Miracles, the Temptations, Edwin Starr, Marvin Gaye, "Little Stevie" Wonder, the Marvelettes, and Martha and the Vandellas played a grueling itinerary of ninety one-night stands. With rare exceptions, the singers slept on the tour bus. Cautioned by Gordy that they were representing "not only Motown records but all of Detroit," the musicians made it work in the face of difficulties, both grave and comic. Shots were fired at the tour bus; at one rest stop, a hostile gas station attendant refused to let the "niggers" use the toilets. On the other hand, tour participants laughed about the elaborate ruses they employed to get around the chaperons assigned to prevent private meetings between male and female singers; the chimpanzee Edwin Starr snuck onto the bus; and the incessant harmonica playing that led to good-natured threats to drop Little Stevie off at the next godforsaken roadside stop.

Remembering Gordy as a "very spiritual" man with "visions far beyond any of our imaginations," Martha Reeves sums up Motown in the early days as "an exciting place where magic was created." Otis Williams describes a community where everyone "was young and driven by the same dreams. You didn't have to explain yourself. We all had that passion about music and success. You wouldn't think twice about pitching in to help with whatever had to be done, whether it was singing backgrounds or mopping the floor. Joining Motown was more like being adopted by a big loving family than being hired by a company. This isn't just nostalgia talking either. It really was a magical time."

# 5
## *The Big Chill* vs. *Cooley High*:
## Two out of Three Falls for the Soul of Motown

By the time Motown achieved cliché status with *The 25th Anniversary TV Special* and the *Big Chill* sound track, anyone who had trouble seeing past the glitter could be forgiven. By the mid-eighties, the entertainment industry had shrunk Motown to video size, turned Levi Stubbs's agony into a condiment for yuppie angst.

Five Motown classics punctuate the sound track of *The Big Chill* alongside sixties classics by the Rolling Stones, Creedence Clearwater Revival, the Band, the Young Rascals, and the Spencer Davis Group, which featured a young Stevie Winwood, the one white singer whose voice James Baldwin admitted misidentifying as black. In the world of *The Big Chill*, Motown provides the black part of a white mix. It's not precisely a contradiction, more like a no-man's-land of half-acknowledged emotional yearnings. Repeatedly, *The Big Chill* uses Motown cuts at moments of maximum emotional complexity. Marvin Gaye's "I Heard It Through the Grapevine" sounds over the opening titles, which juxtapose the stark reality of suicide with a panorama of yuppie prosperity in the mid-Reagan era. Smokey Robinson's "The Tracks of My Tears" underscores the characters' agonized regrets over not having intervened to save their dead friend. "I Second That Emotion" fuels the celebratory catharsis of the morning after. As musical commentary on the characters' psychological struggles, the cuts work well.

But they don't communicate the gospel energy they carried for large parts of their original audience. In *The Big Chill,* black folk exist *only* in the past. Although the film takes place in a small Southern town, not a single black face appears on screen. Characters refer to blacks only when talking about what they've given up. When Mary Kay Place and Jeff Goldblum get into a conversation about Place's experience in a public defender's office, Place laments the fact that her clients usually deserve their punishments. When Goldblum asks, "Who'd you think your clients were gonna be? Grumpy and Sneezy?" Tom Berenger interjects, "No, Huey and Bobby." Similarly, Goldblum acknowledges that he's lost the part of himself that "made me want to go to Harlem and teach those ghetto kids." But there's no sense that gospel politics means anything at all in the mid-eighties. And there's less sense that the characters or the filmmakers hear the Motown music that accompanies their personal predicaments as a call to engage in any ongoing struggle. For them, Motown looks backward through an affable haze. The label's willingness to cash in with an avalanche of recycled "Greatest Hits" compilations during the eighties did nothing to resist the lucrative nostalgia.

Motown looks and sounds a bit different if you track it through *Cooley High* (1975), a very different movie. On the West Side of Chicago, and in the imagination of director Michael Schultz, Motown explodes with kinetic energy. Whatever the surface message, the underlying dynamic demands assertiveness. *Cooley High* tells the story of a group of high school students growing up in black Chicago during the mid-sixties. The movie pulses with an energy and hope recalling the gospel politics that energized the beloved communities of the South.

The connection wasn't accidental. Most black Chicagoans had family roots in the South, most frequently Mississippi and New Orleans. When Chicago industries, especially meatpacking and the slaughterhouses, faced labor shortages, they recruited workers from the other end of the Illinois Central Railroad line. Robert Abbott, publisher of the nationally circulated black newspaper the *Chicago Defender,* did everything in his power to accelerate the exodus. Describing a place more myth than economic reality, the *Defender* presented Chicago as Mahalia's Jerusalem, a respite from the lynching and poverty of the South. Investigate the family histories of almost any great Chicago musician and you'll find roots in the Delta. Sam Cooke was born in Clarksdale, Muddy Waters in Rolling Fork, Howlin' Wolf from just the other side of the river in Osceola,

Arkansas. Mavis Staples was born in Chicago after her father, Roe-buck "Pops" Staples, moved up from Winona.

Thousands of black Southerners streaming into Chicago during the Great Migration carried their music with them. Mahalia brought the sanctified singing of the New Orleans churches; Howlin' Wolf and Muddy Waters brought the Delta blues from the plantations and, given access to electricity, wasted no time plugging in their guitars. The Rolling Stones and Animals, as well as future Doors organist Ray Manzarek (who grew up in a white enclave on Chicago's South Side), heard their call. Responding to the new experiences of a North that still maintained a romantic aura—a common rhyme declared "I'd rather be a lamppost in Chicago than the king of Mississippi"—the transplanted bluesmen bottlenecked Southern traditions into new forms that the Pullman porters carried back down the rail lines to share with the folks "down home." When Chicago responded to the call of Mississippi, a new black voice was born.

Like its secular cousin, gospel was conceived in the South but some of its classic forms emerged in Chicago. Lifelong Southerners like Dorothy Love Coates and Clarence Fountain might disagree, but Southern-born Chicagoans like Sam Cooke and Mahalia made it clear that black culture could no longer be described solely as Southern. (And the folks who headed out west when the armaments industry needed workers for the Pacific campaign during World War II were already in the game. Specialty Records, the most important gospel label of the fifties, was based in L.A.) When Mahalia, Martin, and the beloved community used gospel to cement the foundation of a political movement, black Chicago, especially the older genera-tion, was very much attuned to what was going on down home.

By the mid-sixties, however, a younger generation was coming into its own, a generation that had never lived in the Jim Crow South. Like the group setting out to fulfill Berry Gordy's dream in Detroit, the young folks in Chicago harbored an expansive sense of possibil-ity. Not that Chicago had turned out to be the promised land. The Windy City's Black Belt, home turf for Sam Cooke and the Staples, not to mention the doomed protagonist of Richard Wright's *Native Son*, was one of the most densely crowded areas in the country. Dur-ing the postwar years, the population density of the Black Belt reached an incredible 300 percent of legal housing capacity. When Mayor Richard Daley welcomed delegates to the 1963 NAACP Con-vention by announcing that there was no longer a ghetto in Chicago, he was booed off the stage. Everyone who lived there knew better.

Preacher and Cochise, the central characters in *Cooley High*, experience Chicago in all its gospel and ghetto complexity; they share the promise and they hear the moan. And Motown provides the sound track. Set in 1964—although the sound track includes songs released as late as 1966—*Cooley High* opens with the Supremes' "Baby Love" playing over a sequence that begins with the Chicago skyline across Lake Michigan and ends up in a ghetto apartment. Picking up on Holland-Dozier-Holland's carefree lyrics and production style, which mirror the "girl group" formula of the Shirelles or the Crystals, these early scenes vibrate with the joy of young black men experiencing a world open to them in ways their parents would never have imagined possible. Energized by Stevie Wonder's "Fingertips," Cochise, Preacher, and their friends hop a ride on the back of a city bus to the Lincoln Park Zoo, a public space of the sort that the movement was fighting to open in the South. In one crucial scene, Cochise organizes a minor theft by staging an argument with a white woman working at a hot-dog stand. In the South, a similar act might well have been fatal, as the citizens of Mississippi had taught Chicago native Emmett Till less than a decade earlier.

Throughout the first half of *Cooley High*, the teenagers live out their own version of the Young American Dream. They dance, joke, and make out to the sounds of the Four Tops' "I Can't Help Myself," the Marvelettes' "Beachwood 4-5789," Smokey Robinson and the Miracles' "Ooo Baby Baby," and the Temptations' "My Girl," which might as well be designated the official anthem of sixties teen lovers, black and white. But where *The Big Chill* uses Motown to endorse an eighties version of escapist personalism, *Cooley High* knows there's something serious behind the pop mask.

One moment in *Cooley High* captures the depth of the gospel impulse about as well as anything in American popular culture. Cochise and his friends are getting ready to share a bottle of wine before heading to a party. When he opens the bottle, Cochise pours a few drops on the ground, saying, "This is for the brothers who ain't here." Defending himself against charges of wasting the wine, Cochise underlines the sense of community that connects Chicago, the black South, and the West African religious traditions he almost certainly doesn't know much about: "There's a lotta brothers who dead or in jail and we got to give them a little respect." The gospel sense of community isn't limited to the present; it reaches back into the deep past, remembers the moan, and helps the characters deal with the blues realities lurking within every Motown classic.

Even as they celebrate the communal energies of black Chicago, the hopes of the Great Migration, the *Cooley High* kids and their real-world counterparts hear the moan much more clearly than the characters in *The Big Chill*, who would have been almost exactly the same age. Where *The Big Chill* refers to political demonstrations and confrontations as part of a romanticized past, *Cooley High* portrays the violence just beneath the surface of everyday black life, even in its most hopeful moments. A party erupts into a free-for-all; Preacher's mother collapses under the burden of her domestic work and her son's unwillingness to do the right thing; a fight at a movie theater culminates in a stunning image of shadows bursting through the screen into reality; Preacher kneels in the twisted shadows beneath the El, calling out in despair over the body of Cochise, whose college scholarship is reduced to meaninglessness by black-on-black murder. As Preacher reenacts Cochise's ritual by spilling whiskey into his open grave, Levi Stubbs's anguished vocal on "Standing in the Shadows of Love" summons up a nightmare of abandonment from the middle of Motown's optimistic pop mix. Whatever happy-talk the official company policy might have touted, Motown spoke to the full reality of black life in the sixties.

Today Coolidge High School, the real-life site of *Cooley High*, presents an emblem of urban hopelessness. The streets where the children hoped and played stand deserted. Mothers do their best to keep their kids off the block, to protect them from a violence unimaginable to the older generations. For a sense of how the Cooley High neighborhood appears today, look at the book *Our America*, a sobering and brilliant montage of photographs, interviews, and meditations assembled by two young black Chicagoans, LeAlan Jones and Lloyd Newman. Like *Our America*, Cochise's fate testifies all too clearly that *The Big Chill*'s lament for youthful idealism addresses the least of our losses.

Motown provided a sound track that was a whole lot more politically charged, more complexly *moving*, for young black Americans than it was for most of the white kids whose money helped realize Berry Gordy's dream. Like gospel, Motown captured both the joy of connection and the pain that gave the joy its edge. But where gospel spoke to the black audience's sense that the joy and pain couldn't be separated, Motown played to the taste of a white audience conditioned to believe that, in James Baldwin's timeless dismissal, "happy songs are happy and sad songs are sad."

Although Motown accentuated the positive, Berry Gordy definitely understood the company's success as part of the movement's struggle against injustice. As part of the masking strategy, Motown avoided saying anything that might turn off record buyers or radio programmers. Where Sam Cooke and James Brown used their popularity to desegregate Southern theaters, however, the Motown Revue accepted racially separate seating areas in Memphis. Singers sang each song twice, once to the white audience on one side of the auditorium and once to the black audience on the other. Motown resisted its artists' desires to create more socially explicit music until it became clear that politics, too, could pay.

And anyway, on street level, the songs had always communicated something fresher, more aggressive than Gordy had in mind. Gordy made generous donations to established civil rights groups and expressed respect for "all people who were fighting against bigotry and oppression." His heart was clearly with King; in 1963, the Gordy label released two albums of King's speeches, *Great March to Freedom* and *Great March to Washington.* "I saw Motown much like the world Dr. King was fighting for—with people of different races and religions, working together harmoniously for a common goal," Gordy wrote. "While I was never too thrilled about that turn-the-other-cheek business, Dr. King showed me the wisdom of nonviolence." Frequently, however, Motown provided part of a sound track for the new black generation that often rejected nonviolence with contempt. When the Detroit ghetto exploded into violence in 1967, Martha and the Vandellas' good-times classic "Dancing in the Street" rose up over the carnage. The thousands of Detroit residents who made the song into a call to arms were responding to Motown in ways that clashed strongly with Gordy's interracial dream. Motown may have presented itself as a Negro enterprise, but it had a black soul.

One of the many things *Cooley High* gets right is that even those insiders—most but not all of them black—who heard the messages in the lower frequencies of James Jamerson's bass and Levi Stubbs's moan didn't have to concentrate on them all the time. Even if you understood Marvin Gaye and Kim Weston's "It Takes Two" as an endorsement of desegregation, you could still groove to it on a date. Responding to "The Tracks of My Tears" as a profound expression of the psychological cost of black masking didn't keep you from singing it when you saw your lover with somebody else. The important point was that there was no dissonance between the personal and the political energies. The power of love you wanted to come down in your own life was the same power that energized Martin and Mahalia and Ella Baker's beloved community. It was all about love and betrayal and the power of connection, which you felt as much when it was gone as when it was there. That was what the gospel impulse was all about.

## A Gospel Impulse Top 40

1. Bob Marley, "Redemption Song," 1980

2. Mahalia Jackson, "Walk in Jerusalem," 1963

3. Aretha Franklin, "Spirit in the Dark," 1970

4. The Impressions, "People Get Ready," 1965

5. Sam Cooke, "A Change is Gonna Come," 1965

6. Staples Singers, "I'll Take You There," 1972

7. Dorothy Love Coates and the Original Gospel Harmonettes, "No Hiding Place," 1954

8. Teddy Pendergrass, "You Can't Hide from Yourself," 1977

9. Martha and the Vandellas, "Nowhere to Run," 1965

10. Swan Silvertones, "Mary Don't You Weep," 1959

11. Jimmy Cliff, "Many Rivers to Cross," 1975

12. John Coltrane, "A Love Supreme," 1964

13. Charles Mingus, "Wednesday Night Prayer Meeting," 1960

14. Marion Williams, "The Moan," 1980

15. Earth, Wind & Fire, "Devotion," 1974

16. Jackie Wilson, "Higher and Higher," 1967

17. Al Green, "Love and Happiness," 1977

## The Gospel Impulse

You're unlikely to find CDs by the Temptations, Bob Marley, or Dianne Reeves in the gospel section of your record store alongside those by Mahalia Jackson, the Swan Silvertones, and God's Property, but you should. Because all of them—along with countless other artists from Curtis Mayfield and Gladys Knight to Aretha Franklin and Earth, Wind & Fire—share a profound sense of the "gospel impulse": the belief that life's burdens can be transformed into hope, salvation, the promise of redemption.

At its best, the gospel impulse helps people experience themselves *in relation to* rather than *on their own*. Gospel makes the feeling of human separateness, which is what the blues are all about, bearable. It's why DJs and the dancers they shape into momentary communities are telling the truth when they describe dance as a religious experience.

> *I have never seen anything to equal the fire and excitement that sometimes, without warning, fill a church, causing the church, as Leadbelly and so many others have testified, to "rock." Nothing that has happened to me since equals the power and the glory that I sometimes felt when, in the middle of a sermon, I knew that I was somehow, by some miracle, really carrying, as they said, "the Word"— when the church and I were one.*
> —James Baldwin

The gospel impulse half-remembers the values brought to the new world by the men and women uprooted from West African cultures: the connection between the spiritual and material worlds; the interdependence of self and community; the honoring of the elders and the ancestors; the recognition of the ever-changing flow of experience that renders all absolute ideologies meaningless. Scholars have traced the spiritual vision of African American culture from

18. Marvin Gaye, "Let's Get It On," 1973

19. Donny Hathaway and Roberta Flack, "Where Is the Love?," 1972

20. Ray Charles, "What'd I Say," 1959

21. Sam and Dave, "I Thank You," 1968

22. Neville Brothers, "My Blood," 1989

23. Edwin Hawkins Singers, "Oh Happy Day," 1969

24. Jerry Butler, "Only the Strong Survive," 1969

25. Stevie Wonder, "Higher Ground," 1973

26. Bruce Springsteen, "The Promised Land," 1978

27. The O'Neal Twins and the Interfaith Choir, "Highway to Heaven," 1983

28. Dianne Reeves, "Old Souls," 1994

29. James Brown, "Soul Power," 1971

30. Parliament, "Star Child (Mothership Connection)," 1976

31. Sly and the Family Stone, "I Want to Take You Higher," 1969

32. Digable Planets, "Where I'm From," 1993

33. Smokey Robinson and the Miracles, "I Second That Emotion," 1967

34. Ben E. King, "Stand by Me," 1961

35. Sister Sledge, "We Are Family," 1979

Africa through the Caribbean and American South to the dance floors of house clubs in Chicago. But there's no question that the gospel impulse found its strongest American voice in the gospel churches, mostly poor and almost entirely black. In church, blacks were unlikely to encounter the prying eyes of potentially hostile whites. Here they could drop the mask. Of course the real people in the gospel churches had to deal with the same problems of hypocrisy, greed, and envy as

> *Gospel songs are the songs of hope. When you sing them you are delivered of your burden. You have a feeling that there is a cure for what's wrong. It always gives me joy to sing gospel songs. I get to singing and I feel better right away. When you get through with the blues, you've got nothing to rest on. I tell people that the person who sings only the blues is like someone in a deep pit yelling for help, and I'm simply not in that position.*
> —Mahalia Jackson

their brothers and sisters out on the block. But even in its inevitable encounters with human frailty, the gospel impulse keeps alive a vision of spiritual community that echoes throughout the music of Sam Cooke and Otis Redding, Bruce Springsteen and A Tribe Called Quest.

The gospel impulse consists of a three-step process: (1) acknowledging the burden; (2) bearing witness; (3) finding redemption. The burden grounds the song

> *Gospel and the blues are really, if you break it down, almost the same thing. It's just a question of whether you're talkin' about a woman or God. I come out of the Baptist church and naturally whatever happened to me in the church is gonna spill over. So I think the blues and gospel music is quite synonymous to each other.*
> —Ray Charles

in the history of suffering that links individual and community experiences. Black folks, like all human beings who let themselves know and feel it, have their crosses to bear. Less likely than whites to subscribe to the facile optimism of America's civic ideology, most blacks maintain an awareness of limitation, of the harsh reality that the man goin' round takin' names doesn't much care whether you've done your best to live in the light of the Lord. We don't choose our burdens; we do choose our responses.

Musicians grounded in the gospel impulse respond by bearing witness to the troubles they've seen, telling the deepest truths they know. The gospel singer testifies to the burden and the power of the spirit in moans or screams or harmonies so sweet they can make you cry. The testimony touches what we share and what we deal with when we're on our own in that dark night of the soul. The word "witness" works partly because the burden involves history, power. There's an evil in the world and, yeah, part of it's inside us, but lots of it comes from the Devil. Call him sex or

> *Music is healing. It's all there to uplift someone. If somebody's burdened down and having a hard time, if they're depressed, gospel music will help them. We were singing about freedom. We were singing about when will we be paid for the work we've done. We were talking about doing right by us. We were down with Martin Luther King. Pops said this is a righteous man. If he can preach this, we can sing it.*
>
> —Mavis Staples

money, hypocrisy or capitalism, the landlord or Governor Wallace, but the Devil's real. You deal with him or he, maybe she, will most definitely deal with you. If you stop right there, you've got the blues.

But gospel doesn't leave it there. Marley, Aretha, Mahalia, and Al Green all testify to the reality of redemption. If the blues give you the strength to face another day but leave you to face it on your own, gospel promises, or at least holds out the possibility, that tomorrow may be different, better. With the help of the spirit and your people—in the church or on the dance floor—you can get over, walk in Jerusalem, dance to the music. But it takes an energy bigger than yourself, the wellspring of healing that South African pianist Abdullah Ibrahim called "water from an ancient well." For the classic gospel singers, the source is God; for soul singers, it's love. Bob Marley calls it Jah. George Clinton envisions Atlantis, the mothership. Arrested Development imagines a tree in Tennessee. Whatever its specific incarnation, gospel redemption breaks down the difference between personal salvation and communal liberation. No one makes it alone. If we're going to bear up under the weight of the cross, find the strength to renounce the Devil, if we're going to survive to bear witness and move on up, we're going to have to connect. The music shows us how.

# 6
# Sam Cooke and the Voice of Change

J. W. Alexander of the legendary gospel quartet the Soul Stirrers remembered the precise moment Sam Cooke found his voice. Recalling the difficulties Cooke faced in trying to match the virtuosity of R. H. Harris, whom he had replaced as the group's lead vocalist, Alexander described the moment of discovery, which occurred in a California auditorium one night in 1953: "in trying to dodge one of those high notes . . . he did a whoa-whoa-whoa type of thing. . . . He just floated under." It was a voice that possessed a unique ability to call forth strong responses from the black folk attending the gospel show that night in California and from the teens, black and white, who heard it on their transistor radios. A pioneer on the path that led from the gospel highway to the top twenty, Cooke envisioned a world where the two audiences might merge into one, where black singers could sing what he called "real gospel" and still get paid.

The circumstances surrounding Cooke's death from gunshots in a South Central Los Angeles motel in December 1964 have never really been explained. He'd gone there with a woman, later identified as a prostitute, who'd stolen his clothes. When he burst into the motel office angrily demanding their return, he was shot by the motel manager, who claimed that she had acted in self-defense. Many in the black community believed he'd been set up. The only sure thing is that his death changed the world of American popular music in ways that delayed the fulfillment of his dream.

Cooke mapped the paths available to singers trying to bring the gospel impulse into the interracial marketplace. He had begun his career in gospel during the formative years of the freedom movement. Beginning in 1953 when "Jesus Gave Me Water" sold sixty-five thousand copies, an extraordinary performance in the all-black gospel market, Cooke's voice floated the Soul Stirrers through a series of hits that confirmed them as a major force in gospel. Moving to the popular marketplace, he recorded a series of seemingly innocuous pop hits including "Cupid," "Wonderful World," and "You Send Me." By the end of his life, he had begun to merge his approaches in the "gospel pop" of "Bring It on Home to Me," "Soothe Me," and the breathtaking "A Change Is Gonna Come."

Born in the heart of the Mississippi Delta and raised in Chicago's Bronzeville, Cooke got a firsthand look at the transition from Southern to Northern forms of African American culture. A preacher in the socially conservative but musically vibrant Holiness Church, Cooke's father, Charles Cook—Sam added the *e* as a none-too-effective disguise when he moved from gospel to pop music—had moved to Chicago and found work in the stockyards. Joining over a hundred thousand other black migrants from the South, he worked alongside many of the fifty thousand whites who belonged to the twenty Chicago-area Ku Klux Klan "klaverns." Despite de facto integration on the lower rungs of the economic ladder, social life and housing in Chicago remained nearly as segregated as they had been in Clarksdale, Mississippi.

Like their counterparts in the South, Chicago's black churches provided centers for community activity. Young Chicagoans raised in the church—among them Cooke, Jerry Butler, and Curtis Mayfield—saw how music could bring their people together. The gospel soul they created succeeded in communicating something of the movement's feel to a surprisingly large white audience. As historian Taylor Branch observed, their achievement carried major political significance. Describing a 1963 concert in Atlanta's Ponce de Leon Park where Cooke performed alongside the Drifters, Solomon Burke, Dionne Warwick, Jerry Butler, and numerous others, Branch writes that the park was "jammed not only with Negro fans but also with young white people, for whom the best Negro pop music reached beneath formal and worldly preoccupations to release elemental emotions of sex, frivolity, love, and sadness." Underscoring the political significance of the music, Branch concludes: "The stars of soul music and the blues stood with King as exemplars of the mysterious Negro church—nearly all of them had been gospel singers—but they were still ahead of him in crossing over to a mass white audience. They unlocked the shared feelings, if not the understanding, that he longed to reach."

Cooke reached that audience with a string of hits beginning with "You Send Me" and culminating in "A Change Is Gonna Come," which was released eleven days after his death. The song expresses the soul of the freedom movement as clearly and powerfully as King's "Letter from a Birmingham Jail." The opening measures verge on melodrama: a searching French horn rises over a lush swell of symphonic strings accompanied by tympani. But Cooke brings it back to earth, bearing witness to the restlessness that keeps him moving like the muddy river bordering the Delta where he was born. Maintaining his belief in something up there beyond the sky, Cooke draws sustenance from his gospel roots. He testifies that it's been a long, long time—the second "long" carries all the weight of a bone-deep gospel weariness. Then he sings the midnight back toward dawn. The hard-won hope that comes through in the way he uses his signature "whoa-whoa-whoa" to emphasize the word "know" in the climactic line—"I *know* that a change is gonna come"—feels as real as anything America has ever been able to imagine.

James Baldwin reached for something similar in his classic story "Sonny's Blues." Thinking of his uncle's death by mindless racial violence, his brother Sonny's struggle with heroin addiction, his young daughter's illness and death, Baldwin's narrator turns to music for something that's not quite consolation and even less understanding. Creole, the bass player in Sonny's band, brings the jazz explorations back home: "He and his boys up there were keeping it new, at the risk of ruin, destruction, madness, and death, in order to find new ways to make us listen. For, while the tale of how we suffer, and how we are delighted, and how we may triumph is never new, it always must be heard. There isn't any other tale to tell, it's the only light we've got in all this darkness."

When he tried to shine some of that light on pop audiences in the late fifties, Cooke encountered cultural dissonances that demanded extraordinary skills of translation and negotiation, as well as some masking. The interracial rock and roll explosion ignited by Chuck Berry, Little Richard, Buddy Holly, and Elvis a few years earlier had run up against serious resistance. Hypersensitive to the threat of international communism, mainstream politicians painted any challenge to American "normalcy" as part of an all-encompassing communist plot. Even when their methods attracted some timorous and belated criticism, J. Edgar Hoover and Senator Joseph McCarthy did not defy the mainstream in their ideology. John F. Kennedy defeated Richard Nixon in large part because his anticommunism was *more* extreme. In this political climate, any agitation on social issues, including any challenge to conventional racial or sexual roles, drew sustained fire. In the South, where most whites colored King's movement dark red, that wasn't a metaphor.

The new "mongrel music" provided an inviting target. In the mid-fifties, rock and roll rattled a staid McCarthy-era America with disconcerting images of unfettered sexual energy that frequently brought blacks and whites together on suddenly integrated dance floors. Pictures of Little Richard, eyes rolled back underneath a distinctly bizarre mountain of hair, confronted cold war–era America with images from one of its worst nightmares. It didn't help that he seemed at least as interested in the white boys as the sisters they were supposed to be protecting. The hysterical tone of the attacks comes through clearly in a pamphlet distributed to white parents: "Help save the youth of America! Don't let your children buy or listen to these Negro records. The screaming, idiotic words and savage music are undermining the morals of our white American youth."

The authorities cracked down on the interracial music scene. Chuck Berry went to jail; Little Richard "retired" to the ambiguous safety of the church, throwing his diamond rings in the river—"they never would tell us *what* river," laments Solomon Burke—and denouncing rock and roll as the devil's music after he dreamed of his own damnation. Pioneer disc jockey Alan Freed, who made little distinction between rock and roll and rhythm and blues, was hounded into exile in a payola scandal that somehow let clean-cut pop impresario Dick Clark escape unscathed. Sanitized teen idols like Fabian and Frankie Avalon—many of them Italian Americans dark enough to remain exotic without presenting a threat to "racial purity"—channeled the uncontained sexual energy of the pioneers into chaperoned romance guaranteed not to move more than a few steps past first base.

Enter Sam Cooke with a "crossover" vision that helped redefine American popular music. By the time "You Send Me" reached number one in 1957, Cooke had almost a decade of mileage on the gospel highway, first with Chicago's Highway QCs and then with the Soul Stirrers, where he replaced the legendary R. H. Harris as lead vocalist. Like blues guitarists, jazz instrumentalists, and hip-hop vocalists, gospel quartets often fought it out head-to-head for audience approval. A singer had to be on his game or he wasn't going to hold the stage. Just that simple. Never able to stand toe-to-toe with the raw power of gospel veterans like Claude Jeter of the Swan Silvertones, Ira Tucker of the Dixie Hummingbirds, the incomparable Clarence Fountain of the Five Blind Boys of Alabama, or Archie Brownlee of the Five Blind Boys of Mississippi, Cooke finessed the issue. Moving away from Harris's combination of raw power and down-home phrasing, Cooke developed the personal style described perfectly by Daniel Wolff in his definitive biography, *You Send Me: The Life and Times of Sam Cooke:* "When Sam took hold of a note . . . it wasn't the traditional nonverbal moan that Holiness congregations were used to. It wasn't a cry of pain. Instead, he decorated the note, embellishing the melody till it hung, fragile as lace, in the air over the congregation."

Cooke's new approach resulted in the kind of competitive stalemate that might emerge in a one-on-one game between Kareem Abdul-Jabbar and Michael Jordan. Each star kept his supporters, but each had to refine his style. Those who watched Cooke with the Soul Stirrers remembered that for the younger members of the audience, especially the women, he was *the* man. Cooke's audience heard his voice as a response to the power of the moan and the redemptive vision. "Come Go with Me" revives the vision of the promised land while "Pilgrim of Sorrow" testifies to the reality of the burden. But the key to Cooke's success, even within the gospel world, lay in his provocative blending of sex and spirituality in "Jesus Gave Me Water" and "Touch the Hem of His Garment." Mostly Cooke pretended to stay just—and only just—this side of the line from Ray Charles's frankly sexual "I Got a Woman" and "What'd I Say." But, as Willie Dixon, Cooke's contemporary on the blues side of Chicago's musical tracks, put it: "The men don't know but the little girls understand."

The black girls in the gospel audience, the same teenagers who listened to Little Richard and Chuck Berry, understood Cooke's star potential clearly. So did Sam. During his five years of gospel stardom, he developed an ideal crossover style: delicate, almost ethereal, but with enough of Harris's and Fountain's power to provide a clear alternative to pop crooning. He also had the advantage of seeing what had happened to the crossover rock and rollers when they let the mask slip too far. Cooke's foray into the mainstream established the approach refined by Berry Gordy's Motown. There were three basic principles: innocent (if sometimes masked) lyrics; arrangements (frequently built around strings) that emphasized hooks; and smooth background harmonies (often provided by white studio singers).

The call and response on the crossover dream connected singers from Memphis to Manhattan. Recording for New York's Atlantic Records, Clyde McPhatter and the Drifters transformed their gospel roots into a sweet soul style that anticipated Cooke's on hits such as "Such a Night," later covered by Elvis Presley, and "Honey Love." At the same time Cooke was recording "Cupid" and "Only Sixteen," the girl groups, often produced by studio genius Phil Spector, were exploring parallel approaches. The powerful bass line and softly strumming guitar in Jerry Butler and the Impressions' "For Your Precious Love" anticipate the gospel soul of Ben E. King's "Stand by Me," a secularized remake of the gospel standard "Stand By Me Father." Against a deceptively beautiful orchestral backdrop, King's lyrics ride the power of a soul-deep bass line. Looking out on a darkened landscape where "the moon is the only light we'll see," King searches for the strength to overcome his sense of isolation. "I won't be afraid, no I won't be afraid," he repeats, "Just as long as you stand by me." It's a classic case of political masking. Listeners unaware of the violence facing the beloved community can hear the song as a plea for romantic connection. But if you visualize a lone SNCC organizer on a Southern back road, the song grows deeper.

Even while he was appealing to the integrated teen audience of

Dick Clark's *Saturday Night Show,* Cooke continued to play one-nighters for predominantly black audiences in the South. On New Year's Eve 1962, as he was preparing a musical assault on Las Vegas, he more than held his own at a gospel concert in Newark, New Jersey, where he appeared alongside the Dixie Hummingbirds, the Caravan Singers, and the latest incarnation of the Soul Stirrers. Cooke explained his continuing connection with his roots: "When the whites are through with Sammy Davis, Jr., he won't have anywhere to play. I'll always be able to go back to my people 'cause I'm never gonna stop singing to them. No matter how big I get, I'm still gonna do my dates down South. Still gonna do those kind of shows. I'm not gonna leave my base." James Brown—and Ella Baker—would have understood.

If you listen to Cooke's crossover hits with an awareness of masking, some wonderful moments, otherwise invisible, come into focus. One of Cooke's biggest hits, "Wonderful World" (later covered by soul legends Herman's Hermits and James Taylor) opens with what seems to be a high school cliché: "Don't know much about history / don't know much biology." The cliché's worth a second thought. Because, if there are two things that a black man in pop music needed to encourage the white audience to forget, they were history and biology, at least the parts involving skin color and sexuality. If you could do that, who knows? The world just might turn out to be as wonderful as *Leave It to Beaver* and *Camelot* promised.

# 7
# Solid Gold Coffins:
# Phil Spector and the Girl Group Blues

Even when Cooke was creating his pop hits, he remembered his gospel roots. That wasn't easy in the pop world, where the connection was sometimes lost, with tragic results. The girl groups produced by Phil Spector are a case in point. Spector recognized great singing when he heard it, and there's never been a producer who could get denser, more breathtaking sound out of a studio. Many of the singers he recruited for his groups had been trained in the call-and-response traditions of the gospel church.

But when the deal went down, Spector's records were Spector's records. Ronnie Bennett, lead singer of the Ronettes before she married Spector in 1966, recalled "how fanatical Phil was about every detail of what went on in the studio." Spector controlled every aspect of the Ronettes' classic singles, "Walking in the Rain," "Baby I Love You," and "Be My Baby," which provides the title for Ronnie's memoir of her life with Spector. Both in the studio and when the Ronettes performed live, Spector insisted they follow his orders concerning clothes, hair style, movement, and vocal inflection.

Spector's desire to dominate Ronnie wasn't limited to music. The scenes of violence and abuse recounted in *Be My Baby* are overwhelming. Right before Ronnie summoned the courage to break out of the marriage, Spector threatened to kill her and told her mother: "I'm completely prepared for that day. I've already got her coffin. It's solid gold. And it's got a glass top, so I can keep my eyes on her after she's dead." After the divorce, he made the first $1,300 alimony payment in nickels.

Ronnie Bennett wasn't the only one with that kind of story to tell. Almost every female singer of the early sixties had, at the very least, suffered through a series of difficult romantic relationships. Tina Turner accepted Ike's beatings in part because she preferred them to life in the cotton fields where she had grown up. "Cotton, I hated it," said Tina, "picking cotton and chopping it, the sun was so hot. I dreaded those times. That's the only thing that made me change my life. I knew I couldn't do that. As a child, I knew the beginning of hate and can not do and don't want to do and will not do." Ike may have provided an alternative to Nutbush, Tennessee, where Tina grew up as Anna Mae Bullock, but the price of the ticket was high. You can hear it in Tina's voice on "A Fool in Love." After the deep gospel moan that opens the record, Tina and a female chorus engage in a wrenching call and response on a situation that Ronnie would have understood: "You know you love him / you can't understand / why he treat you like he do when he's such a good man." About all you can say is that if Phil Spector and Ike Turner are the working definition of a good man, we're in a world of hurt.

Not even Motown, determined to avoid the slightest hint of anything white Americans could stereotype as "niggerish" behavior, avoided the problem. Sharing none of Spector's tendencies toward violence and disrespect, the Gordy family did its best to provide a positive model. While there's no question that Berry Gordy, Sr.'s mantle as family patriarch passed down to his son, women were deeply involved, as equals, in the family's decision-making process. Before Berry Gordy, Jr., could borrow the $800 he needed to found Motown from the credit union the family funded with required donations from all members, he had to convince the family council he was worth the risk, and that required the support of his mother and sisters. Women made the financial decision that made Motown happen.

But none of that could save Tammi Terrell. Briefly married to boxer Ernie Terrell, who once fought Muhammad Ali for the heavyweight crown, Tammi embodied Motown's ideal of the (black) "girl next door." The duets she recorded with the young Marvin Gaye— "If I Could Build My Whole World Around You," "You're All I Need to Get By," "Ain't Nothing Like the Real Thing"—told a story of fresh and innocent love, and helped Motown establish a presence in the teen magazines. When Tammi collapsed into Marvin's arms on stage during a performance at Hampden-Sydney College in Virginia, the magazines presented her hospitalization as part of a tragic romance.

Real life was quite a bit different. One of many singers attracted to her vibrant energy, James Brown remembered Tammi as "a kid that people ran too fast and took advantage of." Others who knew her described her romantic life as a nightmare of violence and abuse. The problem, according to Marvin Gaye, who never actually had a sexual relationship with his fantasy partner, was that "Tammi was the kind of chick who couldn't be controlled by men." And when men feel control slipping away, they often resort to their fists. Although no legal charges were ever filed, almost everyone who knew her believes the "brain tumor" that finally killed her—she underwent eight brain operations in the year and a half after her collapse—resulted from physical battering. "Tammi was the victim of the violent side of love," Gaye said. "At least that's how it felt. I have no first-hand knowledge of what really killed her, but it was a deep vibe." Although no one at Motown has ever publicly admitted it, the vocals on the "comeback" albums released by "Marvin and Tammi" to capitalize on Tammi's "recovery" and the revitalization of their fantasy romance were actually sung by Valerie Simpson. Tammi Terrell died at age twenty-four.

Closer to the chaos of the blues than the gospel celebrations their records suggested, the experiences of Ronnie Bennett, Tina Turner, and Tammi Terrell point out the unresolvable tension between the gospel energy of their best records and their blues experiences as women in a world where Spector could oversee the Crystals' horrifyingly beautiful "He Hit Me (It Felt Like a Kiss)"; Courtney Love's devastating mid-nineties cover hammered home the horror and let the beauty be. With the possible exception of the great records he made with the Righteous Brothers and Tina Turner's 1966 classic "River Deep Mountain High," there wasn't much real call and response between Spector and his singers. In the end, that left Spector himself isolated and blue. When Spector's musical genius passed over the borderline into paranoid silence and isolation, no one was in a position to call him back.

# 8
# SAR and the Ambiguity of Integration

Always a realist, Sam Cooke shared James Brown's belief that success predicated on the goodwill of white Americans couldn't be trusted. That was why he went out of his way to keep his connections with his original audience. And it was part of the reason why, in the last years of his life, Cooke developed close friendships with Malcolm X and Muhammad Ali, the two black men who accounted for many of white America's worst nightmares. Moments after the then Cassius Clay stunned Sonny Liston to win the heavyweight championship, he called on Cooke to join the celebration in the ring, introducing him as the world's "greatest rock and roll singer." Depending on how you looked at it, it either was or was not a long way from the Copa, where earlier that year Cooke had donned a tux to sing not only "Bill Bailey" and "Tennessee Waltz" but movement standards "If I Had a Hammer" and "This Little Light of Mine."

Cooke's politics were complicated. Even as he endorsed the movement's demand for the removal of all barriers keeping blacks from full participation in the public world, Cooke resisted the idea that, once the walls came tumbling down, blacks would abandon their homes and rush inside. A dedicated desegregationist willing to enter the mainstream to replenish his supply of dollar bills, Cooke insisted that any meaningful concept of integration required an equal amount of white movement toward the black world.

For years before he met Malcolm and Ali, Cooke had willingly used his performing skills to support King's goals. Jerry Butler recalls how Cooke supported student protestors in the South by forcing whites to enter traditionally black spaces, a situation that highlights the difference between *integration,* which assumes a white norm, and *desegregation,* in which cultural exchange can flow both ways. In 1959, Cooke forced promoters in Norfolk, Virginia, to open black seating areas to whites attending his performance. Butler assigns soul singers a place "at the vanguard of the movement" and stresses that "Young people like us, we were at A&T in Greensboro and Johnson: that whole corridor of black schools that starts at Baltimore. The entertainers would go in with the kids because we knew better than anybody that it wasn't about money. It was about color. 'Cause we had the money!" Cooke expressed his commitment to desegregation in a column published in numerous black newspapers in 1960: "I'll never forget the day I was unable to fulfill a one-night singing engagement in Georgia because I wouldn't sit in a Jim Crow bus and because no white taxicab driver would take me from the airport to the city—and Negro cabdrivers were not permitted to bring their cabs into the airport. . . . I have always detested people of any color, religion or nationality who have lacked courage to stand up and be counted."

For Cooke, the concept of desegregation allowed connection, but it didn't require it. It was cool to share your music with white folks, and it definitely paid better than the chitlin circuit, but you didn't have to give up the grits to have the gravy. Even though whites had a disturbing tendency to think that all that history just kinda vanished once they'd changed their own personal minds, Cooke, Malcolm, and Ali knew it didn't. Malcolm inspired Cooke to read widely in what was just beginning to be called "black studies." Cooke's longtime guitarist Cliff White recalls him reading W. E. B. Du Bois and whatever he could find on black history: "Sam was deep, deep into that business."

Bobby Womack, whose career Cooke helped launch, remembers: "Sam was always into reading. He read black history a lot, he read Aristotle, he read *The New Yorker* and *Playboy* magazine, I mean he read all the time. Everywhere he went he would look and see where he could get a book—he didn't care what it was about, he would get something." Womack remembers Cooke telling him, "That's the only way you can grow. Otherwise you're going to write love songs for the rest of your life. But everything ain't about love. If you in a situation that you thought was supposed to be a certain way, you can write in a way where it's like an abstract painting."

While he maintained an active interest in "white" culture, Cooke never passed, as black novelist Julian Mayfield phrased it, "into the mainstream, and oblivion." His commitment to black culture and black people culminated in his work with the SAR record label, which he founded with Soul Stirrer manager Roy Crain and gospel singer J. W. Alexander of the Pilgrim Travellers. Once Cooke established a solid financial base with his crossover hits, he worked to realize his vision of bringing real gospel music to a pop audience. His brother L. C. remembers Sam insisting that "Real gospel music has GOT to make a comeback." According to Bobby Womack, Cooke was also determined to bring the political meanings masked by his pop lyrics closer to the surface: "He said, 'Bobby, let me tell you something. People will buy the news if it's sung with a melody.' He said, 'News is cold. Only bad news makes the press. But if you sung it with a melody, it would lighten the burden a little bit, and people would understand.' "

At SAR, Cooke sought to help both new talent and established gospel acts reach a mixed audience. As Alexander recalls, the label consciously applied Cooke's formula for negotiating the larger culture: "We knew because of our background, it was just a matter of different lyrics." The results were frequently brilliant. On the sides cut by the Valentinos (originally the Womack Brothers) and the revived Soul Stirrers with Johnnie Taylor and Paul Foster sharing lead vocals, the potential of a blacker pop sound shines through clearly. The Soul Stirrers' "Wade in the Water" and "Stand by Me Father" hold their own with most of Cooke's pop hits.

It's something of a mystery why SAR never really connected with a white audience. Maybe it was the distribution problems that constantly plague small labels. Or maybe Cooke simply let the mask slip too much. The Soul Stirrers' "Mary Don't You Weep" doesn't really pretend the Pharaoh who got drowned lived three thousand years ago in Egypt. And the soaring "Free At Last" recasts Cooke's pop composition "Just for You"—which can also be heard as a love song to the Lord—as an explicit tribute to Martin Luther King.

Although the mass white audience wasn't ready for the gospel side of Cooke's vision, the music world was. Smokey Robinson acknowledged that "You Really Got a Hold on Me," later covered by the Beatles, was inspired by Cooke's "Bring It on Home to Me," which features a soulful call and response between Cooke and Lou Rawls, who sang lead for the Pilgrim Travellers before embarking on a solo career. Billy Preston, who did his first recording for SAR, would later play keyboard for both the Beatles and the Stones. His straight-out-of-church organ helps make the Beatles' "Don't Let Me Down" one of the greatest soul songs ever recorded by a "white" group. John Lennon wasn't stretching things when he told Beatles manager Allen Klein: "If you can understand Sam Cooke's music, you can understand mine."

Cooke's impact on soul was equally powerful. The Simms Twins' SAR cut, "Soothe Me," pointed the way toward the call-and-response duets of Memphis soulmen Sam and Dave, who cut their own version of the song; Otis Redding frequently covered Cooke's songs while de-
ng his own style of secular testifying. Curtis Mayfield, who per-
Cooke's style of gospel soul, recalls Cooke as an inspirational
when he was growing up in Chicago's Black Belt: "Oh yeah, I
Sam Cooke fan. With the Northern Jubilees [Mayfield's first
group] we admired the Soul Stirrers so much and tried to du-
some of their sounds, but of course Sam Cooke was Sam
. When 'You Send Me' came out, man, we thought it was just a
ic piece of music." An incident described by Soul Stirrer Le
rume concerning the group's recording of "Lead Me Jesus"
hts the complicated relationship between gospel and soul:

told me, "Le Roy, I got a hit coming out, 'Soothe Me.' " And he said,
nt you to write a gospel to it." I said, "You're not going to let your
number come out first?" He said, "Oh, no, I'll hold it." Man, that
came out before our record, and I said, "Sam, why you do that?"
, we played Atlanta and the promoter was standing out on the steps,
e didn't say hello or nothing, he just said, "Crume, why in the world
ou guys do that?" I said, "What, man? What are you talking about?"
He said, "This rock 'n' roll song. You all recorded a rock 'n' roll song." I said, "No, man, we didn't record a rock 'n' roll song. He said, "Well, it's just *like* a rock 'n' roll song. It's not going to work, man." He said, "You guys used to be #1 in here, but you can forget it. Man, you might get booed off the stage." Oh man, I was so scared. That was the one time I took Jimmie in the dressing room and said, "Jimmie, let's don't even touch that song." I said, "Just sing one line, and let's walk." Well, that's what we did, and, man, the crowd just went crazy, and the promoter came to me and said, "Damn, you guys can do anything you want!"

Cooke was acutely aware that the benefits of a desegregated music scene flowed both ways. When Bobby Womack expressed his anger over the Rolling Stones' cover of "It's All Over Now," Cooke calmed him. "This will be history," Cooke told his protégé. "Bobby, man, this group will change the industry. They ain't like the Beatles, they're the ghetto kids. They gonna make it loose for everybody." Despite the Stones' hard-edged image, the Beatles were a whole lot closer to being real ghetto kids. But Cooke's cultural analysis holds. Just as the Stones, Beatles, and Righteous Brothers drew on black traditions to enrich their music, Cooke was learning something from what the white folks were doing. Modeling "A Change Is Gonna Come" in part on Bob Dylan's "Blowin' in the Wind," Cooke was intrigued by the ragged sincerity of the folk revival. The folk singers "may not sound as good," he observed, "but the people believe them more."

"There's something coming," he told Bobby Womack, "and it's coming fast."

# 9
# "The Times They Are A-Changin' ":
# Port Huron and the Folk Revival

Bob Dylan's "The Times They Are A-Changin' " heralded the new world coming with a warning that tripped quickly from clarion to cliché. But for a brief time in the early sixties, a cluster of mostly white, mostly middle-class students seemed determined to forge a new politics attuned to the ideal of the beloved community. Armed with acoustic guitars and an earnest belief in interracial brotherhood, the musicians connected with the folk revival brought the movement's basic values as close to the pop culture mainstream as they've ever been, before or since. In the early sixties, their energies coalesced around the Students for a Democratic Society (SDS).

Media-fed memory has reduced SDS to a cluster of chaotic images: Tom Hayden endorsing guerrilla warfare in the streets of Newark; the Weathermen rampaging through the Days of Rage; students seizing the administration building at Columbia University; angry hecklers drowning out Ted Kennedy at the University of Wisconsin; the whole world watching blood flow in the streets of Chicago outside the 1968 Democratic Convention. Even when distorted by revisionism and nostalgia, those images nonetheless reflect the passion, confusion, and profoundly misguided ideological romance of the *late* sixties. Sometimes it seemed that no one, not even the people who wrote it, remembered the founding document of SDS, the Port Huron Statement.

The Port Huron Statement bears disquieting signs of its academic origin: turgid prose and telltale indications of the ideological hairsplitting that would tear the New Left apart. But its vision of a living political community dedicated to economic accountability, world peace, and racial justice remains vital in a time when a "liberal" president has overseen the dismantling of the welfare state and widened the yawning chasm between rich and poor. Seen by its framers as an attempt to make America live up to its own betrayed ideals, the statement celebrates the concept of participatory democracy. It envisions politics as a way of "Bringing people out of isolation and into community," helping them find "meaning in personal life." Addressing a political context in which Southern "Dixiecrats" and conservative Republicans controlled Washington, the statement endorses what in retrospect seems a fairly conventional, if unusually hopeful, liberal agenda. Although its calls for nuclear disarmament and corporate reform were never seriously considered, large parts of the statement read like a rough draft of Lyndon Johnson's Great Society.

Expressing an urgency foreign to a Kennedy administration unwilling to risk its shaky power base, the introduction concentrates on two "events too troubling to dismiss": the reality of "human degradation, symbolized by the Southern struggle against racial bigotry" and "the enclosing fact of the Cold War." As New Left historian James Miller observes, the students who founded SDS drew their political theory primarily from "the tradition of civic republicanism that links Aristotle to John Dewey." At the same time, they were acutely aware of how much they owed to the freedom movement, which was "exemplary because it insists there can be a passage out of apathy."

Like King's wing of the movement, the Port Huron Statement maintained a cautious hope that the Kennedy administration might be convinced to play a substantial role in addressing "human degradation." Released several months before Kennedy reluctantly committed federal force to the integration of the University of Mississippi (thereby abandoning all hope for further support from the white South), the statement damns the administration with the very faintest of praise:

> It has been said that the Kennedy administration did more in two years than the Eisenhower administration did in eight. Of this there can be no doubt. But it is analogous to comparing whispers to silence when positively stentorian tones are demanded. President Kennedy leaped ahead of the Eisenhower record when he made his second reference to the racial problem.

Calling for an aggressive alternative to Kennedy's gradualism, the statement emphasizes the need for voter registration, pointing toward the collaboration with black activists that culminated in the Freedom Summer of 1964. Earlier, during SNCC's 1962 voter registration campaign in McComb, Mississippi, SDS leader Tom Hayden had met Bob Moses, whose political philosophy exerted a major impact on the Port Huron deliberations later that year. Transmitted through mimeographed copies of the Port Huron Statement, the vision of participatory democracy fueled the moral imaginations of the students who founded local chapters of SDS in Boston, Ann Arbor, Berkeley, and Madison.

Many of those same imaginations had been attracted to the movement by the political songs on the 1963 folk revival classic *The Freewheelin' Bob Dylan*. Dylan dealt directly with both of SDS's main concerns: "Masters of War" and "A Hard Rain's A-Gonna Fall" focused on the cold war; "Oxford Town" and "Only a Pawn in Their Game" on racial justice. Several other political songs that elicited a strong response when Dylan performed them in concert were omitted from the album: "The Ballad of Emmett Till" and "Talkin' John Birch Paranoid Blues," which Columbia Records vetoed for fear of lawsuits from right-wing lunatics.

Thousands of college students streamed south to help register voters in Mississippi. Often romantic in their politics, sometimes naive about the depth of white supremacy, almost all shared a conviction of righteousness. They were responding to King's plea to let freedom ring and to the folk songs they took with them to the base camps dotting the Mississippi Delta, "looking like a strange mixture of kids going to camp and soldiers off to war," one of them wrote home.

Many of the students looked to the folk revival for perspectives and information excluded from the nightly news. The framers of the Port Huron Statement belonged to the first generation raised on television; many of them were enthralled by the moral dramas the SCLC constructed for the nationwide audience. In the early days of the movement, TV coverage usually placed viewers in a position closer to the demonstrators than to the authorities resisting their demands. White middle-class viewers in the North gazed into the steely eyes of state troopers snatching American flags out of the hands of schoolchildren in Jackson, Mississippi, shared the tension as the Freedom Riders—white ministers wearing clerical collars and well-dressed young black men—were swept away by the hurricane of violence in the Birmingham bus station. In her autobiography, Joan Baez describes King's constant awareness that the whole world was watching his every move. Walking beside King during an SCLC-sponsored campaign in Grenada, Mississippi, Baez responded angrily to the crowd harassing the marchers:

> They looked particularly pasty, frightened, and unhappy on this day, not at all like a "superior race." I whispered to King, "Martin, what in the hell are we doing? You want these magnificent spirits to be like *them?*," indicating the miserable little band on the opposite curb. "We must be nuts!" King nodded majestically at an overanxious cameraman, and said out of the corner of his mouth, "Ahem . . . Not while the cameras are rollin'."

The SCLC's most effective use of the media strategy occurred in Birmingham, Alabama, where fire hoses and police dogs deployed against black schoolchildren made a clear moral statement in living rooms and dens throughout white America.

However biased in favor of the movement TV coverage might have seemed to George Wallace or Spiro Agnew—the godfathers of Rush Limbaugh's "liberal media" hallucination—white students seeking the meanings behind the SCLC's carefully orchestrated morality plays found television useless. Many of them turned to folk music, to Baez, Dylan, Phil Ochs ("Talking Birmingham Jam," "Too Many Martyrs (The Ballad of Medgar Evers)," and the devastating satire "Love Me, I'm a Liberal") and Peter, Paul & Mary ("Very Last Day," "If I Had a Hammer," and the hit version of "Blowin' in the Wind"). The folk singers provided the kind of insight the students sought.

But there were limits to the folk revival's political vision. Especially after the catharsis of Freedom Summer, the folkies had trouble building bridges to ordinary black people. Despite the presence of Odetta, Josh White, and a few other black folk singers, the folk revival was mostly a white thing. If the goal was brotherhood, this wasn't a problem that could be ignored. The black presence at folk concerts was pretty much limited to the small group of black Bohemians who had decided to check out what was happening over on the newly accessible white side of town. Amiri Baraka, who had been one of them, observed that most of those Bohemians preferred to listen to the R & B on the jukeboxes in the black taverns where they went to loosen up and relish a less contrived sense of community. Part of the problem with the folk revival was that it failed to attract the black listeners who preferred Motown, Sam Cooke, or even less "historically correct" versions of gospel or the blues.

The folk revival's sense of the blues reveals the core of the problem. For the vast majority of the folkies, the blues were something strummed on the front porches of picturesque Southern shacks by grizzled old men descended directly from Mark Twain's Jim. They'd suffered, but they endured, and cool stuff like that. Given the number of humanities majors and aspiring writers in the crowd, the echo of the literary noble savage shouldn't come as any surprise. What the folkies *didn't* want in their blues was electricity, drums, any tinge of the fallen modern world. Which was a real problem since by 1960, a good three quarters of those grizzled old black men were hanging out in Chicago, Detroit, or other points north, trying to get paid while they set out the basics of rock guitar for the more attentive if less earnest rock and rollers. The Folkways record label, probably the definitive source of material for the folk movement, shunned all contact with urban blues, thereby isolating Muddy Waters, Howlin' Wolf, and John Lee Hooker from the American white folks with the greatest theoretical interest in black culture. Anyone getting his or her sense of black life from Folkways liner notes would have been hard-pressed to guess that black folks had ever encountered electricity.

# 10
# Woody and Race

Woody Guthrie spent damn little time worrying about authenticity. If the concept meant anything at all to him, it was backing up the words he'd written on his guitar: "This machine kills fascists." The folk revivalists who looked to Woody as a mythic hero could certainly have learned some things from taking a closer look at how he dealt with race. By the time Woody recorded "This Land Is Your Land," which Lyndon Johnson suggested should be made the national anthem, his concept of America included blacks, Mexicans, and Indians as well as the sometimes virulently racist white folks of the Oklahoma hills where he was born.

The voices Woody heard as a boy in Oklahoma came from all over America's racial map: the black town of Boley lay ten miles down the road from Okemah, where he grew up in what had been called Indian Territory until the white folks developed an interest in the oil pooled beneath what they'd mistaken for a barren wasteland. But like his white companions, Woody was taught to hear the phrase "people" as "white people"; a part of the local Democratic political machine, Woody's father at least condoned and probably participated in several lynchings. One of the turning points of Woody's political development came in 1937, when he received a letter protesting his use of a racial slur on the Los Angeles radio broadcast where he played the role of the naive hillbilly. The listener wrote: "You were getting along quite well in your program this evening until you announced your 'Nigger Blues.' I am a Negro, a young Negro in college, and I certainly resented your remark. No person . . . of any intelligence uses that word over the radio today." Rather than downplaying the situation, Woody admitted his upbringing had blinded him to the issue; he simply hadn't thought about it. He apologized and promised not to do it again.

And he didn't. Which no doubt helped him build friendships

such as the one described in the first chapter of his autobiography, *Bound for Glory*, which opens with the line "I could see men of all colors bouncing along in the boxcar." Strains of the old spiritual "This Train"—"This train is bound for glory, this train"—echo through the chapter, which focuses on Woody and a black companion as they attempt to avoid the railroad bulls.

Like his descendants in the folk revival, Woody wrote dozens of message songs including "Hang Knot," a blistering condemnation of lynching, and "Plane Wreck at Los Gatos (Deportees)," written after he'd read a newspaper story about the crash of a plane carrying migrant farmworkers back to Mexico. The news report identified the Anglo crew members by name but cloaked the migrants in anonymity. Adapted by activists working for immigrant rights in the nineties, the chorus of "Deportees" redresses the dehumanization. Guthrie bids farewell to his "amigos"—Juan and Rosalita, Jesus and Maria—and laments the white world's refusal to value them as anything other than disposable labor: "You won't have a name when you ride the big airplane. / All they will call you will be deportees."

Woody consistently backed up his songs on racial justice with action. Recounting his experiences as Woody's shipmate in the merchant marine during World War II, Jimmy Longhi told a story about his friend's confrontation with segregation in the military. Midway through a particularly perilous Atlantic crossing, their ship came under heavy attack. Jimmy, Woody, and Cisco Houston ventured belowdecks to sing for the troops, hoping to take their minds off the depth charges exploding all around them. During a pause in their performance, Woody heard the sound of a "glorious Negro chorus." Seeking the source of the sound, Woody discovered fifty black soldiers crowded into a toilet room. Longhi described entering the room to encounter an energetic call and response between the group and its commanding officer, Daniel Rutledge. Reaching deep into the shared images of the gospel tradition, Rutledge sang out his sermon on the coming "Judgement Day" and the soldiers responded with cries of "Free! Free!"

Accepting Rutledge's invitation to sing for the troops, Woody surprised them by singing "John Henry," initiating an exchange of songs. When Woody offered to let Rutledge play his guitar, the black officer noticed Woody's slogan and improvised a sermon on the connection between the war against Hitler and the struggle against American racism. Rutledge called out, "An' we know that after we win this war, when the king of slavery is dead, when the king of slavery is dead, things is gonna *change* for the people of Israel!" When the men responded "Change! Change!," Rutledge held Woody's guitar "above his head like a weapon" and hammered home the main point of the movement that returning black veterans would help define and carry through: "An' the walls will come tumblin' down!"

The most immediate wall, Longhi recalls, was the one separating the black and white troops on Woody's ship. Hearing the commotion in the toilet, a white officer arrived to summon Woody back to the white soldiers waiting for him to resume his performance. Woody refused to return unless the black soldiers could come with him. Refusing to accept the officer's insistence that segregation was a policy he didn't support but was powerless to change, Woody insisted on seeing higher and higher ranking officers until he found himself face-to-face with the ship's commander. Determining that the commander was a fan of Benny Goodman's swing band, Woody pointed out that Goodman's group included black musicians Teddy Wilson and Lionel Hampton. Although many of the clubs Goodman played in banned integrated "dance bands," Goodman circumvented the Jim Crow laws by defining Wilson and Hampton as "concert performers." When the commander acquiesced, Woody and Rutledge proudly led the black troops back to the "white" area of the ship, where Woody's "no dancing" pledge lasted about as long as it did in the clubs where Goodman played.

But the part of Woody's life that most directly relates to the folk revival's race problems was his admiration for and work with black musicians including Leadbelly and the duo of Sonny Terry and Brownie McGhee. Woody's music shared the rough edges, intensity, and immediacy of Leadbelly's "The Midnight Special" and "The Bourgeois Blues." Neither Woody nor Leadbelly produced commercially successful popular music, perhaps because neither held a nostalgic ideal of returning to an "authentic" music located in some mythic rural past. While Woody thought of his music as a voice of, from, and for the people, he knew the people's voices changed as their experiences changed. As a committed leftist, he welcomed any change that would reduce the violence and poverty beneath the nostalgic images.

Until Huntington's disease muffled his voice, Woody struggled to make musicians on the American left understand how crucial race was to that change. Once, Woody arrived in North Carolina to perform for a strike fund in the textile mills only to find the union segregated. He refused to play for an all-white audience. As a result, he played for an all-black one when the white union boycotted his "open" performance.

Woody was distressed when folk music began to move toward the mythic notion of authenticity. The first folk group to enjoy major mainstream success was the Weavers, whose lineup included Woody's old leftist friends Pete Seeger and Ronnie Gilbert. Paving the way for the even greater popular success of the even less political Kingston Trio, best known for their version of the Appalachian ballad "Tom Dooley," the Weavers had major hits with Leadbelly's "Goodnight Irene" and Woody's "So Long It's Been Good to Know You." The traditional melodies remained but the politics and the polyrhythmic drive that connected Brownie and Sonny with the South and, at second remove, the electric blues, faded away along with the black presence in the folk scene.

The Weavers' triumph marks the real beginning of what music critic Dave Marsh calls the "rhythm problem" in the folk scene. Woody saw it coming and tried to resist. In response to the Weavers, he announced plans to form an integrated group with Leadbelly, Brownie, and Sonny. But when his illness silenced him, no one pursued the vision of an interracial folk group, maybe because some of the fifties folksingers felt compelled to downplay their leftist pasts in response to McCarthyism. After all, this was an era in which FBI agents were trained to spot "communists" by their comfort around Negroes. Or maybe black/white groups didn't match the folk revival criteria for authenticity. Whatever the cause, by the early sixties not many of the politically serious folk revivalists were willing or able to get down with the sounds coming out of Sam Cooke's Chicago or Berry Gordy's Detroit. And even though folk drew on black sources, it had precious little appeal among young blacks. Which was a shame because the folkies and their black contemporaries really did share a commitment to freedom and dignity. But they were living in different worlds.

# 11
# "Blowin' in the Wind": Politics and Authenticity

A well-known image from the closing concert of the 1963 Newport Folk Festival sums up the folk revival's sense of its political mission. The concert culminated with Joan Baez, Bob Dylan, Pete Seeger, the SNCC Freedom Singers, and Peter, Paul & Mary joining together to sing "We Shall Overcome" and "Blowin' in the Wind." A widely circulated photograph of the performers, arms linked, testifies to the movement's ideal of interracial solidarity. Like so many images from the sixties, the image tells only part of the story.

Although "Blowin' in the Wind" inspired real political activity, its lyrics carried an undertone of romantic passivity that contrasted with the increasingly aggressive approach of the black movement. "How many roads must a man walk down before they call him a man? / How many seas must a white dove sail before she sleeps in the sand?" For black singers like Sam Cooke and Stevie Wonder, who covered the song after Peter, Paul & Mary made it a hit, the last line expresses the yearning for rest after a long and bitter struggle. When King called out "How long?," his black supporters responded "Not long." Even so-called moderates demanded "Freedom Now!" The black SNCC members who would soon ask whites to leave the organization were rapidly losing patience with what they saw as a white willingness to answer Dylan's question with sorrowful resignation to the universality of injustice. For black participants in the Southern movement, moving forward was a matter of life or death. And while the white students who went to Mississippi put themselves at real risk—witness the murders of civil rights workers Goodman, Cheney, and Schwerner—the difference in urgency showed up daily in the sound of the folk revival.

Especially in the years before Dylan arrived in Greenwich Village and announced himself as the second coming of Woody Guthrie, folk music often turned away from the present to gaze back on a half-imagined rural past. John Jacob Niles, a formally trained singer who specialized in reviving traditional music, observed at Newport in 1960 that "My audiences thank all folk singers for comfort, for assurance, for the nostalgia that seems to connect them with times past." For many listeners in those early days, Joan Baez exemplified folk. When she made her national debut at Newport in 1959 singing "We Are Crossing Jordan's River," it's doubtful whether anyone in the audience was particularly attuned to the masked meanings that would have been obvious at movement rallies in Mississippi or South Carolina. There's something mournful, haunting, in the sound of Baez's early albums, which consist almost entirely of traditional ballads lamenting lost love. Her voice filigrees the edges of emotions, evoking a past dimly seen through the mists rising up over the Scottish hills and English moors. Baez's music almost requires silence, freeing listeners for inward-looking reveries that have little in common with either the explosive responsiveness or the expectant silence of a gospel congregation. As folk revival historian Robert Cantwell observes, despite Baez's personal ideals, her ethereal voice and repertoire of what the Newport festival program called "utterly pure, nearly sacrosanct folk songs" was widely received as a "residue of authentic Anglo-American identity."

It wasn't something Baez, who grew up in a pacifist Quaker family and passionately supported the freedom movement, sought. Along with Ochs, she was the most consistently political of the folk revival singers. After Baez met Dylan, her concerts featured movement standards "Oh Freedom" and "We Shall Overcome" alongside Dylan's most piercing political songs "With God on Our Side" and "A Hard Rain's A-Gonna Fall." Inspired by the idealism of the Port Huron Statement and the moral heroism of the Southern movement, she encouraged the folk revival to assume a more aggressive political stance. But Baez could never really overcome the barriers her musical form and voice set up between her and the black listeners whose cause she espoused.

It wasn't just a problem of aesthetics. Even as it highlights the folk revival's commitment to racial justice, Baez's autobiography reflects its somewhat romantic sense of the movement. Her description of a concert she presented at all-black Miles College just outside Birmingham at the height of the SCLC campaign there points to the revival's strengths and its problems. Baez remembered her surprise when whites, who had obviously never been on the Miles campus before, began arriving for her performance. Imagining the spiritual connection between her music and the demonstrators who were being jailed and beaten just a few miles away, Baez writes: "Images of the kids gave me courage, and the concert was beautiful. It ended with 'We Shall Overcome,' and the audience rose and held hands, swaying back and forth while they sang. The singing was soft and tentative and many people were crying."

That was what the folk revival did best. Star performers like Baez and Dylan could bring people who would otherwise have been content with escapist popular entertainment into at least momentary contact with the larger political world. For a few years in the mid-sixties all but the least aware Top 40 fans knew a few movement standards. Despite being banned by numerous Top 40 radio stations, Barry McGuire's "Eve of Destruction" reached number one on the pop charts with a lyric that demanded listeners concerned with the "hate there is in Red China" wake up and "take a look around at Selma, Alabama." No doubt, many of those listeners shed a few tears over violence and injustice and left it at that. But a handful marched out and put their lives on the line.

Within a few years of the Freedom Summer, as the folk revival faded, things had changed in ways very few of the students who'd gathered at Port Huron could have imagined. A Southern president elected on a peace platform solemnly intoned "we shall overcome" while SNCC expelled its white members. A new wave of English bands inspired by R & B and the electric blues forged new connections between black and white music. For the students of Port Huron, the Rolling Stones' "Get Off of My Cloud," the Animals' "We Gotta Get Out of This Place," and the Beatles' "Help" were more authentic than anything the musicologists might recover from old black men toiling in the Delta sun.

# 12
# Music and the Truth:
# The Birth of Southern Soul

The South was at least half myth to the Bob Dylan who carefully placed a copy of Robert Johnson's *King of the Delta Blues* in the background on the cover of *Bringing It All Back Home*. But it was something very real to the homegrown musicians who made Southern soul into something harder, grittier than the sweet sounds coming out of Detroit and Chicago. No doubt it had something to do with the fact that most Southern whites didn't even pretend to accept integration, a word which the Klan used to conjure up visions of bestial black men defiling the flower of Southern womanhood. George Wallace said it about as clearly as it could be said: "Segregation now . . . segregation tomorrow . . . segregation forever."

Almost forty years have passed since Wallace's ringing declaration made him the symbol of Southern white supremacy and lifted him to national prominence in a series of telling presidential campaigns. Few Americans recall that Wallace won 90 percent of the white vote on Maryland's Eastern Shore in 1964, or that he consistently polled more than 20 percent of national support during most of the 1968 presidential campaign. The amnesia concerning everyday life under Jim Crow, encouraged by white indifference to racial problems and a growing tendency among some blacks to see segregation as a golden age of self-sufficiency, is even more disturbing. In his biography of black activist Robert Williams, *Radio Free Dixie*, historian Tim Tyson rips away the veil of nostalgia and forgetfulness cloaking the realities of daily life under segregation:

> The power of white skin in the Jim Crow South was both stark and subtle. White supremacy permeated daily life so deeply that most people could no more ponder it than a fish might discuss the wetness of water. Racial etiquette was at once bizarre, arbitrary and nearly in-

violable. A white man who would never shake hands with a black man would refuse to permit anyone but a black man to shave his face, cut his hair, or give him a shampoo. A white man might share his bed with a black woman but never his table. Black breasts could suckle white babies, black hands would pat out biscuit dough for white mouths, but black heads must not try on a hat in a department store, lest it be rendered unfit for sale to white people. Black maids washed the bodies of the aged and infirm, but the uniforms they wore could never be laundered in the same washing machines that white people used. It was permissible to call a favored black man "Commodore" or "Professor"—a mixture of affection and mockery—but never "mister" or "sir." Black women were "girls" until they were old enough to be called "auntie," but could never hear a white person, regardless of age, address them as "Mrs." or "Miss." Whites regarded black people as inherently lazy and shiftless, but when a white man said he had "worked like a nigger," he meant that he had engaged in dirty, back-breaking labor to the point of collapse.

Jim Crow and white supremacy weren't abstract to the black singers and white musicians who collaborated to make Rick Hall's Muscle Shoals, Alabama, studio one of the two most influential locations in Southern soul. Muscle Shoals wasn't all that far from Birmingham, which may have been the most deeply entrenched bastion of white supremacy. *New York Times* reporter Harrison Salisbury described the city in the early sixties: "Every channel of communication, every medium of mutual interest, every reasoned approach, every inch of middle ground has been fragmented by the emotional dynamite of racism, enforced by the whip, the razor, the gun, the bomb, the torch, the club, the knife, the mob, the police, and many branches of the state's apparatus." Telephones were routinely tapped, mail intercepted and opened—"the eavesdropper, the informer, the spy has become a way of life."

Contact between blacks and whites, in private homes or musical studios, was subjected to intense scrutiny. In his invaluable *Sweet Soul Music,* Southern soul chronicler Peter Guralnick describes the dangers and tensions that went along with making music that redefined racial conventions. Songwriter Donnie Fritts remembered traveling with white organist Spooner Oldham and black soul singer Arthur Alexander to play a date in Birmingham. "Birmingham was dangerous back then, and I mean dangerous, son. As best I can remember the show was for some high school graduation, and it seems to me like it was at the Jewish Community Center. Which was two strikes against us right there. It wasn't long since those three little colored girls had been blown away, and we got some bomb threats that night. . . . Arthur was scared to fucking death. He wouldn't get out of the car."

Fritts recalled another time when Alexander, Oldham, guitarist David Briggs, and a couple of black friends went over to Birmingham. Briggs wanted to stop off and visit a friend in a white section of town. Fritts remembered "waiting on him, and me and Spooner got out and went into this cafe, and the lady behind the counter said, 'Are you guys with those niggers out there?' I said, 'Yeah. Why?' She said, 'Look, it's none of my business, but I been watching this car that's circled the block twice with some guys in it, and if I was you, I wouldn't be here the next time they come around.' I said, 'Nuff said, ma'am.' "

Wallace's words echoed clearly throughout the mid-South—a loosely defined region incorporating northern Alabama, and Mississippi, western Tennessee, and eastern Arkansas. They were in the heads of the white supremacists who used dynamite and guns without a second thought to enforce racial divisions. They thundered beneath the declarations of the Alabama White Citizens Council, which established a committee "to do away with this vulgar animalistic nigger rock and roll bop." The executive secretary of the council declared: "The obscenity and vulgarity of the rock and roll music is obviously a means by which the white man and his children can be driven to the level of the nigger."

That was the racial backdrop for the unlikely group of musicians who came together to mount a challenge to segregation that was less ideological, but more far-reaching, than what the folk revival had in mind. As deeply grounded in the gospel impulse as anything coming out of Chicago or Detroit, Southern soul had no tendency to downplay the harsh realities at the heart of the blues. That might have been because the Southern soul singers stuck closer to their black audiences. Wilson Pickett, Otis Redding, and Sam and Dave always did much better on the R & B than on the pop charts. Redding, for example, never placed a record in the pop top twenty during his lifetime. Careful not to stray from their core audience even when they experienced mainstream success, the Southern soul singers felt much freer to deal with the places where it was hard to tell salvation from damnation than the singers who made Motown's upbeat sound a constant presence in the top ten.

Both the black audiences and the local white folks had their impact on the sound of Southern soul. No one was about to mistake the mid-South for the promised land. When Wilson Pickett, who was born in Alabama but moved to Detroit as a teenager, arrived in Muscle Shoals looking for producer Rick Hall, he was shocked by what he found: "I couldn't believe it. I looked out the plane window, and there's these people picking cotton. I said to myself, 'I ain't getting off this plane, take me back North.' This big Southern guy was at the airport, really big guy, looks like a sheriff. He says he's looking for me. I said, 'I don't want to get off here, they still got black people picking cotton.' The man looked at me and said, 'Fuck that. Come on, Pickett, let's go make some fucking hit records.' I didn't know Rick Hall was white." Recording at Hall's Fame Studio, Pickett laid down the classics "Land of 1000 Dances," "Mustang Sally," and "Funky Broadway."

The history of Southern music contains hundreds of similar scenes involving the sometimes friendly, sometimes tense contact between black and white musicians. Carl Perkins provides the archetypal version of the story when he credits his musical education to a black sharecropper, "Uncle John" Westbrook, who worked in the same cotton fields as Perkins's poor white family. "He used to sit out on the front porch at night with a gallon bucket full of coal oil rags that he'd burn to keep the mosquitoes off him, and I'd ask my daddy if I could go to Uncle John's and hear him pick some." When Perkins began developing his version of the rockabilly style he shared with the young Elvis Presley, he took Uncle John's style to heart. "I just speeded up some of the slow blues licks," he remembered. "I put a little speed and rhythm to what Uncle John had slowed down. That's all. That's what rockabilly music or rock 'n' roll was to begin with: a country man's song with a black man's rhythm." Two decades later Dan Penn, one of the real aces of both Muscle Shoals and Memphis, echoed the point: "We didn't know nothing until black people put us on the right road. I never would have learned nothing if I'd have stayed listening to white people all my life." Putting a slightly sardonic spin on the situation, Memphis drummer Jim Dickinson commented, "Everybody learned it from the yard man."

Which doesn't alter the reality that Southern soul, like early rock and roll, really *was* an interracial collaboration. Soul singer Solomon Burke, whose country/R & B hybrid "Just Out of Reach (Of My Two Empty Arms)" predated Ray Charles's *Modern Sounds in Country and Western Music* by a year, summed up the underlying connection between the musics of the black and white South: "Gospel is the truth. And country music is the truth."

In some ways, what happened musically in Memphis *might* have happened almost anywhere in the South. Several of the central figures in Southern soul—Booker T. Jones, Duck Dunn, Aretha Franklin—were Memphis natives. But most grew up elsewhere: Otis Redding in Macon, Georgia; Sam Moore in Miami; James Brown in South Carolina and Georgia; Wilson Pickett in Alabama. Aretha, Pickett, and Al Green all moved north with their families before they were adults. The same pattern held for the white musicians who helped build the city's musical tradition. Elvis was born in Mississippi, Jerry Lee Lewis in Louisiana, Carl Perkins in rural Tennessee, Steve Cropper in Missouri. Sam Phillips, whose Sun Studio became the magnet for the musicians who established Memphis as the cradle of interracial rock and roll in the fifties, didn't arrive until he'd spent his first sixteen years in northwest Alabama, a hundred miles north of Greenville, where a black street singer named Tee-Tot (Rufus Payne) had taught a young Hank Williams to sing the blues. And the hard truths of Williams's "Six More Miles (to the Graveyard)" and "A Mansion on the Hill" responded to the example of Jimmie Rodgers, the first star of country music, whose "Waiting for a Train," "In the Jailhouse Now," and "T for Texas" echoed the blues and gospel traditions of Louisiana and Texas. Rodgers frequently traveled with black sidemen.

The pieces that came together in Memphis were available elsewhere, in part because the black and white Souths were closer culturally than anyone wanted to admit. In a slightly different universe, you can imagine rock and roll or Southern soul developing out of the Piedmont blues Brownie McGhee and Sonny Terry played for the black and white crowds who thronged to the Carolina tobacco markets every fall. Or as a part of Atlanta's never-ending effort to establish itself as the capital of a "New South" that never quite seemed to arrive. Or in New Orleans, where it kind of did happen. Or Macon, home to both Little Richard and Otis Redding.

But the historical fact is that it happened in Memphis. Sam Phillips's description of his entry into the city in 1939 suggests one of the main reasons. Following a path blazed by thousands of young men growing up in the backwoods South, the sixteen-year-old Phillips "went to Memphis with some friends in a big old Dodge. We drove down Beale Street in the middle of the night and it was *rockin'!* It was so active—musically, socially. God, I loved it!"

If you were looking for good times, Memphis offered plenty. Suspended midway between brutal reality and regional hallucination, Memphis occupies a strange place in the psychic landscape of the region. The Mississippi Delta, it is said, begins on Catfish Row in Vicksburg and ends in the lobby of Memphis's Peabody Hotel. In the semifictional geography created by William Faulkner, who grew up just down the road in Oxford, Mississippi, Memphis provides a safety valve for the tensions created by the hard-shell religious fundamentalism and white supremacist orthodoxy of the small-town white South. When they aren't running off to the wilderness to arm-wrestle enormous mythic animals, Faulkner's Mississippians love nothing better than road-tripping up to Memphis for a few days in the brothels and gambling dens. Like the Harlem where a young Malcolm X made his living guiding whites to whatever sexual adventures they could imagine, Memphis revealed the white obsession with segregation as a pious mask over a moral vacuum. As in Harlem—and Berry Gordy's Detroit for that matter—the bottom line was the dollar bill.

Memphis had a different sort of appeal for the black musicians who brought the musical forms from their Delta homes to the big city. Although black Memphis as a whole was never affluent, it offered far more opportunity than the even poorer rural places most of them came from. Providing semipublic interracial spaces that just weren't available in Sunflower County, Mississippi, or Osceola, Arkansas, Beale Street gave black musicians a chance to cash in on the white folks' desire to walk on the wild side.

The comparatively open racial atmosphere that brought black musicians together with both black and white audiences on Beale Street hadn't happened by accident. Unique in the Jim Crow South, the white power structure in Memphis depended on black votes and black money. The central figure in Memphis politics from 1910 until his death in 1954 was E. H. "Boss" Crump, head of a machine as powerful as Richard Daley's in Chicago or Fiorello La Guardia's in New York.

When Crump arrived in Memphis just after the turn of the century, the city's politics followed the classic Southern pattern: aristocratic white planters manipulated racial animosities to set blacks against poor whites, who were only too eager to be manipulated. Often the aristocrats relied on sanctimonious appeals to religious purity, invoking the ideals of "pure white womanhood" and the "white Christian nation." Such appeals deflected attention from the

Delta's economic system, which enabled Mississippi to rank near the top of the list of millionaires per capita at the same time it held a firm grip on its status as the poorest state in the nation.

Recognizing the economic reality of the city's underground economy—based on gambling, prostitution, and bootlegging—Crump organized a coalition of white and black businessmen with Beale Street interests. Whatever their color, the entrepreneurs were sick of the periodic crackdowns ordered by politicians seeking to maintain their standing with the good Christian voters. The respectable black citizens of Memphis, every bit as dedicated to their churches as their white neighbors, viewed Beale Street with God-fearing suspicion. They most definitely wanted to keep their daughters as far as possible from its dens of sin. But they knew that Crump was preferable to the Klan. If nothing else, he needed their votes to maintain political control. It probably didn't hurt that W. C. Handy, the "Father of the Blues," had written Crump's campaign song.

Rising to power with the support of this bizarre coalition, Crump guaranteed tolerance of the black- and white-owned businesses—mostly bars and brothels—that operated side by side, drawing a mixed crowd to the two-block free zone just off the Mississippi waterfront. Although segregation remained nominally in effect, there was plenty of crossing of racial lines. The Memphis whorehouses were the only ones in the South which condoned black men's access to white prostitutes, though only after three a.m., by which time white men had presumably had sufficient time to exercise their racial privilege. In the Beale Street clubs, Sleepy John Estes, Furry Lewis, and Memphis Minnie took the blues songs from the Delta and reshaped them into something new while playing for customers of all races. It was a perfect workshop for Handy, who deserves his title only in the sense that he wrote down and marketed a form that was taking shape all around him.

If Handy's claim was ambiguous, Memphis had certainly earned its designation as the "murder capital of America." In part because Crump's police tolerated the open sale of cocaine, drug addiction was epidemic. Plenty of dark corners were available for anyone eager to explore the night side of the Southern psyche. Beale Street simmered and sometimes exploded. The 1938 murder of eight prominent white citizens by three black men in a Beale Street turf war precipitated a public outcry that closed down the old wide-open Beale Street. But Memphis musicians never quite forgot the vibrant interracial scene that would resurface at Sam Phillips's Sun Studio in the fifties.

However exhilarating Beale Street could be, black folks recognized its limits. If Faulkner's Memphis signified an ambiguous sort of freedom for small-town whites, black novelist Richard Wright's autobiographical *Black Boy* portrays the city as something more like purgatory, a halfway house for Delta blacks on their way to Chicago. If moral or sexual lines blurred in Memphis, a black man or woman had to be a fool to trust it very far. For anyone paying attention, Memphis history provided plenty of warnings against accepting white fantasies at face value. In 1892, the white citizens of Memphis responded to black journalist Ida B. Wells's antilynching campaign, during which she suggested white women might conceivably be sexually attracted to black men, by destroying the offices of her *Free Speech* newspaper and driving her out of the city.

A half century later, the civil rights movement consistently avoided Memphis, preferring to deal with white supremacy in the small towns of Alabama, Georgia, and Mississippi. Martin Luther King's advisers expressed grave reservations about his decision to engage the garbage collectors' strike, a decision that took him to the balcony of the Lorraine Motel. There was no shortage of whites who thought James Earl Ray was a hero, many of them the same ones who, angry over the Kennedy administration's role in the desegregation of Ole Miss, had cheered the news of JFK's death in Dallas. They had company, of course, throughout the nation.

In Memphis, then, white supremacy coexisted with the most fluid interracial musical heritage in the South (with the complicated exception of New Orleans). The blues were a way of life, not just a musical form. Despite the money black businesses made under Crump, many black citizens simply kept their distance from Beale Street and everything it represented. Holding firmly to the church that provided their rock in a weary land, they tried their best to keep their families and communities together. It wasn't easy: prostitution was by far the most lucrative employment available to black women; their brothers often preferred to take their chances on the street rather than scrambling for manual labor in an economy that didn't pay *white* folks much. The black community was all too familiar with lost souls; it knew that every minute of every day someone you loved was standing at the crossroads, wondering which way to go.

That's one of the reasons why the blues and gospel have such a complicated relationship in Southern soul. When Southern singers strike out to make some money, they're more likely to sing about sex than salvation, violence than the promised land. They don't always bother to distinguish love from hate or sex from death. But almost all of them learned to sing in church. When Wilson Pickett testifies to that moment in the midnight hour when his love comes tumbling down, he's remembering the savior waiting for the sinner in the dark night of the soul. When Sam Moore and Dave Prater whipped their listeners into a frenzy of call and response, the energy came right out of the sanctified church.

Describing the source of Sam and Dave's appeal, Moore pointed to their direct connection with Marion Williams and Mahalia Jackson. "Nobody up to that had never done that kind of stuff," he said, referring to the R & B singers who had adapted gospel to the pop marketplace. "People had taken the gospel harmonies and some of the gospel melodies, gospel songs, and gospel chord progressions and gospel singing inflections—but to actually bring the C. L. Franklin preaching style, no one had done that the way that, in a show, the Stirrers with R. H. Harris or Sam Cooke or whoever, or the Highway QCs would do," Moore continued. "All of them—even Wilson Pickett, when he was in the Violinaires—would preach, evangelize onstage. We incorporated that into soul music. It was really, as the people used to say, 'messing with the Lord. You're messing with God, boy. What are you doing?' "

Where Mahalia and Sam Cooke kept their eyes on the prize, Stax's interracial house band, Booker T. and the MGs, like Sam and Dave in their "messing" mode, worried mostly about keeping the party hot. Listening to them, you couldn't always tell how much of the fire came from the devil and how much from the Lord.

It was a problem Robert Johnson knew well.

# 13
# Down at the Crossroads

If you were white and honest, the blues revealed things the upbeat America of the early sixties assured you didn't exist. That's why so many mid-South white boys—Steve Cropper and Duck Dunn of the MGs, songwriter-producers Dan Penn and Chips Moman, even Elvis before the velvet paintings filled in the blank spaces—fell in love with music that made desegregation sound like something more than an empty dream. Then again, if you were *just* white, the blues could make you swear off mirrors, never mind music with a harder edge than Perry Como. Dozens of white musicians bear witness to how black music helped them escape the suffocating communities they grew up in.

But for most black musicians, the blues evoked a deeper, more agonized relationship between the individual and the community. The crucial difference is that, in the black blues, evil retains its religious significance. Every note Robert Johnson played as he wandered the dark highways of America during the Great Depression reverberates with the reality of exile from a gospel community he knows is real. Widely honored as the most profound of the Delta bluesmen, Johnson wrote songs that testify to his anguished connection with a spiritual force. Johnson's titles resonate with apocalyptic biblical images: "Stones in My Passway," "If I Had Possession over Judgement Day," "Hellhound on My Trail," "Crossroads Blues."

For white rockers like Eric Clapton, the crossroads mark a place of existential decision; for Johnson, they stretch over an abyss that's both theological and social. Like most black Southerners, he knew the choice you make at the crossroads can determine everything. For a fugitive slave or a black man running from the Klan, every crossroads presented a choice of direction that could make the difference between slavery and freedom, life and death. Johnson's anguished blues place the listener at one of the crossroads. You can hear the wind howl; you can't quite be sure whether it's covering the patroller's baying hounds. No question that "Crossroads" points to the grounding of the blues in American racial realities. But there's also no question that the sense you're about to take an irrevocable step is something everyone feels sometime, somewhere. It's the sense, as Robert Penn Warren's narrator in *All the King's Men* puts it, "that you are alone with the Alone, and it is His move." One more cry from the guitar string, one more twisting chord from the gut-bucket, and there's no going back.

It's a place where white folks have a choice of getting past white, of understanding something about what it means to live in a world without options other than the ones you can figure out for yourself right now. And you've got no time to think about where that step might take you, to weigh implications. The blues say you do what you have to do, your act's what you are. It's why Bob Dylan titled his greatest album *Highway 61 Revisited* after the road that carved cross-roads through the heart of the Delta. "Like a Rolling Stone" wasn't named for Mick and Keith. Dylan's at least got a sense of what Johnson and Ma Rainey and Muddy Waters were talking about, of what it means to walk down the road that bends back to where black and white came to pretty much the same thing. If only on Beale Street. And only between three a.m. and dawn.

But there's another dimension of "Crossroads" that remains obscure even to the Dylan of "Just Like Tom Thumb's Blues," stranded in a place where "gravity fails and negativity don't see you through." If Dylan maps the existential wasteland, Johnson's "Crossroads" remembers the routes connecting West Africa with the Delta. For many West African tribes, the crossroads were the place where the spirit world and the material world converged, where you went when you needed spiritual energy. For the Yoruba, the crossroads were a place of power and danger. They were dedicated to and ruled by the spirit, or *orisha*, Esu-Elegba, who walks with a limp, revels in chaos, and carries messages between the material and spiritual worlds.

Like all orisha, Esu-Elegba combines strengths and weaknesses. When the Yoruba tell stories about the orisha, they're initiating discussion, not presenting role models. Unlike the stereotypical Sunday sermon that reveals the meaning of a biblical passage, the Yoruba process requires call and response. Esu's strength lies in his mastery of language and codes, his verbal facility, his literary intelligence. His weakness lies in his amorality. He loves confusion just because he feels at home with it. He's perfectly capable of tearing a community apart because it's interesting, to see what happens. This brother has clearly got to be watched.

But if you need to get closer to the divine presence, to learn the inner meaning of the incomprehensible messages that come in dreams or moments of awe-ful awareness of the spirit, you've got no choice but to deal with Esu. One way or another, Esu—a.k.a. Legba, Papa LaBas, the Signifying Monkey, Brer Rabbit, the Nigga You Love to Hate, Richard Pryor, and Flava Flav—is gonna deal with you.

So you go down to the crossroads. And maybe you meet a man with a limp. Which, legend has it, is how Robert Johnson learned to play the blues. Laughed off the stage at a Delta juke joint, he vanished for a year, some say three. When he returned, he spoke the blues in tongues his elders had never even imagined. Some say he traveled from New Orleans to Chicago, mastering his craft; others say he sold his soul to Beelzebub.

Black Christians had strong reasons for renaming Esu the "devil." They'd seen what happened to folks who chose the wrong road. If Esu bestows creative brilliance, he exacts a price. He brings chaos to a community in desperate need of stability. Esu embodies the spirit of Beale Street: drugs, sex, violent death. All in the name of a good time, good music. Pure deviltry.

Maybe the most basic crossroads for a black Southerner led one way to Beale Street, the other way to church. Robert Johnson made his choice, but his music never lets you forget it was a choice. That somewhere a Sunday-morning sister was singing him back home. Or that she was more than half likely to follow him into the woods when she heard that dark blue moan some lonely Saturday night.

## A Blues Impulse Top 40

1. Grandmaster Flash and the Furious Five, "The Message," 1982

2. Robert Johnson, "Hellhound on My Trail," 1937

3. Ike and Tina Turner, "A Fool in Love," 1960

4. Bessie Smith, "Downhearted Blues," 1923

5. Muddy Waters, "The Same Thing," 1964

6. The Four Tops, "Bernadette," 1967

7. Aretha Franklin, "Chain of Fools," 1967

8. Stevie Wonder, "Living for the City," 1973

9. Wu-Tang Clan, "C.R.E.A.M.," 1994

10. Temptations, "Papa Was a Rollin' Stone," 1972

11. Bob Marley, "Them Belly Full," 1975

12. Sly and the Family Stone, "Family Affair," 1971

13. Bruce Springsteen, "Backstreets," 1975

14. Marvin Gaye, "I Heard It Through the Grapevine," 1968

15. Clarence Carter, "Makin' Love (At the Dark End of the Street)," 1969

16. Ray Charles, "Unchain My Heart," 1961

The blues ain't nothin' but a good man feelin' bad. Hard to beat the definition for clarity, except to note the obvious flip side: the blues ain't nothin' but a good woman feelin' bad. Lord knows, there's a temptation to leave it there. After all, the blues are mostly about what you're feeling here and now.

But, however much the blues resist abstraction, there's a bit more to say. The blues force you to deal with the man with the knife, your lover's wandering eyes, the fact that when the devil comes calling, plenty of good respectable folks are waiting at the door. If you really hear the blues, you know you're one of them, that life's a hell of a lot more complicated than those lines between saints and sinners, or the black and white sides of town, let on.

> Sad as the blues may be, there's almost always something humorous about them—even if it's the kind of humor that laughs to keep from crying.
> —Langston Hughes

Blues guitarist Eddie Kirkland breaks down the blues about as well as they can be broke: "What gives me the blues? Unlucky in love for one, and hard to make a success is two; and when a man have a family and it's hard to survive for." If there isn't enough money in the house, all those little things—the hole in the window screen, the third straight meal of beans—grow real big real fast. By a conservative count, 180 percent of blues deal with sex or money. The extra 80 percent accounts for the times sex and money are the same damn thing. Once the spiral starts—once your man doesn't bring home enough money for the rent, once your woman puts on that red dress and goes out the door—there's no stoppin' it. All you can hope for is the strength to face another day. On the good days, you can laugh about some of it. As bluesman Furry Lewis, who worked as a Memphis street cleaner, recalled: "You know, old folks say, it's a long lane don't have no end and a bad wind don't never change. But one day, back when Hoover was president, I was driving my cart down Beale Street, and I seen a rat, sitting on top of a garbage can, eating a onion, crying." Or, as B. B. King commented, "Singing the blues is like being black twice."

> *The blues is an impulse to keep the painful details and episodes of a brutal experience alive in one's aching consciousness, to finger its jagged grain, and to transcend it, not by the consolation of philosophy but by squeezing from it a near-tragic, near-comic lyricism. As a form the blues is an autobiographical chronicle of personal catastrophe expressed lyrically.*
>
> —Ralph Ellison

For Ralph Ellison, the blues present a philosophy of life, a three-step process that can be used by painters, dancers, or writers as well as musicians. The process consists of (1) fingering the jagged grain of your brutal experience; (2) finding a near-tragic, near-comic voice to express that experience; and (3) reaffirming your existence. The first two steps run parallel to the gospel impulse's determination to bear witness to

> *No wonder Hamlet came to debate with himself whether to be or not to be. Nor was it, or is it, a question of judging whether life is or is not worth living. Not in the academic sense of Albert Camus's concern with the intrinsic absurdity of existence per se. Hamlet's was whether things are worth all the trouble and struggle. Which is also what the question is when you wake up with the blues there again, not only all around your bed but also inside your head as well, as if trying to make you wish that you were dead or had never been born.*
>
> —Albert Murray

the reality of the burden. But where gospel holds out the hope that things will change, that there's a better world coming, the blues settle for making it through the night. As Ellison's friend Albert Murray wrote, they deal with "the most fundamental of all existential imperatives: affirmation, which is to say, reaffirmation and continuity in the face of adversity."

> *Perhaps I love them because the attitude toward life expressed in blues records—that everyone has troubles but they can be endured, that happiness is not lasting, so don't be fooled by your good times—is truly the essence of "blackness." Blues do not promise that people will not be unhappy, but that unhappiness can be transcended, not by faith in God, but by faith in one's own ability to accept unhappiness without ever conceding oneself to it. Blackness is not an Afrocentric lesson, nor a coming together of the tribe in fake unity. It is this: a fatalistic, realistic belief in human transcendence, born in the consciousness of a people who experienced the gut-wrenching harshness of slavery, of absorbing the absolute annihilation of their humanity, and who lived to tell the world and their former masters about it. And it is about how they reinvented their humanity in the meanwhile.*
> —Gerald Early

The blues deal with the unavoidable problems that come with being human. You wake up in the morning and they're waiting for you all around your bed.

It's not a question philosophy can answer. All you can do is reach down inside the pain, finger the jagged grain, tell your story and hope you can find the strength to go on. You never really get away, transcend. If you're lucky, though, if the song's call gets some sort of response, some echo in the parts of your head that believe it may be worthwhile, a smile from that woman at the dark end of the street, that's all you can hope for. Reaffirmation, the strength to say, yeah, I'll *be*. Chicago blues master Willie Dixon stated the blues answer to Hamlet's question with irreducible clarity: "I'm *here*, everybody knows I'm *here*." Knowing all that time that tomorrow morning the blues'll be right there beside his bed. Good morning, blues.

Murray's rephrasing of Ellison's "transcendence" as "reaffirmation" clarifies the meaning of "near-tragic, near-comic lyricism." Sometimes the blues make you laugh, but the real "comedy" resembles Dante as much as Richard Pryor, who, we might note, had his own "inferno" and used it as a source for much grim humor. If tragedy describes a world in which loss is inevitable and irrevocable, comedy describes one where balance, however tenuous, wins out. Dante's point was that hearing the harmony behind the screams required a perspective close to God's; that's why the comedy's "Divine."

And why human life, as Richard Pryor can testify, mostly isn't. On the human level, evil's not something you can change, just something you have to deal with. Singing the blues doesn't reaffirm the brutal experience, it reaffirms the value of life. The blues don't even pretend you're going to escape the cycle. You sing the blues so you can live to sing the blues again. A lot of times the blues are mostly about finding the energy to keep moving. That's why they're such great party music and that's why you hear them echoing through rock and through rap.

The blues tell you that as long as you can hear your voice, as long as you can find even a little bit of the laughter in the tears, you can most likely find the strength to wake up in the morning and deal with the fact that you messed it up again, that the devil's back at the door and you're putting on your shoes, humming his song.

# 14
# Soul Food:
# The Mid-South Mix

Wilson Pickett called it "grits music." King Curtis gave his amen, introducing "Memphis Soul Stew" by announcing, "We sell so much of this, people wonder what we put in it." He went on to serve up a hit single concocted from "a half tea-cup of bass," "a pound of fatback drums," "four tablespoons of boiling Memphis guitar," "a pinch of organ," and "a half pint of horns." "Now place on the burner and bring to a boil," the Texas-born sax man called out. "Beat well." Add a vocalist with the down-home intensity of Otis Redding or the aching soulfulness of James Carr and you have the recipe for the funkiest, grittiest soul music of the sixties. Steve Cropper observed that "It wasn't Chicago, and it wasn't New York, and it sure wasn't Detroit. It was a Southern sound, a below-the-Bible-Belt sound. It was righteous and nasty. Which to our way of thinking was pretty close to life itself."

According to James Brown, who provided most of the ingredients for the Memphis recipe, you couldn't separate Southern soul from gospel: "Gospel is contentment because it's spirit, and you feel that spirit when you sing it. It's the same spirit I feel when I'm on stage today. I feel it when I sing. Period. I make people happy, and *they* feel it." Brown, who'd placed nine songs on the R & B charts before Carla Thomas's "Gee Whiz" and the Mar-Keys' "Last Night" established Stax as a major force in soul music, reflected that "The word soul . . . meant a lot of things—in music and out. It was about the roots of black music, and it was kind of a pride thing, too, being proud of yourself and your people. Soul music and the civil rights movement went hand in hand, sort of grew up together."

It may seem like something of a contradiction that what was almost universally received as the *blackest* of the soul styles had by far the largest amount of white participation. Cropper and bass player

Duck Dunn, both white, joined black organist Booker T. Jones and black drummer Al Jackson to form Booker T. and the MGs, the Stax house band that backed Otis Redding, Sam and Dave, Wilson Pickett, and countless others. Frequently, they were joined by the Memphis Horns, led by white trumpeter Wayne Jackson and black sax man Andrew Love. The top tier of Southern songwriters included Redding, the black team of Isaac Hayes and David Porter, and good old boys Chips Moman and Dan Penn, whose credits include "The Dark End of the Street," "Do Right Woman," "Cry Like a Baby," and "Sweet Inspiration."

Although it was created by Southerners and remained very much rooted in the region, Memphis soul transformed the entire pop music scene. Black singers from the North who'd had trouble adjusting to crossover styles frequently found the Southern approach liberating. Even though Aretha Franklin walked out of the Muscle Shoals Studio after a white session musician used a racial slur with her husband, the song she recorded there—"I Never Loved a Man"—ignited her career, which had floundered for a half decade up North. Having decided she didn't much like recording in the South, Aretha brought the South to Atlantic's New York studios. All of the hits that established her as the "Queen of Soul"—"Respect," "Natural Woman," "Think," "Chain of Fools"—feature white Southern musicians, including bass player Tommy Cogbill, organist Spooner Oldham, drummer Roger Hawkins, and guitarists Jimmy Johnson and Joe South.

Memphis's impact on white pop music was equally profound. Penn and Moman's American Studio became a Mecca for a range of singers that have little in common except that they made their best records in Memphis: Neil Diamond, Dionne Warwick, Lulu, the Box Tops, the Sweet Inspirations, Dusty Springfield, Bobby Womack, B. J. Thomas, James and Bobby Purify, jazzman Herbie Mann. For a sense of what Memphis contributed, listen to Diamond's "Holly Holy," Womack's "Woman's Gotta Have It," the Box Tops' "Soul Deep," or Springfield's *Dusty in Memphis,* highlighted by a beautiful rendition of "Son of a Preacher Man." The sessions Elvis recorded at American are by far the best music he made during the last two decades of his life; they produced the hits "Suspicious Minds," "Kentucky Rain," and "In the Ghetto"—Elvis's single foray into explicit message music. But the real high points are soul standards—"True Love Travels on a Gravel Road," "Only the Strong Survive," and, most tellingly, Percy Mayfield's "Stranger in My Own Home Town."

The Memphis sessions justify James Brown's sincere praise of the "strong spiritual feeling" in Elvis's music.

Penn summed up the interracial complexities of the scene when he told Memphis chronicler Robert Gordon: "There were a lot of white people and black people who had tried to bring the R & B and the white side together. It became a white/black situation, you had white players and black players together. The mixture, who knows what that does to us, but it does something. There was so much respect." Penn went on to contrast the sixties with the eighties. "Now we get all these white people in the studios. Everybody respects each other but it's like you ain't bringing anything different to 'em. We're trying to make a painting here, what color did *you* bring? You're orange and he's orange and we need some red, we need something different, and back then black people brought so much to the whole thing. . . . That cross-color respect was a wonderful thing. It carried a lot of power. We don't seem to have much of that now."

The interracial scene of the sixties originated in the forties and fifties. After Boss Crump closed down Beale Street, musicians continued to participate in interracial networks without public sanction. If whites in fifties Chicago were extremely unlikely to see "real" gospel music live, aspiring white musicians such as the members of the Royal Spades (later the Mar-Keys) attending all-white Messick High School could slip across the river to West Memphis. Royal Spade alumni Cropper and Dunn were among those who learned their approach to music from B. B. King and bandleaders like Ben Branch and Willie Mitchell, who would later help shape the music that lifted Al Green to the top of the soul world. Mar-Key sax player Don Nix remembers sneaking over to the Plantation Inn, "where all the black bands played. And all the black bands had horns. So while everybody else was playing Elvis Presley songs with two guitars and a bass or whatever, we had baritone, tenor, and trumpet, and we played all rhythm and blues music."

When "Last Night" went to the top of the R & B charts in 1961, the white Memphis high school band went out on the road. Black audiences were shocked to discover the band's racial makeup. Wayne Jackson recalls: "We worked the chitlin circuit—black—that's why there weren't any publicity pictures of the group. One place in Texas I remember in particular, we rolled up and they were barbecuing a goat, and you could stand on one side of this club and look through the cracks in the wall to the cotton patch on the other side, and they didn't believe we were the Mar-Keys. 'You can't be the Mar-

Keys!' 'Well, we are,' we said. 'Here's our agent's number; you can call him.' Well, at first they were a little hostile. This was before integration, you know, before a lot of things. But then, when we started playing, they loved us."

While Cropper, Dunn, and Jackson were developing their intimate knowledge of the black musical world, black singers were nurturing the multiracial audience for Southern soul. Even as the white South went to war to maintain the racial purity of its college classrooms, the fraternities of Ole Miss and the University of Alabama encouraged what amounted to cultural miscegenation. Solomon Burke, Percy Sledge, and Otis Redding were among the soul artists who joined salacious novelty acts like Doug Clark and His Hot Nuts and the Thirteen Screaming Niggers as regulars on the fraternity circuit. Rufus Thomas, the grand old man of Memphis soul, fondly remembers playing the college circuit: "I must have played every fraternity house there was in the South. When we played Ole Miss, they'd send the girls home at midnight, and then we'd tell nasty jokes and all that stuff. Oh, man, we used to have some *good* times down there in Oxford. When something was coming, some kind of show, I mean, they'd build themselves up to it, and then, when we got there, they were ready for it. I'd rather play those audiences than for any other."

Not everyone involved with the scene sounds as upbeat about its racial elements as Thomas or Jackson. Sam Moore of Sam and Dave isn't alone in his belief that Stax—at least before black executive Al Bell became a major figure in 1965—amounted to a new kind of plantation where the black singers did the work while the white management made the decisions. White drummer Jim Dickinson underlines the tension between the music's challenge to racial boundaries and the situation outside the studio: "The Memphis sound is something that's produced by a group of social misfits in a dark room in the middle of the night. It's not committees, it's not bankers, not disc jockeys. Every attempt to organize the Memphis music community has been a failure, as righteously it should be. The diametric opposition, the racial collision, the redneck versus the ghetto black is what it is all about, and it can't be brought together. If it could, there wouldn't be any music."

Even if it failed to resolve the oppositions, Memphis music certainly helped develop an audience that was at least interested in listening to the arguments. Along with the chitlin and fraternity circuits, radio played a crucial role in the changes that took place in

American pop music during the postwar years. As late as 1945, radio DJ'ing remained an all-white occupation. In 1947, *Ebony* magazine could identify only sixteen black DJs among the three thousand with regular shows, noting that most of those had been hired in the last couple of years. Memphis-based WDIA played a major role in changing that picture. Unsuccessful in the white market and perhaps inspired by the popularity of Sonny Boy Williamson's *King Biscuit Blues Show*, which was broadcast through the mid-South on KFFA from Helena, Arkansas, WDIA switched to an all-black format in 1948. A year later, all the DJs on WDIA were black. Combining gospel, blues, and jazz with what black cultural historian Nelson George calls its role as "bulletin board" for black Memphis, WDIA's fifty-thousand-watt transmitter carried the voices of DJs B. B. King and Rufus Thomas into over a million black homes.

And who knows how many white ones. If the material that went out on WDIA was black, the picture on the receiving end was more complicated. There's a consensus among the pioneer black DJs that whites constituted at least half their audience, especially during the nighttime hours. The implications for the development of American popular music in the fifties and sixties were immense. Previous generations of white children encountered relatively segregated musical worlds. To get access to the types of black music that were considered too rough or dangerous for crossover audiences required some serious effort. But when "white" radio stations began imitating the successful black formats, blues- and gospel-based sounds could be heard in even the most remote corners of America.

Still, teenagers growing up in the mid-South had an advantage over those in Nebraska, for example, because they could follow up on what they'd heard by riding that well-worn path from the small-town South to Memphis. The Southern soul they helped create differed clearly from the sounds created by black musicians working in the more intensely segregated musical environments of Detroit and Chicago. Memphis soul grew out of a much freer, improvisational process.

The typical Stax session involved building a record out of scraps of lyrics, the idea for a melody, a few chord changes. The MGs, sometimes supplemented by the Memphis Horns, would lay down a groove, talk about what worked and what didn't, incorporate the resulting changes in another version, and repeat the process until they were ready to cut a record. Perhaps the most striking difference between Stax and Motown is the recognition given to the Memphis musicians. From "Last Night" through "Green Onions" and "Memphis Soul Stew," instrumentals played a crucial role in Stax's image. Stax production style gave equal weight to instrumental and vocal tracks, emphasizing distinct voices rather than a wall of sound. When the Stax-Volt Revue toured Europe, Booker T. and the MGs played their own set before backing up the headliner singers. In England, Cropper received almost as much attention from the press as Otis Redding or Sam Moore.

Many Southern soul classics incorporate "mistakes" that Motown would have edited out. The horn section on "Hold On, I'm Coming" gets lost on the second chorus. On Percy Sledge's "When a Man Loves a Woman," the horn section is hopelessly out of tune. Peter Guralnick reports that when Atlantic Records producer Jerry Wexler bought the rights to distribute the single, he specified that he wanted to remaster it in New York; the Atlantic producers spent several weeks working with the master tape. When the song hit the charts, Wexler called Quin Ivy, who had produced the original session, and said: "Aren't you glad you recut it?" Ivy replied, "Jerry, you used the original, out-of-tune horns and all."

There's a temptation to reduce sixties soul music to a competition between Memphis and Detroit for the hearts, minds, and dollars of young America. You can set it up as a paradox: the interracial Memphis scene asserts an uncompromising blackness while the almost-all-black Motown studious play to the taste of the white marketplace. Stax singer William Bell expressed the core diference when he said, "We were basically raw energy, raw emotion. Motown was more slick, more polish." Variations on this approach, which usually treat Chicago as an outpost of Detroit when not ignoring it altogether, circulate freely through many histories of rock and soul.

But they don't have much to do with the truth. Call and response provides a more accurate framework than "battle to the death." For all the differences between the musical approaches of Memphis, Detroit, and Chicago, the musicians associated with each location expressed support and admiration for the "other side." David Porter acknowledged that he and Hayes modeled Sam and Dave's hits on a formula they learned from the Temptations' "Don't Look Back": "Part of what eventually evolved into the magic of Hayes and Porter's writing was my study of the Motown catalogue. That was an ongoing process." Down the road in Muscle Shoals, Penn and Fritts were doing the same thing. As Penn said, "We'd play a Temptations record, we'd write a Temptations song."

Curtis Mayfield echod Porter's sentiments: "It wasn't really a ri-valry. Those guys at Motown were just so much admired and they were so big, there was no need. The best I could do was learn some-thing from them. What with Berry Gordy, Smokey Robinson, they had fantastic writers over there and all you could do was admire those folks for the contribution they made to America." Carla Thomas considered Mayfield one of the "most beautiful guitar play-ers in the world." Mayfield's friend Jerry Butler reached across the mostly imaginary regional lines when he collaborated with Otis Red-ding to write the Southern soul classic "I've Been Loving You Too Long." Redding, who idolized Sam Cooke, filled his albums with songs from Chicago (Butler's "For Your Precious Love," nearly a dozen Cooke songs including "Chain Gang," "Wonderful World," and "A Change Is Gonna Come") and Detroit (the Temptations' "My Girl" and "It's Growing").

Many Motown artists reciprocated the admiration they received from their peers. Marvin Gaye saw the growing popularity of South-ern soul as a harbinger of larger changes: "The era was changing the music. Gutbucket soul – like Aretha and Wilson Pickett and Otis Redding – had gotten popular . . . Anyway, the white kids wanted a different kind of music. They wanted to hear about something be-sides love." By the mid-sixties, Motown's response to Southern soul could be heard in the funk rhythms and the uncompromising lyrics of the records produced by Norman Whitfield for Gaye, Gladys Knight, and the Temptations. Sam Cooke's onetime protégé John-nie Taylor was only one of the Northern singers who capitalized on the changing scene; his number one hits, "Who's Making Love" and "I Believe In You (Believe In Me)," were both released on Stax.

Part of the black community's broader struggle to redefine the ground rules of American society, the dissonant harmonies emanat-ing from Memphis drew on and spoke to the beloved community. Like gospel, Southern soul spoke to the burdens of life and the need to reach for something higher. The rough edges reflect something fundamental about life in a place where rednecks and the children of the ghetto shared enough of a comon culture to challenge everything they'd been taught about race. It wasn't smooth, but nei-ther was the life outside the studio. And, for a while, there was rea-son to think that the dialogue that began in Memphis might spread across the world.

# 15
# Dylan, the Brits, and Blue-Eyed Soul

When he wrote the blues classic "Rolling Stone," Muddy Waters wasn't overly concerned with Hibbing, Minnesota, where Bob Dylan was setting out on a journey that would eventually take him down Highway 61 into the heart of the Mississippi Delta. Muddy certainly didn't lose much sleep over the London School of Economics, where Mick Jagger was studying the Chicago blues as seriously as the Chicago school of economics. At first glance, it's hard to imagine anyone with less in common than the Delta-born bluesman and the young rock and rollers who responded to his call in ways that threatened to change the world.

Which tells you something about the blues impulse: it isn't confined to one musical form, and it isn't, at least literally, about race. The best work of Dylan and the Rolling Stones doesn't suffer when you listen to it back to back with Howlin' Wolf and Tina Turner. The strongest white blues—Dylan's *Highway 61 Revisited,* the Stones' great run of singles from "Satisfaction" through "Paint It Black," the Animals' "It's My Life" and "We Gotta Get Out of This Place"—hold the promise of a conversation built on a more trustworthy foundation than the earnest liberalism of the folk revival. The fact that it didn't work out doesn't mean it was a bad idea.

Dylan's "Like a Rolling Stone" responds to the blues on levels that have nothing to do with liberal politics or nostalgic authenticity. The song returns obsessively to the most fundamental blues question: "How does it feel?" It isn't about the consolations of philosophy or the dodge of ideology. It's about how it feels to be existentially adrift, a broken piece of a fallen world. Muddy knew the feeling well, and about all he had to say in words was "oh well." But his guitar, and the way he bent the syllables around the words that never quite told the whole story, expressed with killing precision how the world felt to a black man who was about to head up Highway 61 toward a Chicago that he knew damn well wasn't the promised land. Dylan reversed the motion, headed down into the mythic heart of darkness, and unleashed a flood of imagery about how it felt to be "on your own with no direction home / a complete unknown / like a rolling stone." As in Muddy's call, the blues intensity of Dylan's response lies in the music, in the things that couldn't quite be said. Devils as real as the ones that stalked Robert Johnson haunt Al Kooper's gospel-organ drone, Mike Bloomfield's Chicago-bred guitar, Dylan's moaning harmonica. Kooper, who'd never played organ before the *Highway 61 Revisited* session, described the sound of "Like a Rolling Stone" as his "twisted Jewish equivalent of gospel" mixed with Dylan's "primitive, twisted equivalent of rock and roll."

You can hear "Like a Rolling Stone" as a blues cry out of the singer's own brutal experience. Or you can hear it as cutting social satire, a classic put-down of a shallow chick who doesn't share the poet's superior insight into the human condition. I hear "Like a Rolling Stone" as pure, deep blues: Dylan's confession that he's as lost as the rest of us. The closest thing to a political message on *Highway 61 Revisited* is from "Ballad of a Thin Man": "There's something happening and you don't know what it is." When asked for a statement opposing the Vietnam War, Dylan sardonically bounced the question back at the interviewer: "How do you know that I'm not, as you say, *for* the war?"

Defying the pious condescension of the folk audience that booed him throughout the 1965–66 tour where he plugged in his guitar and waved good-bye to authenticity, Dylan forged a music that challenged his audience to finger the jagged grain of the blues. Like "Subterranean Homesick Blues," probably the least ideological of the great political rock songs, "Like a Rolling Stone" casts the listener into a vortex of political paranoia where the good guys and the bad guys exchange clothes and read from the same scripts. Dylan's lyrics affirm the tradition of rock poetry that originates with Chuck Berry's "Too Much Monkey Business," "Nadine," and "Brown Eyed Handsome Man." Social satire, the blues impulse, and straight-out rock and roll collide, releasing a burst of poetic energy that would inspire John Fogerty's mythic bayou, Jim Morrison's archetypal apocalypse, and Jimi Hendrix's voodoo soup.

While Dylan was changing the way musicians thought about the possibilities of rock, the British bands that invaded the United States in 1964 and 1965 played an equally crucial role in preparing the audience for the new take on the blues. Much more consciously immersed in the Chicago blues and Southern soul than their contemporaries in the colonies, the Animals, Rolling Stones, and Yardbirds introduced black music to multitudes of white Americans who didn't know John Lee Hooker from John Hope Franklin. However often Dylan *called* his songs blues—"Subterranean Homesick Blues," "Outlaw Blues," "Just Like Tom Thumb's Blues," "Tombstone Blues," "Stuck Inside of Mobile with the Memphis Blues Again"—his electric music wasn't *about* race. At least explicitly.

By the time *Highway 61 Revisited* redefined American rock in the fall of 1965, the Rolling Stones had paid homage to both Chicago and Memphis, the sacred cities of their racially aware genealogy of rock and roll. At least in the early days, the British response to black music took on near-religious overtones. Van Morrison, who began singing with a Belfast blues band when he was fourteen, sounded the dominant note when he said simply, "The blues are the truth." Morrison's pursuit of that truth brought him to something like an Irish version of the gospel impulse. *Astral Weeks, Moondance,* and the underrated *Period of Transition* may not be washed in the blood, exactly, but they are awash in blues and gospel spirit.

At times, the British reverence for Muddy Waters and John Lee Hooker resembled the folk revival's sense of the Delta blues. But there were some crucial differences, most notably an underlying belief that the blues addressed shared experience. The Animals' lead singer, Eric Burdon, observed: "If I heard John Lee Hooker singing things like 'I been working in a steel mill trucking steel like a slave all day, I woke up this morning and my baby's gone away,' I related to that directly because that was happening to grown men on my block." Equally important, the British bands felt none of the aversion to rhythm and volume that drove pacifist Pete Seeger into a violent rage when he threatened to cut the electric cords plugged into Dylan's guitar at the 1965 Newport Folk Festival. Every British group with a harder edge than Herman's Hermits traced its roots to *modern* black American music; and even the Hermits had hits with the Rays' doo-wop classic "Silhouettes" and Sam Cooke's "Wonderful World."

A quick survey of early albums by British bands highlights their role in introducing white American teens to black material. Their songs hit hardest in the vanilla suburbs and cream-of-wheat heartland, where American teens lacked exposure to the real thing. The Stones' first American album included Rufus Thomas's Stax classic "Walking the Dog," Chuck Berry's "Carol," and Muddy Waters's "I

Just Want to Make Love to You"; the Dave Clark Five had big hits with energetic covers of Chris Kenner's "I Like It Like That," Bobby Day's "Over and Over," and Marv Johnson's "You Got What It Takes"; the Searchers rendered the sexual comedy of the Clovers' "Love Potion #9" fit for the top twenty. The Yardbirds popularized the purist approach of the British blues movement led by Alexis Korner and John Mayall; any guitarist who masters the licks on the *John Mayall's Blues Breakers with Eric Clapton* has memorized the Dictionary of the Chicago Blues. Even the Beatles, whose love for Carl Perkins's rockabilly and Buck Owens's country made them the whitest of the first-line British invasion groups, were originally distributed in the United States by Chicago's black-owned and -operated Vee Jay label. They covered the Marvelettes' "Please Mr. Postman," Smokey Robinson and the Miracles' "You Really Got a Hold on Me," Arthur Alexander's "Anna," and Barrett Strong's "Money." The low point of British obsession with black American music came on the near-comic near-tragic cover versions of James Brown's "Please Please Please" and "I Don't Mind" that clutter the Who's first album.

Black music defined British groups in ways that were unusual in the United States. John Fogerty remembered the playlist of Creedence Clearwater Revival's predecessor the Golliwogs—who got their name because it sounded "British" to the PR men in the front office at Fantasy Records—as a typically eclectic American mix in which "Mustang Sally" and "Green Onions" showed up alongside "Wipe Out" and "Louie Louie." In contrast, many of the British bands prided themselves on playing nothing but black music. Burdon remembered the English R & B scene as "a genuine underground. It was amazing to find out that what we were doing in Newcastle, which we thought was strictly our thing, was being done in other places by other people."

In London, the Rolling Stones established their reputation with an approach almost identical to the Animals'. The Stones got together as a direct outgrowth of their shared interest in black music. Keith Richards described the crucial moment: "I get on this train one morning and there's Jagger and under his arm he has four or five albums. I haven't seen him since the time I bought an ice cream off him and we haven't hung around since we were five, six, ten years. We recognized each other straight off. 'Hi, man,' I say. 'Where ya going?' he says. And under his arm, he's got Chuck Berry and Little Walter, Muddy Waters. 'You're into Chuck Berry, man, really?'

That's a coincidence. He said, 'Yeah, I got a few more albums. Been writin' away to this, uh, Chess Records in Chicago.' "

Unlike Dylan, whose acid-etched meditations were as likely to concern Ezra Pound as Howlin' Wolf, most of the English bands went out of their way to pay honor to their sources. Ten days into their first U.S. tour in 1964, the Stones took a break to record at Chess Studios, where they met Chuck Berry, Willie Dixon, and Muddy Waters, who, Stones bass player Bill Wyman remembered, "helped us carry our gear inside." He helped them do a lot more than that. The Stones' early records were filled with Chicago blues, and Muddy's "I Just Want to Make Love to You" was their first U.S. single. They felt equally at home in Memphis. In addition to recording Southern standards like Otis Redding's "Pain in My Heart," the Stones went out of their way to see every Southern soul star playing in the cities where they performed, expressing particular admiration for Wilson Pickett.

The relationship between Jagger and James Brown reflects the nature and the tone of the interactions between the British rockers and their black idols. Brown took genial glee in reporting the origin of Jagger's "distinctive" stage mannerisms. The Stones were scheduled to follow Brown at the filming of a TV special, *The T.A.M.I. Show.* Never one to underestimate the competitive elements of performance—he once booked Solomon Burke as an opening act and then paid his "rival" for the title "King of Soul" to sit and watch his show—Brown remembered:

> The Stones had come out in the wings by then, standing between all those guards. Every time they got ready to start out on the stage, the audience called us back. They couldn't get on—it was too hot out there. By that time I don't think Mick wanted to go on the stage at all. Mick had been watching me do that thing where I shimmy on one leg and when the Stones finally got out there, he tried it a couple of times. He danced a lot that day. Until then I think he used to stand still when he sang, but after that he really started moving around. . . . Later on, Mick used to come up to the Apollo and watch my shows.

Brown didn't resent the interest. He described the Stones as "brothers" rather than "competitors" and emphasized that the British groups—he specified the Animals, Kinks, and Beatles as well as the Stones—"had a real appreciation for where the music came from and knew more about R&B and blues than most Americans."

It wasn't that white American bands were totally ignorant of what was happening in black music. Some pockets of American popular music remained interracial even after the collapse of the first generation of rock and rollers. From the start, white groups in the ethnic enclaves of the East Coast played an active part in the doo-wop scene. The list of doo-wop classics includes records by black groups such as the Penguins ("Earth Angel") and the Five Satins ("In the Still of the Night"); white groups such as the Mystics ("Hushabye") and Dion and the Belmonts ("I Wonder Why"); and integrated groups such as the Dell Vikings ("Come Go with Me") and the Crests ("Sixteen Candles"). The Four Seasons' "Let's Hang On" combines doo-wop harmonies and R & B intensity; their ability to place two singles— "Sherry" and "Big Girls Don't Cry"—at the top of the R & B charts anticipates the "blue-eyed soul" of the mid-sixties. Although no white soul singer came anywhere close to the appeal or power of Otis Redding or James Brown, a somewhat incongruous group of white musicians have succeeded on *Billboard* magazine's "black" charts—which have variously been labeled "Harlem Hit Parade," "Race Records," "Soul," and "R & B," which, Little Richard always joked, stood for "real black."

The success over the years of distinctly "black"-sounding singers like Teena Marie, Hall and Oates, Bobby Caldwell, or even the young Elvis Presley, who had six number one R & B singles, comes as no real surprise. The Righteous Brothers ("You've Lost that Lovin' Feeling," "(You're My) Soul and Inspiration") and the Rascals ("Groovin'," "People Got to Be Free") fit in easily with the soul mix of the mid-sixties. Righteous Brother vocalist Bill Medley credits black audiences with helping the duo overcome the resistance of white programmers who considered their sound "too black." "One thing we're most proud of," Medley said, "is that the black audience accepted us point blank and they didn't have to, they just didn't have to. The great thing about the black audience is that if you are emotionally cuttin' it, that's what it's all about."

But it's anyone's guess why the Beach Boys enjoyed as much "R & B" success as the Rolling Stones. Part of the reason may be that the Stones—whose biggest "crossover" hit, "Satisfaction," peaked at number 19—began to record during the fourteen-month period when *Billboard* eliminated the separate black chart. The magazine explained the decision by observing that the pop and R & B charts had become so similar that there was no point in publishing both. Primarily a testament to Motown's crossover success, the decision suggests a belief that the nation was on the verge of a fundamental change. Three decades later, the idea that race may soon be irrelevant seems as remote as it must have in the 1850s, when Abraham Lincoln argued that the only solution to the race problem would be to return emancipated slaves to Africa. The music of the sixties offered a tantalizing promise of a world where blacks and whites could live together, work out their differences without denying who they are. But the glimpse proved fleeting.

# 16
# The Minstrel Blues

The British Invasion illuminated some shadowy corners of America's multiracial culture. As Ralph Ellison suggests, many black-white cultural exchanges can be understood as an elaborate minstrel show. Even as it perpetuates stereotypes and exploits blacks economically, Ellison argues, the cultural imitation across racial lines reveals connections we usually prefer to deny. Contemplating the minstrel show, Ellison writes: "It was as though I had plunged through the wacky mirrors of a fun house, to discover on the other side a weird distortion of perspective which made for a painful but redeeming rectification of vision."

The early history of minstrelsy anticipates both the painful and redemptive dimensions of the sixties cross-racial musical dialogue. In 1828, a white man named Thomas "Daddy" Rice saw a black man performing a strange but compelling song and dance on a street in Charleston, South Carolina. Rice bought the man's song, dance, cart, and clothes for fifty dollars. Within a decade, Rice had parlayed his imitation of the original into a lucrative show business career, creating a sensation in New York, touring London, and scattering the cultural landscape with land mines that continue to go off on a weekly basis. Already well known as an "Ethiopian Delineator" when he met the black man who would make his fortune, Rice participated in one of the most popular forms of nineteenth-century American popular culture. Groups such as "The Six Original Ethiopian Serenaders" painted themselves in blackface and presented grotesque cartoons of black life. Advertisements for the "Congo Melodists" promised authentic renditions of the "Nubian Jungle Dance," the "Virginia Jungle Dance," and the "African Fling."

Audiences lacking direct contact with African Americans typically confused the parody with the real thing. Visions of comic dandies, childlike Uncles, and sex-crazed ape-men erased the complex black humanity of Frederick Douglass and the grandfathers of the Delta bluesmen. Ida B. Wells and the grandmothers of Mahalia Jackson and Ella Baker were reduced to coal-black Mammies and high yella Jezebels. The situation got so far out of hand that black performers were forced to don blackface and alter their speech because they failed to accord with the "reality" defined by white minstrels. No surprise that many blacks recoiled in anger and disgust from any imitation of black culture by white performers.

The economic impact of minstrelsy was even worse. Rice's ability to parlay the fifty dollars he paid his source into a fortune wouldn't have surprised many of the black musicians of the fifties or sixties. The long-standing segregation of the record charts encouraged white artists to release sanitized "cover" versions of black hits. Pat Boone became a star on the basis of mummified covers of Fats Domino's "Ain't That a Shame," the Charms' "Two Hearts," and the Flamingos' "I'll Be Home." His hit versions of Little Richard's "Long Tall Sally" and "Tutti Frutti" make a significant contribution to American humor.

On many occasions, the black/white minstrel dynamic amounted to something like pure theft. One of the most notorious cases concerned the Beach Boys' rip-off of Chuck Berry. Riding a wave of hits that began with "Surfer Girl," the Beach Boys (whose business affairs were run by the Wilson brothers' father, Murry) released "Surfin' USA." The song's infectious rhythms, sweet harmonies, and celebration of teenage fun as American myth established the group as uncontested rulers of surf music. The only problem was—despite a record label crediting the song to Brian Wilson—it's Berry's "Sweet Little Sixteen" note for note. It took a lawsuit to get Berry songwriting royalties and credit as Brian Wilson's "collaborator."

Although that's one of the worst cases of direct financial exploitation, it's not the only one. And the relationship doesn't have to be that direct. Ben E. King observes that the arrival of the British bands polarized a musical scene in which "there was no separation. We had collected a people to listen to a music but when they came along . . . that changed the whole attitude of the music in the racial way." King expresses a measured anger shared by many other soul singers: "There was a bit of jealousy because we were cut off at a time we was getting ready to become stronger than strong ourselves. All the signs were there that the music that was being created right here at home was gonna be tremendously big. And then all of a sudden these kids came along and stopped all that. It was a strong pill to swallow." Ironically, then, the increased attention the British Invasion brought to the Chicago bluesmen came, in a very real sense, at the expense of their soul brothers and sisters.

The Stones did a decent job of sharing the financial rewards with some of their sources. They consistently chose black acts to open for them on their tours, thereby exposing Ike and Tina Turner and B. B. King, who opened for them in 1969, to new and larger audiences. Still, the elements of minstrelsy in the Stones' music are undeniable. Some of their cover versions re-create the sources almost exactly. Every rhythmic subtlety and vocal glide in Jagger's rendition of "You Better Move On" comes directly out of Arthur Alexander's original. The example takes on additional significance when you realize how very "Jaggeresque" the song sounds. Jagger's odd accent patterns and the drawl dropping off into a quavering blue note sound more than a little familiar to anyone who knows Alexander. The problem isn't that the Stones were covering black material, it's simply that there's no reason to prefer their "You Better Move On" to Alexander's or their remake of "Can I Get a Witness" to Marvin Gaye's original.

That's the basic problem with the British version of the minstrel show. Like the folkies, the Brits were least interesting when they came closest to realizing their goal of authenticity. They sounded best when they quit worrying about how John Lee or Muddy or the Wolf—let alone that master of contrivance Chuck Berry—did it. Not that the straight imitations sounded bad. They just didn't amount to much in the way of response. Even when it was good rock and roll, it didn't have much soul.

Both the Stones and the Animals dealt with the problem by following the basic blues principle of taking a good hard look at their own lives. The Animals' response to the blues is much more convincing in "It's My Life" and "We Gotta Get Out of This Place" than in their workmanlike covers of John Lee Hooker's "Boom Boom" or Jimmy Reed's "Bright Lights, Big City." Like the Chicago blues, the Animals' best music isn't limited to the circumstances it grew out of. "We Gotta Get Out of This Place" spoke to the soldiers in Vietnam and the residents of the Denver barrio as clearly as to Burdon's neighbors "in this dirty old part of the city / where the sun refuse to shine." The Animals' response to a world where "people tell me it ain't no use in trying" echoes, but doesn't imitate, Mahalia's determination to walk in Jerusalem. There's a fierce determination in Burdon's voice when he vows to escape if it's the last thing he ever does. He focuses on the personal level, but the drive for a better life echoes Curtis Mayfield's call to keep on pushin': "We gotta get out of this place. / Girl, there's a better life for me and you."

But there were some differences between British blues and soul and their black antecedents. The most crucial distinctions involve the relationship between individual and community. Like thousands of the white American teenagers who bought their albums, the Animals believed that finding yourself required rejecting the place you came from. That isn't just a white thing, of course, but most black musicians treat the desire for escape as something that binds the blues "I" to the gospel "we." To say this is not to condemn it—"It's My Life" worked precisely because the Animals were singing about their complicated relation to their community, not trying to re-create the one between Muddy Waters and the straw boss on Stovall's Plantation. The song got a resounding amen from white rock and rollers everywhere. Bruce Springsteen used it to explore his tangled feelings about New Jersey during his early tours. For the Animals, for Springsteen, for most of their white audience, voice and self had to be defined *against* community first. Then, maybe, you could think about bringing it all back home.

The Stones' search for a voice that didn't simply imitate or exploit their black mentors, complicated by their enormous long-term financial success, reveals some of the most difficult problems of the minstrel dynamic. Like the Animals, the Stones produced a string of classic sixties hits expressing their highly specific sense of reality: "Satisfaction," "Get Off of My Cloud," "19th Nervous Breakdown." Grounded by drummer Charlie Watts and bassist Bill Wyman (whose precisely embellished runs set the standard for hard-rock bass in part because they never miss the polyrhythmic point), the Stones explored the murky depths of existential ennui in a con-sumer society that all too often confused brand names with the meaning of life. The Stones took the blues to places Jean-Paul Sartre and the electric Dylan knew well. That's probably why French New Wave film director Jean-Luc Godard built one of his greatest films around the recording sessions where "Sympathy for the Devil" grew from country blues riff to a swirling inferno of rock and roll nihilism in fierce debate with gospel despair. Released in Europe as *One Plus One* and in the United States as *Sympathy for the Devil*, the film maps the paths that led the white musicians of the mid-sixties through the mythic South to an existentialist homeland where they could play their own kind of blues.

In "Sympathy for the Devil," "Paint It Black," and "Gimme Shelter," the Stones call out from the heart of a darkness where politics and passion dissolve into pure howl. Balancing their listeners on the razor's edge between smug satire and an empathy you wish you didn't feel, the Stones slam you down in the path of a crossfire hurricane spawned somewhere in Robert Johnson's Delta and raging through the hearts of darkness that define the "white" world. The Stones nailed the core of white life and, with a difference, black life in a world of hedonistic advertising and ninety-nine-floor apartment blocks. "Satisfaction" explodes in anger, rage, at a world where the ads promise fulfillment now, but the women tell you to come back, maybe next week. And you know they're lying. Because chances are you were lying to them. Everybody's on a losing streak. Nobody's even pretending not to know what Muddy Waters meant when he sang "I Can't Be Satisfied." When the Stones called out for satisfaction, they meant yesterday. When Otis Redding and Aretha Franklin covered the song, their responses carried the weight of hundreds of years. The fact that a lot of people understood all three versions held out at least the hope that, a hundred years after Daddy Rice, white listeners might be starting to get the point.

# 17
# Otis, Jimi, and the Summer of Love: From Monterey to Woodstock

Just after he finished a blistering version of "Respect" midway through his set at the Monterey International Pop Festival, Otis Redding slowed down the tempo and announced that it was time for "a soulful number." Behind him, Booker T.—resplendent like the rest of the MGs in a lime green mohair suit no one in the audience would have even considered wearing—whispered a gospel organ chord while Otis launched into a monologue introducing "I've Been Loving You Too Long." "This song is a song, you know, we all ought to sing some time. This is the love crowd, right? We all love each other," Otis began softly, but suddenly his body tensed, he leaned forward, and his voice took on an intensity straight out of the black Georgia churches he'd grown up in. "Am I right?" he called out. "Let me hear you say yeah." The overwhelmingly white crowd of forty thousand roared its response, doing its part to make Otis's performance one of the defining moments of 1967's "Summer of Love."

Mesmerized by a vision of San Francisco as a new kind of community created by and for the "gentle people with flowers in their hair," John Phillips, guiding force of the Mamas and the Papas, joined with producer Lou Adler and a handful of established musicians to organize the Monterey Festival. In many ways, Monterey fulfilled the promise expressed in Scott McKenzie's hit version of Phillips's "San Francisco (Be Sure to Wear Some Flowers in Your Hair)": "Summer time will be a love-in there." The three June days on Big Sur radiated positive vibrations, personal and musical. Despite Phillips's leanings toward benign pop harmonies, Monterey brought together an intriguing cross section of black and white music. Along with McKenzie, the Association, and the Mamas and Papas, the lineup included the Byrds, who made the clearest political statement of the festival with their version of Dylan's "Chimes of Freedom"; San Francisco icons the Jefferson Airplane and Country Joe and the Fish; and a gaggle of blues-rock bands including Canned Heat, the Electric Flag, the Steve Miller Band, and the Paul Butterfield Blues Band. Sam Cooke's old friend Lou Rawls introduced soul to the mix with a moving set of "Love Is a Hurtin' Thing," "Dead End Street," and "Tobacco Road." It was a shame and a pity that the Impressions and Dionne Warwick canceled scheduled appearances and that Smokey Robinson's presence on the festival board failed to overcome Motown's aversion for situations it wasn't sure it could control.

After Otis and Jimi Hendrix played their sets, no one was thinking much about what they *hadn't* seen. Their performances were the unquestionable highlights of the festival. And it wasn't that they lacked competition. Emerging as challengers to the Stones, the Who tore through an incendiary set, panicking Adler when they destroyed their equipment during their patented Theater-of-Cruelty-meets-l'enfant-terrible "My Generation." It was a coming-out party for the new San Francisco bands, many of which followed the Brits into the more psychedelic regions of the blues. Fronting Big Brother and the Holding Company, Janis Joplin screamed her white blues into a major recording contract. As Eric Burdon sang in his tribute to the festival, "Monterey," "the Byrds and the Airplane flew."

And Hendrix looked down on them from above, introducing the rock audience to the jazz innovation and spiritual exploration that would dominate the late sixties. Even though rock critic Robert Christgau dismissed him as a "psychedelic Uncle Tom," Hendrix's Monterey set permanently altered the love generation's idea of what it was all about. And part of it was that no one had any idea just exactly what "it" was. Using every trick he'd learned while serving his apprenticeship on the chitlin circuit backing up Little Richard, Curtis Mayfield, and the Isley Brothers, Hendrix gave the crowd a taste of psychedelic voodoo. Insinuating himself into a mindscape prepared by Dylan and drugs, he set the night, his guitar, and the sexual imaginations of countless members of the counterculture on fire with a mixture of Chicago blues ("Killing Floor"), rock standards ("Like a Rolling Stone," "Wild Thing") and then-unknown songs that would become his standards ("Fire," "Purple Haze").

There was a lot to like about Monterey. But if you slow down the film and look closely, you can see cracks forming in the commune walls, sense the hopes of the New Left and the beloved community beginning to fall apart. Part of the collapse had to do with political vision. As California Dreamer Phillips wrote in "San Francisco," the Summer of Love was all about "people in motion, people in motion." The problem was that motion doesn't make a movement.

The distinction is crucial. Most of the people living in the communes in the Haight supported radical political ideas. Almost everybody believed in some sort of racial equality. Flat everyone wanted to be free. But the politics remained abstract, expressing a belief that you could dream community into being and that somehow things would simply change. Which wasn't something that anyone who'd been paying attention to the South was likely to put much faith in. Whatever their differences, Ella Baker, Martin Luther King, and Huey Newton, who was busy forming the Black Panthers just across the bay, had no illusions that evil was going to go away without a struggle. Even the hippies in Memphis and Atlanta had a harder edge. No one with long hair down South was likely to forget the reality of violence.

The blurred political vision of the Summer of Love marked a distinct retreat from Port Huron. Members of the counterculture experimented with ideas of community, tried them on for size, and, if they didn't fit, put them down and rolled another joint. Pockets of activism developed, dissipated, re-formed. You could see it as participatory democracy in action. Or as solipsistic self-indulgence. Was it a counterculture or a new niche market? Buffalo Springfield nailed it in "For What It's Worth" when they sang, "There's something happening here / what it is ain't exactly clear."

By and large, by 1967, black folk didn't much care. Monterey, and the scene that give birth to it, was mostly a white thing. You could see it—the Monterey Pop crowd shots rarely manage to capture more than a couple of black faces in any frame—but you could also hear it. Janis Joplin, one of the few Southerners to perform, blew the crowd away with "Down on Me" and "Ball and Chain" partly because she didn't have to compete with KoKo Taylor or Aretha Franklin. And if black folk didn't care much about Monterey, which at least had Otis Redding and Lou Rawls to recommend it, they cared even less about Woodstock.

In the mythology of the sixties, Woodstock marks a pinnacle, the moment when the vision of an alternative community—a Woodstock Nation—came into clearest focus. For a few days, the festival bloomed into the third-largest city in New York. Births perfectly balanced deaths (three of each). Despite the chaos—abandoned cars clogging the access roads, shortages of pretty much everything, a rainstorm that basted the scene in mud—people kept their cool.

The music—for anyone close enough to hear it—lived up to the audience. The presence of Joan Baez linked the celebration to the folk revival and the (no longer quite) New Left. Arlo Guthrie brought his father's legacy with him. Blues rockers from Ten Years After and Canned Heat to Country Joe and the Fish showered sparks across the fields. Creedence Clearwater Revival didn't exactly play the blues, but they showed the crowd that a bunch of white boys from California knew the impulse well. Hendrix delivered the keynote speech with his electronic sermon on "The Star-Spangled Banner" as theme song for Vietnam, making rockets explode and napalm light up the dawn. Sly and the Family Stone took everyone higher, ascending into a rarefied atmosphere where the soul Sly picked up in his mother's storefront church in San Francisco turned to vapor and poured back down as the best rock ever made. When the Family Stone, on the upswing of an arc that would descend into the deepest abyss the era had to offer, invited the Nation to dance to the music, Woodstock responded with a kaleidoscope of motion.

It seemed like a dream and, at least if your idea of community involves blacks and whites, it mostly was. The tensions of Monterey had grown. More black musicians performed at Woodstock than at Monterey—Richie Havens, the Chambers Brothers, Hendrix, Santana. But other than Sly *soul* was conspicuous only by its absence. Sly embraced rock in ways Otis might have gotten to if he'd lived. But nothing at Woodstock asked the overwhelmingly white nation to extend its boundaries. As the Summer of Love drew to a close, clear signs of the racial polarization of the late sixties had begun to emerge. Hendrix provided a flash point.

Even the best white guitarists experienced Hendrix's performance as a kind of revelation. Recalling the first time he saw Hendrix play, Mike Bloomfield said: "Hendrix knew who I was, and that day, in front of my eyes, he burned me to death. I didn't even get my guitar out. H-bombs were going off, guided missiles were flying—I can't tell you the sounds he was getting out of his instrument. . . . How he did this, I wish I understood. He just got right up in my face with that axe, and I didn't even want to pick up a guitar for the next year." The Who's Pete Townshend experienced Hendrix's virtuosity as a put-down with distinctly racial undertones. Prior to Monterey, the Who and Hendrix had argued about the order of performance. At the airport after the festival, Townshend walked up to Hendrix and said, "Listen, no hard feelings. I'd love to get a bit of that guitar you smashed." To which, rock critic Charles Shaar Murray reports, Hendrix replied, "Oh yeah? I'll autograph it for you, honkie." "I just crawled away," Townshend admitted. The confrontation both grew out of and deepened Townshend's sense of racial insecurity. Contemplating the differences between his own place in the interracial music scene and that of Eric Clapton, Townshend reflected: "I think the difference is that Eric feels perfectly natural with his adoption of blues music. He feels it inside; I don't. I don't even really feel comfortable with black musicians. It's always been a problem with me, and I think Jimi was so acutely sensitive in his blackness that he picked that up. [After Monterey] I felt a lot of hate, vengeance and frustration. Possibly because of my sensitivity, my uneasiness with black people. I felt I deserved it somehow."

Hendrix's response to Townshend suggests the tensions that would overwhelm the movement in the late sixties; Otis Redding's performance and response to the white counterculture suggests a different set of possibilities. Otis dug the feel of Monterey, reached out to the love vibration, tried to figure out what it had to do with the kind of tenderness he'd learned to coax out of the moan. Exhilarated by the response he received at Monterey, Otis wanted to expand the conversation. He immersed himself in the Beatles' *Sgt. Pepper's Lonely Hearts Club Band* and began to study Bob Dylan's songwriting. On December 7, he went into the studio and recorded "Dock of the Bay." Although Stax wasn't at all sure the record should even be released, it was by far his most popular crossover song. At the same time he was reaching out to a broader audience, Redding maintained his awareness of his roots. He'd spoken with James Brown and Solomon Burke about establishing an organization to provide health care benefits and pensions for older black musicians.

And then, on December 10, his plane went down in Madison, Wisconsin. Every time I look out my front window, I see Lake Monona, where Otis died. Whenever I play his great songs—"Pain in My Heart," "Try a Little Tenderness," "I've Been Loving You Too Long," "Ton of Joy"—I wonder whether Otis might have been able to bring the hippies, my people, into a deeper understanding of the gospel impulse. At times the counterculture closed its mind as tightly as the Rotarians and militarists it despised. But Otis knew full well you couldn't forget the elders, the ancestors, your straying brothers and sisters. If you're going to make it real, you've got to find a way to connect with the folks who have no interest in putting flowers in their hair. Otis was willing to talk to anyone. The crowd at Monterey seemed, for a fleeting moment, to hear.

# 18
# Last Thoughts on the Dream:
# Dot and Diana

The montage of the early sixties unfolds in a series of images, each with its own rhythm, its own story and secret depths. The Cooley High kids liberating the Lincoln Park Zoo; Dylan strumming his acoustic guitar for SNCC; Sam Cooke breaking from the Copa to embrace Muhammad Ali; Sly calling the tribe to disorder; Steve Cropper bending notes around Booker T.'s gospel organ; the beloved community singing down the devil waiting, then and always, just outside the door.

Let's take a closer look at two of the faces in the montage. The first, Diana Ross, needs no introduction to anyone reading this book. The second, Dorothy Love Coates, remains almost unknown outside the world of gospel.

And that's a crying shame.

No disrespect to the divine Ms. Ross, but there isn't any question who's the better singer. Dorothy Love Coates belongs alongside Ray Charles, Aretha, bluegrass elder Ralph Stanley, Al Green, and George Jones on the short list of truly brilliant American singers. She ranks with Mahalia, Claude Jeter, and Marion Williams as the greatest gospel singers of all time. The point isn't to win the "who's number one" parlor game, but to encourage anyone with any interest at all in singing or soul to hustle up a copy of the Specialty CD that combines Dorothy Love Coates and the Original Gospel Harmonettes' two "Best Of" albums. You won't be disappointed.

Those two albums represent the best of what the early sixties offered: a model of call and response rooted in an unflinching engagement with history; an understanding of the world that sends pulses of energy back and forth between gospel and the blues; an unwavering commitment to the beloved community; a refusal to be seduced into a mainstream where the value of life is measured in money; and music so powerful it can change your life.

Dorothy Love Coates grew up in Birmingham, where the strength of her voice carried her from the church choir onto the gospel highway. Powerful with more than an edge of rawness, Coates's voice scrapes the very bottom of whatever it is human beings try to keep hidden and rises up with an insistence that opens pathways in your spirit you didn't know were there. Which may be thrilling, but it isn't always comfortable.

And that's the point. Coates, who lived through some of the major struggles of the freedom movement, knew full well that nothing about freedom, redemption, came easy. She'd seen the clubs crack heads, known the Alabama cops and the good citizens whose will those clubs represented. She had stared into the darkening night where many thousands had vanished long before Goodman, Schwerner, and Cheney's faces appeared on the six o'clock news. However much she might have yearned for peace, success, a world where you could do your own thing, her voice confronted you with the world as it is, challenged you to find the strength to change it.

The songs Coates wrote cut so close to the bone they're often mistaken for traditional. She infused traditional material with an immediacy that demanded action. Her version of "No Hiding Place" warns against moral evasion with supreme clarity, the hard-earned knowledge of the cross aflame: "I went to the rock to hide my face / the rock cried out no hiding place." When the Harmonettes join in, all thought of retreat dissolves into determined confrontation with Pharaoh. When she sings "You better run to the city of refuge," she calls down the Lord's wrath on those who oppress the righteous.

Again and again, Coates gives classic voice to images flowing down the generations. "That's Enough" inspired cover versions by Ray Charles, Johnny Cash, and dozens of gospel groups with its assurance "When my enemies attack me / Heaven sends me help / He won't leave me to fight battles by myself." Coates asserts an unwavering faith, but it's a faith that speaks to the day-to-day labors of life and love. In "I Wouldn't Mind Dying," she takes up the "sword of justice." "99½ Won't Do," like the songs of gospel pioneer Thomas Dorsey, has passed over into the basic vocabulary of black America alongside "Nobody Knows the Trouble I've Seen" and "Go Down, Moses," the songs created by the men and women James Weldon Johnson called the "black and unknown bards." The hundred percent Coates demands renders the distinction between spiritual and political meaningless. Living right and attending to your soul requires awareness of the people around you. And awareness requires action.

The effectiveness of Coates's performances grew equally from the power of her voice and the responses of the Original Gospel Harmonettes: Mildred Miller, Vera Kolb, Willie Mae Newberry, Odessa Edwards, and pianist Evelyn Starks. The Harmonettes were much more than a backup group. Moving from close harmony to personal testifying, they provided a kaleidoscopic sense of community in motion. The brilliant "Get Away Jordan" medley on the CD of the legendary gospel concert at the Shrine Auditorium in Los Angeles feels as immediate today as it did in 1955. You can hear the Harmonettes stretch time, urge Coates on, unite around key phrases that call Coates's solo voice into the night. They never succumb to formulaic response. They bear witness that the struggle, in your soul and on the roads of Birmingham, demands your full attention, your hundred percent. If you really *hear* the call, you've got no choice but to respond. And you can't no ways let yourself be tired.

As much as any singer on or off the gospel highway, Coates explicitly embraced gospel politics, holding close to her home community. A strong supporter of Martin Luther King, Coates acted with the clarity and determination of Ella Baker. "On nights, I'd sing for the people, days I'd work for the white man," she said. She marched beside Martin and spent time in the Birmingham jail without getting famous. She certainly had the chance to record for the mainstream audiences attracted to Ray Charles and Aretha Franklin. But she stayed in Birmingham, rejecting all offers to cross over: "I told them, don't bother about me. The white man don't love any of us. When he quits making his change off me, he'll drop me in a minute. . . . there's some money so dirty you hate to touch it."

Unsparing in her condemnation of individualism and greed, Coates told gospel music historian Anthony Heilbut:

Man thinks he's so grand and great. He's taken everything out of the earth and made money on it, the rubber, the oil, the diamonds, he put his own claim on them. But whatever man possesses, he got it from God's earth. Like General Tire. Mr. General Tire can say it's his, but the rubber came out of the trees, it's just a stone fact. Behind everything man's done to make his own empire, he's created his own jungle which he himself can't control. Man'll steal and lie. The one thing he can't stand is the truth. Like these gospel singers today. When the whole country's collapsing, they go out telling these ungodly, shameless, Mother Goose lies. But that's all right I'm gonna wait on my change, and that's a *fact*.

The beloved community heard her and appreciated her sacrifice. As much as anyone else, Dorothy Love Coates carried the core vision of the early movement into the complicating sixties and seventies. As one movement veteran said, "Mahalia sang for us on the weekends, Dot was there every day."

Diana Ross could have used a little of Coates's fierce dedication to the beloved community, and a whole lot of her awareness that individual stardom exacts a high price. In a sense, Ross's success marks the end of the golden age of American singing, the postwar decades that gave rise to Coates and a host of other powerful black singers: Mahalia, Ray Charles, Levi Stubbs, Gladys Knight, Sam Cooke, Patti LaBelle, Sam Moore.

It's impossible to separate the emotional power of these singers from the political energy of the movement. Both emerged at a unique moment in American history. For a brief time, a substantial majority of blacks managed to balance a deep sense of connection to the beloved community with a real desire to move closer to an American mainstream where blacks and whites would interact more freely and equitably. Martin Luther King's dream was, as he told the world, "very deeply rooted in the American dream." Survival in America didn't necessarily imply bleaching your soul. For that same brief moment, a significant number of whites seemed willing to respond to the vision of democracy and equality. White listeners attracted by the subversive sounds of Motown frequently moved on to the gritty sounds coming out of Memphis, or to Curtis Mayfield's gospel soul. Adding some white folks to your audience didn't require surrendering your voice. And it held out a healing vision of possibility that nostalgia cannot bring back.

You can hear the vision beginning to fade when you listen closely to Diane(a) Ross, whose change of name marks her trajectory from talented Detroit teenager to poster girl for *Entertainment Babylon.* It's certainly not that she lacked authenticity. Ross grew up in Detroit's Brewster-Douglass housing projects. In the fifties, Brewster-Douglass wasn't going to be confused with the hard-core east side ghetto of Paradise Valley. But Cass Technical High School, which Ross attended with fellow Primettes Mary Wilson and Flo Ballard, was closer to Cooley High than Primrose Lane. Ross's father described the Brewster projects as a desirable location: "At that time, a bad stigma hadn't attached to the projects. The front yards had nice lawns, the housing was decent and there were courtyards. The apartment that we were in had three bedrooms, a full basement, a living room, kitchen and dinette. It wasn't so terrible, believe me." Speaking to a television interviewer, his daughter remembered a much bleaker scene: "Not all of us kids survived the ghetto, but the ones who did were a mighty tough lot. You see, the ghetto will get you ready for anything. The first big fight is just gettin' out."

Unlike the gospel singers who dedicated their voices to uplifting their communities, Ross used her voice to escape. The problem with her success certainly wasn't that she couldn't sing. Although Ross's smooth soprano lacked the earthy power that had made Flo the original lead singer, she could filigree rhythms and twist the ends of lines with delicious blue-green glides. At her best, Ross provided a female version of Smokey Robinson in pop mode.

Pop *was* the problem. Marvin Gaye, Levi Stubbs, David Ruffin, Martha Reeves, and Smokey, in his gospel mode, established Motown's soul credibility, assured its rightful place in the great tradition. The Supremes, however, relied exclusively on pop confection. It paid off with an incredible string of hits. Head to head, the Supremes outdueled the Beatles at their peak. Beginning with "Where Did Our Love Go?" in July 1964, they parlayed five consecutive Holland-Dozier-Holland compositions into number one pop hits. Between the summers of 1964 and 1967, they released thirteen singles: ten topped the charts and twelve made the top ten. "Nothing but Heartaches" stalled at eleven, a failure on the order of the baseball season Roberto Clemente hit .291.

Not so curiously, the Supremes performed slightly less well on the black charts, where "only" six of their records made number one. Gradually, Ross's pop genius pushed the gospel roots of her singing deep into the background shadows (where the Motown production team placed Flo during recording sessions, far enough away from the mike to keep her voice from overwhelming Diana's). The overly polished background harmonies eliminated the individual responses that let you know the Temptations still heard the moan. The Four Tops' Levi Stubbs infused even the most formulaic Holland-Dozier-Holland compositions with an edge of blues desperation, a knowledge of what it's like to stand in the shadows of love, how it feels to reach out and close your arms around flat nothing. Ross sang Holland-Dozier-Holland safe. Millions of white teenagers loved the Supremes without feeling any need to change the way they dealt with the world.

There's nothing wrong with popularity. The great singers reached out to anyone who could get to it. You didn't have to be black to respond to Stubbs's desperation or Mahalia's vision of the promised land. Brother Ray made it seem deceptively easy when he painted country classics "I Can't Stop Loving You" and "A Worried Mind," which includes one of his most moving piano solos, the deepest blue on the palette. But they always brought it back home; their voices, if not always their actions, refused to sunder the I from a "we" that included anyone who heard it that way and acted accordingly.

By 1967, however, the beloved community was strictly in Diana Ross's rearview mirror. Moving on up assumed a distinctly individual meaning when Diane changed her name, took top billing for the commercially reconstituted Diana Ross and the Supremes, and finally embarked on a solo career that led her through the silver screen to the disco inferno. Flo Ballard descended into the somewhat more literal hell of welfare and died of heart disease at age thirty-two. The wrong Supreme had the lead in *Lady Sings the Blues*.

Part of the difficulty in understanding an era defined by Dorothy Love Coates *and* Diana Ross, James Brown *and* Joan Baez, involves what happened later. Images of the later sixties obscure the unfulfilled potentials, the things people prayed for, worked for. But the music behind the images continues to ring with the vision that held the early sixties together and made it, for a moment, real. You can hear the hope for, and the belief in, a nation capable of accepting its past, fingering the grain of its brutal experiences, bearing witness and moving toward redemption: together on the highways of Alabama and the streets of Chicago, alone where the spirit moves the soul.

Whatever meaning survives from those days when the movement marched out of the black South into the hearts and minds of a large part of America survives in the traces of melody, the rhythmic figures, the choruses and cries that blend into a haunting and inspirational sound track: "I've Been 'Buked and I've Been Scorned," "Satisfaction," "I Want to Take You Higher," "You've Lost That Lovin' Feeling," "Where Did Our Love Go?," "The Times They Are A-Changin'," "Hold On, I'm Comin'," "A Change Is Gonna Come."

Mahalia summed up the challenge of gospel politics when she sang "I'm Gonna Live the Life I Sing About in My Song." The movement didn't expect people to be saints, at least not in any simple sense. Look closely enough at anyone—Martin, Mahalia, Sam Cooke, Aretha—and you're going to find a human being carrying his burdens and feeling her blues. Rather, the gospel impulse challenges us to bring our actions into line with our values, to reduce the dissonance between our personal and our political experience. Most fundamentally, it requires a commitment to community, a refusal to confuse individual success, especially success measured by money, with redemption.

The music of the early sixties wasn't immune to the tensions that helped produce it. But in a world defined by both unprecedented economic opportunity and historic struggle for human dignity, music helped the beloved community find meaning in the past and possibility in the future. Some people held to music as a way of resisting what they saw as destructive changes, refusing to surrender the values of the gospel impulse. Others set out to imagine new possibilities for the coming world, arguing that black music had always showed you how to make a way out of no way. It was the difference between Martin and Mahalia on the one hand, Malcolm and John Coltrane on the other. The early sixties belonged to gospel; the late sixties would belong to jazz.

# Section Two

## "Love or Confusion?": Black Power, Vietnam, and the Death of the Dream

# 19
# Sly in the Smoke

It's hard to see the late sixties through the smoke. Smoke rose over the shells of Detroit and Newark, the battlefields of Khe Sanh and the tunnels of Cu Chi, the barricades in Paris and Prague. Carried along by the guitar lines that brought Jimi Hendrix and Bob Dylan, Sly Stone and Miles Davis into troubled communion, smoke both sharpened and clouded the best minds of a generation that, with a few exceptions, figured out how to inhale without undue difficulty. While much of the smoke was real, some of it was the kind of blue smoke dispensed by revisionist historians determined to reduce the era to stereotypes of subversive nightmare or revolutionary dream.

The "sixties," as they have passed into both conservative and radical mythology, actually took place between about 1965 and 1974. More than any other period of American history, these years remain inextricably identified with their music. Sharing a belief that they could change the world, musicians who had grown up on gospel and the blues, rock and roll and classical music, shared a sense that music should make it new, help us imagine communities capable of living up to the moment, personal and political, mental and elemental. From Miles Davis and John Coltrane to Aretha Franklin and the Beatles, the most powerful musicians of the late sixties associated their sound with revolutionary social change. Generally avoiding ideological simplification, the music usually made a more compelling case for the new world than the manifestos endorsing the Revolutionary Socialist Workers' Collective, the Transcosmic Commune of the Unbound Id, or a Kingdom of New Ghana carved from the heart of the Black Belt South.

No musical group embodied the late sixties better than Sly and the Family Stone. The band brought together the highest aspirations and the underlying chaos of a time defined equally by the Vietnam War and the "Summer of Love," by Black Power and white backlash. Certainly, no musical act presented a more exhilarating image of what America might become. Even as the political world refragmented along lines of race and ideology, Sly presided over a musical community that obliterated racial designations. It would have been downright silly to call "Stand" or "I Want to Take You Higher" white rock or black soul. The group's visual presence erased boundaries, conjured up something too beautiful to be anything but a dream. The women played instruments and the men sang.

Sly's lyrics perfectly capture the mix of political seriousness and comic irreverence that kept the sixties from disintegrating into dour self-parody. Blues laughter echoed in the background when the Family responded to Sly's menacing "Don't call me nigger, whitey" with "Don't call me whitey, nigger." The willingness to look the devil in the eye, even when the eyes were in the mirror, lifted Sly and the Family Stone well above the self-satisfied righteousness that makes a fair amount of sixties music difficult to listen to today.

Certainly, no other group could have made "Everyday People" and "Family Affair" feel like anything other than a stone contradiction. Riding the wave of positive energy that crested when Sly invited a generation to dance to the music at Woodstock, "Everyday People" celebrated a kind of visionary American family: black and yellow, white and red, male and female. Unimaginably in the land of airbrushed emaciation, it was even all right to be "a fat one trying to be a skinny one." One moment the group set down soul grooves as funky as anything Memphis might imagine, stretching time to make room for things you were just then thinking up. Then they mixed up a gumbo where Hendrix guitar licks added spice to a horn section that remembered Count Basie. The Family could be as weird as San Francisco, where Sly had established himself as a DJ and producer, as deep as the heart of Texas, where he was born, or as stylish as Oakland, where he was raised and where the Black Panthers were redefining fashion as well as freedom. Different strokes for different folks. At the end of "Everyday People"—which hit number one the same month Richard Nixon mouthed the oath of office—Sly reached deep into his gospel roots—when he was four years old, a family group cut "On the Battlefield for My Lord"—and testified "we got to live together." You knew he was right, that the movement *had* changed America, created a place where folks could listen to the Beatles and Aretha, Creedence and Coltrane, Nina Simone and the Doors.

Three years later, when Sly and the Family Stone had their last number one hit with "Family Affair," you knew with equal certainty that something fundamental had changed. You could hear the change in the music, wailing and anguished, pulsing with the rhythms of the riots, Vietnam, the drugs that eventually stopped Sly's song in the middle of a downbeat. And we were in it together whether we liked it or not. If we weren't going to live up to Martin's dream, then we'd have to come up with something else. As Sly sang, "Blood's thicker than the mud."

Blood, way too much of it black blood, ran in the streets. The blood of the soldiers and civilians killed in Vietnam mingled with that of the thirty-two inmates and nine guards slaughtered at the Attica Prison in New York, with the blood of Black Panther leaders Fred Hampton and Mark Clark murdered in their beds by Chicago law enforcement officers, with that of George Jackson and Malcolm X and Martin Luther King and Bobby Kennedy.

There was one hell of a riot going on. Sly reached out for redemption, thanked Africa for letting him be a self he was only beginning to imagine. But there was absolutely no hiding place down here. By the time the last helicopters lifted off from the roof of the Saigon embassy, the only thing most Americans could agree on was the mess we had made of the nation. Polls revealed that the only thing less popular than the Vietnam War was the antiwar movement, to cite only one of the bitter ironies.

It's not hard to reduce it all to a cliché. Things fell apart, the center didn't hold. The worst were filled with passionate intensity and the rough beast slouched into the White House, where it's living still. If you prefer the street-level phrasing, it was too good to be true. It helped if you were—and you probably were—stoned. Comedian Robin Williams got it right when he observed that anyone who remembers the sixties wasn't there.

But it's too easy to evade the questions of how and why the mellow "sha sha"s that linked "Everyday People" with the gospel politics of the early sixties gave way to the anguished moan that fades to black at the end of "Family Affair." There's no question which song offers the better way to live. There's even less question which paints a more accurate picture of the quarter century that's passed since Sly effectively vanished from the world. The right blames the left and the left blames the right. No one in polite society calls anyone nigger or whitey, but race dominates American politics as surely as it did in the years leading up to the Civil War. Carl Rowan, the leading black "establishment" journalist of the sixties, a calm man who once headed the U.S. Information Agency, recently published a book called *The Coming Race War in America*. George Wallace begat Richard Nixon begat Ronald Reagan begat the Contract on America. And there's a good blues argument to be made that Lyndon Johnson, in his finest hour, begat the whole damn bunch.

# 20
# Death Warrants:
# LBJ, Martin, and the Liberal Collapse

Lyndon Johnson understood that when he signed the bills that marked his greatest legislative triumphs, he was signing the death warrant of the Democratic Party. "I think," he said as he handed the pen to Bill Moyers moments after the 1964 Civil Rights Act became law, "we delivered the South to the Republican Party for your lifetime and mine." A veteran of East Texas politics, where no one, including Johnson, hesitated to play the race card if it would help win an election, LBJ harbored few illusions about the place of idealism in American politics. When he described the aftermath of his victorious campaigns to enact the Voting Rights Act and its predecessor, the 1964 Civil Rights Act, he was simply describing a strategy that, in an earlier incarnation, he might have used himself. In his memoirs, LBJ wrote that by 1968, "More and more Republicans tried to base their campaigns on promises to protect the individual from 'LBJ's bureaucrats,' who, they said, would be 'swarming over every neighborhood setting up Negro quotas, forcing homeowners to sell property, and encouraging vicious gangs of rioters and looters to destroy neighborhoods which dared resist."

Yet when he introduced the Voting Rights Act to a joint session of Congress, LBJ made one of the most surprising and idealistic speeches in American political history. Without question the finest moment of a career that spanned nearly a half century, LBJ's speech elicited NAACP leader Roy Wilkins's praise as "the goddamnedest commitment to the civil rights cause I had ever heard." Echoing the movement's vision of a beloved community united in its diversity,

LBJ emphasized that "There is no Negro problem. There is no Southern problem. There is only an American problem." Just before he concluded his speech, Johnson paused, envisioning, as he wrote in his memoirs, "a picture of blacks and whites marching together, side by side, chanting and singing the anthem of the civil rights movement." The president raised his arms and quoted the words of a song that many of the white voters who would soon desert the Democratic Party in droves considered a direct attack on the American way of life: "Their cause must be our cause too. Because it is not just Negroes, but really it is all of us who must overcome the crippling legacy of bigotry and injustice. And . . . we . . . shall . . . overcome."

Lyndon Johnson made civil rights a cornerstone of his Great Society agenda for the most unlikely of political reasons: he simply thought it was right. Shepherding the Voting Rights Act through Congress required heroic effort. Johnson cashed in political chips he had amassed as Democratic whip and majority leader in the Senate; he filled the barrel with the sweetest pork this side of a Texas barbecue. He twisted arms, hard, and refused to listen to Southern congressmen who told him they'd be run out of town as "nigger lovers" if they supported the legislation. According to several who provided swing votes, LBJ responded to their protests by asking them how they'd explain to their constituents why not a nickel of federal money was coming into their districts. "Nigger, nigger, nigger, that's all I hear," Johnson told a group of Southern congressmen. "You might as well stop, because we're going ahead." After meeting with the president in the Oval Office, even George Wallace testified to LBJ's persuasive powers. "If I hadn't left when I did," Wallace said, "he'd have had me coming out *for* civil rights." Seen from a certain angle, LBJ's support of the movement was truly heroic.

From a slightly different angle, however, it was simply the first act of a tragedy worthy of Shakespeare. Before the ink had dried on the "death warrant" signature, LBJ had begun taking actions that would reduce the Great Society agenda to an easy target for Republicans and the Southern Democrats who would provide the keystone of Nixon's Southern strategy. The real death warrant of the Democratic Party may well have been signed when LBJ approved secret increases in military spending for Vietnam during 1964 and early 1965. Johnson had campaigned against Barry Goldwater as a peace candidate, vowing never to send "American boys to die in Asia." But even as he declared a "War on Poverty" to address the economic roots of inequality, LBJ's military budget drained the resources needed to make the domestic war meaningful. Wilbur Mills, the powerful conservative leader of the House Committee on Ways and Means, delighted in observing that "The Administration simply must choose between guns and butter." As Martin Luther King repeatedly observed, LBJ chose guns. Noting that the United States spent five hundred thousand dollars to kill each enemy solider, but only thirty-five dollars a year to assist each American in poverty, King charged that "the bombs in Vietnam explode at home. They destroy the hopes and possibilities of a decent America. . . . The promises of the Great Society have been shot down on the battlefields of Vietnam."

LBJ's own feelings about Vietnam intensify the tragedy. In 1964, with a booming economy that held out the possibility of increasing black opportunity with minimal white resentment, LBJ expressed profound and prophetic doubts about a war that most of the country didn't even know was being fought. In public he downplayed the extent of American involvement while in private he told advisers: "I don't think it's worth fighting for, I don't think that we can get out. It's just the biggest damn mess I ever saw. This is a terrible thing that we're getting ready to do. . . . It's damn easy to get into a war, but it's going to be harder to ever extricate yourself if we get in." On that point, at least, King would have agreed.

The relationship between Johnson and King provides a classic study in the difference between electoral and gospel politics. LBJ assumed that politics worked through trade-offs: you scratch my back, I'll scratch yours. Several of the Western votes that helped pass the Voting Rights Act, for example, came in exchange for riders creating water projects. When LBJ put the power of his office behind legislation King's Southern Christian Leadership Conference had been supporting for years, he fully expected that King would reciprocate when the time came. The time came when Johnson sought King's support for Vietnam.

Sensible of the risks LBJ had taken, King hesitated, remaining silent on the war while Black Power advocates attacked it as a symbol of racist exploitation and liberal hypocrisy. Finally, a year to the day before he was assassinated, King spoke out against the war at New York's Riverside Church. "A time comes when silence is betrayal," King said before launching into one of the most compelling statements of the antiwar position. Speaking in terms which will shock those who remember him only for the "I Have a Dream" speech,

King thundered, "Our only hope today lies in our ability to recapture the revolutionary spirit and go out into a sometimes hostile world declaring eternal hostility to poverty, racism, and militarism."

LBJ viewed King's speech as an act of betrayal. Although the president maintained a discreet public silence, an aide acknowledged that, of all the antiwar voices, "King was the person we were most upset about. Martin was spectacular. The problem with Martin going off with the Hanoi Hawks disturbed us profoundly." Feeling increasingly isolated and besieged by protestors chanting "Hey hey LBJ, how many kids did you kill today?," Johnson withdrew ever further from a movement increasingly defined by the militant voices of Huey Newton, Stokely Carmichael, and H. Rap Brown. He approved intensive surveillance of anyone suspected of involvement with the riots that erupted in Harlem, Newark, Detroit, Watts, and numerous other ghettos. Conservatives launched successful counterattacks on the War on Poverty, charging that funds distributed by the Office of Economic Opportunity had been used to transport and arm rioters. The Johnson White House panicked, at one point concocting a bizarre plan to discredit Carmichael by planting a rumor that he was really white. FBI director J. Edgar Hoover revelled in his mandate to use the counterintelligence program COINTELPRO to harass movement leaders without regard to their specific actions or beliefs.

On April 4, 1968, Martin Luther King, Jr., was gunned down on the balcony of the Lorraine Motel. No one needed to sign yet another death warrant for the liberal movement. Already mortally wounded, it died in Vietnam.

# 21
# "All Along the Watchtower": Jimi Hendrix and the Sound of Vietnam

"There must be some kind of way out of here," sang Jimi Hendrix. For many of the grunts slogging through the mud of Southeast Asia, there wasn't. Many of those who survived and found their way back to what they called, with a mixture of longing and cynical humor, "the world," brought Vietnam with them. While the Vietnamese people and the men and women who fought there took the hardest hits, anyone who thought that Vietnam was about somebody else was stone-cold deluded. The fact that Vietnam affected every corner of American life didn't stop us from blaming the war on political demons from the other side, retreating to communes or suburbs, turning off our hearts and minds.

No one wanted to admit that all of us were lost in a heart of darkness more disturbing than the one Francis Ford Coppola would hallucinate in *Apocalypse Now*. So we didn't. We lied so often that, by the time the war was over, lying had become the accepted, expected centerpiece of our political life. No matter how often LBJ, Nixon, or, for that matter, the Weathermen or the Panthers lied about how profoundly our experiences of Vietnam were connected, the music told the truth.

The truth wasn't primarily about politics, though there's no way to talk honestly about Vietnam without recognizing the accuracy of LBJ's prediction that it would become a political nightmare. Hendrix, who had served in the army's elite "Screaming Eagles" paratrooper unit before the start of the war, had next to nothing to say about the war itself, but his music seethes with the chaotic energy connecting the jungles of Southeast Asia with the streets of America. Explosions, screams, the sounds of mechanized horrors and what poet Wendell Berry called "millions of little deaths" reverberate through "Machine Gun," the Woodstock performance of "The Star-Spangled Banner," "Love or Confusion," and Hendrix's version of Dylan's "All Along the Watchtower," which he transformed from metaphysical parable into the national anthem of America-in-Vietnam and Vietnam-in-America.

Vietnam was America's first truly integrated war. Sort of. Despite the mountains of literature devoted to the conflict, obscenely little attention has been given the specific experiences of black soldiers in Vietnam. After an early period of relative racial harmony—during which blacks suffered a highly disproportionate number of casualties—military units based in Vietnam began to experience the full range of racial tensions that both reflected and fueled the Black Power movement back home. After the Tet offensive and the assassination of Martin Luther King in 1968, black soldiers in Vietnam established a separate culture based on their determination to resist all signs of white supremacy. As the war dragged on, incidents of racially motivated rebellion—including "fragging" (attacks on officers or one's fellow soldiers named after the fragmentation grenades used because they destroyed evidence) and desertion—increased until substantial sections of Vietnam were effectively beyond the control of the military command. Though historians have yet to wade the Big Muddy of classified documents and personal accounts that will verify the fact, I suspect that black soldiers in Vietnam deserved at least as much of the credit for bringing the war to an end as the antiwar movement at home.

During the early days of the war, most black combat soldiers shared their white colleagues' belief that the war was necessary. Although they were aware of the racist attitudes of some white soldiers, most shared the feelings of black combat engineer Harold "Light Bulb" Bryant, who observed: "We didn't have racial incidents like what was happening in the rear area, 'cause we had to depend on each other."

After 1968, however, attitudes shifted rapidly. Don Browne, an air force security officer in Tuy Hoa and Saigon, described his anger over King's assassination:

My first inclination was to run out and punch the first white guy I saw. I was very hurt. All I wanted to do was to go home. I even wrote Lyndon Johnson a letter. I said that I didn't understand how I could be trying to protect foreigners in their country with the possibility of losing my life wherein in my own country people who are my hero, like Martin Luther King, can't even walk the streets in a safe manner.

When a white soldier complained about the constant TV coverage of King's death, saying, "I wish they'd take that nigger's picture off," Browne and two black friends "commenced to give him a lesson in when to use that word and when you should not use that word. A physical lesson."

Reinforced by reports that in the early years of the war blacks had suffered 23 percent of the combat fatalities despite constituting only 12 percent of the military force, black unrest grew. Where most of the black soldiers during the early days were career military men, most who arrived after 1967 had been drafted. Many were acutely aware that the college deferment allowed well-off whites to avoid fighting in a war that most black leaders blamed for shifting resources away from the pressing problems of black communities. In 1970, Wallace Terry surveyed black enlisted men and officers in Vietnam and reported that, however the question was phrased, they were two to three times as likely as their white peers to oppose continuation of the war.

The change in Vietnam was particularly clear to career military men who had served there before. An unapologetic advocate of the "old school" belief that the army provided unmatched opportunities for black advancement, Colin Powell had been stationed in Vietnam as an adviser in 1963. When he returned in 1968, Powell was deeply disturbed by the racial implications of what he saw:

> Bases like Duc Pho were increasingly divided by the same racial polarization that had begun to plague America during the sixties. The bases contained dozens of new men waiting to be sent out to the field and short-timers waiting to go home. For both groups, the unifying force of a shared mission did not exist. Racial friction took its place. Young blacks, particularly draftees, saw the war, not surprisingly, as even less their fight than the whites did. They had less to go home to. This generation was more likely to be reached by the fireworks of H. Rap Brown than the reasonableness of Martin Luther King, Jr.

By the early seventies, the racial situation in Vietnam was explosive. Desertions increased. According to the *Wall Street Journal,* at least 500 GIs deserted every week during May 1970. The *London Express* estimated that throughout the final years of the war, at least 60 soldiers a week, the majority of them black, were crossing over to the National Liberation Front of South Vietnam. At the same time, racial violence was becoming commonplace. The Pentagon, hardly noted for its candor on such questions, *reported* that 209 soldiers had been killed by other Americans during 1970 alone. Many of the killings were directed against officers who forced grunts to carry out missions they considered dangerous and pointless. Powell did not consider himself immune: "Both blacks and whites were increasingly resentful of the authority that kept them here for a dangerous and unclear purpose," he wrote. "The number one goal was to do your time and get home alive. I was living in a large tent and I moved my cot every night, partly to thwart Viet Cong informants who might be tracking me, but also because I did not rule out attacks on authority from within the battalion itself."

Many of the fraggings had racial undertones. One vet who'd served at Da Nang told historian Nick Biddle: "Things got so bad around where I was that we actually had to pull guard on ourselves— does that make sense? We had to pull guard duty around our own hooches, to protect ourselves from ourselves. I'm not saying that all of it was racially motivated, but every time I heard about something going on, it was this black guy fragging this guy he got mad at."

Music served as a frequent flash point for racial incidents. Many blacks complained about the white-dominated playlist of the Armed Forces Vietnam Network, which one vet described as "bland, censorious and programmed-from-Washington." Black grunts noted the preponderance of "rebel flags and hillbilly music" (which reflected the large number of poor Southern whites who ironically found themselves in Vietnam for many of the same reasons as black draftees from the inner cities). *Jet* magazine attributed the shooting death of a white officer in Quang Tri to his attempt to force black soldiers to turn down their stereo. "Unplugged the stereo. Bang, bang," the *Jet* report concluded. Terry Whitmore, whose *Memphis Nam Sweden* is one of the very few black memoirs of Vietnam currently in print, reports a similar incident that exploded into a riot. When the facilities manager at the Freedom Hill PX in Da Nang removed all soul music records from the jukebox, black marines began breaking up tables and chairs. Dozens were arrested.

Although music sometimes contributed to the tensions in Vietnam, it also gave the grunts moments of relaxation, release. Music played in PXs, black soldiers' "soul hooches," and Saigon bars. The best books about the war—Michael Herr's *Dispatches,* Gloria Emerson's *Winners and Losers,* and Wallace Terry's *Bloods*—mention an extensive list of musicians including Aretha Franklin, Wilson Pickett, Bob Dylan, the Rolling Stones, Otis Redding, the Animals, avant-garde saxophonists Eric Dolphy and Pharaoh Sanders, the Mothers of Invention, Johnny Cash, the Supremes and Temptations, Bobbie Gentry, Glen Campbell, Miles Davis, the Miracles, Jefferson Airplane, Paul Revere and the Raiders, Archie Bell and the Drells, Buffalo Springfield, Cream, Junior Walker and the All Stars, the Grateful Dead, and, of course, Jimi Hendrix.

In his memoir "Nine Meditations on Jimi and Nam," Roger Steffens, who was stationed in Pleiku, writes: "Jimi gave us the melody of war, raw and off-key, the ragged guys who'd been shot in the field." Reflecting on Vietnam as a "roomful of mirrors," Steffens sums up why Hendrix—who always had trouble attracting a large black audience back in the world—appealed equally to blacks and whites in Nam. "He represented a way to listen to the sound of your own outer limits. Being there and listening to him, no matter what the kids back home thought his music meant, they could never connect at the level we did. We were in the right zone to tune in. More intensity, more extremism. When we got back to the world, it was the soundtrack of the war; and if you tried to communicate that to people here, you couldn't make them understand, they thought you were crazy."

Back home, Vietnam invaded every corner of American music. Although polls showed Americans almost evenly divided in their opinions of the war, very few singers followed in the footsteps of Staff Sergeant Barry Sadler, whose romanticized "Ballad of the Green Berets" hit number one in 1966. Doves dominated the musical debate on Vietnam. Woody Guthrie's "old left" compatriot Pete Seeger ignited a nationwide debate on the war with a scathing performance of "Waist Deep in the Big Muddy" on the Smothers Brothers television show. Young singer-songwriter Tim Buckley ("No Man Can Find the War") blended his voice with those of folk revival survivors like Joan Baez and Tom Paxton ("Lyndon Johnson Told the Nation," "Talking Vietnam Potluck Blues") and "folk rockers" like the Byrds ("Draft Morning"). The antiwar mix included Creedence Clearwater Revival's "Fortunate Son," "Run Through the Jungle," and "Who'll Stop the Rain"; Country Joe and the Fish's "I Feel Like I'm Fixing to Die"; John Lennon and Yoko Ono's "Give Peace a Chance"; and the Doors' "Five to One" and "The Unknown Soldier." The Turtles brought Dylan's (slightly masked) draft-resistance anthem "It Ain't Me Babe" to the top ten. Addressing themselves to a would-be lover who's looking for someone to "love you and defend you / whether you are right or wrong," the Turtles spoke for many in the generation when they responded, "It ain't me you're looking for." Even bubblegummers Tommy James and the Shondells came out against the war in "Sweet Cherry Wine."

Edwin Starr's Motown classic "War" sounds the dominant response to Vietnam in soul music: "War? What is it good for? Absolutely nothing." Jazzmen Eddie Harris and Les McCann launched a blistering attack in "Compared to What?" Introduced by McCann's ironic invocation of the theme from the Fifth Dimension's love anthem "Aquarius," the cut pounds out a jazz funk groove beneath Harris's screaming condemnation. Railing at a politicians' war lacking even the semblance of justification, Harris concludes bitterly: "Nobody gives us rhyme or reason. / Half of a doubt and they call it treason." Freda Payne called on the powers that be to "Bring the Boys Home"; Jimmy Cliff's "Vietnam" helped introduce reggae to American listeners; the earliest incarnation of George Clinton's

Funkadelic painted nightmarish warscapes in "Wars of Armageddon" and "Maggot Brain," where Eddie Hazel's gospel blues guitar exhumes the nation's lies. J. B. Lenoir's "Vietnam Blues" told the simple truth.

When the war finally ended, Funkadelic's "March to the Witch's Castle" sounded its death knell and offered the vets a somber welcome. For returning veterans, Little Feat's "Mercenary Territory" and the Radiators' "Zigzagging Through Ghostland" took on blues depths. Two of the most moving musical responses to black Vietnam, Curtis Mayfield's *Back to the World* and Marvin Gayes' *What's Going On*, delve into the broader problems faced by returning soldiers. The stereotype of the psychotic Vietnam vet has become so deeply entrenched in the pop culture that it sometimes overshadows the fact that most vets live "normal" lives. Though what normality means in a country that retrospectively embraced Vietnam as a "noble cause," a "failed crusade" betrayed by anti-American agitators, remains open to discussion. Still, there's no question that Vietnam vets, both black and white, encountered intense hostility from those who opposed the war. One white vet remembered being told, "I'm sure you killed babies and women and children and old people and I think it's too bad someone didn't kill you." A black vet experienced a parallel reception: "When I came home, I realy got upset about he way my peers would relate to me. They called me a crazy nigger for going to the war." Another black vet remembered being condemned as Uncle Sam's flunky. "The women," he concluded, "wouldn't talk to you."

Back in the world, black vets either overcame or ignored the coldness and played a central role in the growing Black Power movement. When Wallace Terry asked black combat soldiers whether they planned to join the Black Panthers when they returned home, more than a third responded affirmatively. Edgar Huff, who served with the marines at Da Nang, viewed Vietnam as training for an assault on white supremacy in his native Alabama: "Whenever the Ku Kluxers would come, I would be terrified," he told Terry. "And I thought about that many times when I was overseas, and I had those beautiful machine guns. I would just wish to hell I had somethin' like that back in Alabama when those sonofabitches came through there. I would have laid them out like I did those damn Congs. The same way." Combat paratrooper Gene Woodley was even more explicit about the connection between Vietnam and the revolution at home: "Rifles, guns. I join the Black Panthers group basically because it was a warlike group. With the Panthers we started givin' out free milk and other community help things. But I was thinkin' we needed a revolution. A physical revolution. And I was thinkin' about Vietnam. All the time."

# 22
# 'Retha, Rap, and Revolt

When Aretha Franklin belted out her call for "Respect" in the summer of 1967, *Ebony* magazine, probably the *least* radical black publication, declared it the year of " 'Retha, Rap and Revolt." For the Black Panthers and their supporters, "Respect" sent an unambiguous message to white America: From now on, black folk would take care of business in their own way. The day of the Tom had come to an end. As much as any speech or manifesto, "Respect" defined the energy of the freedom movement as its center of gravity shifted from Martin Luther King's interracial coalition to the unapologetically *black* organizations headed by, to use James Brown's term, a "new breed" of photogenic firebrands including H. Rap Brown, Stokely Carmichael, Eldridge Cleaver, and Huey Newton. If you got your information from television, you would have thought the Black Power movement had been created and defined solely by males.

The black women responding to Aretha's call for a "little respect when I get home" knew that wasn't the whole story. Like most young black women at the time, Aretha expressed her support for the "black revolution." She credited the new movement with forcing "me and the majority of black people to begin taking a second look at ourselves. It wasn't that we were all that ashamed of ourselves, we merely started appreciating our *natural* selves . . . falling in love with ourselves *just as we were.*" But there's no avoiding the fact that even as the male-centered Black Power movement launched an intense attack on white supremacy, it approached gender relationships in ways that contradicted its principles. "Mrs. [Fannie Lou] Hamer," one new SNCC militant announced, "is no longer relevant."

The Black Power movement played an absolutely crucial role in revealing how racist thought patterns permeated American culture.

The core of the thought structure lay in the association of "white" with "good" and "black" with "evil." Black Power theoreticians drew attention to the fact that the hero in western movies always wore the white hat, that conventional paintings of heaven portrayed white angels in white robes walking through an alabaster city. More importantly, the Black Power movement observed that Western thought fell into patterns organized around dichotomies: one term carried a positive connotation, the other negative. Consistently, the positive term was associated with whites, the negative term with blacks. "Civilization" was white, "savagery" black. "Mind" was white, "body" black. "Maturity" white, "childishness" black. "Industriousness" white, "laziness" black.

The list can be extended indefinitely. Generally, characteristics associated with whites were also associated with men, while women found themselves consigned to the negative category. It's important to emphasize that the dichotomies weren't thought out in advance or formalized; they simply express pervasive patterns in American culture. Drawing attention to the psychological and political impact of these patterns, Black Power advocates challenged their validity. Unfortunately, their primary reaction was simply to reverse the value judgment attached to "black," to exchange the positions of black and white atop the list of positive and negative characteristics. The problem with that was that it left the rest of the structure unchanged. Within the movement, black signified positively, but so did "male" and "heterosexual." The deep structures that established a hierarchy of human value remained unchanged. Many of the problems that eventually undercut the promise of the Black Power movement could be traced back to that original failure to make a radical enough break from hierarchical modes of thinking. For Aretha and the brothers and sisters who held on to the gospel vision of redemption, the problems with the new movement were almost inseparable from its contributions.

As historian William L. Van Deburg observes in *New Day in Babylon,* "Black Power" came in several distinctive flavors, each with its own values and agenda. The Nation of Islam and the Republic of New Africa called for complete separation from an American mainstream controlled by white devils. Focusing on culture rather than politics, Maulana Karenga's US Organization called for a new black awareness grounded in traditional African culture. Organized in response to police violence in Oakland, the Black Panthers endorsed revolutionary socialism and called on workers of all colors to overthrow an economic system that manipulated racial animosity to divide and conquer the working class. Other organizations adopted a separatist approach to Black Power. Following the lead of SNCC, which in 1966 became the first movement organization to explicitly embrace a Black Power agenda, the Congress of Racial Equality excluded whites from membership in 1968.

By the end of the decade, Black Power had entered every area of African American society. Black student unions from Madison and Berkeley to Howard University and San Francisco State demanded the creation of black studies programs. The League of Revolutionary Black Workers and the Dodge Revolutionary Union Movement (DRUM) attacked workplace conditions as new incarnations of the plantation system. Black Power organizations sprang up in prisons and on military bases. Although a black boycott of the 1968 Olympics failed to materialize, sprinters John Carlos and Tommie Smith spread their message throughout the world when they stood on the awards platform with heads bowed and gloved fists raised in a Black Power salute.

Whatever their ideological and strategic differences—and they were profound—Black Power advocates shared a belief that it was time for black folks to get rid of their masks. Most agreed that whites had played far too large a role in the movement and that the older generation of black leaders amounted to a school of brainwashed Uncle Toms. The growing dissonance between the old and new movements came to a head following the ambush shooting of James Meredith near the start of his 1966 "March Against Fear" through rural Mississippi. Representatives of both the SCLC and SNCC rushed to Meredith's bedside to plan the continuation of his march. Historian Timothy Tyson presents a clear picture of the emerging tensions:

The three-week trek across Mississippi registered thousands of new black voters, but the media focused on tensions between SNCC and SCLC. SCLC's chants of 'Freedom Now!' competed with SNCC's new call for 'Black Power.' While its meaning remained ambiguous, 'Black Power' took on connotations of separatism, alienation, and violence. Vice-President Hubert Humphrey spoke for many liberals when he said, 'racism is racism—and there is no room in America for racism of any color.' Roy Wilkins called Black Power 'the reverse of Mississippi, a reverse Hitler, and a reverse Ku Klux Klan.' King termed the slogan 'an unfortunate choice of words' but called attention to its roots in traditions of racial pride, economic uplift, and cultural self-affirmation. King conceded Stokely Carmichael's point that other ethnic groups had risen through group solidarity, but pointed out that such groups had acquired clout without chants of Irish or Jewish Power: 'Somehow, we managed to get just the slogan,' King said.

There were times when it seemed that Carmichael's conception of power had as much to do with theater as with politics or economics. When the March Against Fear reached the state capitol in Jackson, Carmichael shot a white SCLC representative between the eyes with a water pistol. Increasingly, black "traitors" were subjected to similar treatment; Amiri Baraka's play *Slave Ship* climaxed with revolutionaries parading across stage carrying the severed head of a docile Christian preacher modeled on King. The stage directions describe the scene as a "Miracles'/Temptations' dancing line," "a new-old dance, the Boogalooyoruba." Probably not what Berry Gordy had in mind.

The Black Power movement's repudiation of the legacy of slavery complicated and deepened its relationship to black music, which was universally recognized as a potentially revolutionary tool. Seeking to imagine purified forms of black being, theorists valorized the experimental jazz of John Coltrane, Pharoah Sanders, Sun Ra, Albert Ayler, and Archie Shepp, whose "Attica Blues" and "Money Blues" blended jazz, soul, and funk to sound a powerful revolutionary call. Shepp understood the revolutionary energy as "The Cry of My People," but the obsession with transformation led some theorists to ill-conceived rejections of the past. Karenga, for example, repudiated the blues. "Therefore, we say," intoned the man whose lasting contribution to black life would be establishing Kwanzaa as an Afrocentric alternative to Christmas, "the blues are invalid; for they teach resignation, in a word acceptance of reality—and we have come to change reality." The idea that the blues were invalid would have come as a surprise to the grunts slogging through the Mekong Delta. Chicago bluesman Willie Dixon was a whole lot closer to the truth when he observed: "as you change the time, it changes the blues. Every time you change the news, you got to change the blues because the news ain't always the same. The blues changes just like everything else changes."

Karenga wasn't a crackpot on the fringes of the movement. His call for a "black aesthetic" had a profound impact on numerous writers, artists, and musicians. In his influential essay "Black Cultural Nationalism," Karenga called for an art which would be "collective. . . .

it must be from the people and must be returned to the people in a form more beautiful and colorful than it was in real life. For that is what art is: everyday life given more form and color." Not all that bad a description of gospel and the blues. Yet Karenga rejected both as reactionary, arguing that "all art must reflect the Black Revolution, and any art that does not discuss and contribute to the revolution is invalid, no matter how many lines and spaces are produced in proportion and symmetry and no matter how many sounds are boxed in or blown out and called music." Valid art must "expose the enemy, praise the people and support the revolution."

Attempting to move beyond Karenga's simplistic application of these principles, Amiri Baraka explored the tension between revolutionary aesthetics and everyday black life. Like most nationalist theorists, Baraka loved free jazz. He heralded the challenging structures and sometimes discordant sounds of Coltrane's "Meditations" and "A Love Supreme" or Ayler's "Spiritual Unity," works that presaged the "emergence also of the new people, the Black people conscious of their strength, in a unified portrait of strength, beauty and contemplation." Baraka understood that while ordinary black folks might admire and theoretically support revolutionary music, they loved and listened to James Brown. They didn't seem to care all that much when Brown endorsed Hubert Humphrey in 1968 and Richard Nixon in 1972.

In his essay "The Changing Same (R&B and New Black Music)," Baraka interpreted the popular preference as part of a dialectical process that would help create the new black world. Unlike Karenga, Baraka heard the new jazz as a response to the calls of gospel and the blues, both of which were "valid" expressions of the black community's struggle to reach a higher plane of political awareness. The gospel moans and blues cries, Baraka wrote, carried a musical energy that transcended their capitalist and Christian origins. He praised Motown, the Impressions, and James Brown for providing "a core of legitimate social feeling, though mainly metaphorical and allegorical." Soul music represented a stage in a larger revolutionary process: "the song and the people is the same. . . . the songs, the music, changed, as the people did." During the last years of the sixties, the most powerful voice of black change belonged to Aretha Franklin.

# 23
# "Spirit in the Dark": Aretha's Gospel Politics

Raised in a household where Mahalia Jackson, Marion Williams, and Clara Ward were frequent visitors, Aretha knew full well that her voice carried on the great tradition of gospel politics. Her music communicated equally powerfully with supporters of H. Rap Brown and Martin Luther King, whom she idolized. Nothing came closer to realizing the Black Power movement's (often betrayed) ideal of "unity without uniformity" than its response to the woman universally recognized as the "Queen of Soul." Black comedian Dick Gregory, who mounted a campaign for the presidency in 1968, testified to the depth of Aretha's impact: "You'd hear Aretha three or four times an hour. You'd only hear King on the news." Soul music historian Peter Guralnick describes the scene at a black record store in Boston the day "I Never Loved a Man" was released: "People were dancing on the frosty street with themselves or with one another and lining up at the counter to get a purchase on that magic sound as the record kept playing over and over. It was as if the millennium had arrived."

Aretha's millennium lasted less than ten years, but no artist has ever had a better decade. Seventeen of her songs reached the top of the soul charts; another eighteen hit the top ten. The Grammy Award in the category "Best R & B Performance, Female" was unofficially rechristened the "Aretha Franklin Award" when the "Queen of Soul" won it the first eight times it was given. More important, Aretha's music charts the evolving energies of the late sixties and early seventies as clearly as any history imaginable. "Respect," "Think," "Rock Steady," and Aretha's joyous celebration of "*black* and Spanish Harlem" earned her her place in the movement's pantheon. Set in motion by Joe South's great guitar introduction, "Chain of Fools" expresses the movement's revolutionary determination with crystalline precision: "One of these mornings that chain is gonna break."

From childhood, Aretha breathed the atmosphere of gospel politics. Her father, C. L. Franklin, was one of the most charismatic preachers of his generation; over fifty of the sermons he preached from beneath the neon blue crucifix over the altar at Detroit's New Bethel Baptist Church were released by Chicago's Chess Records. The best known, "The Eagle Stirreth Her Nest," has been included on countless gospel music collections. In addition to the gospel singers who took Aretha and her sisters under their wing after the death of their mother, Martin Luther King frequently visited the Franklin home when he was in Detroit. "Dr. King was a wonderful, wonderful, fine man as well as a civil rights leader," Aretha said. "He very definitely had an appreciation for gospel music." When Detroit sponsored "Aretha Franklin Day" in February 1968, King presented her with an award from the SCLC. Although he was suffering from a case of laryngitis and couldn't speak, the crowd at Cobo Hall responded in a way that put ideological frictions in their proper perspective. A writer for the *Michigan Chronicle* described the scene: "this was a 'love wave.' Everyone just stood on their feet. He never said a word, because he couldn't. But you could just feel the impact his presence had—just him being there. . . . At the time, people were said to be wishy-washy about King, that he wasn't militant enough. Well, all twelve thousand people in that room cared for him—you could feel it."

Aretha's continuing love for King did nothing to limit her appreciation for the Black Power movement. She created her most powerful music when her sense of connection to the black revolution was at its strongest. Like many in the black community, she was attracted by the Black Power movement's tone rather than its specific ideology. "I suppose the revolution influenced me a great deal," said Aretha, who had begun to dress in African styles such as colorful boubou gowns and towering head-wraps. "But I must say that mine was a very *personal* evolution—an evolution of the *me* in myself. But then I suppose that the whole meaning of the revolution is very much tied up with that sort of thing, so it certainly must have helped what I was trying to do for myself. I know I've improved my overall look and sound."

The five albums she released between 1970 and 1972 speak to the inner depths of what was happening in America with far greater accuracy than any political manifesto of the period. Featuring Aretha's gospel piano playing and the vocal backing of the Sweet Inspirations (whose members included Whitney Houston's mother, Cissy), *This Girl's in Love with You, Spirit in the Dark,* and *Young, Gifted and Black* rank with the best soul albums ever made. *Aretha Live at Fillmore West* showcases her ability to match the rock-oriented sound provided by guitarist Cornell Dupree, organist Billy Preston, drummer Bernard Purdie, and King Curtis's Kingpins. Aretha's greatest triumph, however, came with her return to her gospel roots on *Amazing Grace.* Accompanied by the rhythm section who'd backed her at the Fillmore, along with gospel legend James Cleveland and the Southern California Community Choir, Aretha achieved the nearly unthinkable feat of placing a straight gospel album in the pop top ten.

Aretha's music of the early seventies testifies to the feeling of a community still holding on to a vision of possibility, but aware that the revolutionary moment may be slipping away. Written after Aretha had freed herself from a first marriage that was by all accounts pure blues nightmare, "The Thrill Is Gone (From Yesterday's Kiss)" wrestles with feelings of doubt and desolation before releasing a sense of redemption that speaks to the changing same of her people's history. Like B. B. King, who took a different song with the same title into the pop top twenty the same year, Aretha presents the end of a relationship as a painful but necessary step toward something better. The pain still in her voice, Aretha transforms the lyric from "the thrill is gone" to "I'm free" and the Sweet Inspirations respond with an image King had made into the movement's mantra: "free at last, free at last, great God almighty, free."

Aretha's use of politically charged gospel images both connects her with and underscores her difference from the Black Power movement. Aretha's basic meaning always came through clearly; very few listeners misunderstood the political implications of "Young, Gifted and Black," "Rock Steady," or "Spirit in the Dark." But Aretha never mistook the *option* to speak directly with the *obligation* to do so. She understood double voicing and masking not as impositions of the white masters but as aesthetic strategies developed by generations of brilliant black artists. Precisely because she felt no need to make explicit political statements in every song, Aretha tapped blues depths and gospel visions that were difficult to express in hackneyed political jargon.

Aretha's gospel soul classic, "Spirit in the Dark," employs the mask to evoke a sense of political community too often lost in the confusing ideological crosscurrents of the early seventies. The song opens with Aretha's quiet gospel moan but rapidly settles into a steady rock beat as she asks her sisters and brothers how they feel. Her invitation to get up and start dancing is as much a call to political action as Martha Reeves and the Vandellas' "Dancing in the Street." The groove that carries the first half of the song explores the feel of a community in unified motion. If the song had ended halfway through, it would still be a classic. But Aretha refuses to accept the rock groove as the best of all possible worlds. Almost three minutes into the song, when most singles would be fading out, Aretha inserts a sudden, emphatic gospel piano run. Joyously responding to their sister's sanctified call, the Sweet Inspirations call out, "I think y'all got it." The rock groove explodes with a sanctified energy as powerful as Mahalia's "Walk in Jerusalem." For another minute and a half, Aretha and the Sweet Inspirations take the secular audience to church. The spirits they call down vibrate with a clearer sense of shared purpose, of the concrete struggle for redemption, than anything ideology had to offer.

By the time Aretha released the last of her great secular albums, *Young, Gifted and Black,* the promise of the Black Power movement seemed as elusive as King's dream. Aretha's "Border Song (Holy Moses)" captures the changing tone so clearly it's hard to believe that Elton John, who wrote the song, hadn't conceived it as a response to the sermon Martin Luther King preached in Memphis the night before he was killed. That sermon, "I've Been to the Mountaintop," gave a terrible immediacy to the black community's often retold story of Moses as the visionary leader who never makes it to the promised land. In "Border Song," Aretha testifies that she's living in the land of bondage, surrounded by specters, by people "who ain't my kind." Her tone resonates with the bitter despairing rejection of whites that was gradually replacing the revolutionaries' celebratory, if not always coherent, blueprints for a better, blacker day. Aretha laments having been "deceived," "removed" to a place where the "wind has changed directions" and the only water available to slake her thirst evaporates from a poisoned pool.

Masking allowed Aretha to address the complicated malaise that involved black-white relations, the internal dynamics of the black movement, Vietnam, presidential corruption. Some days it seemed like the healing waters had drained away, leaving nothing but barrenness stretched out ahead of the beloved community. After a brief, cruel heyday of hope, blacks found themselves removed to the desert for no reason save to die. As many a preacher reminded them

from the pulpit, Moses had faced a similar situation when his people despaired of reaching the promised land and built themselves a
golden calf. The cost of their backsliding was forty more years in the
wilderness. The situation cried out for a voice to arise and renew
hope. In "Border Song," Aretha holds up her little light without
lying about how hard the struggle will be, how soon the promised
land will even come into sight. Cornell Dupree's electronically
processed guitar responds to her gospel piano, merging with the call
and response between Aretha and the Sweet Inspirations on the central question: "Can we live in peace?" There's hope—at least
Aretha's still able to share the burden with her community—but no
promise. When the chorus drops suddenly away and the song ends
on an offbeat dissonant piano chord, Aretha's testifying that, however deeply you believe that someday we'll all be free, the burden
never ends. That's just the way it is.

# 24
# Jazz Warriors:
# Malcolm and Coltrane

Malcolm X watched over nearly every black neighborhood during
the late sixties. Testifying to the living presence of the martyred
leader, the murals that transformed the walls of tenements and community centers into pageants of black heroism extending from ancient Africa to a visionary future often portrayed Malcolm as the
central presence. The "Wall of Respect" and "Wall of Meditation" in
Chicago, the "Wall of Consciousness" in Philadelphia, the "Exodus"
mural in Boston, and the "Leaders and Martyrs" mural in Oakland
surrounded Malcolm with a changing cast of politicians, writers, and
musicians. No musician received more attention than John
Coltrane. From the perspective of the revolutionary artists who celebrated their lives, Coltrane and Malcolm shared a determination
that could be boiled down to a clear central message: *"Change the
world. Now."*
Both Malcolm and Coltrane relied primarily on the power of

sound to effect change. Unleashing torrents of expression that called the foundations of the oppressive order into question, both pushed to expand the limits of their people's understanding. Not surprisingly, the response to their calls was sometimes slow in developing. As a result, both Coltrane and Malcolm made their largest impact after they were dead. Malcolm commanded the respect of almost everyone who actually met him, but during his lifetime his power base remained limited to relatively small pockets of supporters in the northern ghettos. Similarly, almost all jazz musicians, including those who rejected his radical approach to free jazz, recognized Coltrane's importance. But no Coltrane album ever even made the top two hundred.

It's the classic jazz situation. The most visionary thinkers create possibilities for those who come after them. But the immediate response to their calls almost always misses the point. Malcolm predicted with certainty that the mainstream media would reduce him to a caricature: "The white man, in his press, is going to identify me with 'hate,' " Malcolm said. "He will make use of me dead, as he has made use of me alive, as a convenient symbol of 'hatred'—and that will help him to escape facing the truth that all I have been doing is holding up a mirror to reflect, to show, the history of unspeakable crimes that his race has committed against my race."

If Malcolm has to serve as a symbol of something—and the main point here is that he shouldn't—he should symbolize politics as a *process*. Over the course of his thirty-nine years, Malcolm experienced a series of transformations, each associated with a different name. As Malcolm Little growing up in Nebraska and Michigan, he developed an intimate knowledge of the frustrations of a black family trying to escape poverty. After his father's death, which Malcolm attributed to white supremacist retribution for his Garveyite beliefs, he watched his mother disintegrate psychologically while the family was torn apart by a demeaning welfare system. Although Malcolm was an excellent student, a white teacher discouraged his interest in law school, telling him he should pursue a career as a carpenter. Moving to the East Coast, Malcolm Little was transformed into Detroit Red, a streetwise hustler who understood the gangsta rappers' ethos from the inside. "The only thing I considered wrong," he told Alex Haley, "was what I got caught doing wrong. I had a jungle mind. I was living in a jungle and everything I did was done by instinct to survive."

Inevitably finding himself imprisoned, Detroit Red received his first exposure to the teachings of the Nation of Islam, which has an unmatched record of reforming black convicts and junkies by providing a highly structured framework for living a disciplined, constructive life. Immersing himself in the study of history and religion, Malcolm found copious evidence to support the Nation's view of whites as "devils" created specifically to torment blacks. Emerging as the Nation's most charismatic spokesman, the newly renamed Malcolm X seized on white America's unwillingness to admit harsh truths: "I'm telling it like it *is!* You *never* have to worry about me biting my tongue if something I know as truth is on my mind. Raw, naked truth exchanged between the black man and the white man is what a whole lot more of is needed in this country—to clear the air of the racial mirages, cliches, and lies that this country's very atmosphere has been filled with for four hundred years."

Malcolm's final transformation came after he fulfilled his duty as a Muslim to make a pilgrimage, or *hajj*, to the holy city of Mecca. For the first time, Malcolm saw people of different colors interacting in contexts relatively free of white supremacy. Rather than rationalizing away his experience, Malcolm—who was soon to assume the orthodox Islamic name El-Hajj Malik el-Shabazz—reworked his vision of the world. "In the past, yes, I have made sweeping indictments of *all* white people," he acknowledged. "I never will be guilty of that again. . . . The true Islam has shown me that a blanket indictment of all white people is as wrong as when whites make blanket indictments against blacks."

Malcolm did not, however, retract his indictment of white America. Although he no longer saw whites as genetically incapable of changing their behavior, he emphasized that most still acted *as if* they were devils. It's a minor rephrasing, but its implications are absolutely crucial, both politically and culturally. If whites *are* devils, that's just the way it is and there's no point trying to work with them. If they simply *act like* devils, however, it becomes possible to imagine redemptive changes that make interracial communication and political coalition viable.

When Malcolm founded the Organization of Afro-American Unity after leaving the Nation of Islam, he limited membership to blacks. But he was willing to accept white support and encouraged whites to create equivalent organizations in their own communities. Malcolm reflected on the change when he reconsidered his response to a white student who had asked him what she could do to support his cause following a lecture on a college campus. Malcolm had responded with a curt "Nothing." After returning from Mecca, however, he said that he would now tell her to " 'Work in conjunction with us—each of us working among our own kind.' Let sincere white individuals find all other white people they can who feel as they do—and let them form their own all-white groups, to work trying to convert other white people who are thinking and acting so racist."

At each stage of his development, Malcolm told the fullest truth he knew, incorporating new information and experience in an expanding understanding of black people's place in the world. His real importance lay in his ability to communicate that expanding understanding to ordinary brothers—he was always at his best with black men—on the street. Films of Malcolm almost always show him interacting with crowds. His wonderful smile and pointed sense of humor served him well in no-holds-barred street-corner debates.

The images on the films contrast sharply with the most famous poster of Malcolm. Solitary and pensive, Malcolm stands by a window, gun in hand. The printed slogan that typically accompanies the picture reduces his fluidity to a militant cliché: "By Any Means Necessary." Not that Malcolm would have repudiated the basic idea. When confronted with violence, he insisted, violence was a proper response. White supremacists must learn that the days when blacks would turn the other cheek had come to an end. But Malcolm came to regret having allowed himself to be photographed with the gun. Ironically, on the day the picture was taken, he had armed himself in response to reports that he would be attacked by black adversaries. After his release from jail, Malcolm did his best to avoid physical conflict. He knew exactly what violence did to the relationships between black people. The last words he spoke before he was killed by black gunmen were "Let's cool it, brothers."

As black liberation theologian James Cone shows in his book *Malcolm and Martin and America,* Malcolm was moving toward a much more conciliatory stance during the last year of his life. Freed from the racist underpinnings of the Nation of Islam's theology, he encouraged coalitions among all types of black groups and, on occasion, radical white organizations. He expressed cautious optimism that black elected officials might effect meaningful change within a system that the Nation of Islam had repudiated as "white tricknology." Cone argues persuasively that it is a mistake to understand Malcolm and Martin as adversaries advocating diametrically opposed ideas of "nonviolence" and "violence." Rather, he suggests, they represent two different voices in the broader dialogue on black life in America.

Malcolm understood black culture as a crucial part of that ongoing conversation. In his speech announcing the formation of the OAAU, he said: "Our cultural revolution must be the means of bringing us closer to our African brothers and sisters. It must begin in the community and be based on community participation. Afro-Americans will be free to create only when they can depend on the Afro-American community for support, and Afro-American artists must realize that they depend on the Afro-American community for inspiration. . . . Culture is an indispensable weapon in the freedom struggle. We must take hold of it and forge the future with the past."

For the Chicago artists who elevated Malcolm and Coltrane to places of honor on the "Wall of Respect," the jazz saxophonist represented an ideal response to Malcolm's call. Like Malcolm, Coltrane passed through several distinct stages before finding his most revolutionary voice. During the late fifties and early sixties, he belonged to a group of emerging sax players that included Ornette Coleman, Wayne Shorter, and Sonny Rollins. Struggling to break a heroin habit, Coltrane served apprenticeships in bands led by Miles Davis and Thelonious Monk. His densely melodic solos provide a perfect foil for Miles's sparse, cool trumpet playing on "So What" and "Bye Bye Blackbird"; he learned to follow Monk's excursions into the non-Euclidean geometries of sound and silence on "Trinkle Trinkle" and "Ruby, My Dear." "Working with Monk brought me close to a musical architect of the highest order," Coltrane said. "I felt I learned from him in every way—through the senses, theoretically, technically. I would talk to Monk about musical problems, and he would sit at the piano and show me the answers just by playing them. I could watch him play and find out the things I wanted to know. Also, I could see a lot of things that I didn't know about at all."

Once Coltrane kicked his habit and began to explore the spiritual traditions of Africa, Asia, and the Middle East, he rapidly moved to the forefront of the new free jazz movement. The group he formed with drummer Elvin Jones, pianist McCoy Tyner, and bass player Jimmy Garrison played with a ferocity and dedication that commanded unmatched political and cultural respect. Although Miles Davis preferred Coltrane's earlier, more conventionally structured playing, he summed up the intense response to Coltrane's later work, which, Miles wrote, represented, for many blacks, the fire and passion and rage and anger and rebellion and love that they felt, especially among the young black intellectuals and revolutionaries of that time. He was expressing through music what H. Rap Brown and Stokely Carmichael and the Black Panthers and Huey Newton were saying with their words, what the Last Poets and Amiri Baraka were saying in poetry. He was their torchbearer in jazz, now ahead of me. He played what they felt inside and were expressing through riots—'burn, baby, burn'—that were taking place everywhere. . . . It was all about revolution for a lot of young black people—Afro hairdos, dashikis, black power, fists raised in the air. Coltrane was their symbol, their pride— their beautiful, black revolutionary pride.

If Malcolm occupied the central position in the muralists' collective re-envisioning of African American heritage, Coltrane elicited an equivalent response from revolutionary poets. The poets disagreed, sometimes angrily, on the precise political meaning of Coltrane's music, but all considered him an ally in their brand of revolution. In Haki Madhubuti's "Don't Cry, Scream," Coltrane embodies black nationalism. Amiri Baraka's "Am/trak," written after the poet had recanted his earlier black nationalist beliefs, appoints Coltrane presiding spirit of an interracial workers' revolution and condemns Madhubuti as a "backward cultural nationalist motherfucker." In "Dear John, Dear Coltrane" and "A Narrative of the Life and Times of John Coltrane: Played by Himself," Michael Harper forgoes ideology and places Coltrane at the center of a centuries-long black struggle for self-definition. Whatever their differences, the poets agree that, in the words of David Henderson's "A Coltrane Memorial," he represents "a way of escape / the underground rails . . . as we ride on up the way."

Although Coltrane said little to encourage anyone attempting to pin him to a particular ideology, he supported the movement's goals. One of his most moving compositions, "Alabama," was written in response to the Birmingham church bombing. Coltrane patterned his saxophone lines on the cadences of Martin Luther King's oration at the funeral of the four girls who died. Midway through the song, mirroring the part of the sermon where King transforms mourning into a statement of renewed determination, Elvin Jones's drums rise up from a whisper to a tumult of directed anger. Propelled by the rhythms, Coltrane's sax summons the people to what can only be understood as a unified assault on Pharaoh's palace.

Coltrane's revolutionary presence had as much to do with his religious vision as his politics. Like Malcolm, who believed that Islam provided a better path to redemption than the "white man's Christianity," Coltrane radiated a profoundly spiritual presence. His greatest music repeatedly asserts the reality of a divine energy that transcends the narrow understandings of human beings. In "Spiritual" and "Song of the Underground Railroad," he linked that energy to the specifically African American religious tradition of gospel politics. But Coltrane constantly expanded his frames of reference, reading incessantly and finding a particular affinity with the works of the Indian thinker J. Krishnamurti. Incorporating elements of African, Asian, and Islamic mysticism, Coltrane's music encompassed the outer reaches of the heavens and the inner recesses of the atom. "Wise One," his tribute to Albert Einstein, intimates a world where even the tension between science and religion dissolves into dance.

"Africa," "India," and the soaring "Ascension" unleash what Coltrane's contemporaries called "sheets of sound." Abandoning conventional musical structures, Coltrane sought to overwhelm his listeners' defenses, allowing them to experience unsuspected types of beauty. The music Coltrane created during the last years of his life provides glimpses of a way of being so radical, so encompassing, that it reduces complaints about the chaotic quality of some passages to irrelevance. It's not difficult to understand where those complaints came from. Based on the notion that the divine presence encompasses absolutely *everything*, that even the greatest discord contributes to the cosmic harmony, "Om" strikes most first-time listeners as unlistenable cacophony. Inside the torrential rhythmic pulses provided by Garrison and Jones, however, Coltrane, Tyner, and saxophonist Pharaoh Sanders exchange calls and responses that seek out each moment's place in an unimaginably intricate divine plan. The music is there, Coltrane seems to be saying, if only we can learn to hear it.

The fullest realization of Coltrane's vision, *A Love Supreme*, radiates a soaring spiritual power comparable to the "Ode to Joy" from Beethoven's Ninth Symphony. Coltrane opens with a blues cry but Garrison's bass immediately establishes the heartbeat riff that keeps Coltrane's spiritual quest in touch with the beloved community. The search unfolds in four movements, each exploring a different landscape on the path toward a higher truth. There's no real point to trying to translate *A Love Supreme* into words. Like Malcolm in his most eloquent visionary moments, Coltrane testifies to somewhere we've never been, somewhere, in our best moments, we can just begin to imagine. That's what jazz is all about.

## A Jazz Impulse Top 40

1. John Coltrane, "Afro-blue," 1963

2. Parliament, "Aqua Boogie (A Psychoalphadisco-betabioaquadoloop)," 1979

3. Miles Davis, "So What," 1959

4. Sly and the Family Stone, "Thank You (Falettinme Be Mice Elf Agin)," 1970; "Thank You (For Talkin to Me Africa)," 1971

5. Charles Mingus, "Haitian Fight Song," 1957

6. Jimi Hendrix, "Peace in Mississippi," 1970

7. Donny Hathaway, "The Ghetto," 1990

8. Eric B and Rakim, "In the Ghetto," 1990

9. Duke Ellington, "Harlem Air Shaft," 1941

10. Public Enemy, "Bring the Noise," 1988

11. Amina Claudine Myers, "African Blues," 1980

12. Karlheinz Stockhausen, "Hymnen," 1964

13. Louis Armstrong, "West End Blues," 1928

14. Cecil Taylor, "Olu Iwa," 1986

15. James Brown, "Papa's Got a Brand New Bag," 1965

16. Cassandra Wilson, "Children of the Night," 1993

## The Jazz Impulse

Jazz, observed Louis Armstrong, is music that's never played the same way once. The world changes, the music changes. Jazz imagines the transitions, distills the deepest meanings of the moment we're in, how it developed from the ones that came before, how it opens up into the multiple possibilities of the ones to come.

Ralph Ellison defines the jazz impulse as a constant process of redefinition. The jazz artist constantly reworks her identity on three levels: (1) as an individual; (2) as a member of a community; and (3) as a "link in the chain of tradition." Nothing is ever a given. Who you are, the people you live with and for, the culture you bear: everything remains open to question, probing, reevaluation. The jazz impulse shapes the sound of numerous musicians who aren't usually thought of alongside Louis and Duke, Bird and Miles. George Clinton's P-Funk empire lives and breathes the spirit of jazz, stretching minds, transgressing every boundary it comes to. Listen to the changes in Jimi Hendrix's treatment of the same songs at different times—there's a wonderful four-disc set titled *Stages* that documents concerts from each year between 1967 and 1970—and you hear an obsession with redefinition that bears comparison with Monk or Ellington. DJs sample the past, recombine it into something a lot closer to the spirit of jazz than Wynton Marsalis's reverent, technically flawless homages to the way it sounded yesterday, when life was clear.

*True jazz is an art of individual assertion within and against the group. Each true jazz moment (as distinct from the uninspired commercial performance) springs from a contest in which each artist challenges all the rest; each solo flight, or improvisation, represents (like the successive canvases of a painter) a definition of his identify: as individual, as member of the collectivity and as a link in the chain of tradition.*

—Ralph Ellison

For jazz artists, music provides a model of the world. "Beautiful" music based on conventions—verse and chorus, triadic harmonies, the familiar combinations of instruments in a bebop quartet or a guitar rock band—implies a set way of perceiving and experiencing the world. You know what's coming next, how you fit. Nothing *wrong* with that.

The jazz impulse asks what about those parts that *don't* fit: the dreams, desires, unanswered questions. Part of the reason jazz comes out of the African American tradition—though it reserves the right to go absolutely anywhere—has to do with what conventions have meant to black folk. Stay in your place, over on the other side of the tracks. Enjoy the back of the bus.

Jazz does its best to blow that kind of complacency away. Which is why jazz sounds

> [T]he slaves were only able to express themselves fully as individuals through the act of music. Thus each man developed his own 'cry' and his own 'personal sound.' The development of 'cries' was thus more than a stylization; it became the basis on which a group of individuals could join together, commit a social act, and remain individuals throughout, and this in the face of overt suppression. It has been suggested that the social act of music was at all times more than it seemed within the black culture. Further, to the extent the black man was involved with black music, he was involved with the black revolution. Black music was in itself revolutionary, if only because it maintained a non-Western orientation in the realms of perception and communication.
>
> —Ben Sidran

revolutionary even when it doesn't pay much attention to next week's election or anybody's party line. Jazz says we don't have to do it the way we've always done it. We can do it like this or like that, or, as soul jazzman Bobby Timmons tweaked it, "This Here" or "Dat Dere." That's also why a lot of people who try to conscript jazz into their own particular revolution wind up experiencing serious doubts. Your cow ain't a damn bit more sacred than theirs.

Jazz transforms noise into music, challenges us to *hear* the music in the noise, open our ears, our minds, our lives to things we hadn't thought about. Monk hits that funky note in "Misterioso" the first time and you think he's made a mistake. He hits it again to tell you he meant it. When he hits it that third time, you realize it was *your* mistake, that it was heartbreakingly beautiful the first time, that you could have heard it all along. And after a while you flash on the fact that Duke Ellington had been playing that note for years, that there's discord,

> *Charlie Parker? Charlie Parker. All the hip white boys scream for Bird. And Bird saying, 'Up your ass, feeble-minded ofay! Up your ass.' And they sit there talking about the tortured genius of Charlie Parker. Bird would've played not a note of music if he just walked up to East Sixty-seventh Street and killed the first ten white people he saw. Not a note!*
> —Amiri Baraka, *Dutchman*

noise, at the heart of "Satin Doll." Only Duke had a different style, a velvet touch that invited you to dream a new world out of the blacks, browns, and beiges of a changing same that *never* stayed in its place. The jazz impulse offers a deeper, sweeter, harsher, and truer sense of the world.

*If* you can get to it. There's no question the jazz impulse demands more from its listeners. You have to pay attention, remember the theme well enough to follow the variations, catch the jokes. It helps to know some music theory, to understand what the meta's for. Jazz loves to think about itself, play changes on ideas as well as sounds. Sometimes the theme that's being varied hasn't even been played. Jazz gets you thinking along one line, then switches directions, breaks apart expectations you didn't even know you had. It digs deep down inside your mind and shows you where the electric paths carrying thought and sensation back and forth between your consciousness and the world have begun to turn to bone. Jazz keeps the world in motion, alive.

Conceptually, not much separates jazz from the (post)modernist avant-garde. Both harbor a fierce desire to make it new, to shatter the idols of the marketplace, to explore the deepest recesses of human experience. It's not hard to imagine conversations between Duke and Béla Bartók, Stravinsky and Charlie Parker, Miles Davis and Karlheinz Stockhausen, Cecil Taylor and Gyorgi Ligeti. DJ Shadow and Tricky deconstruct the simulacra as surely as Derrida or Baudrillard. Anyone who reads Thomas Pynchon ought to be able to get down with the Mothership.

> *A percussive truthfulness. A synthesis of conflict and beauty. A futuristic maturity. An opening out toward multidimensionality through simplicity. . . . music requires an active listener—someone who doesn't have to be told the whole story. A transmutation of mind and sound: a third something is created. He was a deep listener. . . . Clusters of chords. A woman's walk. A man's bluesy cry in the night. Expansion rather than constriction. The listener helps to decide the music's shape—keeping it organic and alive. Always becoming.*
>
> —Yusef Komunyakaa

Whatever the connections, jazz isn't just another cut of meat off the modernist bone. The difference comes down to the way jazz honors the ancestors, remembers its roots in gospel and the blues. While jazz certainly encourages each player to find her own voice without undue regard for the community's cherished illusions, the *histories* of jazz too often confuse finding a voice with technical skill, being able to play high like Louis, fast like Bird, dense like Trane. But at the very most, technique's only half the story. Finding your own voice, in the black jazz tradition, demands knowing where that voice comes from, confronting, without illusion or evasion, who you really are. And that's what the blues are all about. Jazz lore is filled with stories of white (and some black) players who master the licks and show up to challenge the elders, who vanquish the pretenders by playing the blues. Know thy (black) self.

The connection between jazz and gospel may be even more crucial. As Ralph Ellison wrote, true jazz asserts the individual voice against and *within* the group. Very few jazz players reject their connection with the beloved community. Even the most radical, the farthest out, want desperately for their people to hear their call.

Coming at the gospel ideal of redemption from the other side of the cosmos, the jazz impulse envisions realities we've only dimly imagined, offers us new ways of thinking in the hope that they'll carry us a step farther down the road toward what poet Robert Hayden called the "mythic North," the "star-shaped yonder Bible city." The jazz impulse speculates on the paths leading toward it, what it might be like when we arrive, helps us develop into people who might be able to live there in peace.

# 25
# "Black Is an' Black Ain't":
# JB, Miles, and Jimi

"Black is an' black ain't," Ralph Ellison wrote in the prologue to his great jazz novel *Invisible Man*. "Black will git you an' black won't. It do an' it don't." Attempting to reconcile the demands of racial affirmation with their battle against ideological limitations of all kinds, black musicians of the late sixties probed the contradictory meanings of blackness with an intense honesty that responds to the fundamental call of the jazz impulse. In contrast to political discussions that *assumed* blackness as an answer to the most fundamental questions confronting black people, jazz impulse musicians understood racial identity as part of a larger, more complicated mix.

James Brown, Miles Davis, and Jimi Hendrix shared a contempt for simplistic understandings of blackness. Each blew away white stereotypes and embarked on his own quest to reach a higher level of understanding. Juxtaposing their paths helps provide an overview of the complicated racial terrain they were helping to map. Aware of Brown's experiments with African rhythmic approaches, Miles incorporated the aggressively black approach into his own multicultural sound. Aware of Miles's successful blending of "black" and "white" traditions, Hendrix sought to escape the racial dichotomies that made it hard for him to find an audience that would allow him to pursue his visions to their extremes. Together, the three affirm Ellison's sense that blackness can mean everything or nothing at all.

James Brown didn't discover Africa. He didn't actually discover that you could generate a compelling rhythm by accenting the first beat of every measure. But there's no doubt that once the Godfather of Soul took his rhythm stick to "the One," American music became something different, blacker, and more African than it had ever been before. If the jazz impulse is about redefining possibilities, James Brown deserves a place in the pantheon alongside Louis Armstrong, Duke Ellington, and Charlie Parker. Affecting musicians from Miles and Sly Stone to Memphis and Motown, "Cold Sweat" and "Papa's Got a Brand New Bag" unleashed a polyrhythmic ferocity that eventually reconfigured every corner of the American soundscape.

Although most critics traced Brown's musical roots to gospel and the blues, Brown himself emphasized his affinities with jazz: "When people talk about soul music, they talk only about gospel and R&B coming together. That's accurate about a lot of soul, but if you're going to talk about mine, you have to remember the jazz in it. That's what made my music so different and allowed it to change and grow." For Brown, the categories didn't make much difference: "There was one sound I couldn't hear anywhere but in my head. I didn't have a name for it, but I knew it was different. See, musicians don't think about categories and things like that. They don't say, I think I'll invent bebop today or think up rock 'n' roll tomorrow. They just hear different sounds and follow them wherever they lead."

The sound Brown pursued in the late sixties and seventies led to some unmistakably black places. Supported by two of the funkiest drummers who ever lived, Jabo Starks and Clyde Stubblefield, Brown's bands pretty much abandoned melody and harmony. Everything moved to the demands of the rhythmic pulse. Scratch guitarist Jimmy Nolen chopped out rhythms, Maceo Parker led a horn section that punched accents on the beats within the beats without ever losing its hold on the one. Condensing lyric lines into soul shouts and fragments of a sermon on black pride, Brown immersed his crowd in a swirling polyrhythmic texture of calls and responses. However deep Brown took the crowd into the jungle groove, the band never failed to keep the community together, move the party along.

His music spoke as clearly to the throngs that greeted him on his tour of West Africa—which exerted a powerful impact on African popular music—as it did to the ones in Harlem whose feverish responses to "I'll Go Crazy" and "Please Please Please" help make *Live at the Apollo* the greatest live soul album ever recorded. "My whole generation listened to Santana and James Brown," said Nigerian songwriter Herman Asafo-Agyei. Brown's popularity in Africa reached such heights that Nigerian superstar Fela complained that Brown had taken over African music entirely: "The attack was heavy, soul music coming in the country left and right. Man, at one point

I was playing James Brown tunes among the innovative things because everybody was demanding it and we had to eat."

The African response suggests the dual significance of Brown's funk. On the one hand, it affirmed blackness as a core of identity, in Africa as well as the United States. Clearly, blacks needed to take pride in themselves and throw off the shackles of white supremacist stereotypes. But, as Fela's comment reveals, the celebration could become a limitation, enforcing a particular conception of what a black sound was.

Miles Davis never accepted anyone else's idea of what he should sound like. From the late forties on, he had played a crucial part in several distinct movements that transformed the sound of jazz. The *Downbeat* reporter who arrived to interview Miles in 1968 shouldn't really have been shocked to find him surrounded by a pile of popular records by Brown, the Fifth Dimension, Aretha Franklin, and the Byrds (who used a melody from John Coltrane's "India" as the main riff of "Eight Miles High"). When questioned on his favorite music, Miles responded: "My favorite music is Stockhausen, *Tosca* and James Brown."

Miles followed his interest in Brown's experimental funk "down into a deep African thing, a deep African-American groove, with a lot of emphasis on drums and rhythm, and not on individual solos." When Miles added Brown's funk, Sly Stone's rhythmically innovative soul, and Hendrix's rock to his musical mix, the results were spectacular. The new sound came together on *Bitches Brew*, which features an all-star jazz rock orchestra. The music varies from the sparsely syncopated "Miles Runs the Voodoo Down" to the impenetrable density of "Pharaoh's Dance," which rides an ever-changing groove laid down by three keyboardists (Chick Corea, Joe Zawinul, and Larry Young), two bass players (Dave Holland and Harvey Brooks), a bass clarinetist (Bennie Maupin), and a percussion section led by Tony Williams, possibly the most imaginative drummer of his generation. The music ripples over you in waves, voices merge and separate until you're not really sure what you heard and what you only dreamed. Miles's horn emerges from the mix from time to time, but so do Wayne Shorter's saxophone and John McLaughlin's transcendental guitar.

*Bitches Brew* exemplifies Miles's fundamental philosophy of music. "Everyone adds, everyone responds," he observed. "Sometimes you subtract, take away the rhythm and leave just the high sound. Or take out what you know belongs to someone else and keep the feeling. . . . What my musicians have got to do is extend themselves beyond what they think they can do. And they've got to be quick. A soloist comes in when he feels like it. Anyway, that's what he's being paid for. If it's not working out, I just shut them up. How? I set up obstacles, barriers like they do in the streets, but with my horn. I curve them, change their direction." On *Bitches Brew*, Miles adapted the approach to the concept of the musical groove he had picked up in different ways from Brown and the German composer Karlheinz Stockhausen, whose *Hymnen* uses fragments of national anthems to create a stunning meditation on the constantly shifting patterns redefining Europe's place in the world. "I got further and further into his idea of performance as a process," Miles said. "I had always written in a circular way and through Stockhausen I could see that I didn't want to ever play again from eight bars to eight bars, because I never end songs; they just keep going on."

As Miles's invocation of Stockhausen suggests, blackness played an important, but not always definitive, role in his musical sensibility. His public persona was uncompromisingly black. He made frequent references to "white motherfuckers," and many considered him overly sensitive and quick to anger. Attending an honorary dinner for Ray Charles at the Reagan White House, Miles delivered an impromptu speech on the white failure to value the contributions of black musicians: "Jazz is ignored here because the white man likes to win everything. White people like to see other white people win just like you do and they can't win when it comes to jazz and the blues because black people created this." A skilled boxer who never backed down from a verbal or physical fight, Miles refused to accept even a hint of racial condescension. Long before Brown's "Say It Loud" turned the phrase into a slogan, Miles was both black and proud.

But he was never a racist. Like almost every major jazzman, he collaborated freely with any musician who put down an interesting sound. Despite his outspoken criticism of the white-dominated music industry, Miles periodically took heat from black musicians and militants for using white players in his bands. His response was unambiguous: "I just told them if a guy could play as good as Lee Konitz played—that's who they were mad about most, because there were a lot of black alto players around—I would hire him every time and I wouldn't give a damn if he was green with red breath. I'm hiring a motherfucker to play, not for what color he is."

Miles's appreciation of the possibilities of interracial music was both aesthetic and economic. He saw no reason why the funky guitar-driven sound of *Bitches Brew* shouldn't appeal to the rock audience that considered far less creative players minor deities. Although he had some problems with the rock emphasis on spectacle at the expense of sound, he welcomed the chance to play for audiences unfamiliar with his classic jazz albums *Birth of the Cool, Walkin', Kind of Blue,* and *Filles de Kilimanjaro.* After playing several gigs at the Fillmore theaters, Miles commented: "We were playing to all kinds of different people. The crowds that were going to see Laura Nyro and the Grateful Dead were all mixed up with some of the people who were coming to see me. So it was good for everybody."

The intersection of jazz and rock worlds came as a distinctly mixed blessing for Jimi Hendrix. A jazz musician trapped in a rock format, he would have loved to have lived in a world where color really wasn't the controlling factor. Not that Jimi had a problem with being black. It was just that he considered blackness a point of departure rather than a destination in itself. During the last year of his life, he developed an appreciation for how Miles had negotiated the hazardous terrain. But he never encountered an audience that got the point.

Growing up in a household where black music was a constant presence, Hendrix responded deeply to the call of the Delta blues. "The first guitarist I was aware of was Muddy Waters," he said. "I heard one of his records when I was a little boy and it scared me to death, because I heard all those sounds. Wow! What was that all about?" Although Hendrix played the blues throughout his life, his approach came straight out of the jazz impulse. He used music to express a distinctly idiosyncratic sense of the world: "It's not an act, but a state of being. I play and move as I feel. My music, my instrument, my sound, my body, are all one action with my mind." Like Coltrane and Monk, Hendrix sought to unveil the music in the noise: "Music is very serious to me. Other people may think it's a load of junk or senseless, but it's my way of saying what I want to say. My own thing is in my head. I hear sounds and if I don't get them together, nobody else will."

Before he became a central figure in the largely white rock scene of the late sixties, Hendrix had served his musical apprenticeship backing up soul revues featuring Sam Cooke, Jackie Wilson, the Supremes, and the Impressions. Himself a brilliant left-handed guitar player, Curtis Mayfield observed: "With the psychedelics and what have you, he was almost like a scientist studying the effects."

George Clinton shared Mayfield's appreciation for Hendrix's explorations: "Jimi was definitely the one we held up when we wanted to reach for something. The way he could control feedback and make it sound so symphonic truly transcended logic. There were no boundaries to his playing. One minute he would sound like Curtis Mayfield, next thing he'd be doing Ravi Shankar. His music gave me the freedom to go out and be anything I felt like being musically." However far his music might take him, however, Hendrix emphasized its black sources: "The background of our music is a spiritual blues thing. Now I want to bring it down to earth. I want to get back to the blues, because that's what I am."

Given his deep roots in black music, Hendrix found it frustrating that most of his audience, at least outside Vietnam, consisted of young whites with limited appreciation for its affinities with jazz and the blues. He enjoyed playing with Experience drummer Mitch Mitchell, but he found the tight format of the power rock trio and the audience's demands for "Purple Haze" and "Foxy Lady" stifling. The black community's general indifference to his psychedelic style was even more frustrating. Hendrix encountered the problem even before blacks began to identify him with the "white" festivals at Woodstock and Monterey. "When I was staying in Harlem my hair was really long," he remembered. "I'd be walking down the street and all of a sudden the cats, or girls, old ladies—anybody—they're just peekin' out, sayin', 'ough, what's this supposed to be, Black Jesus?' or 'What is this, the circus or something?' God! Even in your own section. Your own people hurt you more."

During the last year of his life, Hendrix began reaching out, experimenting with new settings for his guitar work. After the breakup of the Experience, he organized an all-black band with army buddy Billy Cox on bass and Buddy Miles on drums. His Woodstock performance drew much of its strength from the polyrhythmic ferocity of his Afro-Latin backup band, the Gypsy Sons & Rainbows. But the sound mix used for the Woodstock film and album erased the band. Against his will, Hendrix was forced back into the straight rock mode he was trying to escape.

One of the great lost opportunities in music history involves Hendrix and Miles, who clearly recognized the jazz elements of Hendrix's music: "He liked the way Coltrane played with all those other sheets of sounds and he played the guitar in a similar way. Plus, he said that he had heard the guitar voicing that I used in the way I played the trumpet." When Miles and Hendrix met, they eagerly exchanged ideas. "I'd play him a record of mine or Trane's and explain to him what we were doing," Miles wrote. "Then he started incorporating things I told him into his albums. It was great. He influenced me, and I influenced him, and that's the way great music is always made. Everybody showing everybody else something and then moving on from there."

The call and response between Miles and Hendrix affected the music each made during late 1969 and early 1970. The subtle phrasings and increased harmonic sophistication of "Angel" and "Hey Baby (New Rising Sun)" from Hendrix's unfinished concept album *The First Rays of the New Rising Sun* demonstrate that he had internalized some of Miles's ideas. Similarly, the defining element of Miles's sound from *Bitches Brew* on is the increased prominence of the guitar alongside the saxophone and trumpet. While John McLaughlin played with a piercing purity all his own, Miles often chose guitarists who shared Hendrix's fascination with noise: Sonny Sharrock, Pete Cosey, and finally Foley, whom Miles praised for "playing that funky blues-rock-funk, almost Jimi Hendrix-like music."

Miles and Hendrix seriously considered making an album together. There was talk of collaborating with Miles's longtime arranger Gil Evans, who later released an album of Hendrix compositions. Shortly before his death, Hendrix speculated about his own musical future in terms that blend the instrumental approach of *Bitches Brew* with a philosophy reminiscent of late Coltrane: "When the last American tour finished, I started thinking about the future, thinking this era of music sparked by the Beatles had come to an end. Something new has to come and Jimi Hendrix will be there." Hendrix continued: "I want a big band. I don't mean three harps and 14 violins. I mean a big band full of competent musicians that I can conduct and write for. And with the music we will paint pictures of Earth and space so that the listener can be taken somewhere." It wasn't difficult to imagine Hendrix hooking up with John Coltrane, whose last major album was titled *Interstellar Space*.

But Hendrix joined the long line of jazz artists who succumbed, at least in part, to a public unable or unwilling to follow his explorations. Sometimes jazz finds itself lost, wandering trackless paths where the calls fade into echoes of themselves. The sounds reach out toward the ghosts—Samuel Beckett, Nietzsche, Billie Holiday, Bird—drifting silently in their self-contained orbits. The risks of isolation, alienation, suicide aren't abstract. Play something the world's never heard and chances are it won't hear it this time, either. Which is part of what drives so many jazz men and women to drugs. The needle, the pipe, the bottle, and the tab bestow visions which can, for a vanishing moment, cleanse the doors of perception. But mostly they deaden the pain, make the lack of response—for a long entropic moment—seem, almost, bearable.

Finally, the pain killed Hendrix. Shortly before he died in 1970, he expressed his desire for a deeper audience response: "The main thing that used to bug me was that the people wanted too many visual things from me. I never wanted it to be so much of a visual thing. When I didn't do it, people thought I was being moody, but I can only freak when I really feel like doing so. Now I just want the music to get across, so that people can just sit back and close their eyes and know exactly what is going on without caring a damn about what we are doing while we're on-stage." About all we have to suggest where Miles and Hendrix might have taken us are the jazz rock masterpiece "Right Off" from Miles's sound track to *Jack Johnson*; Sonny Sharrock's *Seize the Rainbow* and *Guitar*, and *Nine to the Universe*, a compilation of jams with Miles's organist Larry Young released a decade after Jimi's death. The tragedy was that however much he longed to play jazz, to transcend the artificial divisions of race and style, Hendrix lived and died the blues.

# 26
# Curtis Mayfield's Gospel Soul

At a time when the dizzying pace of change sometimes made it hard to remember where it had all begun, no one kept the gospel faith more steadfastly than Curtis Mayfield. A clear thinker and sharp businessman who gave concrete meaning to the concept of Black Power, Mayfield had begun his career following the path blazed by Sam Cooke. Expressing a deeply held vision of redemption that accepted white presence while insisting on the beauty of blackness, the classic songs Mayfield wrote for the Impressions—"People Get Ready," "Keep on Pushing," "I'm So Proud," and "We're a Winner"—came as close as anything ever written to bringing real gospel to the top twenty. Amid the rapidly polarizing racial climate of the late sixties, Mayfield's "Choice of Colors" and "This Is My Country" held out that hope that Black Power and democratic brotherhood were, however unlikely it sometimes seemed, profoundly compatible.

So it came as a shock when, speaking over a rumbling bass line like something out of the Book of Revelations, Mayfield opened his first solo album by promising the "sisters, niggers, whities, Jews, crackers": "Don't worry, if there's a hell below we're all gonna go." The scream that followed summons up Mayfield's anguish over the betrayal of the vision he had learned growing up in Chicago's Travelling Souls Spiritualist Church, where his grandmother was the pastor. It was a vision he had heard clearly in Hendrix's "Little Wing" and "Message of Love." "Jimi's approach to music transcends racial barriers," Mayfield observed. "His imagination spoke to people on a deeper level than that." By the time Hendrix died in 1970, enough bad scenes had gone down to make even the most hopeful doubt whether America was capable of responding to any truly inclusive vision.

Mayfield was part of a vibrant Chicago scene in which musicians freely exchanged ideas on how music might contribute to the movement. The jazz composers who assembled around spiritual leader Muhal Richard Abrams's Association for the Advancement of Creative Musicians developed a theoretically sophisticated framework for understanding the political potential of black music; Roscoe Mitchell's "Spiritual" and Abrams's "Blues Forever" delve into the revolutionary energy of gospel and blues respectively. At Chess Studios, Willie Dixon wrote politically charged blues for Little Walter (the wickedly sardonic ode to the power of money, "Dead Presidents"), Koko Taylor ("Insane Asylum"), and Bo Diddley ("You Can't Judge a Book by Its Cover"). Herbie Hancock captured the changing energies of the freedom movement in the exuberant "Watermelon Man," the meditative "Maiden Voyage," and the assertive "Riot." The jazz musician with the closest affinity to Mayfield's sensibility, however, was probably Ramsey Lewis, who placed funky covers of Dobie Gray's pop hit "The In Crowd" and movement standard "Wade in the Water" in the top twenty.

From the beginning, Mayfield modeled the Impressions' sound on the music of the black church: "Gospel was your foundation and there's been many a song coming from the black church." The gospel tradition provided the inspiration for many of Mayfield's songs: "All you had to do was just change some few lyrics. 'Keep on Pushing' was intended, written as a gospel song. But all I needed to do to lock it in with the Impressions was say 'I've got my strength' instead of 'God gave me strength and it don't make sense.' I've got my strength. Nothing else needed to be changed." Similarly, "People Get Ready" welcomes anyone willing to do the right thing onto the "train to Jordan" while warning "there's no hiding place against the kingdom's throne." When the song ends with "you don't need no ticket, you just thank the Lord," you can almost believe that the promise of the movement will be fulfilled.

Responding to the situations he saw around him in the black neighborhoods of Chicago's South and West Sides, Mayfield was deeply committed to the movement. "As a young man I was writing songs like 'Keep on Pushing' and 'This Is My Country' and feeling all the love and all the things I observed politically," Mayfield said, considering the connection between his music and the political energy of the sixties. "Of course with everything I saw on the streets as a young black kid, it wasn't hard during the latter fifties and early sixties for me to write through my own heartfelt way of how I visualized things, how I thought things oughta be."

Profoundly political, but never narrowly ideological, Mayfield's sense of how things ought to be took shape both within his own community and in response to the calls of the leaders. "When you're talking about songs such as 'We're a Winner,' that's locked in with Martin Luther King. It took something from his inspiring message. I was listening to all my preachers and the different leaders of the time. You had your Rap Browns and your Stokely Carmichaels and Martin Luther Kings, all of those people were there right within that same era. They get their credit and rightfully so." But Mayfield insisted that the real strength of the movement lay in the commitment of the larger community, the local people he refers to as "the invisible heroes."

As the movement gathered strength, the Impressions spoke more directly about political concerns without attracting significant resistance, at least until 1968, when several radio stations, including Chicago's number-one-rated WLS, banned the distinctly uplifting "We're a Winner." Mayfield attributed the banning to the song's "social conscience; it was about a mass of people during the time of struggle, and when it broke it was so much out of the ordinary. It had a little gospel feeling and it sort of locked in with the movement of equality. It wouldn't be what you could call a crossover record during those times, but the demand of the people kept it struggling and happening, and it's still one of my favorite tunes."

Even as cries of "Black Power!" began to drown out the earlier movement's calls for "Freedom Now!," Mayfield maintained a gospel-tinged vision of interracial harmony. Closer to King than Malcolm X in sensibility, he emphasizes that the movement's successes required cooperation and shared struggle: "People of all colors were trying to push this along ever since there's been a slavery. Not just the minority or blacks. Everybody in this country at one time or another has been a minority, wherever they come from. We just made a good loud noise as far as congregating."

Mayfield's inclusive view of redemption drew some criticism, most of it relatively respectful, from Black Power advocates. Never confrontational in style, Mayfield responded to the criticism with music that reiterated his major points. "Choice of Colors" rejects unthinking racial hatred—"how long have you hated your white teacher"—while endorsing the Black Power call for unity and respect: "Can you respect your brother's woman friend, and share with black folks not of kin?" The clinching lines keep the faith in the open vision of the earlier movement, seeing the path to a better society in "a little more education, and love for our nation."

Even as he reasserted his gospel politics, Mayfield embraced certain elements of the Black Power movement. For one thing, he loved the era's fashions: "It was a great opening, the style, the clothes, the wide pants and the long German coats. Everything sort of fell in and it hit a real nice fashion. To be fly was to *be*, you know." More importantly, Mayfield responded to the Black Power movement's call for uncompromising confrontation with the history of racism and oppression. In the 1968 single "This Is My Country," Mayfield testifies to "three hundred years of slave driving, sweat and welts on my back" but goes on to reassert the gospel vision, now stated in unmasked political terms: "This is my country." It's an uncompromising rejection of anyone—Elijah Muhammad as well as George Wallace—who would deny blacks full participation in American society: "Some people think we don't have the right to say it's my country." Reminding his listeners that "every brother is a leader," Mayfield promises "our love is gonna help the world be free."

If Mayfield continued to resist separatism, his involvement with the Curtom label—named for Mayfield and his old friend and partner Eddie Thomas—showed a deep understanding of the Black Power movement's call for economic self-determination. For more than a decade, Curtom provided an emblem of Black Power, financially and artistically, that transcended slogans. From the beginning of his career, Mayfield was aware of the tragic stories of gifted musicians who fell victim to predatory record labels. His ability to keep control of the rights to his songs didn't happen by accident. Aware of the exploitation suffered by his elders, Mayfield explored ways of establishing control over his economic fate. "It was important to me to own as much of myself as I could. So I found out where the Library of Congress was and how to record my own publishing company. Turned out it cost nothing to do either one."

After he established Curtom, Mayfield felt free to address the problems of racial polarization and the internal problems of inner-city black neighborhoods that he saw increasing despite the promise of the revolutionary movement. He confronted the blues realities of drug addiction ("Stone Junkie"), racial paranoia ("Mighty Mighty [Spade & Whitey])," and the continuing theft of land from American Indians ("I Plan to Stay a Believer"). The vastly underrated song "The Other Side of Town" addresses the spiritual despair of poor black communities, many of them even more isolated than they had been nearly two decades earlier when the *Brown* v. *Board of Education* decision promised to end segregation "with all deliberate speed." The haunting version of "Mighty Mighty (Spade & Whitey)" that opens *Curtis/Live!* condemns the racist "stupidness we've all been taught" and asserts: "really ain't no difference, if you're cut you're gonna bleed." Asking the audience if he can "get a bit deeper," Mayfield echoes James Brown: "I got to say it loud, I'm black and I'm proud."

Mayfield's balancing of black self-assertion and racial openness reaches deep into the gospel tradition, which recognizes that the ability to accept others, to live out the democratic vision, requires self-acceptance. The same combination of perceptions recurs in "We Gotta Have Peace" and "Beautiful Brother of Mine." A masterful combination of Mayfield's gospel and funk styles, "Beautiful Brother" holds out a vision of a community coming to terms with the real meaning of the slogan "Black is beautiful": "Together we're truly black power, learning to love by the hour."

A major element of Curtom's success had to do with the success of Mayfield's movie sound tracks, beginning with *Superfly*, which helped establish the "blaxploitation" genre's peculiar mixture of ghetto realism and sensationalistic obsession with drugs, violence, and a near-cartoon version of black masculine dominance. *Superfly* brings the political contradictions of blaxploitation into sharp focus. Mayfield jumped at the chance when producer Sig Shore asked him to write the sound track for what would become one of the definitive films of the genre. "I can recall having received the *Superfly* script from Sig Shore and [screenwriter] Philip Fenty at Lincoln Center in New York. I was performing there and they brought this script in between shows and wow, I was so excited. I'd written a song just flying back home from New York. It took me hardly no time to prepare the songs and that's how it began. It was different, it was wearing a new hat. I was fulfilling the dreams of many agents and writers and people who are of the business." The songs Mayfield wrote in that burst of creative activity, especially the title cut and "Freddie's Dead," earn the *Superfly* sound track a place alongside Isaac Hayes's "Shaft," Bobby Womack's "Across 110th Street," and Marvin Gaye's "Trouble Man" as the pinnacles of blaxploitation funk.

From the moment the film was released, however, audiences recognized a dissonance between the movie's celebration of drugs and sex, and the message of Mayfield's sound track, which clearly identifies the "Pusherman" as community enemy number one. Mayfield remembers his surprise at the way director Gordon Parks, Jr., transformed the meaning of Fenty's script: "For me when I first was reading it, it read very well. I mean all this was reality. We're not trying to sell it, but we're telling it to you like it is. But reading the script didn't tell you 'and then he took another hit of cocaine' and then about a minute later 'he took another hit.' So when I saw it visually, I thought, 'This is a cocaine infomercial.' That's all it was." "I don't know whether that was intended or not. It was a great beginning and introduction of cocaine to a lot of people. No one really knew about cocaine at the time. Of course it was going to grow anyway whether there was *Superfly* or not. But it was a great opening."

Rather than backing out of the project, Mayfield set about creating what amounts to a masked dialogue with the surface message. "I made the commitment and of course I wasn't going to let go of my chance to do a movie. Yet I didn't want to be part of that infomercial. So it was important to me that I left the glitter and all the social stuff and tried to go straight in the lyrics. I tried to tell the stories of the people in depth and not insult the intelligence of those who were spending their money."

Mayfield's efforts were aided by the fact that the music hit the charts prior to the film's release. "I released it three months prior to the movie coming out," Mayfield recalled. "So when the kids got in there they knew the music." The strategy meant that even though the film includes only an instrumental version of "Freddie's Dead," audience members familiar with the single could juxtapose the film's images with Mayfield's sober reminder that it all leads to meaningless violence, community destruction.

Mayfield reiterated that the script itself tells a story similar to the one in his lyrics: "I didn't put [the movie's main character] down. He was just trying to get out. However, his deeds weren't noble ones. But he was making money and he had intelligence. And he did survive." Mayfield emphasized the point by concluding the title song with a moment that could be described as gospel funk. While long-time Impressions arranger Johnny Pate's orchestration fades out over one of the decade's catchiest rhythmic grooves, Mayfield repeats the line "trying to get over" again and again, bringing "Superfly" into dialogue with the gospel classic "How I Got Over." Mayfield clearly understands the struggles of the brothers and sisters on the streets as part of a shared history extending back to slavery: "He did survive," he repeated. "In that time and era, most times the black guys don't make it through the movie. For most black folks in that time and era, just making it was tough. So this guy did what he did and he was true to himself and he got out and kept his life."

Even as the Black Power movement disintegrated under the combined pressure of government subversion and internal self-destruction, Mayfield kept his eye on the prize. On the sound track to the grittily realistic prison movie *Short Eyes*, he testified that "Doo doo wop is strong in here." But, as the seventies unfolded, Mayfield's voice sounded more isolated. Mayfield's seventies remake of "It's Alright" underscores the changes in his energy since the high point of the movement. The Impressions' sixties version of the song radiates an energy of connection, especially when the three voices come together at the ends of lines. The seventies remake accentuates the distance between Mayfield and the female backup singers, who sound like they're located in a different room. You can feel the call and response fundamental to what Cornel West called the "audacious hope" of the gospel vision falling apart. Mayfield's best songs of the mid and late seventies—"Never Say You Can't Survive" and the achingly beautiful "Something to Believe In"—demonstrate his continuing belief in the gospel vision. Even as he stands alone on the dance floor, contemplating what came to seem the inevitable collapse of his community, Mayfield testifies to the power of love. Still, whatever the remake of "It's Alright" might have claimed, the underlying message came through clearly: *nothing* was going to be all right. And if even that bitter reality is all right, then gospel has circled back to the blues.

# 27
# John Fogerty and the Mythic South

John Fogerty understood the tension between isolation and community as well as any artist white America has ever produced. Even as Creedence Clearwater Revival assumed near-mythic status as the voice of its generation, Fogerty's songs invoked a more disturbing world where he found himself alone, pursued by spirits more at home in the Mississippi Delta than in the Northern California suburbs where he grew up. The patron saint of garage bands throughout America, Fogerty tapped into the deepest wellsprings of American music, sources of energy that refused to acknowledge the divisions that were tearing America apart during the years CCR was at its peak. When Fogerty's voice drawled out the opening lines of "Green River"—"Take me back down where cool water flows, y'all / Help me remember things I loved"—he was staking a claim to his corner of the mythic American soil where, if race doesn't go away, it at least doesn't keep us from hearing each other's voices. Reflecting on his own ancestors, Fogerty embraced his multiracial heritage: "I think about what Muddy Waters really did and he's every bit as seminal, as groundbreaking, as epochal, as Elvis Presley. It's funny that they're both from Mississippi. It's kind of the same journey, just some years apart. Initially, they went to different parts of our culture, but they ended up in the same place."

It was a place Fogerty would arrive at by his own path. Like many white rockers, he came to his soulful rock and roll through radio rather than regional upbringing. Fogerty's story belongs to a profoundly American mythic tradition that allows you to reinvent yourself as a way of discovering something better and deeper than what you "really" were. It's a way of imagining community into the broken world. Fogerty's music belongs as much to the Louisiana swamps as to the San Francisco Bay area where he was born and raised. Which doesn't change the fact that Creedence's claim to being the quintessential San Francisco band is as strong as the Grateful Dead's and a whole lot stronger than those of the Jefferson Airplane or Big Brother and the Holding Company.

In fact, Fogerty never really considered CCR part of the San Francisco sound. "It was all sort of a concoction. I have to say I looked at it with a bit of a jaundiced eye," he said. "We knew that many of those people came to San Francisco later. I thought the whole myth, the mythology of the San Francisco sound, was a concoction, almost like a Chamber of Commerce thing." Creedence had relatively little contact with the most prominent San Francisco bands: "The Grateful Dead were always a little off from our circle. They did things differently. And the Airplane, at least in those days, gave off this vibe, this attitude like Creedence somehow didn't fit into those circles. It was very real. I could never put my finger on what it was, but we were considered outsiders in our own town."

CCR responded to the situation by building a myth of community. Bassist Stu Cook sounded the keynote when he said: "Creedence to me is four individuals who together make up a fifth person. Outside of the four of us. The whole is bigger than any individual. Like a marriage, only there's four personalities instead of two." Tom Fogerty added: "We've been together for ten years. We've got a unity of minds." The cover of the *Willy and the Poorboys* album gave visual expression to the myth. It portrays CCR on a gritty Oakland side street playing instruments from deep in the American grain: harmonica, washboard, gutbucket bass. The music on the album gave substance to the claim; Fogerty's "Down on the Corner" and "Don't Look Now" blend smoothly into the traditional "Cotton Fields" and Leadbelly's "Midnight Special." No rock band ever made music closer to the restless spirit of Harry Smith's stunning (and recently rereleased) *Anthology of American Folk Music*.

That was both CCR's glory and its irresolvable contradiction. The standard stereotype of folk music presents it as the "authentic" voice of a traditional community. Smith's compilation makes the truth clear. Its best moments—ranging from Clarence Ashley's "Coo Coo Bird" and Dock Boggs's "Sugar Baby" through Furry Lewis's "Kassie Jones" and Mississippi John Hurt's "Frankie" to Blind Willie Johnson's "John the Revelator" and Blind Lemon Jefferson's "See That My Grave Is Kept Clean"—consistently reflect the isolation of artists trying to remake tradition in their own tormented image. In his brilliant analysis of Smith's anthology, Greil Marcus identifies the core of the impulse that connects CCR with the black/white American tradition: "One could experience a freedom from one's physical body, and from one's social body—the mask you wore to go about in public among those who thought they knew you, an unchosen mask of nervousness and tradition, the mask that, when worn too long, makes the face behind it shrivel up and rot away. For some, a spinning record opened up the possibility that one might say anything, in any voice, with any face, the singer's mask now a sign of mastery." The tension between the face and the mask connects Fogerty's best songs with an American tradition that includes Skip James's "Devil Got My Woman" and Tommy Johnson's "Big Road Blues" as well as Ralph Stanley's "Rank Stranger" and Hank Williams's "Lost Highway."

Whatever the myth of CCR might have implied, the reality was that John Fogerty, like all great bluesmen, found himself engaged in a sometimes agonizing struggle to disentangle his personal voice from a community that scarcely understood itself. So it's not really surprising that CCR's mythic community disintegrated amidst personal acrimony and a tangle of lawsuits that dragged on like something out of a novel by Charles Dickens. Nor is it surprising that Fogerty's personal odyssey led him from his literal origins to his creative origins in the American South. Fogerty remembered his surprise when listeners began pointing out that his voice seemed "so Southern, so swampy. I've thought about this for years. Where did that come from? Because I grew up in El Cerrito, California, and there wasn't much Southern about it."

The answer to Fogerty's meditations arrived, appropriately enough, at the 1986 Rock and Roll Hall of Fame dinner, where he delivered the induction speech for Buddy Holly. Holly was part of the initial group of inductees alongside Elvis, Ray Charles, Little Richard, Jerry Lee Lewis, James Brown, and Chuck Berry. "That was when I finally got my answer," Fogerty recalled with a smile. "I'd been thinking about this for twenty-five years. That night I stood there and either the people who were being honored were there at the same time or their posters. There were pictures of everybody all around. I looked and I looked at each one of them and realized they were all from the South. The only one I wasn't sure was from the South was Sam Cooke."

"So it was at least nine out of ten," Fogerty continued. "And I found out later Sam Cooke was from Clarksdale, Mississippi, so it was really ten out of ten. Rock and roll is Southern and that's why

I'm Southern. Because what I learned from was Southern. I rest my case." Fogerty framed the question as one of regional roots that impart a distinct Southern family resemblance to rock and roll everywhere. "If you imitate your father and other people say, hey, you imitated your father, you don't even have a choice. You just do what you see."

Not that Fogerty was totally isolated from the deeper roots of American music. "I grew up with the blues," he said, reemphasizing the role radio played in his musical education. "It's not like I was from Tibet or Mars. But I was doing it from afar. I was listening to Muddy Waters but I barely knew anything about his real life. I knew he had a great band. I mean any rock and roller can appreciate that when everybody else was sitting on their porches playing on their acoustic guitars, he organized it and plugged it in. We call it a blues band, but that was a rock and roll band. It was *loud*." One moment from a 1963 performance at a high school reunion became a touchstone for Fogerty's later thoughts about the relationship between his own music and black traditions. "We'd played 'Green Onions,' " he recalled, "and this black guy came up, his name was R. B. King. He would have been about twenty-eight years old. And he says, 'You boys do that rock and roll pretty good. But when you do "Green Onions" there's this in-between you're missin'.' Later, he would have said 'soul.' He was trying to compliment us, but it was absolutely the truth. We were high school kids and we couldn't play a shuffle to save our lives. It's something most white people can't do. 'There's that little in-between you're missin', when you get that, then you'll have "Green Onions" down.' I thought about that a lot over the years."

While Fogerty recognized volume and what he calls "dirt" as shared elements of rock and the blues, he pointed to some crucial differences in the blues tradition. "The blues has a definite attitude about how you play, at least to my mind. Once you get too citified and become scientific like a college professor then it's not rooted anymore, that's for sure. That's why I always say I'm not a bluesman and I'm not pretending to be a bluesman," Fogerty continued. "I have such reverence for the music. Blues are disciplined, they're regimented, so you have to stay in that format. If you go outside, you can't come back in again. You're just not accepted. I don't really want to buy a blues record by some middle-class white guy from Iowa. I have strong feelings about this. It's just not the blues anymore. It's fine if he calls it something else, but he shouldn't say, any more than I would, it's the blues. Because it's not."

Fogerty's insistence on something like authenticity—the idea that you sing what you're born to—seems strange coming from the man who opened the distinctly bluesy "Wrote a Song for Everyone" with: "Met myself a comin' county welfare line / I was feelin' strung out, hung out on the line." It's a safe bet that the black listeners who made Ike and Tina Turner's remake of "Proud Mary" a major R & B hit heard more than a touch of the blues in Tina's incendiary performance. From the opening guitar riffs through CCR's unforgettable harmonies on "rollin' on the river," Fogerty's original flows down from Memphis through the heart of a mythic South that would have been equally familiar to Howlin' Wolf and Hank Williams.

From the time CCR established itself as one of the defining bands of the sixties, the core of the group's sound lay in a blues rock Fogerty dreamed up out of the mythic Louisiana he'd found in his Southern musical ancestors. On classic swamp rock cuts like "Born on the Bayou," "Proud Mary," and "Bootleg" from the *Bayou Country* album, Fogerty sings in an accent that allowed him to cross over the Mason-Dixon Line without providing proof of identity. There are some specific elements of the accent that place Fogerty in Louisiana, closer to New Orleans rather than, say, Memphis or Charleston. It's in the way he puts the Brooklyn twist on the vowels in the line "woiking for the man every night and day," the way he reduces the word "bootleg" to the near-Cajun "boo-lay." No one ever really talked that way, but no one who came under Fogerty's spell was likely to notice, or mind.

Within a four-month period spanning the turn of the decade, CCR released two of the best blues impulse albums ever made, *Green River* and *Willy and the Poorboys*. Fogerty's personal favorite is *Green River*: "I like where that music is, the sound of it, the cover, everything. It's the style, the sound of the song 'Green River.' It's a little more a Sun record," Fogerty said, referring to the Memphis studio where Sam Phillips brought together blues (Howlin' Wolf, Little Milton), country (Johnny Cash), and rockabilly (Carl Perkins, Jerry Lee Lewis) musicians in the early fifties, providing a perfect setting for the emergence of Elvis Presley's rock and roll. On *Green River*, Fogerty perfected the "spooky" sound that summons up the shadowy bayou as a metaphor for what's going down in Richard Nixon's America, a place where it was getting harder to tell the difference between paranoia and common sense. Sounding like something out of the Old Testament prophets, Fogerty's poetic images tap a power similar to that of Robert Johnson's classic Delta blues. When Creedence sang about that bad moon rising, it meant one thing to the grunts in the Mekong Delta, something else to the crowd at the Denver Pop Festival, which had been tear-gassed three times prior to CCR's closing set. No one listening to "Sinister Purpose" or "Commotion" in 1970 had any trouble at all coming up with a point of reference. It's music that drops you into a world where it's possible to hear the shared conversation between Bob Dylan's "Desolation Row" and Bessie Smith's "Downhearted Blues"; Bruce Springsteen's "Backstreets" and Howlin' Wolf's "Killin' Floor"; Fogerty's "Run Through the Jungle" and Robert Johnson's "Hellhound on My Trail."

At once angrier and more exuberant than *Green River*, *Willy and the Poorboys* includes two of Fogerty's most explicit political statements. "Fortunate Son" calls down a righteous wrath on the heads of the folks who "wave the flag to prove they're red, white and blue." Fogerty sketches a scene where the band plays "Hail to the Chief" as accompaniment while the people who inherited "star-spangled eyes" along with their wealth send the poor boys off to die. The chorus makes Fogerty's feelings clear. "It ain't me," he screams. "I ain't no fortunate son." As he said in 1969, "I see things through lower-class eyes. If you sit around and think about all that money, you can never write a song about where you came from."

Equally clear about the political dynamics of a time when too many people were making promises they had no intention of keeping, "Don't Look Now" lays down a country-tinged variation on the straight-ahead rock and roll of "Fortunate Son." Where Fogerty rips into "Fortunate Son" with Little Richard–style screams, he delivers the crucial lines of "Don't Look Back" in something closer to a whisper: "Don't look now, someone's done your starvin' / don't look now, someone's done your prayin' too."

Fogerty ends the crucial three-song sequence that defines *Willy and the Poorboys'* social vision with "The Midnight Special," bringing back the exuberant sound of "Down on the Corner," which opens the album. Creedence's adaptation of Leadbelly's song, which gives the album a strong African American presence, contrasts an almost cheerful syncopated rhythm—CCR shows definite signs of having figured out "that little shuffle"—with a lyric line that raises images of incarceration, police violence, and death; in the black Southern tradition, the "midnight special" could refer either to a train heading north to freedom or to the suicide that some preferred to life in the fields.

In the early nineties, Fogerty set out on a series of journeys that took him to Mississippi in search of a deeper understanding of the blues. The trips, which he described as pilgrimages, flooded him with new thoughts on the tangled web of history, myth, and his own complicated life. He described leaving Memphis in explicitly mythic terms: "Lula and Robinsonville are just a little south of Memphis. They're the first true Delta towns and it's strong with Robert Johnson and Charlie Patton, their presence and history and lore. It's like learning about Canaan or learning about Galilee. Just the names, you go, 'Yeah and then he went down to Lula.' "

An important moment in Fogerty's quest took place at Robert Johnson's grave. Meditating on Johnson's troubled life, Fogerty experienced an epiphany that helped him come to terms with some of his anger toward those he'd felt betrayed him. Much of his anger centered on record company executive Saul Zaentz, who subjected him to the absurd situation of being sued for plagiarism because he sounded like himself. (The specific case involved "Run Through the Jungle" and Fogerty's 1985 hit "The Old Man Down the Road.") Thinking about the decade he'd spent in withdrawal, Fogerty realized that "there's this guy buried there and maybe some guy named Morris Stealum of Cheatem, Beatem & Whatever owns his songs in some big building in Manhattan. [But] it's Robert Johnson who owns those songs; he's the spiritual owner of those songs. Muddy Waters owns his songs; Howlin' Wolf owns his songs. And someday somebody is gonna be standing where I'm buried, and they won't know about Saul Zaentz—screw him. What they'll know is if they thought the life's work was valuable or not. Standing among all those giants, I went, '*That's* the deal here. It's time to jump back into your own stream.' "

Fogerty's meditations on his Mississippi experiences, like the white blues he created with CCR, belong to an unending song—part celebration, part lament—about what authenticity means in an America where a California boy can sing up a South of his own. Like the songs rolled out by Elvis and Muddy Waters when they set off on their different roads toward the same place—and you can add Mahalia Jackson and Buddy Holly, Bruce Springsteen and Sam Cooke to the list of pilgrims—the song Fogerty's singing reverberates with unanswered questions: about who we are, where we can walk, and the sounds of our voices, together and alone.

## 28
## "Trouble Comin' Every Day":
## Southern Strategies and the Revolution on TV

Gil Scott-Heron was wrong when he announced that the revolution would not be televised. The real story, unfortunately, comes out in the hurricane of angry images in Frank Zappa's "Trouble Comin' Every Day." Zappa feared that racial chaos could break out anywhere, any time some "clown" decided to go to war for an ideology. He saw a televised world of smoke and fire, of women drivers machine-gunned from their seats, of drunken mobs waiting their turn to "stomp and smash and bash and crash and slash and bust and burn."

Zappa invited America to "take your TV tube and eat it," but he was well aware that images of fire in the street would continue to stoke the fires in our hearts. As he concluded, "There won't be many left to see it really end." As the game played out, the only beneficiary of the revolution that *was* televised was an administration conceived in paranoia, dedicated to the proposition that if you didn't look out for yourself no one was going to do it for you, and brought to power by a Southern strategy that brought a smile to the grand dragon's no-longer-hooded face.

The one thing liberals like Zappa and black revolutionaries like Scott-Heron shared was a knowledge that the images transmitted on television in the late sixties had a disastrous effect on the movement for racial justice. Scott-Heron knew how the mass media distorted the significance of what was happening in black America. He also knew how seductive the TV lights could be, even to those who spoke scathingly against any involvement with the corrupt system. Scott-Heron's declaration that "the revolution will not be brought to you by Xerox in four parts without commercial interruption" was as much warning as prediction. When he insisted that "the revolution will be *live*," Scott-Heron was challenging the Black Power movement to live up to its professed ideals of self-determination and community involvement.

Scott-Heron belonged to a group of poets and musicians who believed the key to a successful struggle lay in taking their art directly to the streets. Like the Last Poets and the Watts Prophets, Scott-Heron subscribed to the concept of political performance outlined in Black Panther minister of culture Ed Bullins's "Short Statement on Street Theater." Militant artists, Bullins believed, should concentrate on establishing contact with groups unlikely to enter a theater: working people, gang members, junkies, prostitutes, street people. "Each individual in the crowd," Bullins wrote, "should have his sense of reality confronted, his consciousness assaulted." Recognizing the impact of the media, Bullins created a series of "Black Revolutionary Commercials" that could be presented by a troupe moving through the streets.

Like the Last Poets' *This Is Madness* and the Watts Prophets' *Rappin' Black in a White World*, Scott-Heron's first album, *Small Talk at 125th and Lenox*, subscribes to Bullins's revolutionary aesthetics. Conga drums lay down a rhythmic pulse to attract a crowd while Scott-Heron recites poems that, to recall Maulana Karenga's principles of black art, expose the enemy, praise the people, and support the revolution. One of the most effective, "Whitey on the Moon," employs call and response as a form of political education. "A rat done bit my sister Nell," Scott-Heron begins, "while whitey's on the moon." Repeating the title line as commentary on the brutal realities of ghetto life, Scott-Heron builds to the climax, calling out "I think I'll send these doctor bills, air mail special." He pauses and the audience delivers the punch line: "to whitey on the moon."

Too often, the major figures of the Black Power movement ignored Scott-Heron's warning and lost direct communication with their communities. Part of the problem, of course, was that the whole concept of a "major figure" ran counter to the movement's collective heart. Nonetheless, many took the bait. While the brothers—and with the exception of Angela Davis, the leaders anointed by the media were male—angled for center stage, the sisters too often were left to take care of business in the community. The fate of the Black Panthers in Milwaukee demonstrates the problem's far-reaching impact. The Panthers' popularity in black Milwaukee rested largely on their free breakfast program. Seeing to it that black children arrived at school ready to learn, the Panthers also used the time to instill a sense of black awareness. It was a program Ella Baker would have appreciated. As time went on, however, the women who cooked, shopped, and washed dishes grew increasingly disillusioned with the fact that they were simply doing what they'd always done while the men took the credit. The revolution was being conducted for the benefit of the TV audience rather than the children of the ghetto.

The 1968 Democratic Convention in Chicago realized Zappa's and Scott-Heron's worst fears. Televised images showed yippies nominating a pig for president, angry protestors accusing the Democratic Party leadership of fixing the nomination, and Black Panther leader Bobby Seale calling for a revolution in the streets. The increasingly radical factions of SDS gave a gleeful amen while police clubs cracked down on newsmen as well as hippies. The demonstrators were right when they chanted "The whole world is watching," but they were dead wrong about how most of the world understood what it saw.

Every picture of a ghetto building burning or a group of unkempt demonstrators shouting down a liberal politician benefited Richard Nixon. The architects of the "Southern strategy" that allowed Nixon to capture the White House by the slimmest of margins in 1968 and then swamp George McGovern in 1972 gathered every bit of evidence suggesting that liberal permissiveness bred chaos. They must have been downright gleeful when Eldridge Cleaver announced that raping white women was an acceptable way of taking revenge on their fathers. Not content to quit while he was behind, Cleaver proceeded to endorse "practicing" on black women.

Confident of his ability to manipulate the backlash against the Black Power movement and a white left that preferred Lenin to Lincoln, Nixon crafted a campaign strategy that made brilliant use of approaches pioneered, ironically enough, by the freedom movement. Nixon's 1968 campaign was the first explicitly designed for television. Nixon relied totally on Princeton's Opinion Research Corporation to help him, in the words of campaign adviser H. R. Haldeman, "move out of the dark ages and into the brave new world of the omnipresent eye." Adapting the approach the SCLC used when it staged moral dramas in Birmingham and Selma, Nixon's advisers carefully considered every image for its implicit political meaning. Repeatedly they portrayed Nixon as a figure of calm, "law and order," in the midst of the surging chaos. It certainly helped that the cameras which had filmed the early movement from the perspective of the demonstrators had changed position. News reports of the uprisings in Detroit and Newark inundated viewers with images of black violence. The cameras' position looking in on the riots raised fears that the violence might spill out of the frame to disrupt the white world at any moment.

Everyone knew "law and order" meant keeping the uppity black folk in their place. But no one was saying so. Except George Wallace, who came as a distinctly mixed blessing to the Nixon campaign. On the one hand, Wallace's popularity in the South threatened to throw the 1968 election into the House of Representatives or perhaps even provide Hubert Humphrey with a path to victory. If Wallace had withdrawn from the race, Nixon would certainly have carried the South by a large margin. He did well anyway. Humphrey carried only Texas; Nixon won South Carolina, Florida, Virginia, Tennessee, and North Carolina; and Wallace held the heart of the Deep South: Mississippi, Alabama, Louisiana, Georgia, and Arkansas. Wallace's candidacy, however, let Nixon appeal to white fear without ever mentioning race. Rarely bothering to temper his language, Wallace made the racial subtexts of issues like busing and promiscuity clear. His strong showings in the Wisconsin and Michigan primaries demonstrated unambiguously that race was not simply a Southern issue. Any candidate capable of tapping the fears of white working-class males, especially those living in districts bordered by black ghettos, had an excellent chance of undercutting the traditional Democratic coalition. Despite the problems he presented electorally, Wallace paved the way for Nixon's victory by dislodging the loyalties of long-term Democratic voters.

Relying on Wallace to stir up white racial anger, Nixon played the role of diplomat, invoking ideas of unity and civic responsibility. All the while, however, he used the code words "forced busing," "welfare reform," "quotas." The terms seemed neutral—not a hint of "nigger," rarely even a mention of the segregationist mantra "states' rights"—but it was all about what Nixon strategist Kevin Phillips identified as the "secret" of American politics: who hates whom.

Nowhere was the inner meaning of the Nixon campaign clearer than in the ads targeted toward the Southern market in the final weeks before the 1968 election. As longtime civil rights supporter Humphrey came out against the war and insisted on full implementation of the Supreme Court's *Brown* decision on school desegregation, Nixon endorsed "freedom of choice." Unlike "states' rights," the term was not widely recognized as a synonym for segregation. Yet every white voter in the South understood its implications. Like the singers who had expressed their gospel politics through religious images, Nixon communicated clearly with the people he wanted to reach.

One of the ways Nixon communicated with those people was through country-and-western music. Again, he was following the lead of Wallace, whose campaign rallies opened with Nashville gospel star Wally Fowler singing "God Bless America." In the final weeks of the campaign, Nixon bought advertising time on Southern country stations, specifically targeting shows hosted by Buck Owens and Ernest Tubb. Roy Acuff and Tex Ritter joined Elvis Presley in endorsing Nixon. Although Nixon's national strategists expressed doubts about the strategy, C & W was a good fit for the campaign's treatment of racial issues.

Like most mainstream popular music, country almost never said anything that could be construed as actively racist. Loretta Lynn summed up the standard position when she said: "Really, all kinds of prejudice bother me. I've heard more than enough color prejudice from other people, but I don't have it. I'm always happy when black people come to my shows or ask for my autograph. . . . I'm very comfortable with blacks." Like every other white American located just slightly to the left of the KKK on the political spectrum, almost every country singer denied all personal racism. Of course, so did George Wallace. The real problem with country's racial politics during the sixties was that they pretended not to exist. Blacks weren't attacked, they simply weren't anywhere to be seen.

Country's avoidance of racial issues was part of a larger pop culture view of politics as a distraction from the serious business of helping people escape from reality. As Loretta Lynn put it when explaining why she'd turned down Wallace's request that she perform at a fund-raising show, "politics and music mix about as well as liquor and love." Even though Lynn's "Coal Miner's Daughter" and "One's on the Way" articulate a fierce working-class feminism, she held to the credo that entertainment is entertainment, politics is politics. Anyone who insisted on mixing them up was simply raising trouble. Things were just fine until the agitators and hippies started stirring things up. Although Merle Haggard always insisted he'd intended the song as a joke, "Okie from Muskogee" set down a vision of reality dead parallel to the one Nixon campaigned on.

The irony was that Haggard knew better than to think Nixon cared much about what happened to the poor white folks—most of them transplanted Southerners—he'd grown up with on the streets of Bakersfield, California. The best of Haggard's songs—"Working Man's Blues," "Hungry Eyes," and the country gangsta classic "Mama Tried"—come from the same place as Woody Guthrie's angry attacks on an economic system that was killing the Okies as surely as the blacks they distrusted and feared. Haggard's performance at Pat Nixon's White House birthday party revealed the president's lack of connection with the people whose votes had brought him to power. Haggard opened his show with two songs, which drew no response from the audience. "I searched the faces in the crowd, hoping to find just one that seemed at least interested in what I was doing," Haggard wrote in his autobiography. "No luck."

Haggard responded with an anger that Woody would have applauded. "There *he* sat, the President of the United States, the most powerful man in the world. His face was a mask I couldn't read. It was a blank. The least he could do, I thought, on behalf of simple politeness, was to lead his flock of sheep in some hint of appreciation. By the time I finished the third song, I didn't much give a damn." Reaching back into the traditional country repertoire, Haggard played Jimmie Rodgers's "California Blues," thinking sardonically that even though he'd grown up in the same state, Nixon "hadn't hung out at the same place I did." So much for call and response.

One of the few black singers to establish himself in the country world, Charley Pride experienced the contradictions even more deeply. In his autobiography, Pride recalled his childhood in Jim Crow Mississippi without bitterness: "The inequities of segregation were painful, but that was my home and those were my people. I loved Mississippi and do to this day." Still, Pride, whose Nashville-styled hits included "Kiss an Angel Good Morning," "Is Anybody Going to San Antone?," and "The Snakes Crawl Out at Night," acknowledged that "the color issue was always there, hanging around with the unpleasant odor of an old wet dog lying on the doorstep." He recounted the story of an "admirer" who told him after an Atlanta show, "I ain't never heard a nigger sound like you in my life. You put on a hell of a show." Pride's response was not to pass judgment. " 'Nigger' was just a natural part of his vernacular," Pride observed. "It implied nothing. I was coming to realize that many people, particularly Southerners, weren't aware that there was any other way to refer to a person of African descent."

At times Pride found himself caught in a cultural cross fire. Black audiences oriented to soul and jazz often responded to his performances with contempt. One night when he was performing at a USO club in Germany, Pride was confronted with a room divided by "an imaginary fence. . . . All the black soldiers were on one side, all the whites on the other." When a black soldier heckled Pride, asking; "When are you gonna sing one for us brothers?," Pride responded, "I'm singing for my brothers on this side of the room and for my brothers on this side. . . . I told you in the beginning. I'm not James Brown. I'm not Sam Cooke. I'm Charley Pride, country singer." Pride's conclusion echoes Lynn's suspicion of direct political activity: "I didn't set out to be a crusader for racial harmony or change anybody's heart or mind, but I learned early that you can accomplish more with tolerance than with indignation."

And yet, the C & W audience continued to vote overwhelmingly for Nixon and the parade of Republican politicians who played the race card again and again without ever breathing the word "nigger." Waylon Jennings, one of the country singers who by and large avoided slipping into bed with the bosses, provided the perfect comment on the country audience's part in Nixon's 1972 landslide reelection. "The devil made me do it the first time," Waylon sang in "Black Rose": "The second time I done it on my own."

"I'm not black," Frank Zappa sang in "Trouble Comin' Every Day," "but there's a whole lot of times I wish I could say I wasn't white." The Nixon years provided a lot of those moments, and they didn't all come from the country rednecks or the inner circles of the Republican Party. The low point of the whole misguided and evasive discussion of race inside the white community may well have come in the exchange between rockers Neil Young and Lynyrd Skynyrd, both of whom, to be fair, had many better days. Young set the fiasco in motion when he released the self-righteous "Alabama" and "Southern Man." Locating himself in some mythic country where the South monopolized racism, Young conjured up a vision of lynching and bullwhips that effectively absolved the rest of the country (not to mention Young's native Canada) from any moral taint. Responding with understandable, if not particularly well-thought-out, anger and defensiveness, Lynyrd Skynyrd rallied to the defense of George Wallace in "Sweet Home Alabama." Shutting off the sharp street intelligence that makes "Gimme Three Steps" and "That Smell" populist rock classics, Ronnie Van Zant happily helped Young take the fight back out to the mud puddle where it had begun. Not many black folks cared who won.

# 29
# Troubled Souls:
# Wattstax and Motown (West)

On August 20, 1972, Jesse Jackson joined arms with Al Bell and raised his clenched fist in a sign of solidarity with the crowd gathered at the Los Angeles Coliseum for Wattstax, the culminating event of the Watts Summer Festival. A medallion honoring his fallen mentor Martin Luther King hung over Jackson's loose African-style shirt as he joined Stax's black chief executive and over a hundred thousand others in singing "Lift Every Voice and Sing," the black national anthem. Subsidized by several corporate sponsors, Wattstax held ticket prices to one dollar; festival profits benefited Martin Luther King Hospital and the Sickle Cell Anemia Foundation. Featuring every major Stax star—the Soul Children, Isaac Hayes, the Staple Singers, William Bell, Johnnie Taylor—the festival provided a powerful image of what Black Power, at its best, might mean. Wattstax matched the positive energy of Monterey and Woodstock vibe for vibe.

There was, however, trouble beneath the waters. The festival didn't reflect the dominant tone sounding through soul music as the sixties began to fade into memory. The records released by both Stax and Motown during the early seventies reverberate with undertones of doubt, uncertainty, loss. Moving away from the communities which had energized their earlier work, both labels increasingly shifted their attention—and in Motown's case, their corporate offices—to California. Many of the musicians who had shaped the Stax sound resented the decision to hold the Stax festival in Watts rather than Memphis. Their home city most certainly had a sizable ghetto of its own, albeit one located farther away from the movie cameras and music industry players. As MG bass player Duck Dunn said: "Whose cause was it—Wattstax's or Al Bell's? Were they doing it for the people in L.A., or were they doing it to promote Al Bell in L.A.? And what did they ever do for Memphis? Not a goddam thing."

Similarly, when Motown officially relocated to the West Coast in 1972—in large part because of Berry Gordy's interest in the film industry—the magic stayed in Detroit. Motown became, in Nelson George's words, "just another record company." By the time that happened, however, Motown had already undergone major changes, many of which took place against Gordy's will or with his reluctant consent. The most obvious changes concerned Motown's use of the mask. Up until 1968, Motown continued to employ the time-tested formula of avoiding issues that might alienate part of the record-buying public. By that time, however, the mainstream of American popular music had changed substantially. James Brown, Curtis Mayfield, and Aretha had addressed serious issues without jeopardizing their careers. Many Motown songwriters and singers wanted the chance to join in the movement.

Still, Gordy proceeded cautiously. The label's treatment of the Supremes' "Love Child" is a case in point. When songwriter Pam Sawyer brought "Love Child" to the Motown committee that matched songs and artists, the immediate response, Gordy remembered, was that the lyric was "too heavy for the Supremes. . . . They're America's sweethearts." Aware of the changing times, Gordy saw the song's potential. But he shared the committee's concern over the risk of identifying Diana Ross with extramarital sex. The solution was to transform the blues story into moralistic warning. As Gordy wrote, "we arrived at a really touching story about a girl who herself was born out of wedlock and is telling her boyfriend she doesn't want to go the wrong way with him and bring another love child into the world. We had managed to take a negative image and turn it around in a positive way."

The "Love Child" approach didn't last long, in part because Norman Whitfield didn't let it. A longtime Motown staffer, Whitfield had emerged as a distinctive voice through his production work on the Temptations' "Ain't Too Proud to Beg," "Beauty Is Only Skin Deep," "(I Know) I'm Losing You," and "I Wish It Would Rain." Harder-edged than Smokey Robinson and funkier than Holland-Dozier-Holland, who wrote and produced most of the classic Four Tops and Supremes records, Whitfield broke through with "I Heard It Through the Grapevine," which reached number one for *both* Gladys Knight and Marvin Gaye.

On "I Heard It Through the Grapevine," the Motown mask begins to slip. Ostensibly a song about the end of a relationship, "Grapevine" captures the late-sixties obsession with rumor, paranoia. Highly political in its implications, the song introduces a separatist sensibility into the inner sanctum of black economic mainstreaming. As black cultural historian Patricia Turner shows in a book titled after Gaye's masterpiece, rumors have a specific political function in black communities. Rumors preach a separatist sermon: The FBI killed Martin Luther King, Jr.; the CIA dumped drugs in the ghettos to control the revolution; O. J. was framed; welfare doctors are systematically sterilizing black women. It doesn't hurt the separatist case that some of the rumors might be true.

Buoyed by the commercial success of "Grapevine," Whitfield was in a position to overcome Gordy's resistance to the drug references in his next major production, the Temptations' "Cloud Nine." When "Cloud Nine" hit the top ten, Whitfield was free to return Motown to the center of the politicized soul world. Funky, socially aware Whitfield productions like Gaye's "The End of Our Road," Edwin Starr's "War," and the Temptations' blues classic "Papa Was a Rollin' Stone" define the Motown of the late sixties and early seventies in the same way the Supremes and Smokey defined its earlier period.

But Motown's continuing significance as a social force rested primarily on music created by Gaye and Stevie Wonder after they took control of their own creative directions. When Wonder reached his twenty-first birthday, he disavowed the contracts signed for him when he was a minor. Although the demand for renegotiation shocked Gordy, Wonder emphasized at the signing ceremony for his new contract that he had never intended to abandon his mentor: "I'm staying at Motown because it is the only viable surviving black-owned company in the record industry. If it were not for Motown, many of us just wouldn't have had the shot we've had at success and fulfillment. It is vital that people in our business—particularly the black creative community, including artists, writers and producers—make sure that Motown stays emotionally stable, spiritually strong and economically healthy."

"There are faults at Motown," Stevie acknowledged, "but they can be corrected." The primary fault, from his perspective, was the lack of artistic control. Wonder had grown up in a system in which songs and producers were assigned to artists, where every move was subjected to company oversight. By 1971, he was ready to set out on his own, and the brilliant songs on *Talking Book*—"Superstition," "Maybe

Your Baby," "I Believe (When I Fall in Love It Will Be Forever)"—more than justified his confidence.

Similarly, Marvin Gaye was allowed to release *What's Going On* only over Gordy's strenuous objections. When Gaye told Gordy he wanted to release an album protesting "Vietnam, police brutality, social conditions, a lot of stuff," Gordy told him "don't be ridiculous." Gaye insisted, "I'm not happy with the world. I'm angry. I have to sing about that, I have to protest." Convinced *What's Going On* would turn out to be a disastrous mistake, Gordy finally acquiesced. "Marvin, we learn from everything. That's what life's all about. I don't think you're right, but if you really want to do it, do it. And if it doesn't work you'll learn something; and if it does I'll learn something." As Gordy acknowledges in his autobiography, he learned something.

Gaye reported the exchange in less genial terms. "From Jump Street, Motown fought *What's Going On*," he said. "They didn't like it, didn't understand it, and didn't trust it. Management said the songs were too long, too formless, and would get lost on a public looking for easy three-minute stories. . . . Basically I said 'Put it out or I'll never record for you again.' That was my ace in the hole and I had to play it."

The changes at Motown "worried me to death," Gordy acknowledged in retrospect. The cheerful tone of his admission no doubt reflects the fact that the harder-edged music matched the commercial success of the earlier pop sound. For four weeks during December 1968 and January 1969, Gaye's "I Heard It Through the Grapevine," Wonder's "For Once in My Life," and "Love Child" held the top three places on the charts, joined in the top ten by "Cloud Nine" and the Supremes/Temptations collaboration "I'm Gonna Make You Love Me." Later in the year, with the eleven-year-old Michael Jackson coming on like a miniature James Brown, the Jackson Five exploded onto the scene with the first of four consecutive number one records. *Rolling Stone* critic Ralph J. Gleason called "I Want You Back" "the best rock and roll record of all time." But none of it stopped Berry Gordy from setting out in search of the neon green pastures on the other side of the Hollywood fence.

Whatever problems Motown may have had, most of the folks who worked for the label got paid. In contrast, the Stax experience provides a depressing double parable on the dangers of the mainstream and the problems with Black Power. Like Motown, Stax continued to create great music. Songwriter Isaac Hayes emerged from behind the scenes and resurrected the spirit of Phil Spector on *Hot Buttered Soul*. Lush strings, dramatic horn sections, and gospel choruses surround Hayes's drawling raps on the themes of loss and betrayal: "By the Time I Get to Phoenix," "One Woman," and "Walk on By." The Soul Children ("I'll Be the Other Woman"), Frederick Knight ("I've Been Lonely for So Long"), and the Dramatics ("Whatcha See Is Whatcha Get," "In the Rain") actually gave Stax more hits after 1968 than it had in its early years.

The finest of Stax's seventies acts, the Staple Singers brought gospel intensity back home to Southern soul. Established as one of Chicago's leading gospel groups, the Staples shocked part of their audience when they crossed over, even though hits such as "Respect Yourself," "If You're Ready (Come Go with Me)," "City in the Sky," "Touch a Hand, Make a Friend," and "I'll Take You There" expressed clear spiritual messages. Mavis Staples found the resistance hard to understand: "They were sayin' we'd gone to the devil 'cause the people weren't listening to what we were saying. A song like 'I'll Take You There'—what do you think we talking about? Taking you nowhere but to heaven. 'I know a place ain't nobody crying / ain't nobody worried / ain't no smiling faces lying to the races / I'll take you there.' Where else could that be?"

There was a reason that the vast majority of seventies Stax stars were new to the label. In 1968, the label was forced in effect to start all over. In May 1965, Atlantic and Stax signed an agreement that allowed Atlantic to distribute all Stax releases, although Stax maintained complete creative control. Soon, Atlantic began to send its own soul artists to Memphis. Although Stax benefited from Atlantic's distribution network, Atlantic never financed production of the music. Stax president Jim Stewart claims that "Their total investment in Stax Records—*ever*—was $5000."

Which makes the next act of the story absolutely outrageous. In 1967 and early 1968, Stax sought to renegotiate the distribution agreement. At the same time, Atlantic announced an "agreement in principle" with Warner Brothers–Seven Arts that would lead to its absorption within the larger corporation. When Otis Redding died, Atlantic lost interest in the negotiations and Stax decided to move ahead as an independent label. That's when the fist came down. The distribution agreement signed in 1965 had given Atlantic all rights to Stax's catalog of songs and master recordings. Caught up in the music, no one at Stax had read, or understood, the contract. "I've got to tell you that we made a contract with him that probably was unfair," pioneering Atlantic R & B producer Jerry Wexler admitted. "I tried to give them back their catalog, but I couldn't, because the lawyers had put it over. The name of the game was whatever the traffic would bear."

Seven years later, after Stax had risen from the ashes to reestablish itself as the leading Southern soul label, another set of disastrous business decisions resulted in the label's demise. Without belaboring the grimy details, suffice it to say that the label's deals with Gulf + Western and CBS worked out every bit as well as the one with Atlantic. By late 1974, Stax was effectively out of business. Curtis Mayfield stated the moral of the story precisely when he said, in words Berry Gordy would most certainly have endorsed, "Own as much of yourself as you can."

Stax couldn't blame all of its problems on corporate adversaries. After Martin Luther King's assassination—which took place just down the street from the label's studios at a motel that had frequently served as a retreat and gathering place for Stax staffers—Stax began to associate itself with the growing Black Power movement. Both the assassination and the ideological shift disrupted the collaborative atmosphere of the earlier days. Isaac Hayes remembered that King's death set off a lengthy creative paralysis: "I went blank. I couldn't write for about a year—I was filled with so much bitterness and anguish I couldn't deal with it." The impact was different, but at least as powerful, on the white musicians who worked at Stax. Steve Cropper identified the assassination as the turning point in the racial atmosphere. Before King was murdered, Cropper said, "going to Stax was like going to church." But, he continued, "after that happened everything changed."

Many credited or blamed the changes at Stax on Al Bell, a former DJ who became Stax's first black executive and eventually assumed control of almost all operations. Under Bell's direction, Stax became much more politically active than it had been under its original white owners. The label sponsored a reprinting of SNCC's manifesto "All Roads Must Lead to Revolution" and released several spoken-word albums, including Jesse Jackson's *I Am Somebody*. The film based on the Wattstax Festival endorsed a Black Power agenda, juxtaposing musical performances with images underscoring the brutal realities of ghetto life.

But there was a more disturbing side to Stax's Black Power story. Almost from the moment of Bell's ascendance, the grapevine filled with rumors of violence and extortion. White employees no longer felt physically safe coming to work in the ghetto, in part because of the mysterious gun-carrying figures who began to haunt the studio. For Cropper, the final straw came when he and Booker T. were physically pressured to work on sessions they had turned down. "You don't stick a gun in Steve Cropper's back and say, 'You're going to play on this record'—that's not the way you do business," Cropper said. "I don't play with guns—that's stupid—and neither did Booker." A little over a year after King's death, both Cropper and Booker T. severed their ties with the label they had helped build.

The situation came to a head at a 1968 Miami convention organized by the National Association of Television and Radio Announcers (NATRA). The announced purpose was to promote better communication between the white-dominated industry and black radio announcers. Jesse Jackson and Coretta Scott King were among those lobbying for increased industry involvement in the black community. Some tension was inherent in the situation. But the conference collapsed in a chaos of threats and accusations directed against white industry executives and blacks, including Al Bell, who refused to go along with the most radical demands. A "black militant" group identified as the "Fairplay Committee" dominated the proceedings. Many who attended the conference—black and white—viewed the Fairplay Committee as a group of thugs with no real interest in music. The convention disintegrated amid rumors that Al Bell had been beaten, kidnapped, or killed. In fact, he left in the middle of the convention and stayed out of public view for several weeks. As Wexler, himself a target of fierce nationalist criticism, reports, "The people who came to the fore were con men, street-smart guys, extortionists, and racketeers." It was the industry equivalent of the shooting war that broke out between cultural and political nationalists on the UCLA campus. By the early seventies, factionalism and thuggery within the Black Power movement created a growing sense that, however much the leaders might posture, no one had the ghost of an idea which way to go.

# 30
# "Where Is the Love?":
# Donny Hathaway and the End of the Dream

As the sixties faded into the seventies, the smoke thinned over a changed nation. A sound track that had exploded with the demands of "Say It Loud (I'm Black and I'm Proud)," "Respect," and "We're a Winner" increasingly reverberated with the sounds of loss, betrayal, paranoia. The O'Jays kept a suspicious eye on the friendly people waiting to stab them in the back; the Undisputed Truth saw the lies behind the smiling faces; Gladys Knight called on her imagination to make the best of "a bad situation"; Aretha cried out to Moses from her own wilderness. The Chi-Lites called on God to give more power to the people, but their elegiac "Have You Seen Her?" comes closer to capturing the tone of the time. No one filming a documentary on how the sixties ended in black America should have any trouble coming up with a theme song.

My choice would be Donny Hathaway's "The Ghetto." Hathaway begins the song with a gospel moan that resolves into a compelling funk rhythm spiced with his piano improvisations. It's easy to surrender entirely to the groove, to lose yourself in the ebb and flow of life on the streets. But there's that hint of something else in the melody Donny lays on top of the groove two minutes and thirty-seven seconds into the version included on *A Donny Hathaway Collection*. The song vanishes almost before you know it's there. But listen carefully and you can hear "We Shall Overcome," the song the beloved community sang as it marched into battle. Hathaway reminds his listeners—and he was enormously popular with black audiences during the early seventies—to keep the faith, not to give up the dream of redemption, no matter how bleak the world might seem.

Hathaway's ability to blend jazz exploration with heartrending blues ("Giving Up") and moaning, soaring, gospel soul ("Someday

We'll All Be Free") expresses something very near to the heart of black music. The struggle to find the redemption in the brutal experience, to envision a freedom that could transform the ghetto into a black community, is precisely what Amiri Baraka had in mind when he called black music the "changing same." That's the upside. The downside is that the blues never go away. Even after two decades of the freedom movement, one of them dedicated to revolutionary change, there was plenty of brutal experience to go around.

Nina Simone, whom Stokely Carmichael called the "true singer of the civil rights movement," added her amen. A classically trained pianist, Simone redefined the possibilities of material from "I Loves You Porgy" and the traditional spiritual "Sinnerman" to Screamin' Jay Hawkins's "I Put a Spell on You" and Bob Dylan's "I Shall Be Released." Simone expressed the anger beneath the gospel soul of the early movement in "Mississippi Goddam" and the aspirations of the Black Power movement in "Young, Gifted and Black." She plumbed the depths of black women's blues in "Four Women." But Simone never deserved Stokely's praise more than when she sang the gospel depths of the gathering storm in "Why? The King of Love Is Dead." Recorded live just three days after King was killed, the song voices what Simone called "the love and quiet despair we all felt at our loss."

"Where Is the Love?" reflects the love and despair with devastating precision. Performed by Hathaway and Roberta Flack (who among other things collaborated with Jesse Jackson to write the nearly forgotten Black Power classic "Go Up Moses"), the song is so beautiful it's easy to miss the desperation at its heart. Caressing each other's voices in a call and response that erases the distance between "God" and "love," Hathaway and Flack look out on a world of broken promises and fading hopes. They wear the mask with a beauty that twists your soul. Where *is* the love? You can hear their question as an indictment of the white world that reneged on LBJ's promises. Or you can hear it as a blues on the theme of Black Power, a lament for the love promised, but not delivered, by a revolution that never really happened on TV or anywhere else.

# Section Three

## "I Will Survive": Disco, Irony, and the Sound of Resistance

# 31
# Reflections in a Mirror Ball

The mirror ball revolves, slowly at first. Each tiny fragment of glass reflects a discrete image from the seventies: a smiling Jimmy Carter raising Andrew Young's hand in victory; a steel mill closing its doors; a chorus line of smiling gay men on Christopher Street; enraged Iranians calling down the wrath of Allah on the Great American Satan; Stevie Wonder swaying to a song in the key of life. As the glittering globe gathers speed, the images blur, merge in a dance of broken light, cascade into an inferno of contempt, distortion, loss.

No decade has fared worse in our collective memory. Garry Trudeau ushered out the seventies with a *Doonesbury* cartoon in which his sixties survivor characters, unaware that the eighties were on the way, toasted the departure of "a kidneystone of a decade." About the only thing Republicans and Democrats have been able to agree on since Nixon left the White House is that the sooner we forget the Carter years the better. We haven't even begun to come to terms with the meaning of a decade that began with the sixties at their height and ended with Ronald Reagan on his way to the White House.

The mirror ball rotates. Catch the reflections from the right angle and all you can see is hundreds of little me's. Some of them smile, come out of the closet, celebrate their newly won sexual freedom on the dance floors of the underground clubs where disco found its voice. Some wander off into the neon cocaine glow, lose their bearings, vanish into the night. Some of them just sit back and enjoy the show. Christopher Lasch called the seventies a "culture of narcissism," and he wasn't wrong.

Look at the spinning mirror from another angle and a gallery of faces emerges from the shadows: Mexican Americans answering the call of La Raza Unida; Indians on the urban reservations of Minneapolis, L.A., and Chicago; Asian Americans venturing out of Chinatowns revitalized by the Hart-Celler Immigration Act. Jesse Jackson saw the reflections and called for a Rainbow Coalition that took us beyond black and white.

The mirror ball turns again and you see the faces of musicians set in expressions of devotion, determination, and celebration. Even as white rock and black funk parted ways, the seventies gave rise to some of the most intelligently political music ever made. Bruce Springsteen and Stevie Wonder, Bob Marley and the Clash, Al Green and Earth, Wind & Fire all refused to accept the idea that the dream had always been a lie.

Just when you think the fragments might be coming together, the mosaic shatters into images of political turmoil, chaos. Economic advisers with sour expressions contemplating stagflation; the uproar surrounding United Nations ambassador Andrew Young's meeting with a representative of the PLO; hostages marching blindfolded through the streets of Tehran. Images from the world of music echo the politics: a bloodied crowd at a heavy-metal concert tears a chicken to pieces; coke-fueled robots move in unison to a metronomic beat; an antidisco rally at a Chicago ballpark explodes into an orgy of white male rage.

Freeze the motion and focus on the images of two black men wearing robes, standing in the middle of the spinning mirrors. Smiling out at the surging dance floor as he steps down the walkway from the newly arrived Mothership, George Clinton wears the white robes of a funk visionary, part stand-up comic, part conjure man, part priest. Look back out at the world from Dr. Funkenstein's angle and the mirror ball's a bubble bouncing on the nose of a seal that might be training you. Serious, but not somber, the man he faces has passed through the darkness at the heart of the seventies dance and emerged carrying the gospel flame. The black robes with yellow trim draping his slender shoulders announce him as pastor of the Full Gospel Tabernacle of Memphis, Tennessee.

## 32
## Reverend Green
## and the Return of Jim Crow

In 1979, Al Green put aside the gold chains and satin pants that had helped make him the biggest soul star of the decade. Reverend Green has always explained his decision in the most straightforward terms: The Lord called and, after difficult years of hesitation, he answered. Reflecting on the connection between secular hits like "Let's Stay Together" and his religious calling, Green echoes the basic premise of the gospel impulse: "Love between man and God, between husband and wife, between boyfriend and girlfriend, all love comes from God. We have a wonderful Creator, he's blessed us with these things, so we know where our hope lies."

There's no reason to doubt Green's professions of faith. But it's hard not to speculate that factors other than the call from above, which he first heard after a 1973 midnight show at Disneyland, might have contributed to his decision six years later to devote all his energy to spreading the faith. He'd suffered through a bad marriage and he now admits that he physically abused his wife. In the highly publicized "grits" incident, a (married) woman severely burned Green and then killed herself after he refused her proposal of marriage. And, by the end of the seventies, Green's music was receiving only a tepid response from the rapidly resegregating musical audience. The gospel blues classic "Love and Happiness," for example, failed even to break the top one hundred.

Green's turning away from secular music seems emblematic, a statement from black America that it just wasn't worth it to keep on swimming against a current that had gathered strength almost from the moment Jimmy Carter walked through the White House doors. During the mid-seventies, Green had been on top of the world of soul. Almost everything he released—"Tired of Being Alone," "Let's Stay Together," "I'm Still in Love with You," "Call Me," "Here I

Am"—reached the pop top ten. Combining a silky voice that ranged from gritty baritone to delicate falsetto with a seductive sexuality that earned him a huge female following, Green was widely recognized as the heir to Sam Cooke and Otis Redding. As Syl Johnson, who had a hit record with Green's "Take Me to the River," commented, "He was like a black Elvis Presley to the black people."

Drawing on his gospel roots, Green forged a distinctive style that combined characteristics of Stax and Motown. Gospel music historian Anthony Heilbut once observed that on his first major hit, a cover of the Temptations' "I Can't Get Next to You," Green sang in "three voices—a limpid falsetto, a streetwise crooner, a growling preacher." Although Green spent hundreds of hours perfecting his vocals on individual songs, each performance felt spontaneous. As rock critic Robert Christgau commented: "The miracle is that once you're aware of this contradiction, it disappears. Fabricated or improvised? You can't tell, and it doesn't matter—he seems to inhabit a state of late-night hyperconsciousness in which obsessive calculation and unmoored inspiration meet on the other side of the moon."

Born in Forrest City, Arkansas, Green sang with a family gospel group until his father, who forbade all contact with secular music, caught him listening to Jackie Wilson and threw him out. When Green was in his teens, he moved to Michigan, where he recorded a minor hit, "Back Up Train." Unable to follow up on his recording success, Green toured the chitlin circuit, where he crossed paths with Memphis bandleader and producer Willie Mitchell. Impressed with the young singer's voice, Mitchell told Green he could make him a star in eighteen months. Although that seemed too slow for Green at the time, he eventually found his way back to Mitchell and began recording at the Hi Studios in Memphis. Like its friendly crosstown rival Stax, Hi boasted a familial atmosphere and a comfortable working process based on a brilliant house band, Hi Rhythm. Three brothers—guitarist Mabon ("Teenie"), bass player Leroy ("Flick"), and keyboard player Charles Hodges—anchored a group that also included a horn section led by Stax veterans Andrew Love and Wayne Jackson, and either Howard Grimes or former MG Al Jackson on drums. Recording on obsolete equipment that precluded multiple tracking, Hi Rhythm laid down simmering rhythmic grooves for Green's vocal explorations.

Like Stax during the early days, Hi's style blended blues, gospel, and country and western. Teenie Hodges, who had grown up with his brothers picking cotton with their sharecropper father a few miles east of Memphis, remembered: "We were born and raised on a 200 acre farm and we did all the country things. I first noticed singing in the cotton fields when I was picking cotton. A song called 'Ain't No Chains Strong Enough to Bind Me.' Blacks used to say it sounded like country and western, and asked us why would we sing like that. But I'd say it sounds good to me. I don't care what it is, music is music." Another element of the interracial mix at Hi was the singing team of Rhodes, Chalmers, Rhodes, who provided the background vocals on Green's secular hits. The Rhodes sisters, Donna and Sandy, had grown up in a musical family; their father, Dusty, was a country fiddle champion. Charlie [Chalmers] was a session saxophonist who happened to be in the Hi studio when Mitchell needed backing vocals for "Tired of Being Alone." No one who's made the call purely on the basis of sound has ever guessed that the gospel response to Green's call came from three Southern whites.

If Hi belongs unmistakably to the Southern soul tradition, certain elements of its approach link it to the more polished Motown sound. In addition to Green's vocal perfectionism, Hi featured Mitchell's complex approach to harmony, which reflected his jazz training. "I used half-jazz chords, semi-jazz chords. Free chords," Mitchell said. "When people used three notes, we used ten. Big chords, fat chords. Things that weren't supposed to be. The chords were so weird, that's what made the music happen."

If Green was Hi's equivalent of Otis Redding, Ann Peebles deserves a place in the pantheon of soul sisters headed by Aretha Franklin. Recording with Mitchell and Hi Rhythm at the same time Green was starting out, Peebles released three records—"I Can't Stand the Rain," "(I Feel Like) Breaking Up Somebody's Home," and the ferocious "I'm Gonna Tear Your Playhouse Down"—that reiterate, in angrier tones, the messages of "Chain of Fools" and "Respect." Like the most powerful gospel soul from the early sixties, "I'm Gonna Tear Your Playhouse Down" serves notice on a cheating lover (white America? the brothers in the Black Power movement?) that the free ride has come to an end. It's a restatement of the revolutionary gospel anthem "Samson and Delilah," and the message, on every level, is the same: "If I had my way, I would tear this building down."

Green rarely expressed rage as directly as Peebles, but the songs he recorded at Hi provide a strong sense of the emotional changes sweeping black America. Mingling blues confession and gospel testimony, "Tired of Being Alone," "Let's Stay Together," and "I'm Still in Love with You" chart an emotional terrain where you can't tell love from doubt. Memory of a past connection adds an unbearable edge to the feeling of loss; knowledge of separation inspires a renewed search for a love that doesn't even try to separate sex from spirit. From the opening organ riff that carries the listener into a groove haunted by Rhodes, Chalmers, Rhodes's gospel moans, "Love and Happiness" leaves no room for evasion. For anyone who's ever come home at three in the morning unable to tell the difference between sin and salvation, the song tells a nearly unbearable, and unbearably beautiful, emotional truth. On the social level, it's perfect music for a community aware the movement's nearly gone and unsure what, if anything, will take its place.

Increasingly, Green turned to the gospel tradition in his search for an answer. It's not difficult to hear ostensibly secular songs like "Call Me (Come Back Home)" and "Here I Am (Come and Take Me)" as calls for divine help. In "Take Me to the River," the secular mask comes almost all the way off and Green immerses himself in the healing waters that flow from the river religions of West Africa to the black Baptist churches of the South. Green's ethereal self-produced masterpiece *The Belle Album* marks the final step back toward the church. Addressing a woman he desperately loves, Green sings with a wistful, joyous sadness, "It's you I want, but it's Him that I need."

When Green finally responded to the call of the ministry, it brought the deep soul tradition full circle, back to the moment in 1957 when Sam Cooke set out for the promised land of the top ten. Green had spent time in that land and decided it didn't offer the bedrock he wanted for the house he wanted to build. Reverend Green went back home to a black community that hastened to wrap him in its love. The gospel albums he recorded during the eighties consistently won Grammys and sold well, given the limitations of the almost entirely black gospel market. For the true believers who always distrusted the riches of the world, Green was simply assuming his rightful place alongside the gospel stars whose names remain almost unknown in white America: the Reverend James Cleveland, Andrae Crouch, John P. Kee, Inez Andrews, Richard Smallwood, and Shirley Caeser, with whom Green recorded one of the most inspiring gospel hits of the eighties, "Sailing (On the Sea of Your Love)." It's a tradition that lives on in the music of Anointed, Commissioned, the Sounds of Blackness, Kirk Franklin, and the many offshoots of the first family of contemporary gospel, the Winans.

There's no good reason that gospel remains *black* music. Sam Cooke and Curtis Mayfield, Aretha and Al Green have done everything in human power to bring the redemptive vision to anyone who takes the time to listen. You don't have to travel far to get from Cooke's "Touch the Hem of His Garment" to Aretha's "I Never Loved a Man," from the music Reverend Green made for Hi to the sounds emanating from the Full Gospel Tabernacle. "He was doing it so simple," reflected Charles Hodges, whose organ riffs made Green's love songs sound like they were recorded in church. "What it was was to reach people and make people happy in our work. It was because of love. It was all because of love."

Yet when Al Green returned to the church, it marked the end of a concerted effort to let white America in on the secret, the burden and the joy. By the end of the seventies, enough evidence had accumulated to convince a whole lot of black folks that whites simply didn't want to know. For the first time since Little Richard and Ray Charles got America's attention in the fifties, the music that spoke most clearly to the brothers and sisters struggling to make a living had come back home to the ghetto. Ronald Reagan's star was rising on the political horizon and Jim Crow was back in town.

# 33
# Demographics 101:
# Hard Times in Chocolate City

Putting a madcap spin on the situation, as always, George Clinton greeted Brother Crow as the avatar of a dawning age which would witness Muhammad Ali as president, Richard Pryor as minister of education, and Aretha Franklin as the *first* lady. "They still call it the white house," the political metaphysician of the funk rapped over a tribal organ drone spiced with funky horns and a touch of crisscrossing Thelonious Monk piano, "but that's a temporary condition too." Tempering the vision of the new black world with a blues reminder of the brutal history that shaped it, Clinton chuckled, "We didn't get our 40 acres and a mule, but we did get you, C.C."

C.C. was "Chocolate City," Clinton's term for the new, increasingly black, urban landscape created by the massive demographic changes that had swept America since the fifties. In the early sixties, the government of every large American city remained under white control. Even then, however, the working-class whites who formed the power base of the old-line political machines had begun to abandon the cities for the manicured lawns and patios of what Clinton called "the vanilla suburbs." As the decade wore on, "white flight" from riots and the specter of "forced busing" resulted in black majorities in cities throughout the country. Accompanied by Parliament's chant of "gainin' on ya," Clinton celebrated the new black political order: "There's a lot of Chocolate Cities around. We got Newark, we got Gary, someone told me we got L.A. And we're workin' on Atlanta." Parliament imagined the new city as a place of Black Power, black love: "They say you're jive and game and can't be tamed but on the positive side, you're my piece of the rock and I love you C.C."

The realities, however, were more complicated and a good deal more disturbing. The cities of the seventies were not just black, they were poor. As whites moved to the suburbs, they took large amounts of wealth with them. Suburbanization redistributed the tax base away from the cities where most of the commuters continued to work and attend cultural or sports events (though many stadiums would soon be relocated to "safer" outlying areas). The movement of the upwardly mobile middle classes into enclaves with well-funded public services and schools drained resources from areas where an aging infrastructure was in need of replacement or repairs.

When Coleman Young was elected mayor of Detroit in 1973, he assumed control of a city on the brink of economic disaster. Young pinpointed the paradox of white flight when he observed that "The same people who left the city for racial reasons still want to control what they've left." Young sardonically responded to claims that Detroit's problems stemmed from black incompetence by underlining the economic and historical realities: "It starts with economic pressure, and the first economic pressure was slavery. . . . It reminds me of something Martin Luther King said. 'How do you expect us to pull ourselves up by our bootstraps when we don't even have boots?' " Young concluded bitterly, "The motherfuckers *stole* our boots."

Not all of the Chocolate Cities' problems could be attributed to *white* flight. Numerous black Americans, though nothing resembling a majority, had benefited economically from the new opportunities created by the freedom movement. In the thirty years following the *Brown* v. *Board of Education* decision, the income gap separating the black and white middle classes narrowed substantially. In its massive statistical study *A Common Destiny,* the National Research Council reported that by the end of the seventies black men aged twenty-five to thirty-four with some college education could expect to earn 80 to 85 percent as much as their white counterparts. Motivated primarily by the desire to provide a better world for their children—a drive they shared with the new white suburbanites—many members of the new black middle class joined the exodus from the neighborhoods where they had grown up. The primary difference between the black and white movements lay in the fact that, even when they moved out of the cities, black suburbanites usually maintained some direct contact with their less fortunate friends and family members who remained.

Nonetheless, the relocation of successful blacks contributed to significant changes in black neighborhoods, which could be referred to with increasing accuracy as ghettos. The NRC tempered any optimism over the growth of the black middle class with the observation that the seventies had seen an even more dramatic increase in the number of blacks living below the poverty line. Economic conditions in many of the new black cities bore comparison with those in the third world. A survey of fourteen major metropolitan areas revealed that in 1980 *all* had black poverty rates of at least 23 percent. The average was 32 percent and the rates rose as high as 38 percent in New Orleans, 37 percent in Philadelphia, and 36 percent in New York.

In *The Truly Disadvantaged,* black sociologist William Julius Wilson draws attention to the problems created by this increasing *concentration* of poverty. Focusing his analysis on Chicago, Wilson examines the changing relationship between housing segregation and economic conditions between 1970 and 1980. The patterns Wilson presents are stunning. In 1970, only one of Chicago's seventy-seven neighborhoods had a poverty rate as high as 40 percent. Similarly, only one district (a different one) had an unemployment rate as high as 15 percent. By 1980, a radically different pattern had emerged. In two overwhelmingly black neighborhoods, more than half of the residents now lived below the poverty line. In seven others, the rate was above 40 percent. In ten districts, unemployment hovered above 20 percent. Not surprisingly, the concentrations of poverty were *all* centered in the black and Latin neighborhoods of the South and West Sides.

In economic terms, Chocolate City was hurting bad. And, as Wilson pointed out, the numbers only began to tell the story. As long as segregation had forced the vast majority of black people to live within rigidly delineated geographical boundaries, black neighborhoods brought together a rich cross section of economic conditions and social attitudes. In "mixed" black neighborhoods where a large majority of households included at least one member with steady employment, *every* black child—including those from the most disadvantaged families—had regular contact with the norms and behavior patterns expected by the larger society. Although it's important not to overplay the Horatio Alger myth, a highly motivated black child usually had access to at least the lower rungs of the ladder leading to mainstream success.

When the grudging enforcement of civil rights legislation opened new areas to the black working class, however, the situation in the old neighborhoods changed drastically. Almost overnight, many poor black children found themselves cut off from the mentors who could teach them how to negotiate the economic world without denying their blackness. Wilson describes the vicious cycle set in motion by the demographic changes of the seventies:

> [T]he less frequent the regular contact with those who have steady and full-time employment (that is, the greater the degree of social isolation), the more likely that initial job performance will be characterized by tardiness, absenteeism, and, thereby, low retention. . . . Since the jobs that are available to the inner-city poor are the very ones that alienate even persons with long and stable work histories, the combination of unattractive jobs and lack of community norms to re-enforce work increases the likelihood that individuals will turn to either underground illegal activity or idleness or both.

Careful to distance himself from the neoconservatives who railed at stereotypical cartoons of welfare queens and lazy bucks buying porterhouse steak with food stamps, Wilson stresses that "the key theoretical concept is not *culture of poverty* but *social isolation*."

Anyone listening to the music escaping the rebuilt walls of the ghetto wouldn't have had to be told. From Reverend Green's gospel soul to Clinton's P-Funk extravaganzas, black music of the seventies celebrated a gospel vision that helped the isolated residents of the Chocolate Cities survive once it became clear most of them weren't gaining on anyone. Earth, Wind & Fire preached a soul sermon on the theme that united the new black cities, the most serious sixties revolutionaries, and the members of Ella Baker's beloved community: the moral imperative of creating a better world for the blessed children. Throughout the seventies, no one sounded the call for what EW&F called "true devotion" louder or more clearly than the man Clinton nominated as Chocolate City's minister of fine arts, Stevie Wonder.

# 34
# Black Love in the Key of Life

"Dr. King left an unfinished symphony which we must finish," Stevie Wonder told a crowd of fifty thousand that had gathered on the Capitol Mall on January 15, 1982, to push for a national holiday honoring the movement leader and his vision. "We must harmonize our notes and chords and create love and life. We need a day to celebrate our work on the unfinished symphony, a day for a dress rehearsal for our solidarity." No music of the seventies contributed more to finishing King's symphony than the albums Wonder released once he had established his creative independence within the Motown empire. The speech Paul Simon delivered when accepting the 1975 best album Grammy for *Still Crazy After All These Years* gives a clear sense of Wonder's stature. "I'd like to thank Stevie Wonder," Simon said, a smile on his face, "for not making an album this year."

Many of Wonder's songs—"Heaven Help Us All," "Higher Ground," "Love's in Need of Love Today"—directly affirm King's dream of interracial harmony. The list of heroes he catalogs in "Black Man" includes blacks, whites, Asians, Indians, and Chicanos, women and men. Drawing on rock and funk, classical music and jazz, Wonder's inclusive sensibility provided a rallying point for those convinced that music could help bring us together. He acknowledged the Beach Boys' "Good Vibrations," *Sgt. Pepper's Lonely Hearts Club Band,* and Walter Carlos's *Switched On Bach* as influences; he appreciated Cream's adaptation of traditional blues on "Strange Brew" and "Tales of Brave Ulysses." "Some of that psychedelic music is really fantastic," he told an interviewer. "It shows the creativeness of young people. I believe that music is bringing younger people closer together."

Adapting his rock influences to the soul music he'd grown up with, Wonder developed a sound that responded deeply to the explorations of blackness conducted by James Brown, Sly Stone, and Miles Davis, who added Wonder's bass player, Michael Henderson, to his band in the mid-seventies. Wonder was one of the first musicians to use the word "funkadelic" when he described the Temptations' "Cloud Nine" as "a combination of R&B, psychedelic and funky African-type beat. I'm experimenting. A lot of things I've done recently are funkadelic." In addition to transforming the Beatles' "We Can Work It Out" into a funkadelic expression of the gospel vision, Wonder reached out to a white audience when he opened for the Rolling Stones on their 1972 tour. The audience responded warmly, making Wonder one of the few artists whose success transcended the growing racial divisions of the mid-seventies.

Without contradicting its inclusive vision, Wonder's music reaffirmed black love and unity at a time when the best ideals of the Black Power movement seemed to be slipping away. *Songs in the Key of Life* injected a much-needed sense of hope into black America when it was released in 1976. Expanding on the themes of his classic vignette "Living for the City," *Songs in the Key of Life* sketches the complicated realities of ghetto life in a way that denies neither the reality of suffering nor the power of black love. Wonder frames the album with gospel statements, opening with the explicitly spiritual "Love's in Need of Love Today" and closing with the celebration of black community, "Easy Goin' Evening (My Mama's Call)." "Village Ghetto Land," "Ordinary Pain," "Pastime Paradise," and "Joy Inside My Tears" sound blue notes. "As" and "Sir Duke," Wonder's exuberant tribute to his jazz ancestors, envision new and better worlds. Everyone living in a black neighborhood in 1976 and 1977 found themselves immersed in the healing energies of *Songs in the Key of Life.*

Raised from age three in Detroit's east side ghetto, Wonder knew the blues experiences and gospel aspirations of his black audience from the inside. Named Steveland Morris, Wonder was blind from the time he left the incubator. Given the high infant mortality rates in Saginaw, where he was born, Wonder and his mother Lula Mae Hardaway were thankful he lived. "A girl who was born that same day I was was also put into the incubator and she died," Wonder remembered. "I personally think I'm lucky to be alive." More than half the students in Wonder's Detroit school district came from single-parent homes, in part because Michigan welfare rules denied economic assistance to households in which the father was present. Wonder remembered times when he and his brothers stole coal to keep the family warm: "To a poor person that is not stealing, that is not crime. It's a necessity."

By the time he was ten, Wonder had established himself as a fixture in his neighborhood, playing the harmonica on Twenty-fifth and Twenty-sixth Streets and singing on porches, in alleys, and at the Whitestone Baptist Church. Berry Gordy's offer to sign the precocious youngster to a long-term contract took him by surprise. "I hadn't really taken it serious because I was thinking of getting into other things," Wonder recalled. "I wanted to be a minister, or maybe a sinner." Wonder's sense of humor became a Motown legend. An expert vocal mimic by the time he was in his midteens, he would frequently call Gordy's secretary and, speaking in the company president's voice, tell her to buy Stevie a tape recorder or prepare an advance check, once for fifty thousand dollars. Never sensitive about his blindness, Wonder loved to amaze young women by praising the color of their dress or eyes (information he had received in advance from his partners in comedy). Once he volunteered to judge a beauty contest.

Which isn't as silly as it might sound. There's probably never been a more moving celebration of black beauty than "Isn't She Lovely." The short list of runners-up would include "Golden Lady" and "Dark n' Lovely." Maybe Wonder developed his encompassing sensibility because he can't be distracted by the different shades of "black," which in this most rational of nations can refer to skin that's brown, beige, red-brown, golden, cocoa, ebony, or the kind of pink we've decided to glorify as "white."

Although Wonder remained a staunch supporter of Martin Luther King, his music responded to the Black Power movement's call for an art that exposes the enemy, praises the people, and supports the revolution. Wonder consistently celebrated black pride as the necessary basis for a unified community; he embraced his African heritage by braiding his hair and wearing loose African robes. He understood his support of the King holiday as an attempt to heal a community that remained fragmented. "Black people have a serious problem," he said in an interview published in black newspapers across the country. "Everybody else is together. We must learn to appreciate ourselves. We have to learn to appreciate the accomplishments of our forefathers." In another interview, Wonder made his commitment to Black Power clear: "If I can do anything to help my people in respect to black pride, help the black people, then I'll do it."

In addition, Wonder struck out angrily against a range of political enemies. "Big Brother" lashes out at both the Nixon administration and the liberal politicians who visit the ghetto only at election time. He reiterated the point on "Village Ghetto Land" and "You Haven't Done Nothing," which may be the most explicit statement of black anger ever to reach number one; one of the funkiest rhythm tracks this side of "Superstition" and a wonderful cameo by the Jackson Five no doubt helped the white audience overcome any reluctance it might have had about buying a record that didn't even pretend to wear a mask. Although Wonder never wavered in his support for Martin Luther King, he willingly endorsed more militant perspectives when circumstances warranted: "I hate to sound pessimistic, but it will take people many years to realize the true meaning of Malcolm X's message," he said. "That man in D.C. [Nixon] is cutting off all these programs and holding back funds. Who do you think it's hurting? The black man . . . we have always been the last to get and the first to have it taken away."

Wonder's ability to maintain a large white audience while commanding the near-universal love of the black community rested on the fact that, however angry and uncompromising his political statements, he never forgot the healing power of music. Where Wonder's approach differed from that of the Black Power movement—and no doubt where it became less threatening to his white listeners—is in its conception of revolutionary change. As the seventies came to an end, Wonder turned increasingly to mystical meditations such as the intriguing, and elusive, explorations on *Journey Through the Secret Life of Plants*. Reaching for an entirely new way of conceiving the life force, Wonder articulated a kind of New Age/gospel synthesis in the liner notes to *In Square Circle*: "Their hearts were recalling the cycles of love, while their minds were exploring the square root of the universe."

No one with any sense of history or gratitude was going to begrudge Wonder the right to choose his own path through the world. But a striking gap developed between his precisely honed awareness of black life and the vague political vocabulary he used to respond. Where Gil Scott-Heron called for revolutionary action, Wonder sought reform within the existing system. Like his mentor, Berry Gordy, Wonder believed in ascent: Work hard enough, master the rules of the game and you'll succeed, don't let disappointment stop you. As he sang over one of his most convincing funk grooves, you've got to keep on pushin' till you reach the higher ground. Psychologically, the message makes sense as an antidote to the despair of ghetto life. The black children listening to *Innervisions* and *Songs in the Key of Life* certainly needed inspiration to help keep hope alive.

Considered as a political strategy, however, Wonder's approach raises serious questions about the potential effectiveness of *protest*. Songs like "Happy Birthday Martin," "It's Wrong (Apartheid)," and "Front Line," one of the only songs to address the exposure of Vietnam vets to Agent Orange, draw attention to injustices, suggesting that they can be remedied without fundamental alterations in social arrangements. Attributing the problems of the world primarily to ignorance, the strategy depends on the goodwill of those with the power to redress grievances. The problem was that by the end of the seventies even the powerful white folks who were aware of the problems didn't seem to be in a position to do much about them. One of those powerless white people was the president.

# 35
# Jimmy Carter and
# the Great Quota Disaster of 1978

Jimmy Carter understood some things about race, America, and the world that no previous president had even been willing to consider. Or at least it seemed that way for a few months during the primary campaign of 1976. No other American president had ever felt truly at home speaking to black crowds; it was refreshing to see Carter's obvious enjoyment of call-and-response exchanges in Baptist churches and black community centers. His wife, Rosalynn, visited dozens of black neighborhoods, ate in black restaurants, and slept at black hotels. Carter received enthusiastic endorsements from Martin Luther King, Sr., Coretta Scott King, and Andrew Young, who drew attention to the fact that Carter had grown up in an almost all-black rural Georgia community. Bestowing a kind of blues authority on the candidate, Young observed that "John Kennedy read about racism and poverty in a sociology class at Harvard but Jimmy Carter lived it." At least during the campaign, Carter's positions seemed to follow through on Young's implied promise. Committing himself to a far-reaching crusade for human rights, Carter acknowledged connections between minorities in the United States and the oppressed peoples of the third world.

Carter's appeal to the black community paid off in the 1976 election. Black voters provided Carter's margin of victory in twelve states, including several in his native South, where Gerald Ford's version of the Southern strategy delivered nearly two-thirds of the white vote to the Republicans. James Baldwin expressed a cautious optimism shared with many in an open letter to Carter published in the *New York Times*. Baldwin had maintained a profound skepticism about politicians ever since a well-publicized 1963 "summit conference" with Bobby Kennedy had disintegrated in acrimony and accusations of bad faith. Baldwin's gesture took on special symbolic significance in a community that shared his doubts about the mainstream political system. Asking Carter to pardon the Wilmington Ten, a group of North Carolina prisoners convicted of a firebombing during a racial disturbance, Baldwin concluded his letter: "I must add, in honor, that I write to you because I love our country: And you, in my lifetime, are the only president to whom I would have written."

So it was a major disappointment when, shortly after taking the oath of office, Carter marched out, took careful aim at his own feet, and opened fire. To be fair, not all of the wounds were self-inflicted. Changes in the global economy probably made a painful (from the consumer/voter standpoint) escalation of American prices to reflect actual energy costs inevitable. The bills simply came due and somebody had to pay. Similarly, the Ayatollah probably wouldn't have felt more kindly toward the Great American Satan if Gerald Ford had been in office. The most devout man to occupy the White House in at least a century, Carter certainly wasn't responsible for the growing sense of moral aimlessness reflected in sharp increases in crime, pornography, and drug use.

Nonetheless, Carter missed no opportunity to misplay the political game. By midway through his term of office, Carter had alienated most of his black supporters. Despite the appointments of Young, Eleanor Holmes Norton, and former SNCC activist John Lewis to significant posts, Carter received harsh criticism for excluding blacks from his immediate circle of advisers. Contrasting Carter's administration unfavorably with Nixon's, Roger Wilkins claimed that "Black access to the White House is more limited than it has been since the days of Franklin Roosevelt." Carter's handling of Young's forced resignation from his post as UN ambassador cost him any political advantage the appointment might have earned him.

The debacle began when Young met with a representative of the Palestine Liberation Organization. Immediately, Young came under fire from Israeli lobbyists and American Jewish organizations that considered the PLO absolute anathema. Anticipating the rhetorical tactics Ronald Reagan would use so effectively in the 1980 campaign, Barry Goldwater referred to "Young and his 'Manson family' at the United Nations" as "leftovers from the hippie generation. They were what some of us called 'looney tunes.' " When Carter caved in to the pressures and angrily dismissed Young as a "disgrace" to the administration, Jesse Jackson added his voice to the chorus of criticism. Coming full circle, Baldwin concluded an open letter on Young's dismissal with: "My friend, Mr. Andrew Young, out of tremendous love and courage, and with a silent, irreproachable nobility, has attempted to ward off a holocaust, and I proclaim him a hero, betrayed by cowards."

Carter's most far-reaching failure, however, concerned affirmative action, or, as the Republicans phrased it, "quotas." Quotas and affirmative action aren't, of course, the same thing. But you never would have known it from the way the administration responded to the lawsuit brought by Allan Bakke challenging the use of racial preferences in the admissions system used by the Medical School at the University of California–Davis. Attempting to support affirmative action without endorsing quotas, Carter temporized. Misplaying the situation to perfection, he managed to alienate both sides of the most important civil rights case since *Brown* v. *Board of Education*. A veteran of LBJ's civil rights campaign, Carter's secretary of health, education, and welfare, Joseph Califano, wanted to seize the case as a chance to confirm the administration's commitment to racial justice. When he sensed the opportunity slipping away, Califano angrily argued that "The Justice Department's *Bakke* brief would set civil rights back a generation." At the same time, Carter's Republican opponents gleefully saddled him with the title of "quota king." As Carter press secretary Hamilton Jordan mournfully observed in a White House memorandum, "We are going to suffer the worst of both worlds."

The Supreme Court issued almost exactly the ruling Carter desired, upholding the concept of affirmative action while ruling against UC–Davis's use of quotas. Yet the *Bakke* case was an unmitigated disaster for racial progress. Before *Bakke*, the burden of proof in civil rights cases rested on those opposed to affirmative action programs designed to redress historical inequities. The decision shifted the burden of proof onto civil rights advocates by requiring "strict scrutiny" of the logic used to justify any type of racial preference.

The *Bakke* case also provided new ammunition to white supremacists determined to rewrite the history of the freedom movement for their own political purposes. The coalition that had made passage of the 1964 Civil Rights Act and the 1965 Voting Rights Act possible had always been fragile. Although the primary gains of the movement were won through the daily struggles of thousands of ordinary local people, broad public acceptance rested largely on the brilliant rhetorical strategies used by Martin Luther King and, somewhat less eloquently, Lyndon Johnson. Both King and Johnson presented the movement as the fulfillment of shared American ideals of simple fairness and individual opportunity. As Cornel West has shown, King mixed references to Christian ethics and democratic ideals while muting his fundamental commitment to radical economic change. When King centered the Poor People's Campaign on the insistence that real change would demand redistribution of economic resources, it became clear that the progressive coalition was in deep political trouble.

Richard Nixon's Southern strategy had been based on the realization that white acceptance of civil rights legislation was at best grudging. Nixon capitalized on the fact that not only in the South but in a thousand little Souths that ringed cities across the nation, the "silent majority" was seething. Once white supremacists shifted their tactics, substituting campaign contributions to supporters of "law and order" for dynamite and open race-baiting, the progressive coalition was probably facing insurmountable odds even if it had played its hand well.

It didn't. As black sociologist William Julius Wilson demonstrates in *The Truly Disadvantaged*, during the seventies supporters of racial justice achieved the almost unthinkable feat of turning the moral high ground over to Ronald Reagan. A gradual change in the terms of the public debate on affirmative action played a crucial role. The primary goals of the movement remained unchanged—a desire for justice and human dignity, equal opportunity, a better life for one's children. But, Wilson shows, the terms of the debate shifted gradually from an emphasis on *individual opportunity* to an emphasis on *group results*. The shift was obviously in the best interests of those who had no intention of supporting any sort of equal opportunity.

But it was furthered by the ill-considered words and actions of movement supporters who took the Black Power movement's demands for an end to masking all too literally. Black activists found it politically expedient to issue extreme demands to placate the least compromising members of their constituencies. Any evidence of continuing discrimination—and there was no shortage of evidence— was righteously attacked; demands for immediate measurable results were issued without regard for how they would play on the six o'clock news. Wilson traces the shift in the public debate through three phases: a phase emphasizing equal opportunity for equally qualified individuals, the vocabulary consistently employed by King during the early days of the movement; a phase emphasizing equal opportunity for historically disadvantaged groups, the issue which in fact deserved, and continues to deserve, our most serious attention; and a phase emphasizing equal results for groups, an emphasis which is both politically and conceptually indefensible. As Stalin once said in another context, it was worse than a crime—it was a mistake.

If generating a politically viable approach supporting equal opportunity was tricky, the increasing pressure to measure the success of affirmative action programs by quantifying results was a screaming disaster. Those seeking to dismantle affirmative action programs had no trouble finding cases of obvious individual injustice. Individual achievement, they said, counted for nothing. Only making the quota mattered.

And they weren't entirely wrong. Colleges found themselves under pressure to graduate roughly equal percentages of black and white students; police forces were evaluated on how many blacks were promoted to higher ranks. The problems with the group-results approach are both practical and political. If the premises behind equal opportunity are accurate, then it is extremely unlikely that an equal percentage of blacks will be able to make up all of the lost ground and achieve at the same level as a white control group. The best-case scenario, which requires hard work and good faith from all concerned, is that the gap will close gradually over a period of time. It's not something Americans want to hear, but most research indicates that the time required to overcome the long-term effects of a caste system such as that involved in segregation should be measured in generations, not years.

Practically, the demand for equal results combined with a political psychology that rarely thought in months and *never* in generations to effect an inexorable lowering of standards, a reality proponents of affirmative action remain unwilling to acknowledge. Nothing is easier than graduating black students if you don't care about what they've learned. The "gentleman's C" given students of the elite attending prestigious universities has metamorphosed into the "affirmative action C" given out by teachers afraid they'll be criticized for "racism" and unwilling to spend the time it takes to make the promise of opportunity meaningful. The alternative approach to meeting quotas, adapted by most elite private universities in the United States, is to recruit heavily from among the sons and daughters of successful black professionals. The graduation rates will look better and standards can be maintained. But the net increase in opportunity is close to zero.

Nineteen seventy-eight marks a turning point in American racial history. Since that time, every appeal for racial justice has been attacked for giving "special consideration" to "groups." The crucial debate on equal opportunity never really began. Carter's failure to focus attention on the serious questions raised by the concept of group opportunity ceded the moral high ground and the political majority to Ronald Reagan. The movement has never recovered.

## 36
## Roots:
## The Messages in the Music

MFSB stood for Mother, Father, Sister, Brother. Or maybe it was Mighty Fine Soul Band. Street wisdom put a slightly different twist on the MF. Whatever the initials stood for, they referred to the great studio band that powered the last of the soul music empires: Philly International, the brainchild of lyricist Kenny Gamble, his songwriting partner, Leon Huff, and producer Thom Bell, the maestro of "symphonic soul." Philly International's slogan—The Message in the Music—signaled its goal of picking up Motown's legacy by creating a socially uplifting music that would appeal to everyone in the black community and as many as possible on the other side of the rapidly re-forming racial line.

Philly International holds a special place in the hearts of many black artists who see it as a perfect expression of the decade's complicated crosscurrents. Stevie Wonder, who'd done his part in keeping the Motown faith, praised Gamble and Huff for mixing "the joy of love with the pain of oppression. They let it marinate and it was sweet." Curtis Mayfield saw them as "young, proud black men" who shared Berry Gordy's ability to negotiate with "the powers that be." "They walked a tight line in many directions," Mayfield said, "but you always knew Gamble and Huff were steering that ship." Looking back at what Philly meant to black communities in the seventies, poet Nikki Giovanni captured the energies that made Philly a link between the gospel politics of the fifties and the Black Power movement:

> that's when in some wild and wonderful way we were courageous
> enough to still fall in love and crazy enough not to hold back and sen-
> sible enough not to cry when it was over nor whine nor beg and plead
> and threaten but just find another love for another day and even if

people thought we were trite and silly we knew we were just expressing a brand new us and oh you had better believe the people were
ready for that train a coming. that's when we were strong and determined to change the world and if not change it leave it different from
when we first met it and i like black people for that.

When MFSB's driving instrumental "The Sound of Philadelphia"
(a.k.a. the theme from *Soul Train*), which defined the Philly sound
in the same way "Green Onions" defined early Stax, hit the air during the spring of 1974, Gamble, Huff, and Bell were already record
industry veterans. Gamble and Bell had known each other while
they were growing up in Philadelphia, but pursued different paths
early in their careers. While Gamble fronted a soul act called the
Romeos, Bell developed his approach to symphonic soul by produc-
ing the lushly orchestrated Delfonics hits "La La Means I Love You,"
"I'm Sorry," and "Didn't I (Blow Your Mind This Time)." Meanwhile
Huff moved from his birthplace across the river in Camden, New
Jersey, to New York, where he played piano on sessions supervised by
Phil Spector, Mike Leiber, and Jerry Stoller. "I'm still thrilled about
it," Huff recalled. "Playing on the Ronettes' things was one of the
real highlights of my career. And I'll never forget Leiber and Stoller
because they helped me get the knack of the studios."

The founders' extensive experience proved crucial to the success
of Philly International and helped them overcome Philadelphia's
reputation as a second-line presence in the music world. Over the
years many important musicians had been born or made their
homes in Philadelphia, among them gospel singers Clara Ward,
Marion Williams, and Ira Tucker; jazzmen John Coltrane, Bobby
Timmons, and Jimmy Smith; and soul singers Solomon Burke, Patti
LaBelle, and Garnett Mims. But Philly had never managed to establish itself as a significant recording center. The city's gospel label,
Gotham, lost its stars to Newark-based Savoy; the jazzmen all went up
the road to New York; and New York–based Atlantic overshadowed
every Philly soul label until the advent of Philly International. The
turning point for Philadelphia came when Huff left New York and
began collaborating with Gamble on songs for local soul groups, including the Three Degrees, the blue-eyed soul group Soul Survivors,
and the Intruders, whose "Cowboys to Girls" provided the team with
its first number one hit.

The Philly sound first came together on the records Gamble and
Huff produced when they were asked to help save the careers of vet-

eran soulmen who had fallen on hard times. Wilson Pickett's "Don't Let the Green Grass Fool You" and several Jerry Butler records capped by the Black Power anthem "Only the Strong Survive" pioneered what was to become the standard Philly formula: socially relevant, but nonconfrontational, lyrics; swirling string arrangements; and a mix emphasizing the rhythmic accents. It was an approach that would be employed on Philly classics including Harold Melvin and the Blue Notes' "Wake Up Everybody" and "Bad Luck"; the O'Jays' "Put Your Hands Together," "Don't Call Me Brother," and "Love Train"; Lou Rawls's "You'll Never Find Another Love Like Mine"; and the Three Degrees' "When Will I See You Again?"

By the time Gamble, Huff, and Bell established Philly International in late 1971, they had perfected their approach. The key to their consistency was the MFSB band, whose sound longtime James Brown sideman Fred Wesley called "funk with a bow tie." Like Booker T. and the MGs and Hi Rhythm in Memphis and the Funk Brothers at Motown, MFSB was organized around a central group of musicians that changed very little over the years. Incorporating Latin influences more frequently than their counterparts in the South and Midwest, bass player Ronnie Baker and drummer Earl Young kept the rhythms pulsing beneath the guitar work of Bobby Eli and Norman Harris. Huff on piano, Vince Montana on vibes, and a string section recruited from the Philadelphia Symphony Orchestra supplemented MFSB when an arrangement called for a different flavor. Eli attributed the label's broad appeal to the open atmosphere in the studio: "The MFSB band is something special. Now that band's got more ethnic groups in it than the United Nations. Yet they've made it through all that 'say, ain't some of these guys white?' shit. They get played on the black radio stations consistently. And that's justice. MFSB put Philadelphia on top in the first place."

As vocalist Teddy Pendergrass observed, the Philly sound was "a force so powerful that white stations couldn't ignore us." In fact, no one even distantly connected with the soul scene ignored Gamble and Huff. The Commodores ("Sail On"), Spinners ("I'll Be Around," "Ghetto Child," "Could It Be I'm Falling in Love," all produced by Thom Bell), Manhattans ("Kiss and Say Goodbye"), and Chi-Lites ("Have You Seen Her," "Oh Girl") were the black side of a Philly-inflected mix that extended through Hall and Oates ("She's Gone") and Fleetwood Mac ("Rhiannon") to the Eagles, whose producer, Bill Scymzyk, acknowledged that the first orchestral note of

"Take It to the Limit" was a direct imitation of the opening chord of Harold Melvin and the Blue Notes' "If You Don't Know Me by Now." If anything, Philly's impact increased during the eighties when R & B acts from Luther Vandross ("Never Too Much") and Anita Baker ("Angel") to Phyllis Hyman ("Living All Alone") and Maze ("Joy and Pain") mixed gospel vocals, subtle polyrhythms, and lush string arrangements. As Jimmy Jam and Terry Lewis, the most influential R & B producers of the Reagan era, acknowledged, "There wouldn't be a Jam and Lewis if it weren't for Gamble and Huff."

Although Philly International's success rested primarily on the distinctive sound Richard Torres called "velvet with a spine," Gamble believed deeply in music as a way of transmitting healing messages. In the liner notes to the O'Jays' *Family Reunion* album, Gamble wrote that the growing divisions within black communities were "creating a halt to the flow of wisdom from the wise to the young, and stifling the energy of the young which is the equalizer to wisdom and age." Gamble's response to the situation restated the basic principles of the gospel impulse: "Being of truth and understanding of all things, we must recapture the family structure—Mother, Father, Sister, Brother—and give respect to everyone. Remember the family that prays together stays together. Put the 'Unity' back into the family."

The specific messages transmitted by Philly International reflected the growing tensions within black America. On one hand, the label shared Motown's commitment to ascent, mainstream success. Even though the O'Jays warned against the sins committed "For the Love of Money," Philly International was most definitely concerned with financial success. Gene McFadden and John Whitehead's "Ain't No Stoppin' Us Now" expressed a dedication to making it on all levels. Never revolutionary, the label avoided explicit ideological statements that might have alienated segments of the audience. Although Gamble converted to Islam, his commitment to a morally upright, patriarchal community was acceptable to the most conservative SCLC leaders. The keynote of Philly International's universalist agenda, the O'Jays' "Love Train" celebrates an absolutely inclusive vision of human unity. Expanding the Impressions' "People Get Ready," the train picks up passengers not just "coast to coast," but also in Africa, India, the Middle East, China, and Russia.

Other Philly International records, however, reflected an increasing tendency to turn away from white society and look to the black past for solutions to the problems of life after ascent. Observ-

ing that individuals who make successful ascents often find themselves isolated from black life, literary critic Robert Stepto identifies
a second major pattern, which he calls "immersion." If ascent can be
described as the movement "up from slavery," immersion represents
a "return to the roots." Where ascent requires that individuals master mainstream "literacy"—the rules of the white man's game—
immersion requires the recapturing of "communal literacy." During
ascent, individuals move from the "symbolic South"—the rural
South, or the inner city—to the "symbolic North"—a job in the Pittsburgh steel mills or a place in a prestigious university. In the process,
they often lose contact with the changing forms of communication
used back home: dance, music, slang. When they return home, they
find they no longer speak the same language, literally or conceptually. All the book knowledge in the world does them no good in their
attempts to fit in on the street. The key to a successful immersion is
being able to get back into the flow, accept the black-defined rules
of the game.

During the seventies, black artists in many forms responded to
these tensions by creating a popular genre of works exploring the
crosscurrents of ascent and immersion in African American history.
The most popular, Alex Haley's *Roots* and Ernest Gaines's *The Autobiography of Miss Jane Pittman,* attracted even larger audiences when
they were made into television movies. Setting the pattern for seventies immersion narratives, both celebrate black survival and success. Ascent, they imply, need not cut black people off from their
heritage. A successful immersion, as portrayed by Haley and Gaines,
inspires the beloved community to make its own ascent. If all black
people make it into the mainstream, the mainstream won't be such
an isolated place. Haley concludes his epic with a celebration of a
new interracial American family. Similarly, *The Autobiography of Miss
Jane Pittman* reaches its climax when the hundred-year-old protagonist takes an inspirational step toward freedom. As Robert Hayden
wrote in his great poem "Middle Passage," African American history
charts a "voyage through death to life upon these shores."

Philly International's contribution to the discussion was the O'Jays'
"Ship Ahoy," a ten-minute mini-epic that preceded Alex Haley's
*Roots* by some three years. Despite Philly International's upbeat ideology, the song shares little of Hayden's or Haley's sense of hope. A
potentially explosive tension, nearly a contradiction, haunts the center of the song and Philly International as a whole. Even as Gamble
and Huff reached their zenith, the society around them seemed on

the verge of resegregation. It became harder and harder to believe that the legacy of slavery could be consigned to the past. Beginning with the sound of water washing against the side of a slave ship, "Ship Ahoy" recounts the brutal experiences of the Middle Passage as clearly as the early episodes of *Roots*. Eddie Levert's groans insist on the bitter irony of "men women and baby slaves coming to the land of liberty." The sun may be shining over the horizon, but the O'Jays refuse to look away from the reality of Middle Passage and there's no sense that things are going to work out fine. There's no equivalent in "Ship Ahoy" to the black/white family gathering that confirms Haley's endorsement of ascent. Whatever the optimism of Philly International's official message, "Ship Ahoy" fades out on a harsh note as the O'Jays trade ominous calls of "waiting," "waiting," "waiting."

A surprising number of Philly International's biggest hits echo the emotional tone of "Ship Ahoy." Featuring the gritty gospel vocals of Teddy Pendergrass, who would become a major star as a solo act, Harold Melvin and the Blue Notes sang about separation, loss, emotional devastation. Although the lyrics of "I Miss You," "If You Don't Know Me by Now," and "Don't Leave Me This Way" all deal with personal relationships, it's not hard to hear them as masked warnings of the chasm opening between black and white, young and old, rich and poor. We've given it our best shot, Pendergrass testifies, and it's come to nothing. Pendergrass's gospel moan at the beginning of "Don't Leave Me This Way" wouldn't have been out of place in the poorest church in the most destitute part of Philly's south side ghetto. The fact that it comes on top of a disco beat simply tells you that the party had a tormented soul.

## 37
## God Love Sex:
## Disco and the Gospel Impulse

The word "disco" conjures up its own parody: John Travolta preening for the mirror in *Saturday Night Fever*, Margaret Trudeau collapsing on the front page of the tabloids; the Village People prancing out of the ruins of the Stonewall Inn and into a strobe-lit YMCA. In memory, the music fares no better than the scene as the Bee Gees, Rod Stewart, Mick Jagger, the Bee Gees, Dolly Parton, Frank Sinatra, and (believe it or not) Ethel Merman join the greatest of them all, the Disco Duck, in a monorhythmic drone throbbing on and on into a coke-and-quaaluded night.

All of that happened, but it happened after 1977. The early history of disco has been almost forgotten. The crucial moment in the transformation of disco into its own worst enemy was the opening of Studio 54, the exclusive Manhattan club where the beautiful people gathered to prove their superiority to the unfashionable or, worse, would-be-fashionable masses. In *The Last Party: Studio 54, Disco, and the Culture of the Night*, Anthony Haden-Guest tells a story as harrowing as *The Shining* or *Helter Skelter*. The doorkeepers at Studio 54 possessed the power to separate the elect from the damned, granting access to a fantasy realm where the blues realities of the outside world had been declared magically irrelevant. Often they would tell women seeking admission to strip and provide sexual favors only to renege on their part of the devil's bargain.

Haden-Guest quotes the sixteenth-century libertine François Rabelais to reveal the nature of the Studio 54 "Nightworld": "*En leur regle n'estoit que ceste clause: Fais ce que vouldras* (Do what you want shall be the whole of their law)." "Exactly. Perfect," responded Don Rubell, brother of Studio 54 owner Steve Rubell. "It was do what you will. And there was no concept of punishment. And no new morality that was in existence at that time. . . . Was it abused? Yes. Were bad things done in the name of good? Yes. But it was a moment of ultimate freedom." If the pop culture dream of sex, drugs, and a certain sort of rock and roll was ever literally fulfilled, it was on the dance floor and in the back rooms of Studio 54. After less than two years, the fantasy collapsed in an unholy mess. The IRS played the role of avenging angel. On the morning of December 14, 1978, agents arrived to cart away the "secret" set of books and nearly a million dollars in cash that had been hidden in the club's walls and false ceilings. Studio 54 clones of all social descriptions kept the party going for a while, but the end of disco's reign had begun.

From a musical perspective, that was just as well. Although music played constantly in the clubs, it served primarily as a kind of decoration. Musicians *were* important, but for the most part, not disco musicians. Mick Jagger, Diana Ross, and Cher sprinkled their glitter on Studio 54. Almost every musician visiting New York stopped in: Stevie Wonder, Michael Jackson, Dolly Parton. They were admitted not for their music, but for their star quality. Most revealing in terms of the Nightworld's relationship to music was the experience of Nile Rodgers and Bernard Edwards, the creative forces behind Chic. Chic's "Dance, Dance, Dance (Yowsah Yowsah Yowsah)" and "Everybody's Dancing" were among the most popular records on the Studio 54 dance floor. But when Rodgers and Edwards, decked out in wing-collar shirts, two-tone Spectator shoes, and towering Afros, showed up at Studio 54 to attend a party hosted by Grace Jones, the doorkeepers shut them out.

After waiting several hours, they retreated to Rodgers's apartment. "We resorted to using music therapeutically," Rodgers reported. "Bernard and I started jamming, just guitar and bass. We were just yelling obscenities . . . *Fuck Studio 54 . . . Fuck 'em . . . Fuck off! . . . Fuck those scumbags . . . Fuck them!* And we were just laughing. We were entertaining the hell out of ourselves. We had a blast. And finally it hit Bernard. He said, 'Hey, Nile! What you're playing sounds really good.' " After a few lyrical transformations with the demands of radio airplay in mind, the song became "Le Freak," one of the biggest hits of the disco era.

During the Studio 54 years, Chic provided a living heartbeat in a musical scene increasingly threatened by minstrel vultures. Supported by versatile drummer Tony Thompson and vocalists Alfa Anderson and Luci Martin, Rodgers and Edwards developed a distinctive variation on the Philly International sound. Rodgers's guitar lines flowed in and out of string arrangements that were usually sparser and more nuanced than Philly's. The trilogy of songs Chic produced for Sister Sledge presents, to use disco chronicler Ken Barnes's phrase, "the definitive disco manifesto." The first, "He's the Greatest Dancer," introduces the dance floor as a kind of ritual ground while the last, "Lost in Music," testifies to the transformative power of music. The real triumph, however, comes in "We Are Family." Whatever the song might have meant in the Studio 54 Nightworld, it reasserted a gospel vision of harmony and unity at the precise moment Jimmy Carter was unceremoniously showing Andrew Young to the door. Driven by a bass line that would be imitated by everyone from Queen ("Another One Bites the Dust") to the Sugar Hill Gang ("Rapper's Delight"), Chic's own "Good Times" delivers a eulogy for the era in the guise of a celebration.

The redemptive energies of "We Are Family" and the blues realism of "Good Times" served as a reminder of disco's social origins and musical roots. For Rodgers, the vision transcended the disco scene. "As a guitarist, I was into Jimi Hendrix; as a person, the Black Panthers," he said. "So I just wanted to make music that felt like revolution." Disco had in fact grown out of two distinct revolutionary movements of the late sixties. Musically, disco developed out of the main styles of early seventies black dance music: the polyrhythmic funk inspired by James Brown and George Clinton, and up-tempo soul music, especially extended versions of Philly International hits. Socially, its primary sources lay in the gay rights movement that gathered momentum following the Stonewall Riot of 1969.

The most popular bar on Christopher Street, the Stonewall Inn brought together a crowd of blacks, whites, and Puerto Ricans who put up with its abysmal sanitary conditions largely because it was the only gay bar in New York which permitted dancing. In the summer of 1969, Martin Duberman reports in his book *Stonewall,* the jukebox featured an eclectic mix of Motown hits and slow dance standards such as "Smoke Gets in Your Eyes." Even at the Stonewall, however, the freedom to dance was limited by the threat of police raids. In addition to confiscating unstamped liquor, the vice squad enforced laws requiring dress "appropriate to one's gender" and forbidding intimate touching—including dancing—between members of the same sex. At the beginning of raids—many of which were tipped off in advance in return for graft payments—a flashing white light warned the men on the floors to stop dancing and resume "normal" conversations.

In the early morning of June 28, 1969, the crowd at the Stonewall included veterans of the civil rights movement, members of Students for a Democratic Society, and a cross section of antiwar activists. No one who was there that evening suggests that what transpired represented a conscious political rebellion. But there's no question about what happened when the police raided the bar. Rather than passively accepting the almost ritualistic harassment that had forced gay life underground, the crowd on Christopher Street exploded in anger. Shouting "Gay Power!," bystanders began throwing coins, bottles, and beer cans at the police, who responded with clubs and a fire hose. The scene devolved or advanced, depending on your perspective, into a near-parody of a riot when a group of cross-dressing queens formed a chorus line and, kicking their legs in the air, taunted the police with a song proudly announcing: "We wear no underwear / We show our pubic hair."

Inspired by Stonewall, the gay rights movement made an increasingly aggressive and effective assault on the laws and customs that kept gays closeted. By the mid-seventies, while antigay ordinances remained in effect through most of the country, major changes had occurred in a few locations, most notably Manhattan and San Francisco. Gay clubs played a central role in the New York club culture that gave birth to Studio 54. Within a year of Stonewall, David Mancuso opened the prototypical gay dance club, the Loft, which was followed by the Flamingo, Nepenthe, Le Jardin, Hippopotamus, and Infinity, which featured a glowing neon penis. Several of the clubs pioneered the use of the "Translator," a system that coordinated the flashes of the light system with the beats of the music on the club's sound system. Throughout the seventies, gay life remained much more racially mixed than the American norm. One of the results was that the music played at Studio 54's gay precursors placed a heavy emphasis on black dance sounds.

Before 1976, no clear line separated "disco" from "funk." A club dance mix might include former Temptation Eddie Kendricks's "Keep on Truckin' " or "Boogie Down"; the Jacksons' "Dancing Machine"; the most recent Philly International hits; Chaka Khan and Rufus's "You Got the Love" or "Sweet Thing"; James Brown's "Doing It to Death"; Lyn Collins's JB-produced feminist anthem "Think"; and Kool & the Gang's jazzy "Jungle Boogie," "Higher Plane," or "Spirit of the Boogie." Not until the second half of the decade did the live drummers and polyrhythmic intensities give way to the standardized studio production style that gave disco its bad name. The metronomic disco beat amounted to a concession to the "outsider" audiences that thronged to the scene without understanding its music. Gloria Gaynor attributed the loss of rhythmic complexity specifically to the needs of the white audience: "I think it was kind of hard for white people to get into R & B because the beat is so sophisticated and hard for the kind of dancing white people were doing. The kind of clearly defined beat that's in disco music now makes it easier to learn our kind of dancing."

For black dancers, and gay dancers of all races who shared their appreciation of style (as opposed to fashion), a challenging rhythmic mix encouraged the expression of individuality within a knowledgeable community. As they would in the house music scene that developed out of "real" disco, dancers engaged in elaborate calls and responses with each other and the DJs who kept the music flowing. Music critic Iain Chambers described the disco tradition as a seventies expression of black music's changing same:

> In disco the musical pulse is freed from the claustrophobic interiors of the blues and the tight scaffolding of R&B and early soul music. A looser, explicitly polyrhythmic attack pushes the blues, gospel and soul heritage into an apparently endless cycle where there is no beginning or end, just an ever-present "now." Disco music does not come to a halt . . . restricted to a three-minute single, the music would be rendered senseless. The power of disco lay in saturating dancers and the dance floor in the continual explosion of its presence.

Given the emphasis on process and flow, there are obvious dangers in focusing too much attention on individual disco songs. Nonetheless, the parts frequently reflected the whole. Many disco hits shared Philly International's blend of gospel hope and blues pessimism. Disco was without question the most powerful forum for women's expression during the seventies. Like Aretha Franklin, Donna Summer learned to sing in church. After the novelty record "Love to Love You Baby" made her a star, Summer demonstrated her powerful voice and hard-edged blues sensibility on "Hot Stuff," "Bad Girls," and "She Works Hard for the Money," the latter two wry comments on her own position as disco diva. Gloria Gaynor did not share Summer's church background: "My grandmother was very religious and she inundated my mother with church, so my mother decided if she had children she would never make them go to church." Still, Gaynor's treatment of the feminist anthem "I Will Survive" testified to the possibility of transforming the burden into strength in a way that hearkened back to Mahalia's "Keep Your Hand on the Plow."

If disco retained strong similarities to gospel, its movement into the Studio 54 Nightworld underscored some already existing differences. Nile Rodgers described the evolution of the music away from gospel's communal ideals:

> It was definitely R&B dance music. That was where it originated. Then it took on more blatant sexual overtones because of the gay movement. . . . It seems to me that disco—from when I first recognized it as a musical form—was the most hedonistic music I had ever heard in my life. It was really all about Me! Me! Me! Me!
>
> It was the exact antithesis of the hippie music that had preceded it. It wasn't about save the world! It was about get yourself a mate, and have fun, and forget the rest of the world. In a strange way that was very therapeutic. When I was political, and a hippie, we talked about freedom and individuality, and it was all bullshit! You could tell a hippie a mile away. We conformed to our non-conformity. Whereas disco really *was* about individuality. And the freakier, the better.

More often than not, the hedonistic expressions of individuality focused on physical pleasure. Gospel music sang about salvation through God; soul music sang about the power of love. Taking the progression another step into the secular world, disco translated "love" as "sex." The great soul singers had usually been willing to grant the point; sexual healer Marvin Gaye wanted to follow up his classic of spiritual seduction "Let's Get It On" (also recorded in a gospel version titled "Keep Gettin' It On") with a song he called "Sanctified Pussy" (fortunately retitled "Sanctified Lady" when it was finally released).

In a social scene where cocaine was considered a harmless party favor, trouble soon came knocking. The tensions between hedonistic pleasure and communal aspiration were particularly clear among gays. On the one hand, many gays responded to the relaxation of legal strictures by plunging into a joyous celebration of sexual freedom. By the end of the decade, the bathhouses and Christopher Street clubs had become sexual playgrounds; some men had sex with hundreds of different partners. Although the new scene ostensibly celebrated the gay community as a whole, there were obvious problems—including the early stages of the AIDS epidemic—for individuals seeking relationships combining pleasure with long-term spiritual growth.

No artist expressed the tension more powerfully than the flamboyantly gay San Francisco disco diva Sylvester. Blessed with a voice that could have made him a star in any musical form, Sylvester expressed the connection between personal and communal fulfillment in "Dance (Disco Heat)," "Power of Love," and "You Make Me Feel (Mighty Real)." But "Trouble in Paradise" and "Cry Me a River" reveal an equally intense awareness that after the disco closed and yesterday's lover vanished into the dawn, you still had to deal with your personal burdens. The community's shared knowledge of that morning-after letdown kept Teddy Pendergrass's Philly International hit "You Can't Hide from Yourself" active in dance mixes for over a decade. A searing cry for love backed by a gospel chorus situated near the heart of the disco inferno, Sylvester's "Sell My Soul" made no attempt to deny the cost of the new freedom. Sylvester, who died of AIDS in 1988, testified that, if only someone was buying, he would have sold his soul for love.

# 38
# Disco Sucks

On July 12, 1979, straight America took its revenge. Between games of a doubleheader at Chicago's Comiskey Park, the throng gathered in support of DJ Steve Dahl's antidisco crusade joined in a thunderous chant of "Disco sucks!" In center field, Dahl approached a wooden box overflowing with disco records doused in lighter fluid. As the crowd cheered, Dahl set the altar ablaze, igniting a drunken rampage that trashed the field and resulted in the cancellation of the second game.

Far from an anomaly, the Comiskey Park riot gave voice to the ugliest undertones of the antidisco sentiment that united segments of the population with almost nothing else in common. By the time the craze had faded in the early eighties, it began to seem as if *everyone* hated disco. (Which raised the interesting question of how the *Saturday Night Fever* sound track had managed to sell twenty-five million copies.) At one extreme, political progressives, of a distinctly puritanical sort, condemned disco as an expression of commodity culture, capitalism at its worst. Even though disco was the only pop-

ular music other than country in which women played a large role,
many feminists felt that disco reduced women to sexual playthings.
Easily confirmed reports of women bartering sex for drugs or admission to clubs certainly buttressed the feminist case.

Although antidisco feeling in black communities rarely matched
the ferocity displayed at Comiskey Park, many doubted its musical
and/or moral value. Taking a stand against what he labeled "sex-
rock," Jesse Jackson condemned disco as "garbage and pollution
which is corrupting the minds and morals of our youth." Threatening a boycott against records and distributors, Jackson's Operation
PUSH convened several conferences on the evils of disco. Less
heated and a good deal less puritanical than Jackson, George Clinton simply found the standardized late disco rhythm boring. "Nothing get on your nerves more than some rhythm that's the same thing
over and over again," commented the master of polyrhythms. "It's
like makin' love with one stroke. You can fax that in." By the time
the Rolling Stones cashed in with their disco minstrel classic "Miss
You"—which comes complete with the obligatory, if ironic, stereo-
typing of black and Puerto Rican women as objects of sexual
taboo—many black listeners had turned away from disco and picked
up on the new generation of funk bands that remembered how to
get up for the downstroke.

Even as funk founder James Brown marketed himself as the "original disco man," groups such as the Ohio Players ("I Wanna Be
Free," "Fire"), the Isley Brothers ("Harvest for the World," "Take It
to the Next Phase"), Brass Construction ("Movin' "), the Bar-Kays
("Cozy," "Holy Ghost"), Slave ("Slide"), and War ("The World Is a
Ghetto," "Cinco de Mayo," "Low Rider") kept the faith with the Godfather's vision of socially aware polyrhythmic complexity. Carrying
on Jimi Hendrix's tradition of guitar-driven rock and soul, the Isley
Brothers rallied their listeners to "Fight the Power." While the actual
musicians faded further and further away into the shadows of the
disco studios, funk musicians stretched out and improvised their way
through the rapidly changing landscape of the Carter collapse.

The true keepers of the jazz flame in the seventies—"jazz" itself
had wandered off into the soul-deadening commercial fusion of
George Benson and Spyro Gyra—the funk bands were at their best
in live performance. The most effective live funk album, Earth,
Wind & Fire's Gratitude opens with a scorching medley ("Africano/
Power") that sets a political framework for responding to the
group's hits, which often worked their way into the disco mix. "Sun

Goddess," "Gratitude," and "Celebrate" stir the crowd to a peak of gospel togetherness; "New World Symphony" extends the vision to its fullest democratic extent; and the stunning call and response between Andrew Woolfolk's sax and Philip Bailey's searching tenor lifts "Reasons" to heights rarely reached outside the church. With Earth, Wind & Fire, the Ohio Players, Brass Construction, and Lakeside as alternatives, it was no wonder large parts of the black audience turned away from the increasingly commercial disco of the late seventies.

The core of the antidisco movement, however, was both more aggressive and more disturbing. Most of the Comiskey Park rioters were young white men. While nobody conducted a survey of their sexual preferences, they certainly projected a distinctly straight male energy. Most of the disco stars were black, female, and/or gay. The conclusions are inescapable. White rockers plunged into the antidisco crusade with an eagerness bordering on obsession. "Our goal in the seventies was to destroy disco," reflected Tom Petty. "We saw that as a terrible menace to music." Steely Dan guitarist Skunk Baxter elaborated on the evils of disco: "The machine age sort of took its revenge on music and disco music became the antithesis of what music used to be. The music instead of being a voice became an accompaniment. It was almost the anthem of alienation." The attacks weren't just about musical style. Few rockers bothered to comment one way or another on funk, which was musically even more remote from rock. For that matter, huge stylistic differences separated the major styles of seventies rock—punk, glam, country rock, art rock—from one another, but that kind of venomous disdain was only directed at disco.

The antidisco movement represented an unholy alliance of funkateers and feminists, progressives and puritans, rockers and reactionaries. Nonetheless, the attacks on disco gave respectable voice to the ugliest kinds of unacknowledged racism, sexism, and homophobia. Driving disco from the charts, the alliance also succeeded in destroying the last remaining musical scene that was in any meaningful sense racially mixed. After nearly a quarter century of doubt, white America had recovered its sense of self.

# 39
# Punks and Pretenders

Lou Reed was joking in 1977 when he announced that on the cover of his next album he'd be wearing blackface and eating a watermelon. The song that opened the second side of the album, *Street Hassle,* however, made it clear that Reed hadn't lost interest in the bizarre racial fantasies playing themselves out in hip white America. Deliberately ragged, "I Wanna Be Black" confronts the contradiction between white America's theoretical fascination with blackness and its lack of contact with real black life. The contradiction was never more pronounced than in the late seventies.

In "I Wanna Be Black," Reed casts himself in the role of what Norman Mailer called the "white Negro," a hipster turning to black life for a sense of danger and authenticity lacking in his own. White Negroes weren't new in the late fifties when Mailer wrote the essay that popularized the term; ever since the Harlem Renaissance of the twenties, fashionable young whites had sought out forbidden thrills on the other side of the racial tracks. The young Malcolm X made his living "guiding" whites to illicit sexual liaisons. Lashing out against white Negroism, James Baldwin pointed out that the phenomenon relied on stereotypes of blacks as mindless animals controlled by physical passion. Whenever white folks needed to avoid the unpleasantness in their own heads, Baldwin noted, they projected the "dark side" onto any available colored folks.

Reed shared Baldwin's feelings about psychic slumming; "I Wanna Be Black" does its best to force the issue. A rhythmically ragged blues fantasy, the song runs down the full litany of white Negro projections. Reed's persona imagines himself with "a big prick" and a "stable of foxy little whores." He fantasizes himself as Malcolm X casting a hex on President Kennedy's tomb, and then as Martin Luther King, tragically martyred. The main point, as Reed hammers home in a chorus complete with parody gospel response, is what he *doesn't* want to be: a "fucked-up middle-class college student." Himself. Blackness, for the white Negro, has no content other than what's already there in his own screwed-up head.

There's no doubt that Reed intended "I Wanna Be Black" as ironic commentary on white racism. The precise meaning of the irony, however, wasn't clear. Reed's relationship to the "I" in the song can be understood several different ways. You could hear it as an admission of guilt; in "Walk on the Wild Side," Reed had used an icily distant chorus of "colored girls" to symbolize life outside the straight world. But he had struggled to find his voice as a gay male in post-Stonewall New York, so he could legitimately claim his own blues knowledge of life in the shadows. But if Reed *didn't* share the guilt, "I Wanna Be Black" became a vicious attack on someone else's problems, delivered from a position of self-righteous moral superiority. The song hit hard, but it wasn't clear who was taking the punches.

The problems with "I Wanna Be Black," which are no doubt inseparable from its effectiveness, reflected more general patterns in the rock community of the late seventies. Outside of disco, musical communication across racial lines had almost stopped. The major currents of commercial rock and roll attracted an almost exclusively white audience. Record labels had discovered that rock could be truly big business. The sales of the most popular acts—Fleetwood Mac, Carole King, Kiss, the Eagles, Queen, Peter Frampton, Elton John—dwarfed those of their sixties predecessors. The marketing departments couldn't have cared less what the music sounded like as long as it sold. The conventional wisdom dictated that it was far more important to appeal to *everyone* in the white audience than to worry about the black record buyers, who once again found themselves listening to "their own" music pretty much among themselves. As Nelson George points out, the percentage of black acts on the pop charts steadily declined throughout the late seventies and almost all of the black acts who held their place were clearly identified with disco.

Punk rockers hated the whole mess. Equally nauseated by what they saw as the hypocritical sincerity of the hippies, the slick commercialization of the rock mainstream, and the brainless vapidity of the disco robots, the punks let loose a resounding scream of repugnance. English bands, most notably the Sex Pistols, had introduced punk to the masses as an anti-fashion statement based on the Ramones' abrasive lyrics, raw vocal delivery, and deliberately unpolished production style; many punks took fierce pride in *not* being able to play their instruments well. Picked up by downtown New York bands such as Television and the New York Dolls, punk rapidly and ironically became the center of its own strangely fashionable anti–Studio 54 scene centered on the Mudd Club and CBGBs. Like their English cousins, the American punks did their best to shock the mainstream audience. Sarcasm, alienation, and obscenity were the keynotes of the punk sensibility.

A few black Bohemians participated in the downtown scene, among them the brilliant painter Jean-Michel Basquiat, who played clarinet and synthesizer for "noise music" bands Channel 9, Test Pattern, and Gray between 1978 and 1980. In a classic case of white Negro hallucination, Basquiat was often described as a "primitive genius." In reality he had been raised in an economically secure, culturally aware home by his Haitian father and Puerto Rican mother. His mother had taken him to the opera and all of the major New York museums before he was ten. More intellectually polished than the vast majority of the downtown crowd, Basquiat carefully studied the work of the great modernist painters. At the same time, he listened to all sorts of Caribbean and African American music, developing an "Afro-Modernist" sensibility that made it difficult for him to find an audience capable of responding to his distinctly eclectic call.

The Mudd Club, where Basquiat was a regular, provided only a partial solution. His friend Fred Braithwaite, a black artist who provided him with contacts in the developing hip-hop scenes of Harlem and the South Bronx, described the downtown racial makeup: "The scene downtown was pretty much all white except for me, Jean-Michel, and a few other people." At times, Basquiat expressed his impatience with downtown's white aesthetic: "There's not enough black people downtown in this, whatever it is, pseudo-art bullshit." Still, he was willing to play the "pseudo-art" game well enough to become an art-world star, especially after his early work attracted the attention of Andy Warhol. The graffiti-style works Basquiat created on brick walls in lower Manhattan disturbed conventional notions of art's relation to its environment and shared more than a little of punk's iconoclastic attitude. Basquiat's sense of disruption, however, grew directly out of African American musical traditions that implied a vastly different attitude toward community. Specifically, Basquiat placed himself in the jazz tradition of his musical heroes, Jimi Hendrix and Charlie Parker. The point of his art, like theirs, was to transform the community, not to destroy it. Like theirs, Basquiat's work was only partially understood, and, like them, he died an early death.

Punk's failure to resist the growing racial divisions of the seventies—clearly reflected in its followers' inability to comprehend the jazz dimensions of Basquiat's work—resulted from a conscious repudiation of call and response. The rejection ran counter to every major form of black music. From gospel and soul to disco and funk, almost all black musicians shared a belief in the power of community. Even when they addressed the most alienating experiences, they sought an active dialogue, a back-and-forth between the individual and the community. Most of the time, no one was excluded. Although some notion of community lay near the heart of punk, it was a sense of community almost antithetical to gospel politics. Punk viewed supportive dialogue with extreme suspicion. When people agreed, it observed, it was usually because they were avoiding something or flat-out lying. Punk spit in its audience's face, sometimes literally. From a certain angle, you could see that as an act of love, an invitation to join in a community based on shared disgust over the mainstream. But, as Mick Jones of the Clash said in response to critic Lester Bangs's suggestion that "gobbing" might add to "the general atmosphere of chaos and anarchy": "No. It's fucking disgusting."

Still, music critic Greil Marcus insisted on the reality of the "secret yes the punk no has never banished," arguing that punk should be understood "as a force with the capacity to change, or simply momentarily redeem, a life that all unknowing was waiting for it." Bangs, who was without doubt the critic most closely attuned to the underlying energy of the movement, pursued a similar line of thought:

> You see, dear reader, so much of what's doled out as punk merely amounts to saying I suck, you suck, the world sucks, and who gives a damn—which is, er, ah, *insufficient.*
>
> Don't ask *me* why; I'm just an observer, really. But any observer could tell that, to put it in terms of Us vs. Them, saying the above is exactly what They want you to do, because it amounts to capitulation. It *is* unutterably boring and disheartening to try to find some fun or meaning while shoveling through all the shit we've been handed the last few years, but merely puking on yourself is not gonna change anything. (I know, 'cause I tried it.) I guess what it all boils down to is:
>
> (a) You can't like people who don't like themselves; and
>
> (b) You gotta like people who stand up for what they believe in, as long as what they believe in is
>
> (c) Righteous.

Repudiating the society that had spawned it, but unsure of just what righteous might mean, the punk audience was situated perfectly to understand what Reed was getting at in "I Wanna Be Black." The combination of intense interest in black culture and ironic self-awareness contributed to several interesting engagements with white Negroism. Poet turned punk rocker Patti Smith circled back obsessively to racial themes in "Rock n' Roll Nigger" and the "Radio Ethiopia Medley"; the art school refugees who came together as Talking Heads explored African rhythmic patterns; Brian Eno and David Byrne collaborated on a provocative postmodern soundscape in response to Nigerian novelist Amos Tutuola's *My Life in the Bush of Ghosts*. By 1980, when Talking Heads released their African-inflected *Remain in Light* album, however, they'd left the punk aesthetic almost entirely behind, as had Blondie, whose infectious hits "Rapture," "The Tide Is High," and "Heart of Glass" managed to split the difference between CBGBs and Studio 54.

None of the engagements with (a mostly symbolic) blackness changed the fact that punk and its offshoots had almost no appeal to black folks who weren't part of the scene. Part of it was the approach to call and response and part of it was simply the sound. At least in the early days, punk made amateurism an article of faith, part of an attempt to reclaim the music from the corporations who prized polish and competence above honesty and energy. Which was fine, conceptually. But for black audiences used to Clyde Stubblefield, Al Jackson, or Earl Young, the clatter and thrash of punk drumming bordered on painful. At times, you couldn't be sure if punk was striving for polyrhythms or if the drummer had simply lost control and knocked over the trap. And the drummers were usually better than the bass players. To be fair, punk's do-it-yourself aesthetic shared some principles with a black tradition that never over-valued formal training. But you'd never hear a soul or jazz musician say what Mick Jones said about punk: "It's not about getting the bloody chords right."

The singer-songwriters who distanced themselves from punk's grating sound and its contempt for the audience always got the chords right. But by and large, they were no more successful than their barbarian cousins in establishing an interracial dialogue. Several years before Byrne's African journey, Paul Simon had embarked on his own musical tour of the world. Expanding the soft rock sound he'd popularized with Simon & Garfunkel, whose first album includes folk revival versions of freedom movement standards "The

Times They Are A-Changin' " and "Go Tell It on the Mountain," he'd explored Latin rhythms on "Me and Julio down by the School- yard," gone to Jamaica for the reggae flavor of "Mother and Child Reunion," and sung with Ira Tucker's Dixie Hummingbirds on the hilariously uplifting blues "Love Me Like a Rock." On his *Live Rhymin'* album, Simon collaborated with both the South American group Urubamba and gospel's Jessy Dixon Singers. Simon's gospel version of "Bridge over Troubled Water" responds lovingly to Aretha Franklin's rendition of Simon & Garfunkel's ethereal classic. The only comparable moment in the dialogue between rock and pop came when the Staple Singers joined the Band, who demonstrated a deep feeling for gospel on "This Wheel's on Fire" and "I Shall Be Released," to perform "The Weight" on *The Last Waltz.* However much Simon or the Band might have reached out to black musicians and traditions, however, the black audience, if it was aware of them at all, seemed singularly unimpressed.

Jackson Browne didn't have any illusions about reaching a black audience, but his understanding of the reasons for the racial divi- sion reached close to the core of the problem. The cover photo on his masterpiece album *The Pretender* emphasizes Browne's whiteness in a more complex, darker America. Dressed in a blindingly white T- shirt, Browne walks across a busy city street filled with blacks, Asians, Latins, and a few people of indeterminate race. He knows what America actually looks like and he knows the dissonance between white folks and the world they're not quite living in. Although the album's title track makes no explicit reference to race, it cuts to the heart of the white problem. Stating his intention to flee the city— "I'm gonna rent myself a house in the shade of the freeway"— Browne bears witness to the erosion of the belief in love that en- abled white America to take a few tentative steps toward the beloved community during the sixties: "I want to know what became of the changes we waited for love to bring / Were they only the fitful dreams of some greater awakening?" His image of the ships bearing our dreams sailing out of sight echoes, perhaps consciously, the great black abolitionist Frederick Douglass's despair as he sat look- ing out over Baltimore Harbor, at the low point of his life, when he had resigned himself to slavery.

Browne doesn't pretend to have the answers. But he knows that the only hope lies in renewed faith. There's an ironic distance be- tween Browne and his character, but it's a gentle irony. Where "I Wanna Be Black" burns with punk contempt, "The Pretender" calls for the type of response based on a shared burden: "Are you there? Say a prayer for the pretender / who started out so young and strong only to surrender." It's the most moving elegy for the sixties imaginable. But it had little to say about what white folks needed if they were going to carry on the fight in the seventies.

# 40
# Rebellion or Revolution:
# Bruce Springsteen and the Clash

Bruce Springsteen and the Clash agreed on one thing: irony wasn't enough. Beyond that, the last of the great American romantics and the first of the political punks were about as different as white boys on the same side of the fight could be. Nothing could be further away from the young Springsteen's commitment to pure rock and roll energy than the slogan Joe Strummer chose for the mechanic's uniform he wore as a punk statement: "Passion is a Fashion."

There's a temptation to contrast Springsteen's quintessentially American rebellion with the Clash's commitment to revolution. Albert Camus observed that the rebel defines himself in opposition to an oppressive system but has no alternative in mind beyond self-assertion or the celebration of a rebel community, usually on the margins of society. The revolutionary, on the other hand, dedicates himself to overthrowing the corrupt system and replacing it with something better, usually shaped in accord with a well-defined political ideology. The difference, for Camus, involved more than politics. "The revolutionary must change the world," he wrote, "because he cannot change himself." That was the core issue for white rockers struggling to move beyond the racial impasse of the seventies. Do you start with your own experience, forging a life and voice responsive to the underlying calls of black music and history? Or do you first struggle to establish a new order, trusting that revolutionary changes in human behavior will follow?

Through the seventies, Springsteen gave an intimate intensity to the archetype of the rebel without a cause. Showing less than no interest in cool withdrawal or its first cousin, punk irony, Springsteen tore into "Rosalita" and "Born to Run" with a fierce passion that turned his concerts into celebrations of community. During the eighties and nineties, he would address political issues more directly. When he was starting out, however, his politics were almost entirely a matter of voice and presence. A blues politician who refused to give in to the growing divisions, he sang about a dying industrial economy where blacks and whites shared more than they seemed to realize. From "Incident on 57th Street" to "Jungleland," Springsteen populated his songs with a mixture of whites, blacks, and Latins that reflects street-level realities better than the black-and-white images of the world crowding the heads of both whites and blacks.

More important, Springsteen's sound testified to the cultural interaction he described. At a time when white rock was sounding whiter and black music was sounding blacker (with the crucial exception of George Clinton, who certainly wasn't sounding *less* black), Springsteen refused to surrender the populist energy of sixties rock and soul. Even an abridged list of the artists whose records Springsteen covered in concert gives a sense of his eclectic taste. Like every other rock and roller who came up in the sixties, he paid homage to rock's first interracial generation, performing Chuck Berry's "Around and Around," Buddy Holly's "Rave On," Elvis's "I Can't Help Falling in Love with You," and Little Richard's "Good Golly Miss Molly" and "Jenny Jenny" as part of the "Detroit Medley," a tribute to Mitch Ryder and the Detroit Wheels that also included "Devil with a Blue Dress." He covered British Invasion records by the artists who had carried that tradition into the sixties (Manfred Mann's "Pretty Flamingo," the Yardbirds' "Heart Full of Soul," the Searchers' "Needles and Pins"). He gave equal respect to soul, covering Sam Cooke's "Shake," the Temptations' "Ain't Too Proud to Beg," Jackie Wilson's "Higher and Higher," Solomon Burke's "Cry to Me," and Eddie Floyd's "Raise Your Hand" and "Knock on Wood," which he performed with Floyd at a Memphis concert in 1975. He paid tribute to Phil Spector and the girl groups with the Crystals' "Then He Kissed Me" and Darlene Love's "Fine Fine Boy."

Just about everyone who heard Springsteen perform live in the early days agrees that his seventies records—including the classics *Born to Run* and *Darkness on the Edge of Town*—provide only a pale reflection of what happened live. Every night—and he almost never had an off night—Springsteen created a sense of community that said no in thunder to what was happening in the outside world. Thinking back on the racial makeup of the scene around Asbury Park, Springsteen said: "There was racial tension, but it was also a place where people mixed. I walked into the Upstage and saw [black pianist] David Sancious. I met [black sax player] Clarence [Clemons] here. We had one of the first integrated bands in rock music—that was something that grew up around Asbury Park." Including Sancious and Clemons, along with Latin drummer Vini "Mad Dog" Lopez, Springsteen's band was even more diverse than the crowds they played for at the beach clubs, which were mostly white, but always included what one black veteran of the scene called "a handful or two of brothers." Clemons's saxophone would have fit in perfectly with the Memphis Horns; Springsteen's vocals reached deep down into the gospel moan, summoning up the spirit of Marion Williams as passed down through her sometimes straying spiritual son Little Richard.

Springsteen's sense of community began with the inner circle of Jersey shoreline musicians. On the liner notes to Southside Johnny and the Asbury Jukes' *I Don't Want to Go Home* (for which he wrote several soul-based songs), Springsteen paid tribute to the guys who didn't make it: Big Danny, Fast Eddie Larachi and his brother Little John, Margaret and the Distractions, Black Tiny and White Tiny. Every rock and roll scene has them and I would add the names of Terry Gonzalez and Jim Allen to Springsteen's list; add your own if you'd like. Like the Asbury Parkers, their names, as Bruce wrote,

> should be spoken in reverence at least once, not 'cause they were great musicians (truth is, some of them couldn't play nothin' at all) but because they were each in their own way a living spirit of what to me, rock and roll is all about. It was music as survival and they lived it down in their souls, night after night. These guys were their own heroes and they never forgot.

Springsteen knew that the power of rock and roll didn't come from the stars, but from the people—musicians and audiences—who turned to it for the strength to go on, for blues reaffirmation. If you didn't have the energy to get up and face tomorrow, you could forget about anything else. Even before he began to deepen his knowledge of American history and incorporate a broader perspective in *The River* and *Nebraska,* Springsteen understood his music as a contribution to the community that made it possible:

I write a lot about action moments, moments when people are pushed to take a certain action, to do something, to do anything to get out of their present situation or circumstances or predicament—to step out, to get out of that boring thing, to break loose. And I think there's a certain romanticism and a certain kind of everyday heroism that is inherent in this. It's something that is very real to me.

During the seventies, Springsteen communicated clearly to his audience that the world he imagined into reality each night from the stage was as much about them as him. It was as far away from the neomilitaristic rituals of Kiss, who called their fan club their "army," or the punk contempt of the Ramones as you could imagine. Springsteen kept the tradition of call and response alive in white music. And he paid homage to the ancestors. The hilariously energetic set piece "Prisoner of Rock 'n' Roll"—one of the high points of his early concerts—pays tribute to James Brown's impact on Springsteen's performance style. The hardest-working man in rock and roll—JB never relinquished claim to his show business championship—Springsteen collapsed in mock exhaustion near the end of his three- or four-hour concerts. As Clarence and Miami Steve Van Zandt worked feverishly to revive him, Springsteen would raise his head, peering out in amazement at the world around him, before exploding back to life. The audience went with him all the way. It was the age-old blues solution to the existential dilemma. Reaffirm the power of life. The system may try to do you in. But it isn't going to win.

Which from a punk perspective was both precisely the point and a lot of bollocks. While both the Manhattan and London punk scenes subscribed to their own ideas of community, both viewed the romantic idealism at the center of Springsteen's vision as a lie. The sixties had failed. Rock and roll had become another product. As the Clash phrased it on the chorus of "1977": "No Elvis, Beatles or the Rolling Stones / In 1977." Strummer put it even more succinctly on the legend of a shirt he wore in late 1976: "CHUCK BERRY IS DEAD."

The English punks had an even worse problem with call and response than their American cousins at CBGBs. The creative forces behind the Clash, Strummer and Mick Jones, had been heavily influenced by sixties British bands who traced their roots to American blues or R & B. When punk emerged from the underground in 1976 and 1977, it directed its most vituperative attacks against the older rockers who had sold the music into corporate bondage. Distancing themselves as far as possible from their ancestors, the punks faced the very real problem of where to go next.

It was the classic rebel problem. In a 1976 interview, Strummer attacked bands and audiences who used music for enjoyment, saying: "Look, the situation is far too serious for enjoyment, man." Jones seconded him: "If you wanna fuckin' enjoy yourselves, you sit in an armchair and watch TV, but if you wanna get actively involved, rock-'n'roll's about rebellion." In an article published in the influential British music magazine *Melody Maker*, Caroline Coon introduced the Clash to the world beneath the headline "Punk rock: rebels against the system?" Alongside Coon's article, which answered the question with a resounding yes, *Melody Maker* ran a counterpoint piece titled "But does nihilism constitute revolt?"

Judging by their continued reliance on juvenile gestures designed to infuriate the middle class, most punks didn't care. The movement's generic commitment to rebellion resulted in numerous flirtations with Nazi imagery and the right-wing National Front, an extreme expression of the reactionary movement that swept Margaret Thatcher into the prime minister's office. Disgusted with punk's flirtation with fascism, frequently expressed through racially motivated attacks on nonwhite immigrants, the Clash attempted to move from rebellion to revolution. Their homegrown revolutionary ideology frequently hints at Marxist affinities; *Sandinista!* honors the Nicaraguan revolutionaries who overthrew the corrupt Somoza regime, while "Washington Bullets" condemns the U.S.–backed overthrow of Salvador Allende's democratically elected Marxist government in Chile. Especially when yet another Strummer shirt slogan seemingly endorsed the Red Brigade, the most extreme of Italy's communist terrorist groups, the Clash acquired a reputation as a supporter of socialist revolution. But neither Jones nor Strummer, whose teenage heroes included Woody Guthrie, seemed to have much interest in or knowledge of political theory of any sort. When a roadie asked him what the "Brigade Rossi" on his shirt meant, Strummer joked, "It's a pizza place."

The Clash did, however, have a sharp sense of street politics. In the London of the seventies, that involved a much higher awareness of race than it had in the fifties, when the Beatles, Animals, and Rolling Stones encountered blacks primarily through imported records. The nonwhite population of London increased dramatically during the sixties. As in the United States, colored populations tended to cluster together and to occupy the lower rungs of the socioeconomic ladder. Nowhere was that clearer than in the public school system, where, in some areas, enrollments were as high as 90 percent black. The demographic changes affected the members of the Clash in different ways. Although he downplayed his relatively comfortable economic origins, Mick Jones attended an essentially all-white grammar school next door to a comprehensive school that was nearly all black. As a childhood friend of Jones's told Clash biographer Marcus Gray: "We were like a plantation, almost. We inherited this 'They're the white kids, let's kill them' sort of thing. Every Friday they used to gather outside the school. Really heavy. We had to run the gauntlet." One member of the Clash, bassist Paul Simonon, experienced the scene from an entirely different angle as one of the ten percent of white students at a majority black school. There, he was caught up in the white working-class skinhead movement, whose members often indulged in "Paki-bashing" (attacking "colored" South Asian immigrants) and provided an ideal recruiting base for English fascists.

Whatever their angle of vision, the members of the Clash all came into direct contact with the music that would help them escape the impasse of punk's anti-ancestral stance: Jamaican reggae. When Simonon was in school, the most popular music among both blacks and skinheads was "ska," a precursor of the more familiar reggae popularized by Bob Marley and Toots and the Maytals. Gray provides a succinct overview of the musical history that had led punk away from its black roots:

> If Sixties punk rock was an American version of a British version of American R&B, then Seventies punk rock was a British version of *that*. Whatever the tangled web of its genealogy, in both its Sixties and Seventies guises punk was an almost exclusively white musical form, so far removed from its roots in the blues that nearly all the black influence had been lost: it was noisy, uptight and aggressive, the very antithesis of funky.

For anyone even pretending to think seriously about revolution in either Thatcher's England or pre-Reagan America, the lack of a shared black/white language presented some serious problems.

More than any other British punk band, the Clash confronted the racial problem in ways that had deep implications for American rockers. They began by dealing honestly with the fact that they were, after all, a *white* band. There was a tinge of white Negroism in Mick Jones's comment, "We know the blacks've got their thing sewn up. They've got their own culture, but the young white kids don't have nothing." The group's name may have been derived from the title of Culture's classic reggae album *Two Sevens Clash*, a prediction of apocalypse in the year 1977. Clearly, the band sought to associate itself with black revolutionary energy.

But the Clash's first songs addressing race resisted the escapist temptation. Both "White Riot" and "White Man in Hammersmith Palais" grew out of Strummer's personal experiences in black cultural settings. In August 1976, he had gone to the Notting Hill Carnival, a street festival organized by London's inner-city West Indian community. An incident involving the police and a young black man set off a full-scale riot that resulted in sixty arrests and 450 injuries. Considering the revolutionary potential of the anger unleashed at Notting Hill, Strummer wrote what he thought of as a call to whites to join in the revolution. Because punk as a whole had failed to distance itself from the National Front, however, many listeners heard "White Riot" as its evil opposite: a call on whites to strike back.

By the time the group released Strummer's second major racial statement, "White Man in Hammersmith Palais," the band's political persona was deeply enough established to make similar confusion unlikely. One of the most honest blues dealing with white presence in black cultural settings, "White Man in Hammersmith Palais" was written after Strummer attended an all-night reggae show headlined by Dillinger. Disappointed in the music, Strummer found himself watching a scene of racial chaos where "black sticksmen were running around trying to snatch these white girls' handbags." Strummer understood the lack of unity as a call for increased political awareness. "I was trying to talk about revolution, and how we weren't ever going to have one, because who had an answer to the British Army?" he recalled. "I was really getting at the division between the black rebels and the white rebels, and the fact that we gotta have some unity or we're just going to get stomped on." The song he wrote after the experience, however, focuses specifically on the potential pitfalls of white Negroism and culminates in an angry tirade against those who "think it's funny / turning revolution into money."

The Clash's strongest calls for racial unity came in the songs that had least in common with the hardcore punk scene, especially those that engaged in a direct call and response with reggae. They covered a number of reggae songs including Toots and the Maytals' "Pressure Drop," the Rulers' "Wrong 'Em, Boyo," and, most important, Junior Murvin's "Police and Thieves." Sung in a pleading falsetto reminiscent of Curtis Mayfield, Murvin's original was a moving lament over the strife that rendered Jamaica a nightmare of violence in the seventies. Classic gospel call and response, it sounded a deeply felt plea for the community to come back together. Attacking the chords and hammering the rhythms Murvin's producer Lee Perry understated, the Clash transformed "Police and Thieves" into an angry blues. They attacked the complacency of the audience willing to turn revolution into money and refused to play the game.

The Clash continued to experiment with reggae over the next few years, especially on the sides produced by Mikey Dread and the "dub" experiments included on the *Sandinista!* album. But the real impact of their dialogue with reggae came through most strongly on their masterpiece, *London Calling*. In place of the confrontational, alienating sound of their first two albums, *London Calling* returned to the rock and soul roots the punk ideology rejected. From the first notes of the title cut, which opens the album with an apocalyptic vision of nuclear destruction, the album demands a response from beyond the choir. The Clash mix reggae rockers ("Rudie Can't Fail"), social satire ("Lost in the Supermarket"), and calls for political action ("Clampdown," "The Guns of Brixton") with anthems that wouldn't have been out of place at a Springsteen concert ("Death or Glory," "Revolution Rock"). Although the core punk audience viewed the album as a betrayal—a sellout to popularity—it deserves its reputation as one of the best dozen or so rock albums.

No one answered the Clash's revolutionary call. Part of the problem was inherent in the call itself. While they felt a need to move beyond rebellion, especially in its London punk forms, Strummer and Jones never really decided what the new world they wanted might look like. In the end, their solution sounded surprisingly like Springsteen's. Be honest about who you are; ignore the divisions imposed by those in power; reach out to the people whose burdens you share. It was a vision with few undertones of white Negroism. As critic Lester Bangs observed, "Somewhere in their assimilation of reggae is the closest thing yet to the lost chord, the missing link between black and white noise, rock capable of making a bow to black forms without smearing on the blackface." It was a fitting tribute that Bob Marley wrote "Punky Reggae Party" after he heard the Clash's version of "Police and Thieves." "Listen, punk love reggae,"

Marley said, "and some a dem seh things that Babylon no like. I thought dem was badness first, but now me give dem nine hundred percent right. Dem resist the society and seh, 'Me a punk cos I don't want you to shove me where I don't like it.' Because him nuh feel like we inferior—white man feel inferior to the black man, that's why him try kill the black man. And the punk seh, 'No! We wanna join wit the Rastaman and get something outta life.' "

# 41
# P-Funkentelechy

George Clinton thought the whole thing about splitting up into warring camps—black and white, straight and gay, male and female—was pretty damn silly. "Who says a jazz band can't play dance music?" he sang, following up immediately with the corollaries "Who says a rock band can't play funk music? Who says a funk band can't play rock music?" Backed up by a cast of thousands, Clinton's funky dance band Parliament and his equally funky rock band Funkadelic provided the most convincing answer imaginable. Mixing the catchy rhythms and infectious hooks Clinton picked up working as a staff writer for Motown with the nastiest, loudest guitar this side of Jimi Hendrix, the overlapping bands gathered together in the Parliament-Funkadelic clan kept the jazz faith as the resegregating seventies staggered to an end.

Guitarist James Blood Ulmer had it right when he said, "Jazz is the teacher, funk is the preacher." Or, as Clinton phrased it in the title of a Funkadelic album, "Free Your Mind and Your Ass Will Follow." To make sure the congregation didn't wander off in the middle of the sermon, P-Funk kept everything grounded in bass grooves that got the dead to dancing. With Bootsy Collins's monster bass and Bernie Worrell's outer-space keyboard and synthesizer lines leading the way, P-Funk laid down dozens of classic dance floor rhythms: "Up for the Down Stroke," "Standing on the Verge of Getting It On," "P Funk (Wants to Get Funked Up)," "Give Up the Funk (Tear the Roof Off the Sucker)," "Bop Gun," and the immortal "Flash Light."

A blues jester who dressed in space suits, cowboy outfits, giant baby diapers, and, occasionally, nothing at all, Clinton understood the symbiosis of jazz speculation and funk groove: "The rhythm is so hip that it can complement all that intellectual shit that's been going on, which is cool to a point. But first we have to put some rhythm in it, and then later on we can add some metafoolishness, too—like the Chinese and the Indian." Reconstituting cultural bits and pieces like a mad scientist run amok in the studio—one of his personas was the genius Dr. Funkenstein—Clinton took the classic jazz impulse angle on what multiculturalism was all about: "Everybody got somethin'— they probably all into the same place—but no one people has the power to do all that is needed to be done, like lead a planet. I think that when all that shit just gets together in an orgy, really mingles, you'll find out what are the best possible answers to all of our problems. I mean that's *my* chess game."

Nobody ever played it better. During its marathon live performances, P-Funk kept the bass line going without interruption for hours on end. In part because Clinton had learned the musical value of pure volume while backing up acid rockers Vanilla Fudge— "we became the loudest black band in the world, the Temptations on acid"—no one resisted for long. Raising the ante on the extravagant rock shows of Kiss, Queen, and David Bowie, P-Funk's "Mothership Tour" set a standard for multimedia music performance that's certainly never been surpassed. The spaceship prop that descended at the beginning of the show billowing smoke metamorphosed into a cosmic playground for the dozens of singers, instrumentalists, and all-purpose funkateers that moved on and off the stage, blurring the lines between audience and performers.

Once they had the bodies moving, P-Funk seized the opportunity to comment on everything from politics and pop culture to the theory of relativity. It was enough to make black cultural critic Greg Tate dream of "a populist black poststructuralism" based on the "war and peacetime use of the fusion funkbomb Einstein Clinton's theorems made possible." Most of P-Funk's direct political commentary appeared on Funkadelic albums, which frequently took their titles from the hardest-edge cut: *Maggot Brain, America Eats Its Young, Cosmic Slop.* Clinton felt special empathy for precisely the people who had come under attack as examples of the "culture of poverty." One of Funkadelic's most compassionate songs, "Cosmic Slop" focuses on a prostitute trying to shield her children from the blues world that condemns her and them. As Clinton told Living

Colour guitarist Vernon Reid, "See, you're a damn fool if you see somebody starving and poor and you think they should just stay starving and poor and not take care of them. . . . And if I got some little bit of money and I ain't making sure that you got some, I'm a damn fool if I don't expect you to come and try to take it. It's not as easy as each person is responsible for being in their predicament."

If Funkadelic kept up a conversation with a Black Power movement which had moved on to the realm of the ancestors, Parliament envisioned a more fundamental change. Clinton understood the problems with the either/or approach shared by mainstream politicians and their "revolutionary" doubles. From Clinton's perspective, *any* approach that divided the world into comfortable little categories needed serious rethinking. On the great concept albums released by Parliament—*Mothership Connection, Funkentelechy vs. the Placebo Syndrome,* and *The Motor-Booty Affair*—Clinton sheds his "metafoolish" cocoon and emerges a high-order (if no less metafoolish) philosopher of funkentelechy.

The dictionary definition of *entelechy* reads "the realization of form-giving cause as contrasted with potential existence." And if that ain't funky, nothing is. The relationship between cause, form, and possibility sounds the major themes of the jazz impulse. We're always taking form and the form we take was caused by something. The question is: How much freedom do we have to alter the form we become? Can we change our own future, or is the path laid out for us by form givers in advance?

Each of the concept albums mixes up a funny and fascinating cast of characters including Rumpofsteelskin, Sir Nose D'Voidoffunk, Mr. Wiggles, and the Star Child, who get down in a cosmic chess match in which Grandmaster Clinton beats the binary at its own game. Clinton most definitely plays the black pieces, although he shares James Baldwin's sense of "blackness" as an approach to life rather than a color of skin. The "white" pieces represent a frowning, judgmental, static, uptight, nondancing, unfunky world. In short, "reality." The "other" side really isn't. It isn't "real" in any simple sense and it isn't "other" in any sense at all. Clinton's vision of funkentelechy recognizes the funk as the fundamental principle of being, the source of the forms we become. That's partly about sex, without which we just flat ain't here. (Although Clinton knows the clones are coming, and he's determined to get them up for the downstroke too.) But it's also about possibility, play, the jazz world where things keep changing inside the changes. There are all sorts of Atomic Dogs creeping around trading licks with whoever's licking. Ain't nothin' but a party. Free your ass and your mind will follow.

Clinton refuses to respond to the either/or system in or/either terms. The white folks think Freudian; it's all about conflict, fathers killing sons, accumulating shit, as he points out in "Doo Doo Chasers." The black thang's Jungian; it's about the search for integration, reconciliation with the mother and father, getting past the lines that divide the world in two. P-Funk mini-epics overflow with images of psychic unity: spaceships, the lost continent of Atlantis. Everybody's invited on board the Mothership. Doesn't mean they're going to get on board, but that's their call. Never getting too far away from the beat, P-Funk's vision of redemption incorporates encyclopedias of cultural references and in-jokes, as in "Aqua Boogie" from *The Motor-Booty Affair*. The subtitle is "A Psychoalphadisco-betabioaquadoloop" which, if you take it apart, articulates a theory of musical neurophysics or physio neuromusicology. Or something. Clinton weaves in references to different types of brain waves—the alpha and the beta—with mind/body references: psycho for thinking, disco for dancing. You think and you dance and you get *all* of your brain operating, let the energies flow across the mind/body barrier and you'll find yourself in places you didn't even know were there. It's the key to life. And you don't just do it to get it over with. When you get to the end, you do it again. It's a computer do-loop like the one Clinton celebrates in "Loopzilla." Almost alone among male-led musical groups, P-Funk plays with a feminine sexual energy. It isn't about reaching a climax and moving on; it's about building it up, relaxing, riding the wave, climaxing, and doing it all some more. It's healing and it's fun. When it's all working right, as Clinton sings in "Aqua Boogie," "You can dance under water and not get wet." Because, after all, water's a form of matter and matter, on the subatomic and intergalactic levels, is mostly nothing at all.

You can keep associating off of and into P-Funk songs more or less forever. Instruments and voices leave and enter unpredictably; the cast of musicians changed but the crew kept the mothership aloft. The unlimited sense of possibility released by P-Funk's music—the best answer to the rigidity of the seventies—reflects the absolute openness of Clinton's process. As the Grandmaster said: "This is the type of thing they say can't be done; too much ego or somethin' like that. But I don't care whose record it appears on, or what label. Don't make no difference to me. What counts is that every time someone plugs in, it helps the nation. That's what the Mothership Connection is all about—connecting all those people who've been disconnected." One Nation Under a Groove.

# 42
# Redemption Songs:
# Bob Marley in Babylon

"Music is music," said Bob Marley. "It heals the scars." Fully aware of the Babylonian devils inflicting the scars on the community he called "I and I," Marley's music testifies, above all else, to the redemptive power of Jah, the Rastafarian God. Nowhere does the message shine through more clearly than in "One Love," Marley's reworking of the Impressions' "People Get Ready." His voice perfectly complementing the bass-heavy music he described as "a happy rhythm with a sad sound with a good vibration," Marley sings: "One love, one heart, let's get together and feel all right." Like the gospel soul music of the early and mid-sixties, Marley maintained an unswerving commitment to the specific struggles of the poor black people whose blues he shared. Like gospel soul, he saw no contradiction between that commitment and his all-encompassing understanding of "Jah love." "The god who mek I and I," said Marley, "him create technicolor people."

The family resemblance between reggae and black American soul wasn't coincidental. Like his friends in the rural Jamaican countryside and the ghettos surrounding Kingston, Marley grew up listening to black American music on WINZ and WGBS, the powerful Miami radio stations that blanketed the Caribbean with sounds excluded from the government-controlled radio stations on the islands. When asked to name the music that had made the deepest impression on him as a youth, Marley testified to his love for the Drifters, Stevie Wonder, Marvin Gaye, and Curtis Mayfield. As "One Love/People Get Ready" suggests, the Wailers' closest affinity may be with Mayfield's Impressions. Working with legendary reggae producer Lee "Scratch" Perry, Marley and fellow Wailers Peter Tosh and

Bunny Livingston (a.k.a. Bunny Wailer) merged their distinctive voices in a three-part harmony that perfectly expressed "I and I."

If reggae and soul spoke a common language, their dialects differed. Marley shared a specific vocabulary—derived from the Jamaican vernacular and the Rastafarian religion—with other reggae musicians: the Mighty Diamonds, Jimmy Cliff, the Melodians, the Heptones, Burning Spear, and Ras Michael and the Sons of Negus. Some of the concepts—"downpression" or "Jah love"—are relatively easy to comprehend for anyone who gets past the initial barrier of the Jamaican accent, which at first listen seems impenetrable to ears accustomed to hearing Boston, Memphis, or Nebraska as "normal." Like soul, reggae combines elements of gospel and the blues; many of the unfamiliar terms point to either the brutal experience or the goal of redemption.

Another set of reggae terms, however, points to the specific spiritual and political geography of Rastafarianism. The roots of Rastafarianism extend back to the early thirties, when Ras (a designation for a member of the Ethiopian aristocracy) Tafari was crowned emperor (or Negus) of Ethiopia. Assuming the name Haile Selassie ("Mighty of the Trinity"), Ras Tafari was also known by the traditional titles of "King of Kings" and "Lion of the Tribe of Judah," the latter placing him in the succession of King Solomon. Early Rastafarian leaders such as Leonard Howell and Joseph Hibbert hailed Selassie's ascendancy as the fulfillment of the prophecy of Psalms 68:31: "Princes shall come out of Egypt; Ethiopia shall soon stretch out her hands unto God." Disaffected from the British colonial rulers, the Rastafarians modeled themselves partly on the "Maroons," communities of fugitive slaves who eluded capture by establishing strongholds in the Jamaican mountains. By 1940, Howell had established the Pinnacle community, where many of the practices associated with Rastafarianism—the use of ganja (marijuana) as a sacrament, the wearing of dreadlocks—took shape.

During the early fifties, increasing police harassment of Pinnacle forced most Rastafarians to relocate to Kingston. Many located in "Back-o-Wall" or "Shanty Town," both important areas in the growth of reggae. By 1962, when Jamaica gained its independence from England, Rastafarians had held their first large-scale meetings, called *Grounation* or *Nyabangi*. A jointly held spiritual vision more than a church in a traditional Western sense, Rastafarianism took root among the poorest segments of Jamaican society and, not surprisingly, was viewed by the new ruling elites as a political threat.

Part of the reason for the government's uneasiness about Rastafarianism had to do with the movement's celebration of black nationalist leader Marcus Garvey as a hero second only to Haile Selassie. Born in Jamaica in 1887, Garvey had founded a pan-Africanist organization, the Universal Negro Improvement Association in 1914, shortly before he departed for the United States in hopes of visiting Booker T. Washington, whom he viewed as a model of black self-sufficiency. Although Washington died before Garvey could meet him, Garvey soon built the UNIA into a black political organization with unprecedented popular support. The core of Garvey's appeal was simple. "The world has made being black a crime," he wrote. "I hope to make it a virtue." Although trustworthy numbers are difficult to find, Garvey's movement probably attracted more supporters than SNCC, the SCLC, and the NAACP combined. Those surprised at the popularity of Louis Farrakhan and nostalgic for Martin Luther King should take careful note of the enduring appeal of Garveyism. The historical rhythm in black political life between optimism and despair all too clearly gives the stronger hand to the latter. Anticipating the attacks of the Jamaican authorities on his spiritual descendants, Garvey was subjected to intense harassment by U.S. authorities. Ultimately he was convicted of tax fraud—on very doubtful evidence—and deported to London, where he died in 1940.

Much of reggae's specific vocabulary relates directly to Haile Selassie and Garvey. The reggae group Burning Spear, named after the battle name of African independence leader Jomo Kenyatta, employed a near-chanting style derived from the *Nyabangi* ceremonies on "Marcus Garvey," the centerpiece of a powerful album dedicated to fulfilling the leader's vision. In "Worth His Weight in Gold," Steel Pulse urges its listeners to heed "Sir Marcus" 's words and rally around the UNIA colors of black, green, and gold. Garvey's Black Star Line steamship company—financed by sales of stock to ordinary black people—provides a symbol of the escape from captivity in Babylon and the return to the African motherland. Although Garvey seems to have conceived of his rallying cry—"Back to Africa!"—as a mixture of spiritual metaphor and political slogan, many of his followers took the image literally.

The centrality of Africa in reggae was the primary difference between the soul music of the sixties and seventies and the reggae of the same period. As long as black Americans and black Jamaicans focused on the hardships of daily life, the visions ran close together. As

Marley observed, the Wailers' name pointed to the shared realities of the blues: "Name Wailers come from the Bible. There's plenty places you meet up with weeping and wailing. Children always wail y'know, cryin' out for justice."

Making relatively little mention of the religious dimensions of reggae, the first reggae album to make a major impact on American listeners was the sound track to the 1973 film *The Harder They Come*, which succeeded in part because its basic story parallels that of blaxploitation movies such as *Shaft* and *Superfly*. A struggling black man from the ghetto, in this case a reggae musician played by Jimmy Cliff, rises to the stature of legendary outlaw hero. Cliff's "Sitting in Limbo" and the title song, along with the Maytals' "Pressure Drop," portray the brutal realities of life in "Babylon" in terms that would have been familiar to residents of America's Chocolate Cities.

The gospel-oriented songs on *The Harder They Come*, Cliff's "You Can Get It If You Really Want" and the Melodians' gorgeous "By the Rivers of Babylon," reflect the difference between soul and reggae's understanding of the path to redemption. When the Melodians ask, "How can we sing our holy song in a strange land?" they emphasize the Rastafarian belief that Babylon—whether Jamaica, London, or the United States—is not and cannot be a home. Black cultural critic Judylyn Ryan, who was born in Trinidad, explains the emphasis on Africa in black Caribbean culture as an expansion of Robert Stepto's ideas of ascent and immersion. Ryan points out that the ascent-immersion pattern implies that black experience *begins* in slavery, in the "symbolic South." Individuals who make the ascent have no choice but to live in Babylon; their financial success comes at the risk of spiritual death. For Ryan, immersion—the return to the roots of one's family and culture—offers at best a partial solution. Immersion takes one back to the symbolic South, where one again confronts the realities of, to use the Rasta term for the combination of psychological and economic exploitation, downpression. Worse, the ascent-immersion approach offers nowhere to go other than the symbolic North, which has already been proved wanting.

The solution, for Ryan and Bob Marley, lies in understanding the central importance of the "symbolic East," Africa. The story begins with a wholesome African culture; Marley's references to the "Congo Bongo Man" and "Congo Bongo I" affirm an African self which has never accepted Babylon as anything other than a place of exile. The first movement in black culture is not from South to

North but from East to West, through the Middle Passage. Ryan refers to the movement west as a "dispersion" of blacks from their homeland. The symbolic West—the place of exile—and the symbolic South—the place of slavery—are the same place. What's different is the self-understanding of the black people living there. Are you an exile or are you a slave? The answer determines your options for life today and life in the future. For Marley, the answer is obvious: Jah's people are in exile and must, certainly spiritually and preferably physically, return to the motherland. Ryan calls the movement from West back to East *recuperation*. Or, as Afrocentric rappers X Clan phrased it in the title to their first album, *To the East, Blackwards*.

The Wailers' epic "Exodus" provides a sense of what the journey might feel like. Grounded in the rhythm section of brothers Aston "Familyman" (bass) and Carlton (drums) Barrett, the cut pounds through seven and a half minutes of surging polyrhythm, driven by Junior Marvin's ferocious lead guitar. Marley's words can be heard as "we're leaving Babylon" or as "we live in Babylon." Either way, the point is precisely the need for change. The crucial question is the most basic: "Are you satisfied with the life you're living?" And the answer is equally clear. Calling on his people to leave Babylon and return to "our father's land," Marley cries out, "Move!" The voices and instruments swell in response.

The battle against Babylon occupied Marley's consciousness up to the moment of his tragic death from lung cancer and a brain tumor at age thirty-six in 1981. Many of his most powerful songs cry out against the downpressors. Marley's first internationally marketed album, *Catch a Fire*, opens with the blues sequence of "Concrete Jungle," "Slave Driver," and "400 Years," the period of black exile in Babylon. Although Marley repudiated politics (in the electoral sense) as "Devil business," he spoke clearly and forcefully in the tones of an Old Testament prophet: "Like Jah say, the West must perish. It's Devil's country all right. Devils are real people and capitalism and penalism a type of devilism and Draculazing. It's Devil controlling, Devil running part of the earth while God is in Africa waiting for we to agree that there's Devil running this."

Without question, however, Marley's worldwide impact derived from the positive vibration released by the many songs dedicated to his vision of redemption. Of all Marley's albums, *Kaya* is rooted most deeply in the mellow feelings of love, sunshine, and the sense of spiritual well-being offered by ganja. Although white listeners in the West sometimes trivialized the role of marijuana in reggae and seized on the music as an excuse for getting high, Rastafarians understood smoking "herb" as a sacramental action based on Genesis 1:12 and Psalms 104:14, which reads, "He causeth the grass to grow for the cattle, and herb for the service of man." One of Marley's most beautiful love songs, "No Woman No Cry," passes through the hardships of Trench Town, the Kingston ghetto where Marley lived, and into the kind of peace evoked by Toots and the Maytals' "Spiritual Healing," a cover of Marvin Gaye's "Sexual Healing."

While he valued the moments of oneness with Jah and his people, Marley knew that such moments required deep struggle. On the *Natty Dread* album that established him as an international star, "No Woman No Cry" is followed by "Them Belly Full (But We Hungry)" and "Rebel Music (Three O'Clock Road Block)," two of his angriest attacks on the Devils who gorge themselves while the downpressed starve. The title cut reiterates Marley's identification with the exiled hero struggling to release his people from their captivity: "Dread natty dread now dreadlock congo bongo I / Natty dreadlock in a Babylon / dreadlock congo bongo I." Marley conducts a recuperative tour of the ghetto streets, calling his people to follow Natty Dread back to the roots.

In "Redemption Song," Marley demonstrates the difference between journeys to the roots that begin in the symbolic South and those that begin in the symbolic West. Like Alex Haley and the O'Jays in "Ship Ahoy," he acknowledges the reality of slavery: "Old Pirates yes they rob I," he sings, "Sold I to the merchant ships." But Marley has little interest in Haley's celebration of ascent, which, from a Rastafarian perspective, amounts to little more than a picnic in Babylon. Rather, Marley sings, the challenge is to throw off the chains, beginning with the ones that constrain our minds. "Free yourself from mental slavery," he sings. "None but ourselves can free our minds."

For Marley, mental liberation comes through acceptance of Jah, who reveals the deviltry at the heart of white supremacy: "Reggae can't do anything on its own," he said. "God say: until the philosophy which places one race superior and another inferior is permanently discredited and abandoned, then we won't have no peace." The inner meaning of recuperation, the return to Africa, derives not from a physical journey, but from the transformation of our spiritual lives. As Marley said, "Ya cyaan [can't] return to the roots, you must be the roots. Guy think he can return to the roots when he was a leaf, he drop off and that how he return to the roots. We must be the roots."

# 43
# The Message:
# Hip-hop and the South Bronx

In 1979, the South Bronx, the most destitute corner of Babylon, looked like ground zero. Burned-out buildings surrounded by heaps of rubble dotted the landscape. Although things would get worse in the eighties, drug addiction, unemployment, and violence created an environment in which the idea of life as a series of brutal experiences made way too much sense. So it's not surprising that the South Bronx gave birth to the most powerful expression of the blues impulse since Muddy Waters and the transplanted Delta bluesmen plugged in their guitars on the South Side of Chicago. The first generation of hip-hop DJs and rappers knew the blues and they believed in the power of music. For a long time, it didn't look like anyone outside the projects gave a damn.

At one point, New York City commissioned paintings of cheerful airy environments for the sides of South Bronx projects facing the Cross-Bronx Expressway. Presumably commuters driving to work would accept the reassuring images and go on with their lives without giving a thought to what actually went on inside those buildings. Like Chicago's Black Belt, the South Bronx was profoundly isolated from mainstream America. There was, however, a crucial difference between the Chicago of the late forties and the South Bronx of the mid-seventies. Most of the migrants from the South came to Chicago for work. The economy of the seventies rendered dreams of economic advancement less and less realistic. Combined with the demographic shifts that made the area a case study of social isolation, the collapse of New York's industrial economy transformed the South Bronx into an emblem of urban despair.

Although some commentators persist in attributing the rise of rap to Reaganism, pioneer DJs Afrika Bambaata, DJ Kool Herc, and Grandmaster Flash had already established the music's fundamental

characteristics by about 1976. As far as the South Bronx was concerned, Reagan's Republicans and Carter's Democrats amounted to
pretty much the same thing. By the end of the seventies, residents of
the area had taken up referring to it as "Vietnam." It's not at all surprising that, as the eighties wore on, more and more rappers would
explore the possibilities of separatist politics.

Two connected, but distinct, genealogies came together in hip-hop,
one involving the rapper (the performer who spoke the words), the
other the DJ (the one who mixed the music). Rapping really wasn't
anything new in black culture. African Americans had been playing
the dozens—engaging in verbal duels—for decades, if not centuries.
Creatively reconstructing the actual speech of rural blacks during the
1920s, Zora Neale Hurston's 1935 book *Mules and Men* reads like a
guidebook on rap techniques. Various commentators have pointed to
Memphis radio DJs, Chuck Berry, and Isaac Hayes's spoken introduction to "By the Time I Get to Phoenix" as rap precursors. Afrika Bambaata provided a list of sources including African call-and-response
music, the dozens, Cab Calloway's "Minnie the Moocher," the Last
Poets, Muhammad Ali, Shirley Ellis's "The Name Game," comedian
Pigmeat Markham, the political speeches of Malcolm X and Louis Farrakhan, and the Jamaican tradition of "toasting."

The Jamaican connection played an even more important role in
the development of hip-hop DJ'ing. The most immediate precursors
of the DJ crews were the "sound systems" that developed in Jamaica
in response to the government-sponsored radio station's refusal to
play reggae. Loading their speakers and turntables onto flatbed
trucks, reggae DJs would venture into rural areas or the slums surrounding Kingston where they would set up and hold dance parties.
Battling for control of desirable locations and audience loyalties,
sound system DJs engaged in energetic verbal and musical combat.
Most Jamaican records were released with an instrumental, or "dub"
version of the featured song on the flip side. Sound system DJs would
play a hit and then flip the record over, which allowed them to speak
to the crowd without breaking the flow. As the groove continued,
they would plug upcoming appearances, recognize friends in the
crowd, and detail the shortcomings of their competitors. On occasion, the DJs commented on political issues, frequently from a separatist Rastafarian perspective. U Roy is generally recognized as the
first Jamaican DJ to bring the talk-over approach to record; Prince
Jazzbo and I Roy engaged in an exchange of recorded insults that anticipated the rap battle between LL Cool J and Kool Moe Dee.

The similarity between early hip-hop and the sound systems wasn't accidental. Most of the South Bronx DJs came from families with West Indian roots. The DJ generally honored as the founder of hip-hop, DJ Kool Herc (Clive Campbell), was born in Kingston and moved to the Bronx when he was twelve. Herc described the transition to the United States to hip-hop historian S. H. Fernando: "A man named George inspirate I from Jamaica, yunno, and he lived 'pon Victoria Street, yunno, and used to come with the big sound system. It was devastating 'cause it was open air, when it rained that's the dance. I did a lot of things from Jamaica, and I brought it here and turned it into my own little style."

Like the sound systems, South Bronx DJs set up and played wherever they could: in housing project recreation rooms, high school auditoriums, on street corners where they ran electrical cords out from nearby buildings, and eventually in clubs like the Hevalo, where Herc established his reputation. Grandmaster Flash described the competitive atmosphere:

> You had to be entertaining to throw block parties. It was always a rough crowd and there was never any security. If the crowd wasn't entertained, the situation could get very dangerous. I would go to the Hevalo sometimes to check Herc out, but Herc used to embarrass me quite a bit. He'd say "Grandmaster Flash in the house," over the mike, and then he'd cut off the highs and lows on his system and just play the mid-range. "Flash," he'd say, "in order to be a qualified disc jockey, there is one thing you must have . . . highs." Then Herc would crank up his highs and the high hat would be sizzling. "And most of all, Flash," he'd say, "you must have bass." Well, when Herc's bass came in the whole place would be shaking. I'd get so embarrassed that I'd have to leave. My system couldn't compare.

Flash compensated for his technological disadvantages by developing a superior ability to manipulate the turntables. His virtuosic performances played a crucial role in creating the main difference between Jamaican and American systems: the division of labor between DJ and rapper. Sound system DJs, like American disco DJs, usually played entire records. Hip-hop developed a more radical musical approach. Relying on technological advances such as the "single pole, double throw switch," better known as the "fader," DJs switched back and forth between turntables, often dropping in instrumental breaks designed to let break dancers show their moves.

Based on surprising, often humorous, juxtapositions and a polyrhythmic chorus of voices, the resulting mix provided a stark alternative to disco. Socially, the South Bronx felt itself isolated from the interracial, upwardly mobile Studio 54 scene. Given access to the affluent Manhattan clubs, disco artists very rarely performed in ghetto clubs, creating an opening for a new style of community-based black dance music. As Bambaata observed, "The Bronx wasn't really into radio music no more. It was an anti-disco movement. Like you had a lot of new wavers and other people coming out and saying, 'Disco sucks.' Well, the same thing with hip hop, 'cos they was against the disco that was being played on the radio. Everybody wanted the funky style Kool Herc was playing."

Refusing to accept the social isolation of the South Bronx as a limitation on their creativity, the early DJs consistently emphasized the inclusiveness of the hip-hop sensibility. "Hip-hop is all kinds of forms," Bambaata observed. "The music itself is colorless, 'cause you can't say, I don't like R&B, I don't like heavy metal, when half the shit that's out comes from all the different styles of records that's out there. So those who don't have a true knowledge of hip-hop, the true form of it, then they just speak from ignorance. You know, the hell with R&B, the hell with jazz, the hell with this, but hip-hop included all these musics to take a beat, a groove, a bassline." One of the most revealing stories concerning the DJs' jazz-inflected attempt to expand their community's consciousness concerns the particular mix Bambaata played at the parties that earned his reputation. Bambaata told hip-hop historian David Toop:

I used to like to catch the people who'd say, "I don't like rock. I don't like Latin." I'd throw on Mick Jagger—you'd see the blacks and Spanish just *throwing* down, dancing crazy. I'd say, "I thought you said you didn't like rock." They'd say "Get out of here." I'd say, "Well, you were just dancing to the Rolling Stones." "You're kidding!"

I'd throw on "Sgt. Pepper's Lonely Hearts Club Band"—just that drum part. One, two, three, BAM—and they'd be screaming and partying. I'd throw on the Monkees, "Mary Mary"—just the beat part where they'd go "Mary, Mary, where are you going?"—and they'd start going crazy. I'd say, "You just danced to the Monkees." They'd say, "You liar. I didn't dance to no Monkees." I'd like to catch people who categorize records.

At the same time, Bambaata had a highly developed political awareness which he traces in part to James Brown's "Say It Loud

(I'm Black and I'm Proud)" and Sly Stone's "Stand." Those who
were present at his seventies shows—which are documented only by
hard-to-find cassette tapes—remember that his mixes included segments of speeches by Malcolm X, Martin Luther King, and Louis
Farrakhan.

The incongruity between hip-hop's inclusive aesthetic and the
blasted South Bronx landscape where it grew up comes through
clearly in the contrast between the two records that did the most to
establish the music's public image: the Sugar Hill Gang's "Rapper's
Delight" and "The Message" by Grandmaster Flash and the Furious
Five featuring rapper Melle Mel. The first, recorded by a group assembled by New Jersey–based record producer Sylvia Robinson,
projects rap's verbal playfulness as a novelty offshoot of disco. Con-
versely, Flash and Melle Mel sound a blues call that has remained a
checkpoint for hip-hop ever since. Every time rap has wandered into
the popular wasteland, the voice of the South Bronx reminds it of
the problems back home.

Living in a middle-class New Jersey suburb, Sylvia Robinson had
been involved in the music business for two decades when she became aware of the new sound through tapes her teenage children
brought home from the city. As part of the soul duo Mickey and
Sylvia, Robinson had sung on the sixties soul hit "Love Is Strange."
More recently, she had produced Shirley and Company's disco hit
"Shame Shame Shame." Realizing the commercial potential of the
new sound, she recruited three would-be rappers from the fringes of
the scene and recorded "Rapper's Delight," a playful record set to
the beat of Chic's "Good Times." The sound of "Rapper's Delight"
was almost pure disco and the tag line "Guess what America? We
love you!" pretty much sums up its political message.

When the South Bronx rappers heard "Rapper's Delight" on the
radio, their response was predictably dubious. Grandmaster Caz,
whose tape directly inspired the style and lyrics of "Rapper's Delight," commented: "It's like if Greg Louganis is gonna dive, right,
and then Greg Louganis's cousin gonna come dive right after him.
You know what I'm saying, it's like he might have dove, too, but that
ain't diving. So it was like that kind of thing, and it didn't represent
that what MCing was, what rap and hip-hop was." Prior to the Sugar
Hill Gang's success, rap had been recorded only sporadically, usually
on back-of-the-shop labels like Paul Winley Records and Bobby
Robinson's Enjoy Records. Soon, however, Sylvia Robinson (no relation to Bobby) had signed most of the South Bronx rappers to Sugar

Hill Records and a more representative style of rap became available. It took almost three years, however, for hip-hop to even begin to make a significant impression on a broad listening audience.

"The Message" changed the game. The pulsing bass pulls the haunting synthesizer line back down to the charred and smoking city. The drums hammer home the dangers of trying to make it home from the subway when home's in the middle of a war zone. In the unforgettable first verse of what remains rap's greatest blues, Melle Mel immerses his listeners in an urban nightmare of broken glass, rank smells, and unescapable noise. As he encounters the "people pissing on the stairs" and "the junkie in the alley with a baseball bat," Melle Mel's response is to the point: "It's like a jungle sometimes, it makes me wonder how I keep from going under." Way too many black Americans knew exactly what he was talking about. The first time I saw the song performed was at the Bar-Kays' homecoming concert at the Midsouth Coliseum in Memphis; Grandmaster Flash and the Furious Five were one of the opening acts. I'd driven up from Mississippi with three black friends. On the way, we'd been pulled over twice by the cops, presumably on suspicion of race mixing. When Melle Mel called out "don't push me cause I'm close to the edge," the response from my friends and the rest of the fifteen thousand people gathered there, almost all of them black, was thunderous. We were pulled over again on the way back home. A few months later, I saw the group again, this time at the Ritz, an upscale postdisco club in downtown New York. The audience was racially mixed, but obviously affluent. When Flash performed "The Message," it fell flat. Which told you most of what you needed, but didn't want, to know about where the seventies had taken us.

A half decade before the birth of gangsta rap, "The Message" came to the obvious conclusion that the kids growing up in the projects, their eyes singing a "song of deep hate," would idolize the thugs, pimps, and pushers, the only ones in their neighborhoods with any cash. Long before KRS-One and Eric B and Rakim made the same point, Melle Mel played out the game to its logical, losing conclusion. The "stick-up kid" gets busted, sentenced to eight years in prison. Melle Mel sketches a graphic picture of his fate behind bars: "Now your manhood is took and you're a Maytag / Spend the next two years as an undercover fag / Being used and abused to serve like hell / 'Til one day you was found hung dead in your cell."

"The Message" distills the essence of what had happened in America during the seventies. Some black folks had made it, at least financially. But in places like the South Bronx—and they were there in every city—the gospel hopes and jazz visions of the sixties had faded away. What was left was a kind of blues you couldn't always distinguish from pure despair. The new world looked a lot like hell. Grandmaster Flash and the Furious Five saw it coming, but they couldn't stop it. By the time "The Message" started receiving airplay in 1982, black America was two years into the Reagan administration. The edge loomed close and it was a long long fall.

# Section Four

## "And That's the Way That It Is": The Reagan Rules, Hip-hop, and the Megastars

# 44
# Welcome to the Terrordome

The Reagan years were hard times for healing. The worst period in racial relations since the 1890s, the era bombarded Americans with images of racial chaos: a desperate chase on the bridge at Howard Beach; Reagan opening his 1980 campaign in the county where three civil rights workers had been murdered in 1964; a circle of angry whites battering the body of Yusef Hawkins, murdered for the crime of walking with a white woman in Brooklyn's Bensonhurst. The Bush years, beginning with the rampaging hallucination of Willie Horton at the center of the election campaign, weren't much better. A successful black Supreme Court nominee presented himself as a victim of lynching; angry crowds of blacks and Jews filled the streets of Crown Heights; LAPD batons rained down on Rodney King; a white driver was pulled from his truck and savagely beaten; Los Angeles erupted in flames.

So it's not really surprising that the period marks a low point in the story I'm trying to tell about music as a healing force. It's not that the music of the eighties was bad. Hip-hop emerged from the underground to revitalize the collective sound track; megastars like Prince and Madonna, Michael Jackson and Bruce Springsteen created rock and soul hybrids of unsurpassed popularity; underground rock and dance music scenes pointed the way to an intriguing, and sometimes contradictory, set of futures.

But in the end, none of it seemed to matter. Faced with a public world in which *image* was everything, even the most conscious musicians were out of their league. When Reagan convinced us that empty nostalgia was preferable to grim realities, especially the realities of a black America sinking into profound social chaos and despair, we were in bad trouble. Like the realities, the responses were desperate. While the megastars tried to figure out how to create communities that were about something other than the marketing of their own images, the rappers said—to phrase it more politely than was usually the case—"The hell with all y'all." It took about ten minutes for the music industry to figure out how to market *that* image too. In the waning years of the Reagan-Bush era, an album by N.W.A. (Niggaz with Attitude), who had made their big splash with "Fuck tha Police," *entered* the charts at number two. It wasn't about healing.

As rapper Chuck D of Public Enemy put it: "Welcome to the Terrordome."

# 45
# Springsteen and the Reagan Rules

There have been some strange moments in the musical history of the American presidency. Richard Nixon playing "The Eyes of Texas Are upon You" on one piano while Spiro Agnew banged out "Dixie" for accompaniment comes to mind. Jimmy Carter singing "Salt Peanuts" with Dizzy Gillespie. The surrealistic moment when B. B. King joined Lee Atwater, mastermind of the infamous Willie Horton campaign, to celebrate the Bush victory at the White House.

But for flat-out bizarre, nothing can match Reagan's invocation of Bruce Springsteen during a 1984 campaign speech in Hammonton, New Jersey. No doubt impressed by the presence of the American flag on the cover of *Born in the U.S.A.*, and oblivious of the fact that the street take on the cover was that the Boss was taking a leak on the Stars and Stripes, Reagan tapped into his familiar sentimentality: "America's future rests in a thousand dreams inside your hearts; it rests in the message of hope in songs so many young Americans admire: New Jersey's own Bruce Springsteen. And helping you make those dreams come true is what this job of mine is all about." Only slightly embarrassed by the fact that the president couldn't name a single Springsteen song, his campaign staff decided a day later that Reagan's favorite was "Born to Run."

Well, okay. The song *did* refer to the "American dream." Never mind that it was "runaway," a "suicide rap." The day after Reagan's election, Springsteen had introduced "Badlands" by telling an Arizona crowd, "I don't know what you thought about what happened last night. But I thought it was pretty terrifying." The lyrics of "Born in the U.S.A." slammed the romantic mythology of the American dream back down onto the charred earth of a postindustrial north Jersey devastated by Reagan's economic policies. As Springsteen sang in "My Hometown," a song that traces the decay of a small New Jersey town like the one he'd grown up in: "These jobs are going, boys, and they ain't comin' back."

Despite his reluctance to engage in "political" debate, Springsteen eventually responded to Reagan explicitly, referring repeatedly to his presidency as "mythical." In a *Rolling Stone* interview, Springsteen sounded a direct political note:

> I think what's happening now is people want to forget. There was Vietnam, there was Watergate, there was Iran—we were beaten, we were hustled, and then we were humiliated. And I think people have a need to feel good about the country they live in. But what's happening, I think, is that the need which is a good thing is gettin' manipulated and exploited. And you see the Reagan reelection ads on TV—you know, "It's morning in America"—and you say, Well, it's not morning in Pittsburgh. It's not morning above 125th Street in New York. It's midnight and, like, there's a bad moon risin'. And that's why when Reagan mentioned my name in New Jersey, I felt it was another manipulation and I had to disassociate myself from the President's kind words.

A year later, Springsteen introduced his version of Edwin Starr's Motown classic "War" with a clear statement against Reagan foreign policy: "In 1985 blind faith in your leaders, or in anything, will get you killed. What I'm talkin' about here is . . . ," breaking into his best soul shout, "War? What is it good for? Absolutely nothing."

But in Reagan's America, none of it seemed to matter much. There were days when it felt like *nothing* mattered, that it was all a matter of image.

There's one school of thought that says Americans put too much emphasis on the presidency, that what happens is going to happen no matter who's pretending to be in charge. From this perspective, inexorable economic and political forces dictate events within a narrow range. In ways, this is true. But any kind of clear-eyed look at the eighties shows that Reagan earned his starring role, that things would *not* have worked out the same with, say, Alexander Haig "in control." Because, as commentators from all over the political spectrum have pointed out, the economic realities of the era had little immediate impact on voting patterns. Conservative strategist Kevin Phillips provided the most incisive analysis of Reagan-era economic policies in his book *The Politics of Rich and Poor: Wealth and the American Electorate in the Reagan Aftermath*. Looking at the redistribution of wealth that resulted from Reagan tax policies, the Republican analyst arrived at the obvious conclusion that the people who benefited were the rich, especially the very rich. "The 1980s," wrote Phillips, one of the leading architects of Richard Nixon's Southern strategy, "were the triumph of upper America—an ostentatious celebration of wealth, the political ascendancy of the richest third of the population. . . . money, greed and luxury had become the stuff of popular culture, hardly anyone asked why such great wealth had concentrated at the top." The middle class, especially in its lower reaches, was hurting; workers in the deindustrializing urban economy, many of them "Reagan Democrats," were hurting bad. Poor whites? Poor blacks? Don't recall having seen many of them around. They certainly didn't show up much on *Dallas*. Or the six o'clock news. Or in the voting booths when Americans reelected a president who had himself "endorsed" by Bruce Springsteen.

So Reagan flat-out won. And we're not just talking about elections. The America of the eighties was profoundly divided. From the streets of Compton to the boardrooms of the Fortune 500, Reagan set down the rules of the game:

1. **"There's no 'there' there and there never was,"** or, **reality is determined by image and anecdote.** Reagan was absolute master of the ability to transform a single example, however far removed it might have been from any representative situation, into proof of a sweeping generality. By the time he was finished putting the proper "spin" on a situation, it was almost impossible to get anyone to pay attention to concrete realities. A black woman who had been convicted of fraud in a case involving $8,000 was transformed into a "welfare queen" with a fleet of Cadillacs and a tax-free income of $150,000, thus proving that the poor were getting too much help. Ketchup is a vegetable. As long as it sounded good, we bought it.

2. **"First pig to the trough wins,"** or, **the purpose of life is to make a lot of money.** From the junk bond dealers of Wall Street to the scores of administration appointees involved in financial scandals to the athletes going on strike over their right to make multimillions of dollars, the message was clear: "Too much is never enough." And if

it was sad that some little piggies had none, it wasn't sad enough to make any of their big brothers think seriously about passing the roast beef.

**3. "Go ahead, make my day," or, violence is the core of American, which is to say male, identity.** John Wayne, Sylvester Stallone, Eazy-E, Clint Eastwood, Mike Tyson. Who could really tell the difference? People were sick of being pushed around by little countries like Vietnam and Iran and they were ready to blow it all to hell and gone to prove they weren't going to take it anymore. The gangsta rappers, who sold as many albums to white fraternity brothers as they did to the boyz in the hood, were down with it. As long as you could beat someone up, there wasn't any real reason to engage in boring intellectual discussions of trivial issues like hatred or hypocrisy.

**4. "AIDS is God's judgment on the Evil Empire of liberal gay draft dodgers," or, the world is divided into "us" and "them."** Springsteen nailed it when he observed that there were a lot of people whose dreams didn't make any difference during the Reagan era. Worse, there were a lot of people whose *lives* didn't make any difference. The homeless were sleeping on heat grates because that's what they wanted. AIDS was punishment for an immoral lifestyle. "We" certainly never got high or slept around.

In thinking about Reaganism's ability to contain the energies of so many different types of music, it's useful to remember the blues and gospel impulses. Gospel testifies that to seek redemption is to embrace connection, to see the dividing lines for the illusions they are. You bear witness to the troubles you've seen and to how you got over. Then you do your damnedest to live the life you sing about in your song. As the flip side of gospel, the blues confront the reality of evil. The blues know about how money can mess up your relationship with your man or woman, but they refuse to let you lie about your own part in the game. As Robert Johnson sang: "Early this morning, you knocked upon my door. And I said hello Satan, I believe it's time to go."

Black music sings about the complexity of who we are, the ways we can't separate our gospel impulses from our blues realities. Evil isn't out *there*, it's in *here*. Salvation isn't about getting away from where we are, it's about dealing with it. Yeah, the world's a bitch. It would be nice to have enough money to take the edge off. But when the last fair deal's gone down, to quote soul singer Teddy Pendergrass: "You can't hide from yourself. / Everywhere you go, there you are."

In Reagan's America, on the other hand, you apparently *could* hide from yourself. From all accounts, Reagan was seriously upset by suggestions that he was a racist. As his wife, Nancy, said, "A lot of lies are told about people who go into politics, but the only one that ever got Ronnie steamed up was the occasional allegation that he was a bigot." Against such allegations, Reagan offered several anecdotes establishing his Brotherhood Week credentials. His brother's best friend had been black; his father had detested the Klan; he had a black friend on the football team at Eureka College; he supported Jackie Robinson when he broke the color barrier in major-league baseball. How could anyone possibly think he wasn't a friend to black America? As governor of California, he had appointed blacks to state jobs (9 out of 3,709 positions); as president, he appointed blacks to the federal bench (2 out of 160). He hadn't needed quotas to make him do it.

In blues terms, what Reagan did was miss the point entirely. First, he refused to deal with the gritty reality of his own experience. A couple of anecdotes from thirty years ago were sufficient to blot out the reality of his life in public office. The fact that the anecdotes were fundamentally nostalgic and sentimental only underlines how far it was from Reagan's world to the world of the blues. For Reagan, the evil in America was imposed by forces with which he had no connection: the special-interest groups that refused to understand how he had the country's best interests at heart; the Soviet "evil empire" which spread violence throughout the world; the homosexuals who were being visited by God's wrath in the form of a nameless new disease. "We" were pure. "They" just didn't understand.

On every level, Reagan operated from a world where the values of black music could not even be voiced, much less turned into action. And it created a monster problem for the musicians. If you argued with Reagan, you almost inevitably wound up defending "us" against "them." At worst, you tried to hit them the same way they hit us; but they had bigger sticks. If you embraced the blues, dealt with the fact that you weren't quite as pure as Reagan claimed he was, you simply furnished testimony that could be used against you. Acknowledging the blues realities of the inner city—violence, drugs, despair—provided images that reinforced exactly what Reagan was saying about you in the first place. But, as the bluesmen and -women always knew, if you *didn't* tell the truth, you'd die or go crazy. So it should come as no surprise that, in the ghettos, a lot of people did just that. As Public Enemy rapped, for blues-black America, morning in Reagan's America looked more like the "Night of the Living Base-heads."

# 46
# The Problem of Healing in the Hall of Mirrors

The generally unsuccessful struggle of eighties musicians to find a healing voice can't be understood without an awareness of how the Reagan rules played out.

It certainly wasn't a matter of indifference or a lack of awareness. All of the megastars, in their own strange ways, knew that their music grew out of traditions that were black *and* white, that on some level it was about bringing America together. Prince sang silky sexy soul *and* rocked out; Tina Turner played heavy metal gospel games with the white boys' heads; Eddie Van Halen backed up Michael Jackson; Whitney Houston sang Vegas; U2 celebrated Martin Luther King and Woody Guthrie; radical black writer Amiri Baraka recognized Springsteen as a bluesman par excellence.

Closer to street level, a dizzying number of local musical communities desperately struggled to hold on to their own realities, to form supportive communities standing apart from a corrupt mainstream. Rap, which in 1983 was clearly centered in New York City, developed styles specific to California, Miami, Chicago, Atlanta, Philadelphia. One of the ironies of the teapot tempest over the "obscenity" of 2 Live Crew was that Luke Skywalker's Miami sound had almost no connection with the form or content of the music being produced by, to take one example, New Jersey's B-Boy label. Rock's fragmentation was as much stylistic as geographic. Heavy metal, post-punk, thrash, hardcore, and countless subvarieties played to their own inner circles. For their fans, the differences between Metallica, Slayer, the Meat Puppets, and Hüsker Dü were crucial, but few outside the inner circles cared about the distinctions. As the 1980s wore on, the betting line on which city would dominate the future of rock shifted from Athens, Georgia (R.E.M.) to Minneapolis (Hüsker Dü, the Replacements) to the eventual winner, Seattle (Nirvana, Pearl Jam). Nearly every city seemed to develop its own dance music subculture: local versions of house in Chicago (Marshall Jefferson, Frankie Knuckles) and New Jersey (Blaze, Larry Levan), techno in Detroit (Derrick May, Kevin Saunderson), go-go in D.C. (Trouble Funk, E.U.), the diasporic synthesis of London's "Black Britain" (Soul II Soul, Groove Collective). Musically, it was a lively and creative period.

The problem was that neither the megastars nor the local heroes could separate themselves from the Reagan Rules. To put it simply, the megastars got caught up in a big-money game that forced them to spend huge amounts of energy dealing with their own images. Michael Jackson literally changed faces; Tina Turner sensuously embraced heavy metal's comic-book hallucinations; Madonna's music was only one part of the world's longest-running postmodern girlie show; Prince became a chameleon, always a half step ahead of his audience's attempt to freeze him in an easily consumable form, finally un-renaming himself as a hieroglyph. It was hard to bring together communities when everyone on both sides of the TV screen seemed lost in their own hall of mirrors. The flip side of the problem was that the local music communities, whether defining themselves geographically or stylistically, inevitably reinforced the "us/them" logic that made effective political coalitions almost unthinkable. Holding on to your own blues realities meant protecting your community's boundaries fiercely against anyone who didn't know the turf. Refusing to deny the rage they felt as they looked at the wasteland around them, many rap and rock subcultures internalized and perpetuated the underlying violence of the era, all too often directing it against the women who played the role of "them" within a community that was already on the outside.

# 47
# The View from Black America

So what *was* going on on the other side of town while the cameras cut from *Lifestyles of the Rich and Famous* to the menacing image of Willie Horton rampaging through the suburbs like a black beast escaped from *Birth of a Nation?*

For one thing, it was definitely the *other* side. With great regularity, the most comprehensive studies of race in the United States conclude that white and black Americans in effect occupy different nations. Visiting an America organized economically around slavery, Alexis de Tocqueville observed that whites "scarcely acknowledge the common features of humanity" in blacks. Eight decades after abolition, not much had changed. Swedish sociologist Gunnar Myrdal's classic study *An American Dilemma* (1944) provided overwhelming statistical evidence of the chasm that continued to separate blacks and whites in education, employment, housing, and every other area of American life. Two decades down the road, same story. The Kerner Commission concluded its 1968 report on the causes of the riots with the warning that America "was moving toward two societies, one black, one white—separate and unequal." And the beat goes on. In 1992, Andrew Hacker titled his overview of race in American society *Two Nations: Black and White, Separate, Hostile, Unequal.*

So it should come as no surprise that West Coast rap group WC and the MAAD Circle projected the trend into the future at the beginning of their 1991 album *Ain't a Damn Thing Changed:* "Yeah, it's 1997 y'all and ain't a damn thing changed. Unemployment's at a all time high and livin' in L.A. is like death row, you're bound to die. It ain't nothin' but modern day slavery."

By the early nineties, this type of rhetoric was common in rap. Self-styled Black Panther rapper Paris drew a firestorm of criticism for his album *Sleeping with the Enemy* which included "Bush Killa," a fantasy focusing on the assassination of the president. The Bush campaign's exploitation of the "Willie" Horton image elicited extreme bitterness on all socioeconomic levels of black America. The quotes around "Willie" highlight the fact that the criminal in question was named William and never went by the "black" nickname bestowed on him by the Republican spin doctors. Horton was a convicted murderer who had committed assault and rape while out of jail on a Massachusetts furlough program. Of the five similar cases detailed in the original newspaper series on the furlough program, Horton's was the only one with a racial element. Which didn't stop Republican strategist and black music aficionado Lee Atwater from carefully crafting a campaign around the same vicious stereotypes exploited by proslavery apologists, the KKK of the twenties, and the White Citizens Councils of the segregationist South. To cite just one instance, the Maryland Republican Party sent out a fund-raising letter warning that "You, your spouse, your children and your friends can have a visit from someone like Willie Horton if Mike Dukakis becomes president." After seeing the picture of himself chosen for a television commercial by the Conservative Victory Committee, Horton himself said: "I looked like a zombie. They chose the perfect picture for the ads. I looked incredibly wicked."

Hacker's *Two Nations* is the best overview of the sociological realities of race in America at the end of the Reagan-Bush era. But before we take a look at his details, a few words about statistics are in order. Liberal academics pioneered the use of social scientific research to support political agendas. Statistics demonstrating the negative impact of segregation on black children, for example, played a significant role in the legal battles leading up to the *Brown* v. *Board of Education* decision. The policy makers who shaped Lyndon Johnson's Great Society programs and the War on Poverty made extensive use of statistics. During the fifties and sixties, statistics provided an effective weapon in some battles against injustice.

By the eighties, however, it was clear that social science was a two-edged sword. Any undergraduate econ major with a C average will recognize the truth of Mark Twain's division of humanity into liars, damned liars, and statisticians. To some extent, this is a matter of manipulation; the attorneys who argued the *Bakke* case armed themselves with reams of statistics, as did Clarence Pendleton and Linda Chavez when they began to dismantle the U.S. Civil Rights Commission. There was always an expert witness on sale to the highest bidder and the liberals matched the conservatives bid for bid. The general level of statistical illiteracy in the body politic made it very unlikely that anyone would really be able to figure out who was lying to whom about what.

But on a deeper level, the problem with statistics is that they often obscure large parts of the picture they present as reality. Like individual people. Like differences within groups. Any generality about any group is just that: a generality. It's not always easy to see the difference between sociological generalizations, however precise or preposterous their coefficients, and stereotypes. The moral of the story is almost always, to use a bit of economic jargon, *disaggregate.* Take the numbers apart. See what the categories hide. This isn't the place for an extended discussion of how numbers lie, but be aware they do. Almost always. And, in looking at Hacker's sociological portrait of America, remember that this is just a background, that the important thing is the struggle of individuals and communities to do things the numbers say are beyond their reach. This is the flip side of Reagan's use of anecdotes. Where he presented singular cases as typical, it's equally important to remember that what actually *is* typical doesn't set limits.

Yet and still, what Hacker reveals about the situation in black America in the wake of Reagan is a nightmare. *Two Nations* breaks down the numbers on black family structure, income, employment, education, crime, and politics. And the moral of the story is: Ain't a damn thing changed. Except maybe for the worse. One of the real strengths of Hacker's analysis is that it discourages ideological evasions. He provides precious little comfort to those with pat answers from either left or right. Some of what he says is uncomfortable for anyone who wants to minimize the realities that gave the Willie Horton campaign its punch. Whites *are* victimized by black crime. Even at a time when the reality of black-on-black violence is horrifying, nearly three times as many whites are murdered by blacks as blacks are murdered by whites. Over a third of all robberies are committed by blacks against whites.

On the other hand, Hacker reveals the total unreality of the conservative hysteria whipped up by the Jesse Helms campaign ad: "You needed that job and you were the best qualified, but they had to give it to a minority because of a racial quota." What actually happened during the eighties was that, by every measure, black men lost economic ground relative to white men. Black unemployment under Reagan *never* dipped below double digits, while even at the depths of the 1982 recession white unemployment never rose above 8.6 percent. In a nation where blacks account for 12.1 percent of the population, they received only 7.3 percent of the income. Black union members averaged $490 weekly paychecks as compared to the $589 average for whites. As for the "quotas" which the conservatives blamed for white economic frustration, there simply weren't enough blacks in desirable jobs for affirmative action to have had much of an impact except on the all-important anecdotal level, where white men screamed about their victimization. Only 3.7 percent of engineers, 3.7 percent of physicians, 3.1 percent of architects, 2.7 percent of lawyers, and 2.5 percent of realtors were black. At the other end of the spectrum, 30.7 percent of nurses and orderlies, 27.3 percent of maids, 22.6 percent of security guards, 21.5 percent of janitors, and 19.1 percent of vehicle washers were black. You may have needed a job, but *those* probably weren't the jobs you were thinking about.

So the job situation was bad. As Kevin Phillips pointed out, it was bad for everyone. But as the saying goes, when white America sneezes, black America gets pneumonia. And on the streets of inner-city black America, where people were living out the human meaning of the numbers, the plague literally struck home. You could see it in the statistics on AIDS, on infant mortality, on life expectancy. By 1992, there were over a half million black men in jail, another million on probation or with felony convictions on their records. No major surprise so many black children grew up with their mothers or grandmothers in neighborhoods you lived in only if you had no other choice.

Traditional support systems—youth clubs, neighborhood centers—collapsed under the impact of Reagan era cuts to social services. Rapper Tone Loc, best known for his massively popular "mainstream" hit "Wild Thing," described the changes in street reality during the Reagan years. Looking back on the early 1980s when he was growing up in west L.A., Loc said: "When we was doin' the shit, we just drink and fight and whatever. It wasn't too much of no gun activity, you know what I'm saying? We ain't have the money for a high-powered rifle." But, he continued, things changed when crack hit the streets: "That's when these L.A. gangs really came up, like the mid eighties and shit, and that's when they started making all the money, and that's when the shit got out of control. 'Cause with the money they had the power, and with the power they got a lot of respect." So it made a surreal kind of sense that in a few years gangsta rapper Eazy-E (Eric Wright), who died of AIDS, would be making contributions to the Republican Party.

## 48
## The Way It Was and the Way It Is

In the midst of the chaos, a lot of folks got mad and a few got political. Some turned to memories of the Panthers, some to myths of African warriors, some to Jesse Jackson. Very few to the Republican National Committee. Many turned to the Nation of Islam. Not always, or even often, out of theological conviction. Quite a few just liked the way Minister Farrakhan scared the white folks. Just as many were impressed with the members of the Nation who fought it out with the crack dealers, block by block, for control of black communities everyone else had abandoned. If it was a matter of trying to convince a brother to put down the pipe, it no doubt helped to have a white devil standing in for the enemy in his head.

Almost all of the political responses were motivated by the profound hatred of Reagan that permeated inner-city black communities. Always one of the most insightful rappers, Ice T stressed the connection between the gangsta ethos and mainstream values when he introduced "Squeeze the Trigger": "they won't play our records on the radio, man, sayin' we violent, man, they need to look at the news, know what I'm sayin?" Later in the rap, he names names, castigating Reagan for sending "guns where they don't belong" even as a literal shooting war rages on city streets filled with the hungry and the homeless. As Ice T sums it up, "Cops hate kids, kids hate cops, cops kill kids with warnin' shots / What is crime and what is not? what is justice? I think I forgot."

Making it clear that he hadn't lost the hard edge of "Cortez the Killer" and "My My Hey Hey (Out of the Blue)," Neil Young came to pretty much the same conclusion on his Reagan-era masterpiece *Freedom*. The keynote of *Freedom* is Young's version of "On Broadway," which relocates the Drifters' hymn to mainstream success—a secular version of what gospel's Swan Silvertones called the "Milky White Way"—in the real world of crack and crime. Recalling memories of

Frank Zappa's "I'm not black but there's a whole lotta times I wish I could say I wasn't white," Young bitterly lamented in "Rockin' in the Free World": "don't feel like Satan, but I am to them." In "Crime in the City," a policeman spits out "I take my orders from fools" and surrenders himself to a game he knows is corrupt.

The conclusion was clear, as Gil Scott-Heron rapped in his 1984 election song "Re-Ron": "You ask us would we take Jesse Jackson? Hell, we'd take Michael Jackson." The nominations of Clarence Pendleton and Clarence Thomas didn't seem to convince anyone black folks were on their way to the top. Scott-Heron sounded the basic themes of black music's political response to Reagan in "B Movie." Acutely aware of the ways American pop culture uses nostalgia to escape from the complicated blues reality, Scott-Heron greeted the first Reagan administration: "This country wants nostalgia / they want to go back as far as they can / even if it's just as far as last week." If Americans had had their choice, they would have preferred John Wayne as their leader on the march to yesterday, but "Since John Wayne was no longer available / they settled for Ronald Reagan." Before concluding the cut with the sardonic observation that "we're all starring in a B Movie," Scott-Heron assumed the voice of the Reagan era's collective American self longing for a return to "a time when movies were in black and white and so was everything else."

The worst part of the eighties was how thoroughly America— black and white, conservative and liberal, straight and gay, us and them—saw the world through Reagan's rose-tinted bifocals with the black-and-white lenses. Despite its flaws, which were inextricably linked to the harsh social and psychological realities of the period, rap provided a clearer vision.

If rock and roll occupied the dangerous frontier of racial reality in the mid-fifties, thirty years later rap had assumed the position. In the wake of "Rapper's Delight" and "The Message," the nature and future of "rap" was by no means clear; there was a believable, if not quite convincing, argument to be made that rap was simply another musical fad whose time had come and gone. The Chicago Bears Shuffling Crew got down for Mickey D while UTFO and a parade of Roxannes exhumed the tradition of boy/girl answer records.

Which is where Run-D.M.C. comes in.

From the Lower East Side of Manhattan to the South Bronx, from Brooklyn's Red Hook to Long Island City in Queens, "It's Like That" dominated the sound track of the New York streets during the summer of 1983. Not "long and hot" in the classic burn-the-motherfucker-down sense, it was the summer when it became clear that Reagan wasn't an accident. The recession of 1981–82—which was as close to a true depression as we've had since the thirties—was forgotten, if not precisely gone. The real estate industry was priming to reclaim Manhattan, sending the post-punk downtown art scene, along with countless poor blacks and Latins, scattering for shelter in Brooklyn. The old-school rappers and DJs were on the verge of disappearance. DJ Kool Herc and Afrika Bambaata made no impact on hip-hop after 1984; Flash and Melle Mel warned against those "White Lines," but it didn't stop Sugar Hill's most vital artists from vanishing into the cocaine mists.

For people who heard the syncopated minimalist beat echoing through the concrete jungles of New York City, Run-D.M.C.'s lyrics seemed like cinema verité. As the song spread from New York to Philly to L.A., a lot of people who weren't even aware of the underground hip-hop scene responded strongly to its clarity about what was going down in Reagan's America. Run-D.M.C. juxtaposed images of the "war going on across the sea" with those of "street soldiers killing the elderly." Asking "whatever happened to unity?," they concluded simply, "it's like that and that's the way it is." "The Message," take two. In Reagan's America, if there was one thing definitely needed, it was clarity, because there were lots of people unwilling to see what was going down. Run-D.M.C. took a clear look at the blues reality. And the stripped-down beat said it as clearly as the words. Cut away all the bullshit and deal with it. It's like that and that's the way it is.

Like most of the early hip-hop classics, "It's Like That" established itself on the street. Even before the song began to receive limited radio play, lots of people had it memorized. During the summer of 1983, there was no visual image of the group's style to go with the reverberating beats and the in-your-face angry words. Which made what followed seem even stranger.

From the start, most listeners assumed that Run-D.M.C. came out of the same ghetto neighborhoods as Grandmaster Flash and Afrika Bambaata. Not quite. Turns out that the trio of DJ Jam Master Jay (Jason Mizell), Run (Joey Simmons), and D.M.C. (Darryl McDaniels, whose initials, in good Reagan-era fashion, stood for "Darryl Makes Cash") came out of the relatively affluent neighborhood of Hollis, Queens. Joey's older brother Russell Simmons, an old-school hip-hop promoter who developed into a major force in the rap industry, commented on the significance of the group's suburban background: "It's the difference between fantasy and reality. In Queens you could hang out on the corner, but there was safety in the house. . . . The early rappers were from the ghetto, so their stories reflected their lives, but it was important when rap began coming out of the suburbs 'cause these niggers had something else to talk about."

It didn't take long for Run-D.M.C. to meet the tar baby.

# 49
# Brer Rabbit and Tar Baby

The tar baby story is a classic of the African diaspora. In one form or another, it circulates in black communities of West Africa, the Caribbean, Mississippi, Chicago, and London. It's almost certainly making the rounds in the black communities of Berlin and Stockholm. Its influence on popular culture—black, white, and other—has been immense. The story's been used by writers from Joel Chandler Harris and Charles Chesnutt to Toni Morrison and the hilarious funk novelist Darius James (*Negrophobia*). It's been raided by the cartoon makers who don't even seem to know that Bugs Bunny's older cousin Brer Rabbit was born in the African bush, transformed into films by Walt Disney (*Song of the South*) and Ralph Bakshi (*Streetfight*). It provided the plot structure for Michael Jackson's "Billie Jean" video.

And almost no one recognizes it for the separatist parable it is. Whatever the version, the basic elements of the story remain the same. The symbolically black Brer Rabbit encounters a tar baby placed in the road by Brer Fox or a white farmer. When the tar baby refuses to respond to his greeting, Brer Rabbit slaps or kicks it, becoming more and more entangled until he can no longer move at all. When his captors begin to torment him, Brer Rabbit regains his freedom by convincing them that he dreads being thrown in the briar patch more than any other torment. So they throw him in. Manipulating their (white) cruelty and shallow knowledge of his (black) character, he escapes and runs off taunting them that the briar patch is his home.

Both parts of the story have separatist implications. Created by whites as a trap for blacks, the tar baby is a racist stereotype: very black, brainless, immobile, dressed in rags. Brer Rabbit's best move would be simply to ignore it, to walk on down the road and take care of his own business. Once he gets involved, his best move would be to disengage as quickly as possible. As long as only one hand is stuck, he could use his remaining physical power to pull out and *then* go his own way. Harshly realistic like all folktales, however, the tar baby story acknowledges that not very many black folks are simply going to ignore the white world. Most are going to get caught.

So the question becomes, how do you handle it once you've gotten yourself into the mess? If part one of the story warns blacks that it's safer just to stay away from whites in the first place, part two says that once they've got you, you'd better *use* the brain the tar baby says you don't have. It's a manual for psychological guerrilla warfare. What black folks *don't* have is the physical strength to break the white image. So forget about beating tar baby up; you may get over for a while, but after that have a nice time with your brothers in the joint. What black people *do* have is superior knowledge and the ability to use it. Brer Rabbit escapes not because he's strong, but because he knows how to talk. To quote the Rastas, "word sound have power." And he knows how white folks really are; sure, they're going to *say* they have your best interests at heart but what Brer Fox really wants is to hurt black folks as bad as he possibly can. Fortunately, he doesn't know anything at all about black folks. Hell, he doesn't even know Brer Rabbit lives in the briar patch. As the growing isolation of inner cities in the 1980s made clear, Brer Fox didn't spend much time in Compton or the South Bronx.

# 50
# Run-D.M.C. Negotiates the Mainstream

Back to Run-D.M.C., whom we left admiring tar baby's threads: black hats, unlaced Adidas, gold chains.

To understand what happened to Run-D.M.C. during their meteoric rise to media prominence and precipitous decline into self-parody, it helps to remember where they came in. If the polarized reality of the Reagan era was coming into clear focus in the projects by 1983, the view was nowhere near as clear from downtown Manhattan or Hollis, much less from the America where MTV was beginning to take shape around the racially complicated images of Michael Jackson, Madonna, and Prince. From very early on, the majority white "rock" culture in both its avant-garde and media-circus versions had shown an intense interest in the new sounds from the black streets. Plenty of producers knew enough history to understand that almost every new development in black music eventually translated into something that made a lot of money, and that most of the money wasn't going to wind up back in the ghetto. The ongoing, halting cross-pollination of the white avant-garde and hip-hop resulted in a hothouse of exotic hybrids including Sinead O'Connor and MC Lyte's "I Want Your Hands on Me," the Talking Heads' "Stop Making Sense" tour, dozens of hip-hop remixes of Suzanne Vega's ennui-rap "Tom's Diner," and, most peculiarly appropriate of all, Time Zone, a "group" pairing pioneering South Bronx DJ Afrika Bambaata with former Sex Pistol John Lydon (a.k.a. Johnny Rotten).

Run-D.M.C., upwardly mobile suburban kids with a big brother/mentor very much interested in entering the economic fast lane, can hardly be blamed for saying howdy to tar baby, who, this time, said howdy back. The success of Run's first album resulted in equal parts from the "authentic ghetto voice" of "It's Like That" and "Hard Times" and from Eddie Martinez's guitar work on "Rock Box," which would have been at home on a seventies FM track by AC/DC or Aerosmith. Invited into the mix, the white audience came, and Run responded by highlighting Martinez even more on "Rock the House" and "Can You Rock It Like This" on its second album. All of this culminated in the collaboration with Aerosmith on a remake of dinosaur-rock classic "Walk This Way." Notable mostly for "breaking" rap on MTV, the video has earned an undying place in the "It Seemed Like a Good Idea at the Time" Hall of Fame.

The title of Run-D.M.C.'s second album, by the way, was *King of Rock.* As Havelock Nelson and Michael A. Gonzales wrote in *Bring the Noise: A Guide to Rap Music and Hip-Hop Culture,* "the sound you hear is Elvis turning in his grave."

# 51
# "A Hero to Most":
# Elvis in the Eighties

If Run-D.M.C. made Elvis howl in his sleep, it was just the start. Beginning in the mid-eighties, a full-fledged cultural battle broke out for possession of the King's corpse. It was a classic illustration of the Reagan Rules. While black artists projected visions of Elvis as the incarnation of white oppression, his white descendants looked to him for an image of spiritual salvation. Us, meet them. What was most interesting, and ultimately disturbing, about the battle was how clearly it reflected the Reagan era obsession with image and how little any of it had to do with Elvis's actual life.

The story of Elvis's rise from white trash obscurity in Tupelo, Mississippi, to unprecedented rock and roll stardom and his fall to beached whale crooning out his addled last years in a sequined jumpsuit has been told again and again. Every credible history of American popular music credits Elvis with creating a synthesis of country, gospel, and rhythm and blues that brought the energy of black music to a white audience. Never reluctant to claim his own status as the founder of the dynasty, Little Richard acknowledged that Elvis was the one who "got white folks to singing rock and roll."

During the formative years of his career, Elvis mixed freely with his black contemporaries. B. B. King, Presley's labelmate at Sam Phillips's legendary Sun Records, recalled: "I liked Elvis. I saw him as a fellow Mississippian. . . . Elvis didn't steal any music from anyone. He just had his own interpretation of the music he'd grown up on. Same was true for me; the same's true for everyone. I think Elvis had integrity." After Elvis had established himself as a major star, he met R & B vocalist Ivory Joe Hunter, who admitted "frankly, I'd heard he was color prejudiced." Direct contact with Elvis changed Hunter's mind: "He is very spiritually minded. . . . he showed me every courtesy, and I think he's one of the greatest." Combining his firsthand knowledge of the Memphis blues scene with the gospel tradition he had absorbed growing up in Tupelo, Elvis created a music that was profoundly subversive of the racial divisions still legally enforced during his youth.

Which doesn't necessarily resolve the lingering questions about Elvis's racial attitudes. During 1957, a rumor—which you still hear from time to time—circulated in black communities quoting Elvis as saying: "The only thing Negroes can do for me is buy my records and shine my shoes." When directly questioned about the rumor, Elvis replied: "I never said anything like that, and people who know me know I wouldn't have said it." A reporter for *Jet* magazine interviewed black citizens of Memphis and Tupelo, who provided uniformly positive commentary on Elvis's lack of prejudice. *Jet* concluded that "To Elvis, people are people, regardless of race, color or creed." In another reflection of how the reality of racial divisions in the United States can lend credibility to rumors and lies, Sam Phillips is often quoted as having said "I could make a million dollars if I could find me a white boy who could sing like a nigger." Every black musician who ever worked with Phillips—and there were dozens—staunchly denies that Phillips ever used racial slurs.

More to the point, there's no question that Phillips was conscious of both the economic potential and the larger social implications of what was happening musically in Memphis. Setting out to provide a home for "Negro artists in the South who wanted to make a record but just had no place to go," Phillips cut some of the first records by B. B. King, Howlin' Wolf, and Bobby "Blue" Bland as well as Johnny Cash, Jerry Lee Lewis, and Elvis. Looking back at his desire to find a white singer with a black sound, Phillips describes the complicated racial politics of the time:

I wasn't looking for no tall stumps to preach from. And I sensed in [Elvis] the same kind of empathy. I don't think he was aware of my motivation for doing what I was trying to do—not consciously anyway—but *intuitively* he felt it. I never discussed it—I don't think it would have been very wise to talk about it, for me to say, "Hey, man, we're going against—." Or, "We're trying to put pop music down and bring in black—." The lack of prejudice on the part of Elvis Presley had to be one of the biggest things that ever could have happened to us, though. It was almost subversive, sneaking around through the music—but we hit things a little bit, don't you think? I went out into this no-man's-land, and I knocked the shit out of the color line.

Elvis had company in no-man's-land: Chuck Berry, Fats Domino, Little Richard, Carl Perkins. Perkins, a white Sun artist who had literally grown up picking cotton alongside black sharecroppers in the Delta, recalls a conversation with Berry during the early days of rock and roll:

> There was no [segregation] in music. When you walked up to an old 54 or 55 Wurlitzer jukebox and it said "Blue Suede Shoes," Carl Perkins, white. "Blueberry Hill," Fats Domino, black. No. There was no difference. Kids danced to Little Richard, Chuck Berry, Elvis, Carl. Chuck Berry said to me one time, he said, you know Carl, we just might be doing as much with our music as our leaders are in Washington to break down the barriers. He was right.

The music coming out of no-man's-land broke down all kinds of barriers. Oddly enough, the segregationists were right that rock and roll was a threat to the color line. It drew on country, gospel, the Delta blues, the rhythm and blues coming out of the Northern ghettos. Elvis's Memphis recordings—"Mystery Train," "Good Rockin' Tonight," "Milkcow Blues Boogie"—stand alongside Berry's "Roll Over Beethoven," "Maybellene," and "Johnny B. Goode" and Little Richard's "Rip It Up" or "Slippin' and Slidin' (Peepin' and Hidin')" as examples of the subversive, celebratory power of rock and roll before it became "white" music.

What happened during the last half of the fifties was an American tragedy. It didn't take long for the cold war culture—which viewed interracial sexually aggressive rock and roll as part of a communist conspiracy—to defuse Elvis. With the help of Elvis's manager, Colonel Tom Parker, the authorities put him in a suit, cut him off at the waist, drafted him, put him in the movies, and finally turned him into pure myth. It could have been worse, and for black rock and rollers it often was. Chuck Berry went to jail and Little Richard turned to the church. Pat Boone moved to the center of the stage and, to quote Amiri Baraka's diagnosis of white America, "you cannot fail to recognize the difference between Boone, Daniel and Boone, Pat." In one of the most profound passages in American cultural criticism, Greil Marcus describes Elvis's fate in terms that illuminate the problems faced by the megastars of the eighties:

> Elvis has dissolved into a presentation of his myth, and so has his music. The emotion of the best music is open, liberating in its commitment and intangibility; Elvis's presentation is fixed. The glorious oppression of that presentation parallels the all-but-complete assimilation of a revolutionary musical style into the mainstream of American culture, where no one is challenged and no one is threatened.
>
> History without myth is surely a wasteland; but myths are compelling only when they are at odds with history. When they replace the need to make history, they too are a dead end, and merely smug. Elvis's performance of his myth is so satisfying to his audience that he is left with no musical identity whatsoever, and thus he has no way to define himself, or his audience—except to expand himself, and his audience. Elvis is a man whose task it is to dramatize the fact of his existence; he does not have to create something new (or try, and fail), and thus test the worth of his existence, or the worth of his audience.

By the end of the eighties, it had become painfully clear that the myth of Elvis meant one thing to the most self-aware white musicians and something quite different to their black counterparts. For every white rocker grappling with the social and/or spiritual significance of Elvis's life and death, there was a rapper ready to give an amen to Da Lench Mob's "You and Your Heroes." Lashing out at a world he divided in proper Reagan era fashion into black "us" and white "them," lyricist Ice Cube made Elvis the central symbol of an exploitative tradition extending from George Washington to Larry Bird and Madonna. Da Lench Mob's conclusion, if not fully responsive to the complexities of history, had the virtue of clarity: "Elvis, fuck him with my shotgun."

The defense case was less direct. The major images of "Elvis, the Tormented Soul of America" and "Saint Elvis, Our Day-Glo Savior" both emerge in U2's "Elvis Presley and America." This overstates the clarity only slightly. What comes through producer Brian Eno's evocations of a rainswept haunted soundscape are fragmentary images which vocalist Bono improvised in the studio. While "the rain beats down" and a nameless "you" walks under ominous skies, Bono meditates on images of broken language, of aimless motion, unfulfilled yearning: "don't talk to me don't talk to me don't talk to me"; "outskirts, we fade away drop me down but don't break me"; "in your heart it feels like something." But the key may be the phrase that sounds most clearly early in the song: "and I believe in you." Eno later told Bono he should think of the song as a "rap." At last word, he was still waiting for Ice Cube's "amen." But the hip white boys heard and responded with a whole gallery of "serious" rock versions of those velvet paintings of Elvis in heaven.

It would be dangerous to overstate the specific influence of "Elvis Presley and America"; white male rock musicians come by their Elvis obsession honestly. But both Nick Cave's "Tupelo" and Paul Simon's "Graceland" echo U2's quest and salvation themes. Beginning with an apocalyptic thunder roll of percussion, Cave's "Tupelo" sets us down somewhere in a biblical landscape where black clouds roll in over Elvis's birthplace, the Mississippi River runs dry, and distant thunder rumbles like a hungry beast out of Revelation. Against a chorus stretching out the syllables of Tupelo into something that feels closer to hell than paradise, Cave describes the birth of Elvis and his stillborn twin brother in terms that mingle social realism and biblical allusions. "Saturday gives what Sunday steals," and the firstborn is buried in a shoe box wrapped in a "ribbon of red." As "Tupelo" crashes to its end, Cave calls forth an apocalyptic hallucination of Elvis carrying "the burden of Tupelo" in his tormented voice. Aware of how Presley's religious vision grew out of the cotton field grime of the poor white South where infant mortality was as real as it was in the ghettos of Reagan's America, Cave's "Tupelo" remains the most profound version of Saint Elvis.

But it was Paul Simon who gave the religious myth sufficient public presence to draw return fire from Ice Cube and Public Enemy. Aware of the complexities of history, Simon knew that the pilgrimage he set off on in "Graceland" took him "through the cradle of the Civil War." Although Simon's use of South African musicians on the *Graceland* album elicited a certain amount of silly criticism, the album was clearly intended as a statement against racism and apartheid. So it's ironic that the song came to represent, in the increasingly polarized racial climate, the white tendency to substitute abstract mythology for a history of racial oppression. Moving away from the Civil War, Simon meditates on the inchoate spiritual malaise that draws him to Memphis. Aware that he may be using the myth to evade reality, Simon's persona—he's never so simple as to present a clearly autobiographical "I"—concludes that he has "reason to believe / We all will be received / In Graceland." Speaking for the black help, Living Colour expressed some doubts. As lead vocalist Corey Glover sang, *he* had "reason to believe we all won't be received at Graceland."

By the time Simon released "Graceland," Chuck D had had about all of Saint Elvis he could take. Showcased in Spike Lee's movie *Do the Right Thing,* Public Enemy's attack on Elvis in "Fight the Power" received extensive attention outside the rap community. Striking out against Simon's style of liberalism, Chuck D and sidekick Flavor Flav engage in a discussion of "universalism." "We are the same," raps Chuck, while the court jester counters "we're not the same / cause we don't know the game." Contemplating the U.S. Postal Service's plans for a stamp commemorating the King, Chuck D got straight to the point, not bothering to make subtle distinctions between Simon and the other pilgrims to Graceland: "Elvis was a hero to most / But he never meant shit to me you see / Straight up racist that sucker was / Simple and plain / Motherfuck him and John Wayne."

If Elvis was simple, it was the most complicated kind of simple there is. In the early days, Elvis played a crucial role in crafting a new interracial musical style. But in the late sixties, he was an open supporter of both Richard Nixon and George Wallace. Public Enemy wasn't entirely right, but they weren't entirely wrong either. What was most interesting about their take was how much it, like Simon's and U2's, reflected the Reagan era confusion of image and reality. No one even bothered to pretend that what Elvis actually *was* matters. By 1988, what he meant to anyone seemed strictly a function of race. White Elvis the savior meets Black Elvis the enslaver.

So the appearance of Living Colour's "Elvis Is Dead" in 1990 came as a major relief. Founded by Black Rock Coalition member Vernon Reid, who had already established himself as an important post-Hendrix guitarist in the downtown New York avant-garde, Living Colour, which had launched one of the most caustic attacks on the era's obsession with image in "Cult of Personality," played an important role in the argument over Elvis by mediating between the "white" and "black" myths. No doubt influenced by their unique position as a black hard rock band with major MTV visibility, the group did its level best to bring history back into the discussion. When they expressed their doubts about Southern hospitality, Graceland style, the group echoed Chuck D's dismissal of Simon's liberalism. But they immédiately shifted attention to PE: "Elvis was a hero to most / But that's beside the point." For Living Colour the point was that the liberating energies of Elvis's performances had been thoroughly contained. Recognizing Elvis's sexuality as "too dangerous for the masses," Glover describes how the authorities used his sanitized image to enslave the masses, "even from the grave." As a subversive force, Elvis is most definitely dead. The white boy from Tupelo met the tar baby, too. To make sure no one missed the point, Living Colour repeats the line "Elvis is dead" over and over in a variety of voices, black and white, before the closing announcement that "Elvis has left the building."

If "Elvis Is Dead" takes a step beyond Reagan dichotomies, it took someone who was neither "us" nor "them" to bring history back into contact with myth. Best known as spokesperson for the American Indian Movement at Wounded Knee, American Indian activist John Trudell felt no sentimental affection for mainstream American heroes. Although no legal action was ever taken, the death of his family in a fire on the Pine Ridge Reservation was part of a pattern of vigilante violence against Indian activists. Trudell "retired" from political action in the seventies because, as he said, "it was getting to be too dangerous for my friends." When director Michael Apted recruited Trudell for a part in *Thunderheart,* he asked him whether he thought he could play an "angry Indian." Trudell simply nodded and said, "I think I can handle that."

The fact that Trudell's radical political credentials were beyond question made his tribute to Elvis all the more compelling. Set to a medley of riffs from Elvis's "pre-containment" songs, "Baby Boom Che" places Presley's music in the historical context of a post–World War II America suffering under a "psychic pall so widespread as to be assumed normal." "Baby Boom Che" testifies to how Presley's music helped lift the pall. "He raised our voice," Trudell raps, "and when we heard ourselves, something was changing." Calling the battle Presley fought with the help of his "commandants"—Chuck Berry, Little Richard, Buddy Holly, Gene Vincent, and Bo Diddley— "a different civil war," Trudell invokes "Don't Be Cruel," "I Want You, I Need You, I Love You," and "Jailhouse Rock" to stress the political dimensions of Elvis's music. "Wanting and needing and imprisonment / we've all been to those places," he sings. "For a while we had a breath of fresh energy to keep us from falling into the big sleep."

It would provide a neat little parable if the cultural battle for possession of Elvis's corpse came to an end with "Baby Boom Che." The moral of the story would have been that the way to break down an us/them system is to introduce a third term. But it isn't quite that simple. So we're going to wind up where we started out in 1984, with U2's semireligious obsessions. Joined by producer Brian Eno and recording as the "Passengers," Bono and his bandmates wanted to make it clear that they'd been listening to what everyone else had been saying. The result was "Elvis Ate America." While a low voice puts down a background mantra of "Elvis," Bono recites key verses from the book of the King. In a voice energized by hipster self-parody, Bono mingles his vision of the resurrection of Saint Elvis with the racial politics which never emerged from the murk of "Elvis Presley and America": "Ain't gonna rot in a Memphis plot / didn't hear the shot / Dr. King died just across the lot." Whomever and whatever Elvis may have saved, it wasn't Dr. King and his dream of interracial harmony.

Bono goes on to acknowledge some of the other voices in the choir, alluding to Greil Marcus's commentary on Presley's "American Trilogy"—"Dixie," "The Battle Hymn of the Republic," and the old slave spiritual "All My Trials"—as a bizarre attempt to erase racial divisions without acknowledging the blood and pain and despair. Referring to Elvis as a "white nigger," Bono equates Elvis's devouring of America's mythic music with an attempt to eat America "before America ate him." The final line may or may not be a response to Living Colour's take on the Elvis who enslaves America from the grave, but there's no doubt that the next lines clearly respond to the rap attacks. Bono refers to Elvis as a "public enemy" and drawls that he "don't mean shit to Chuck D." So, unlike "Elvis Presley and America," with its images of broken communication, "Elvis Ate America" knows there's an actual historical conversation in progress. But in the end, as it always seemed to with the white rockers, it came back to Saint Elvis.

Maybe the best way to take leave of the never-ending argument on Elvis is with a piece that doesn't take it all quite so seriously: Mojo Nixon and Skid Roper's "Elvis Is Everywhere," a hilarious rocker delivered in mock sermon style that pokes fun at white celebrations of the King. Elvis is in your jeans, your cheeseburgers, your nutty buddies, and your mom, not to mention people of all colors: white, black, brown, and blue. There's only one exception, "the anti-Elvis," who has "no Elvis in him." Michael J. Fox. Which is about as likely to elicit a universal "amen" as anything we're likely to get.

# 52
# Megastardom and Its Discontents: Michael and Madonna

From its vantage point in the midst of a racial catastrophe of biblical proportions, the entertainment industry somehow came to the conclusion that everything was just fine. When you got down to it, people were people, race didn't make all that much difference, and, most important, friendship would conquer all.

During the late eighties and early nineties, as Benjamin DeMott demonstrates in his insightful book *The Trouble with Friendship: Why Americans Can't Think Straight About Race,* Hollywood movies created a fantasy world of interracial friendship and goodwill. As evidence, DeMott cites *Driving Miss Daisy, Pulp Fiction, White Men Can't Jump, Sister Act, 48 Hours, Die Hard with a Vengeance, Fried Green Tomatoes, The Shawshank Redemption,* and over thirty other movies. The same week I read his book, I saw *Crimson Tide* and *Mississippi Burning,* both of which fit comfortably into his approach.

DeMott emphasizes that the friendship movies bear almost no resemblance to most Americans' actual experience of race. "What's dreamed of and gained," he writes, "is a place where whites are unafraid of blacks, where blacks ask for and need nothing from whites, and where the sameness of the races creates a common fund of sweet content." DeMott describes the deep logic behind the idea that friendship can overcome the blues realities of Reagan and post-Reagan America:

> Yesterday white people didn't like black people, and accordingly suffered guilt, knowing that the dislike was racist and knowing also that as moral persons they would have to atone for the guilt. They would have to ante up for welfare and Head Start and halfway houses and free vaccine and midnight basketball and summer jobs for schoolkids and graduate fellowships for promising scholars and craft-union ap-

prenticeships and so on, endlessly. A considerable and wasteful expense. But at length came the realization that by ending dislike or hatred it would be possible to end guilt, which in turn would mean an end to redress: no more wasteful ransom money. There would be but one requirement: the regular production and continuous showing forth of evidence indisputably proving that hatred has totally vanished from the land.

The pattern DeMott identifies originated not in film, but in the marketing (though not necessarily the music) of the musical megastars of the eighties: Michael Jackson, Madonna, and Prince. At the peaks of their popularity, each reached enormous audiences. During late 1984, "Purple Rain" made Prince the first artist since the Beatles to have the number one single, album, and movie the same week; capping Jackson's ascent to a level of stardom reached only by Elvis, *Thriller* sold forty million copies; *Rolling Stone*'s claim that Madonna was "the most famous woman alive" probably wasn't an exaggeration. What's striking about their popularity in the context of Reagan's America is how completely it appeared to transcend racial divisions.

As a product of Motown, Michael had always attracted both black and white listeners. Madonna was the only major white star of the decade with a substantial black following, attracted primarily by dance-oriented remixes of her hits. Prince was a different story, and we'll get back to him later. Michael and Madonna benefited enormously from the emergence of MTV as a central force in the music industry. The perfect manifestation of the Reagan Rule elevating image over concrete reality, MTV's visuals determined the cultural significance of Michael and Madonna more than the music they created.

In line with the developing racial friendship ideology, the megastars' images consistently ignored or erased potentially divisive interracial conflict. Crowd shots from concerts *always* portrayed an integrated audience; the backing dance troupes included dancers of all races. In their behavior and appearance, the megastars refused to accept constraints on their personal identity. Michael's skin grew lighter, his nose thinner; Prince combed out his Afro, changed costume every few hours; Madonna transgressed every boundary she encountered. Race and gender became fluid, matters of personal choice. Historical and social forces lost their defining power. Come with us, their images whispered, and you can be free.

The freedom was precisely the same sort offered by Elvis's "American Trilogy." It consisted of membership in the largest imaginable community. Anyone, regardless of race or gender, could join. We could all be friends. All you had to give up was history. The message fit right in with the rest of Reagan's America.

It wasn't, however, the message of the megastars' music. Each maintained a much deeper awareness of the complexities of the outside world than their marketed images implied. That isn't to say they managed to solve the problem. But each developed a distinctive way of dealing with the problems posed by their popularity. While Michael and Madonna explored ways of raising and lowering their masks while standing in the spotlight, Prince refused the terms of the game.

Michael Jackson's awareness of the mask was clear at least as early as "Billie Jean," which was released just at the point where he was making the transition from stardom to something larger. One of the best albums of the late seventies, *Off the Wall* had reestablished Jackson as both a commercial and a creative force. Highlighted by "Rock with You" and the tellingly titled "Don't Stop Til You Get Enough," *Off the Wall* served notice that he had bigger things in mind. The video for "Billie Jean," the first single release from 1983's *Thriller,* could easily be understood as an astute, and unmistakably black, rejection of the Reagan Rules. The video opens with images of a windswept urban scene dominated by a sign reading "Ron's Drugs and Watches." The plot centers around Jackson's successful attempt to escape from a pursuing authority figure. Playing the role of Brer Rabbit-as-urban-trickster, he dances away into the briar patch, leaving Ron's world behind.

As things worked out, Jackson didn't actually make such a clean escape. The unprecedented popularity of his videos complemented a musical strategy crafted to increase the white rock audience that heard *Off the Wall* as near-disco. The center of the strategy was drafting first-line rock guitarists to contribute solos to Jackson's hits. Eddie Van Halen played guitar on "Beat It"; a few years later Slash of Guns n' Roses played on "Black or White." But the success of the strategy was double-edged. In his book *Trapped: Michael Jackson and the Crossover Dream,* Dave Marsh pinpoints the problem in an open letter to Jackson. On one hand, Marsh acknowledges the importance of overcoming Reagan era racial divisions: "To me, your real victory with *Thriller* came when you united an audience of almost unprecedented diversity and forced blacks and whites, rich and poor, young and old, boys and girls, and all the rest, to recognize each other for an instant." But, Marsh continues, the cost of the victory was to initiate precisely the pattern DeMott saw climaxing in the nineties:

> In this sense, if *Thriller* made a difference in history, it was a negative one. Its contribution was to make the people who bought it think that everything was all right, when it was anything but. That may have been the most masterful of all the illusions you spread, and I'd guess that it's the real reason that Ronald Reagan wanted you to come to the White House. Wherever Michael Jackson went in 1983 and 1984, things were all right.

The 1991 video for "Black or White" raises a set of fascinating and complicated questions concerning Jackson's awareness of megastardom, masking, and the friendship ideology. On the surface, "Black or White" seems the clearest possible endorsement of the friendship ideology. The video fades out with a sequence of multicolored faces morphing into one another. Asian women become black men become white men become Latinas become black women and on and on into a sunshine world where we celebrate diversity and music heals all wounds. Throughout the video, Michael reduces cultural differences to part of a dance that unites his own moves with American Indian ceremonial dancing, stylized African performances, and Hindu temple dancing. No cultural tradition seems to signify anything in particular, to refer us back to a history of brutal experiences. It's a perfect celebration of the friendship approach to racial problems.

But there's a catch. After the initial showing of "Black or White"—which was broadcast simultaneously on Fox, BET, MTV, and BBC-1 in England—few viewers saw the entire video. Following the morphing sequence, the full-length video continued with a stunning sequence in which Jackson unleashes a hurricane of anger, smashing car windows, screaming, and growling in unrestrained fury. It amounts to a glimpse behind the mask. The blues explosion gives the lie to the friendly surface. The entertainment industry, committed to the idea that hatred had vanished from the land, asked that the violent sequence be omitted, and Michael complied. Whether you consider that an intelligent commercial compromise or a failure of nerve depends on your sense of the game. If he'd insisted on the original version of the video, it certainly wouldn't have received the attention it did. And the full-length version is available to anyone who wants to buy or rent a compilation from a video store.

Is the audience aware of the anger behind the mask? The one thing you can be sure of is that the industry won't ask.

Madonna's relationship to the mask is, if possible, more complicated than Michael's. When "Lucky Star," "Like a Virgin," and "Material Girl" catapulted her into the spotlight, Madonna had developed both a fierce desire for stardom and a deep awareness of how that desire contributed to its own kind of blues. During the late seventies and early eighties, she'd spent time in discos and the downtown New York punk clubs. From the gay men who have always remained among her closest friends, she learned a great deal about the use of irony as weapon and defense; from the punk scene, she learned the value of pure toughness for women confronting a male-dominated scene. She understood the significance of the fact that both Deborah Harry of Blondie and Chrissie Hynde of the Pretenders had had to leave the punk sound behind in order to make it big in the music world.

Combining the various sides of her awareness and drawing on her dance experience with several New York troupes, Madonna developed a public persona that parodied pop culture definitions of women as sexual objects while maintaining a deep blues awareness. Produced by Chic's Nile Rodgers, "Material Girl" announces Madonna's intention to play the game better than it plays her. Her next album, *True Blue,* featured "Live to Tell" and "Papa Don't Preach," two of the most powerful women's blues of the Reagan era. Although Madonna's Catholic upbringing complicated her relationship with the black gospel tradition, which usually worked from a Protestant foundation, she clearly understood the value of community. In her movie, *Truth or Dare,* Madonna leads the members of her troupe in an impromptu rendition of the movement standard "We Shall Overcome" when censors threaten to stop their performance.

It was never easy to place Madonna in either a "white" or "black" tradition. Her songs echoed the aggressiveness of white women rockers such as Patti Smith ("Gloria") and Chrissie Hynde ("Stop Your Sobbing," "Brass in Pocket [I'm Special]") and point ahead to Liz Phair ("Whip-Smart") and Alanis Morisette ("All I Really Want," "Hand in My Pocket"). As Phair commented, "Madonna kicked a huge rough-hewn patch through the jungle and we're all tiptoeing behind her saying, 'Look at all the pretty flowers.' Madonna made it possible for me to be interpreted properly."

While Madonna deserves her central place in the history of white women's music, a full understanding of her approach requires an awareness of the black women singers who had a very different relationship to both silence and the mask. From the time Ma Rainey invited anyone who didn't like her performance to kiss her black bottom, women sang the blues with as much humor and aggressiveness as their male counterparts. Their descendants in R & B followed their example. Ruth Brown ("Mama, He Treats Your Daughter Mean"), KoKo Taylor ("Wang Dang Doodle"), Jan Bradley ("Mama Didn't Lie"), LaBelle ("Lady Marmalade"), and Tina Turner ("What's Love Got to Do with It?") all gave as good as they got in their verbal battles with black men. Not that black women were free of social pressures. It was simply that they had learned how to make their own choices about whether and when to put on a mask.

Madonna's most fascinating video, "Like a Prayer," explores the complicated relationship between masking, race, and sexuality. A morality play on the theme of racial injustice, the video focuses on the conflict between a gang of white supremacists who frame a saintly black man for the stabbing (and by implication, rape) of Madonna. Against a backdrop of burning crosses, Madonna dances in her trademark lingerie while a gospel choir adds power to her pleading vocal. Until almost the end, the video seems to be confronting precisely the issue the friendship ideology sought to avoid: the continuing reality of racial violence grounded in unacknowledged sexual fears. The drama at the center of "Like a Prayer" is both serious and compelling.

But the ending turns it all sideways, if not quite upside down. Recovering from her wound, Madonna goes to the jail and explains what really happened to the police, who readily release the black man from his cell. The good white folk, it seems, only want to see justice done. Only the bad skinheads are bothered by the possibility of interracial sex. The black women in the gospel chorus, in an unlikely turn of plot, are pleased as punch to see the black man together with his white boy toy. The curtain closes over an image of a tear on the face of the black man, who has been transformed to wooden icon.

And then another ending gives it all another turn. The curtain opens, and the cast takes a bow. It's a standard postmodern gesture, reminding us it was *all* a fantasy. A sufficiently creative viewer is free to respond to the emancipation scene as a forced compromise with the video format. Or to see the curtain call as a cynical dismissal of the entire production as just another piece in the pop culture flow, worth whatever the market says it's worth. The whole point of pop, as Madonna well knew, is that it won't force issues the audience doesn't want forced.

## 53
## Duke Ellington for Our Time:
## The Symbol Formerly Known as Prince

Miles Davis offered Prince the highest praise one jazzman can give another when he wrote: "he can be the new Duke Ellington of our times." The comparison should be understood literally. In addition to changing the way the world heard music, Duke's great bands were dance bands, profoundly in sync with the changing rhythms of black America. The divergence between "art" and "entertainment" in black culture didn't gather any momentum until Charlie Parker and Dizzy Gillespie's bebop rebelled against minstrel dilutions of swing after World War II. From the twenties on, Duke worked his magic on every form of black popular music. So has Prince.

More complicated in his use of the mask than either Michael or Madonna, Prince has presented himself as soul balladeer, psychedelic guitarist, funkmaster, hippie survivor, seducer supreme, gender bender extraordinaire, behind-the-scenes genius, and spiritual visionary. Miles understood the centrality of gospel to Prince's jazz-oriented creative process. In an insightful comment on Prince's eclectic redefinition of his musical heritage, Miles wrote:

> I really love Prince, and after I heard him, I wanted to play with him sometime. Prince is from the school of James Brown. . . . But Prince got some Marvin Gaye and Jimi Hendrix and Sly in him, also, even Little Richard. He's a mixture of all those guys and Duke Ellington. He reminds me, in a way, of Charlie Chaplin. . . . But it's the church thing I hear in his music that makes him special.

The most striking difference between Duke Ellington and Prince concerns visual style, and reflects the difference in the racial politics of their eras. Throughout his life, Ellington embodied *class*. An immaculate dresser in Jim Crow America, he quietly revealed the foolishness of stereotypes that implied blacks were incapable of meeting the most demanding standards of white society. Because he had no illusions about either the reality or the superiority of those standards, Ellington never made the mistake of losing touch with his people. Even when his journey took him to Carnegie Hall and the White House, he remembered that the A train had carried him to stardom.

Reaching megastardom at the height of the Reagan era, Prince confronted a different set of problems. But he developed a parallel solution: Refuse to accept the terms of the game, don't lose track of your own voice, stay in touch with the sounds of the street. Prince spent the first few years of his career confined to the R & B ghetto, attracting little response from white listeners before *Dirty Mind* and *Controversy*. From the start, the pop audience concentrated primarily on erotic songs like "Head" and "Do Me, Baby." No question about it, Prince was playing the sex for all it was worth. The problem came from his white audience's lack of cultural literacy. When many listeners heard a song "about" sex, they heard a song about sex. Grounded in the gospel impulse and clearly aware of the spiritual sexuality of Al Green and Marvin Gaye, Prince was (usually) testifying to sex and love *and* the power of the Lord.

The problem became particularly acute once Prince attained true megastardom with the success of "Purple Rain" as single, album, video, and movie. Although Miles identified Prince's sound as "a black thing and not a white thing," he pointed to Prince's connections with the interracial music of the late sixties. Like Sly and the Family Stone, Prince's band, the Revolution, featured blacks, whites, men and women. The guitar solo that concludes the album version of "Purple Rain" (edited out of the video) stakes his claim as Hendrix's musical heir. "Purple Rain" threatened to lock Prince into a static, marketable form. The devil offered him the kingdom of the world. Prince refused. He never even toyed with repeating "Purple Rain." His next album, *Around the World in a Day*, reworked the psychedelic visions of the Beatles' *Sgt. Pepper's* and *Magical Mystery Tour.* Significantly, it concluded with "The Ladder" and "Temptation." Prince responded to the lures of the world by restating his spiritual vision, equal parts gospel and jazz.

Not that Prince ever abandoned his roots in black popular music. "Housequake" from *Sign of the Times* may well be the best James Brown cut of the eighties; "The Most Beautiful Girl in the World" reminds you that Prince's first two albums caressed your soul like Marvin or Smokey Robinson. Like most jazzmen, Prince is both prolific and erratic. To get a real sense of his range, you have to listen to the albums he wrote, produced, and played on for the Time, Vanity 6, and Madhouse alongside his own. When he's off, he's off. But he never denies his process and it's generated some of the most profoundly subversive music of our time. Combining crystalline realism and metaphorical density, "Sign of the Times" attacks Reaganism at its core. Backed by a sparse funky beat and his brilliant guitar, the song insists on the blues realities of poverty, addiction, violence, and AIDS. Image, the master of shifting images tells Reagan, shifting images, *ain't* what it's about.

Ultimately, Prince doesn't change as much as it might seem. Miles was the same way. He changed the members of his bands and kept responding to different musical styles. He refused to be locked into a dialogue with anyone's preconceptions about who he should be or how he should look. But at the center of a changing soundscape, Miles's vision of the world, the sound of his voice, remained remarkably consistent. You can always tell it's Miles's horn, no matter whether the rest of the band's playing hard bop, fusion jazz, or orchestrations of Spanish classical concertos.

The same is true with Prince. Through all the changes, he's maintained a central concern with the meaning of spiritual experience in a changing world. Like every other soulman (and for that matter, Madonna), he refuses to separate his explorations of the spirit from his experiences of love and sex. Although the movie *Purple Rain* presented Prince as the embodiment of the most fundamental rock myth—the kid who makes it—the music strained for redemption. "When Doves Cry" and the title cut transform the blues realities of the world where he's been left standing all alone into a plea for understanding and forgiveness. On the "Lovesexy" tour, Prince played "Purple Rain" and his breakthrough hit "1999" as part of a sexual/spiritual mix including "The Cross," "I Wish U Heaven," and "Kiss." They fit perfectly. As the tour developed, Prince frequently delivered sermons on his jazz vision of sex and the spirit:

Who's interested to go on? Who's interested to get up out of this consciousness? Who's interested to try my new drug? It's called "Lovesexy." The feeling you get when you fall in love, not with a girl or boy, but with the heavens above. "Lovesexy." I did not come to preach. I came to have a good time, but from now on let's have a good time for the right reasons. What do you say? I wanna know, who's with me tonight?

Prince didn't exactly mask his meanings. But his jazz sensibility was so rare in the pop world of the eighties, he was impossible to contain. Whatever box the industry might try to put him in, it wasn't big enough. By the time the image caught up with where he'd been, he was somewhere else. Prince invited the audience attracted by his mastery of rock and soul styles to join in the jazz quest for gospel redemption. But he was never coercive. The flip side of "Purple Rain" was a song named "God." It's a perfect expression of how Prince dealt with his stardom. At the precise moment he reached the peak of the megastar system, he reconfirmed his fundamental quest. The song combines one of Prince's best gospel vocals—his voice climbs until it breaks and drops deep down into the moan—with his most adventurous piano playing. The chord clusters he hammers out sound like a spiritual duet with Thelonious Monk or Cecil Taylor. The God of Prince's music can't be contained in an image.

Neither can the symbol formerly known as Prince. When he declared his old self dead and assigned himself the new identity represented by a glyph combining images representing male, female, and music, he was simply reiterating the basic principles of the jazz impulse. Prince's jazz presence was particularly important since the seventies and eighties had raised serious questions about whether jazz retained its subversive force or whether it had passed over to the status of "Cultural Monument," distant, foreboding, and politically inert. The most popular "jazz" musician of the eighties, Wynton Marsalis, and his theoretical sidekick, Stanley Crouch, have done their best to elevate jazz to "art." Wynton, they claim, is Duke Ellington's heir. The Pulitzer Prize he received for *Blood on the Fields* proves it.

Duke, of course, never won a Pulitzer. He was too close to the streets and too far away from the cultural power brokers. The difference for Wynton is that the cultural elite now listens to the jazz of forty years ago, which sounds pretty much like what Wynton's doing today.

Miles was right. Duke's real heir is Prince, who hasn't forgotten the dance. And he hasn't forgotten that the dance is a way of summoning the Lord, transcending the separation of body and spirit. If you're already a member of Wynton's church, he's not a bad preacher, at least when he lets his horn do the testifying. But in a world where not many people are still scuffling to figure out how to make sense of a changing world, Prince has a hell of a lot better chance of saving souls.

## 54
## West Africa Is in the House

While the megastars mesmerized their immense audiences, aggressively *local* music scenes provided alternatives to pop anonymity. In Athens, Georgia, and Austin, Texas, as well as Seattle, Detroit, Minneapolis, Chicago, and Washington, D.C., distinctive musical subcultures asserted the reality of group experiences that couldn't be reduced to decorations in the Reagan era fantasy world where differences no longer mattered. Determined to resist outside definitions, the scenes generated a dizzying array of sounds, each with a flavor distilled from its social location and community mix. Where most of the rock scenes expressed a blues anger at an unfair world, the dance scenes sought ways to renew spiritual community as an alternative to Reagan era puritanism and materialism.

The reason house music never broke through to a larger audience is that records don't even begin to catch the feel of what happened in the clubs where dance music communities came together. While DJ tapes get a little bit closer, they're both hard to find and extremely ephemeral. Unless you've been keeping an archive since the seventies, there's no way to get a sense of what the music played at legendary house clubs like Chicago's Warehouse, New Jersey's Zanzibar, or New York's Loft and Garage actually sounded like. Each city built its own house, its own sonic environment reflecting the specific mix of the community and the imagination of the leading DJs. Shaped by DJs Juan Atkins, Derrick May, and Kevin Saunderson, Detroit's jazzy "Techno" sound reflected the city's fascination with European techno pop like Kraftwerk's "Trans-Europe Express," which had broken into the U.S. market on Detroit's black radio stations. Another chapter in Chicago's long-standing gospel soul tradition, the city's "deep house" sound mixed Philly International and disco "classics" with the celebratory productions of Marshall Jefferson and Frankie Knuckles. A strong Latin presence spiced the house mixes in New Jersey and Chicago, home to the "Queen of Deep House," Liz Torres, and the group "2 Puerto Ricans, A Blackman, and A Dominican."

In contrast to hip-hop, which was dominated by aggressively heterosexual (and often openly homophobic) male voices, eighties house celebrated a free-flowing sexual energy that welcomed the voices of women and gays. In Chicago, house had originated largely in black gay dance clubs which refused to surrender disco to the upscale mainstream. DJ Frankie Knuckles described his approach to house music as a conscious attempt to transcend the racial divisions he experienced when he moved from New York to Chicago: "I grew up with blacks living on top of whites, Italians living on top of them, and Jews living across the hall. I was never ever called a 'nigger' or a 'black motherfucker' until I moved to Chicago. It blew my mind. I decided to stay and do something about it. I was the first Chicago DJ to bring black and white, gay and straight together in one room."

Some of the leading house figures were openly gay, most notably Jamie Principle, whose "We Dance to Political Destruction" brings the political subtext of the music to the surface. There were plenty of straight males in the house scene, too, but few had problems with the music's inclusive energy. House resounded with women's voices responding to their older sisters in gospel, soul, and disco. Adeva's "Respect" reasserted Aretha's call in the changed circumstances of AIDS and the antigay violence that increased dramatically in the mid-eighties. No DJ who refused to play Loleatta Holloway's "Hit and Run," Liz Torres's "Can't Get Enough," or the intense gospel vocals Jocelyn Brown and Alicia Myers recorded with Inner Life and One Way would have made it through a single night at the Garage or the Warehouse.

Brian Chin expressed the house vision in straight gospel terms: "House music surely speaks for itself. Its ideals—peace among all people; sharing thoughts and emotions without self-consciousness; unconditional belonging—emerge inevitably as subtexts, whether it's in your favorite selection of house songs, or in a solitary, uncomplicated line of reassurance: 'We don't really need a crowd to have a party.'" The best house mixes wove tapestries that testified to the continuity of the gospel impulse: MFSB's "Love Is the Message," Blaze's "We Must All Live Together," Sister Sledge's "We Are Family," CeCe Rodgers's "Someday," First Choice's "Let No Man Put Asunder," Inner Life's "Ain't No Mountain High Enough." Fingers, Inc., a Chicago house group consisting of instrumentalist-producer Larry

Heard and brilliant soul vocalist Robert Owens, summed up the house message in the classic revoicing of Martin Luther King's "I Have a Dream" speech, "Our House": "You may be black, you may be white / You may be Jew, you may be gentile / It don't make no difference in *our* house."

But you had to be *in* the house to feel the acceptance. For the DJs and dancers who came together in the clubs, the dance floor signified much the same thing as the "threshing floors" of the sanctified churches. DJs like Larry Levan and Tony Humphries created gospel communities out of the burdened individuals who found their ways onto the dance floor. Calling down the spirit with records that were themselves responses to the brutal world outside, the DJs invited the dancers to share their emotions, their burdens, and their dreams. As Ed Pavlic observes, a good DJ will drop in a bit from a song he's thinking about playing to test the audience response. Recognizing the cues, experienced dancers respond by changing their energy, moving together with other dancers whose movements show they've heard the call. A good DJ hears, and sees, the calls and responses between dancers and records, and broadens the circle, passes them on. When it works, the house club becomes a new version of the beloved community, one of the purest expressions of the gospel impulse. Paying homage to Larry Levan, DJ David DePino observed with wonder, "He was able to get 2,000 people to feel the same emotion and peak at the same time. He could make 2,000 people feel like one."

When the spirit moved through the house clubs, it was almost as if disco had returned to its roots in gospel and soul and then followed those roots back to their West African sources. The Yoruba people of modern Nigeria, whose traditions were transported to the Western Hemisphere during the slave trade, conceive the world in terms of multiple overlapping energies. Each of the Yoruba spirits, or orishas, represents a different type of energy, a different way of being in the world. Individuals become devotees of the orisha whose energy most resembles their own, seeking to attain higher levels of spiritual understanding. Because the fate of the individual, for the Yoruba, cannot be separated from the fate of the community, this spiritual understanding contributes to communal well-being. From this perspective, the point of spiritual development is not to adhere to a rigid set of rules, to become *like* the other believers. Rather, it is to develop your own energy as fully as possible so it will be available to the community when needed. Conceiving of the world in constant motion, the Yoruba know that *all* energies, all types of people, contribute to the health of the larger community.

That's exactly the approach to life that allowed the house clubs of the eighties to present a real alternative to the Reagan Rules. Reaching back to the gospel vision, the house scenes were almost always *inc*lusive in their energy. It wasn't really a contradiction that that energy grew out of the specific rituals of membership clubs, all-gay nights, and the sense of an underground community under siege. Even though the music originated in black and/or gay and/or Latin clubs, whites and/or straights and/or Latins and/or Asians sharing the underlying acceptance of diversity had little trouble finding a place in the dance.

# 55
# "Bring the Noise":
# The New School Rap Game

As the eighties passed from the giddy cocaine high of the junk bond boom to the quagmire of the Iran-contra scandal and the drive-by war in the Persian Gulf, it became increasingly clear that inclusive visions were under siege. If Run-D.M.C.'s stylized B-Boy image dominated rap's center stage in 1984, by the end of Reagan's second term, the spotlight had shifted to Public Enemy. Public Enemy's struggle to escape the Reagan Rules presented a kind of morality play on the theme of good versus evil. Their response to Elvis reflected the most disturbing current in their work: the tendency to see the world in terms of black and white. But on other levels, PE sounded the strongest call of refusal to emerge during the decade, screaming out the theoretical corollary to Run-D.M.C.'s "It's Like That": "Don't Believe the Hype." To a large extent, the group succeeded in realizing their announced plan to "Rock the hard jams—treat it like a seminar / Teach the bourgeois, and rock the boulevards."

The central presence in Public Enemy was rapper Chuck D (Carlton Ridenhour), who met the group's producer and manager Hank

Shocklee at Adelphi University, where he was working at the student radio station and studying graphic design. Two other members played major roles in the group's public image. Sidekick rapper/jester Flavor Flav (William Drayton) was best known for his outrageous sense of humor and bizarre dress; he typically wore a Mad Hatter top hat along with a giant clock around his neck. While Flav provided relief from Chuck D's aggressively serious sensibility, he played an equally important role by grounding the group's political explorations in a firm sense of the blues realities of black life. The third public member of the group was DJ Terminator X (Norman Rogers), who worked alongside the "Bomb Squad" production team of Hank Shocklee, Keith Shocklee, and Eric "Vietnam" Sadler.

The importance of the Bomb Squad becomes clear when you consider that from the start PE's impact came as much from its deeply subversive music as from its overtly political lyrics, which at times perpetuated the us/them phrasing of the Reagan era. Grounding their sound in propulsive bass riffs and topping it with their signature siren wails, the Bomb Squad created sound collages that said amen to George Clinton's funk sermon on the theme "Free your mind and your ass will follow." Like Clinton, PE knew that the primary instrument in modern music is the *studio*. If PE's lyrics sometimes implied black separatism, their approach to sampling made it clear that they listened to everything. There were hard-rock guitars, snatches of jazz. PE could take it into the conceptual stratosphere with Bird, Hendrix, and Coltrane on a cut like "Contract on the World Love Jam." Against a funky bass line, ominous minor chords, and turntable scratches out of the old school, the Bomb Squad montaged sound bites that could be heard as collective autobiography, black nationalist credo, jazz manifesto, and/or the disintegration of community in a media age. The bites juxtaposed terrorist groups and "individual concerns," references to controversies in the rap world and Afrocentric points of view. Warning that "the future of the group is in doubt," PE collapsed the distance between autobiography and social commentary before concluding: "there is something changing in the climate of consciousness on this planet today." Declaring themselves "Rebels Without a Pause," PE envisioned a "new school rap game," a hard-rocking party where people could deal with the realities of politics and the nature of consciousness.

Chuck D was well aware of the challenges PE's music posed, associating himself with the jazz tradition. Taunting "writers [who] treat me like Coltrane insane," he claimed brotherhood with his spiritual ancestor: "we're brothers of the same mind, unblind." The comparison wasn't as much of a reach as it might have seemed to those who associated rap with gold chains and gangsta fantasies. The sound of *It Takes a Nation of Millions to Hold Us Back* and *Fear of a Black Planet* was something new, black and beyond black. PE had company in forging that sound, most notably in Eric B and Rakim, and EPMD, whose "Strictly Business" represents rap's complexity at its best. Like PE's best sides, "Strictly Business" combined an irresistible rhythmic groove with a lyric line that commented on the reality behind the hype. The key to the cut was EPMD's sampling of Bob Marley's "I Shot the Sheriff." Aware that members of oppressed groups are frequently hired to do the dirty work—black deputies frequently handle arrests in black areas—Marley presented himself as a politically conscious outlaw striking out against the true source of oppression: "I shot the sheriff, but I did not shoot the deputy." It's anyone's guess what the song meant to Eric Clapton, whose record company encouraged him to record it as an implicit apology to black fans after he unwittingly lent support to a right-wing political candidate. Clapton's version went to number one. Sampling Clapton rather than Marley, EPMD commented on both the minstrel exploitation of black music and the decay of political awareness among blacks since Marley's time. Lacking a unified movement to channel their energy, they find themselves "one on one in the land of the lost."

At its best, PE expressed a similar combination of political intelligence and street realism. But all too frequently, they found themselves locked in a less constructive, more disturbing struggle with Reagan-style us/them phrasings. Despite the fact that much of the problem stemmed from comments made by "Minister of Information" Professor Griff, who made no contribution to the group's music, PE was forced to expend an enormous amount of energy defending itself against charges of anti-Semitism. "Bring the Noise," the first track on *Nation of Millions*, included a passage that received widespread attention in the mainstream media. The rap presents Chuck D as a black man incarcerated because of his commercial success and because "a brother like me" has declared Farrakhan "a prophet," someone to "listen to" and "follow for now." Far from simply endorsing any aspect of the Nation of Islam's world view or agenda, the verse demonstrates PE's literary complexity, which received no attention at all in the mainstream press. Chuck D ties his imprisonment to the inability of white America to tell one brother from another; he's in jail because a brother *like him* said Farrakhan's a prophet. What's more, even that other brother's endorsement of Farrakhan was limited to "for now." And the point of it all was power for the people.

The public response proved the point. "They" never actually put Chuck D in jail, but the firestorm of criticism directed at the group for anti-Semitism echoed the attacks leveled at Jesse Jackson after he refused to condemn the Nation of Islam's leader. Especially after Jackson's ill-considered use of the phrase "Hymietown" during the 1984 campaign, the media consistently projected any contact with Farrakhan as endorsement and overt anti-Semitism. Despite the growing prestige of the Nation in poor black communities abandoned by Reagan's administration, Chuck D and Jackson were condemned for engaging in dialogue with or about its charismatic leader. As Jackson was aware, however, to break off the dialogue with Farrakhan would have been destructive on several levels. First, in a black community which had internalized the Reagan era divisions, it would have branded Jackson as a leader under the control of the white "they." Whatever the mainstream doubts about Jackson, he was one of the very few political figures able to communicate at all across racial lines. If Jackson's 1984 campaign was directed largely toward issues of racial justice, by 1988 he was attempting to forge a "Rainbow Coalition" based on the economic realities faced by Americans of all races. The loss of a meaningful base in the black community would have rendered his efforts nearly meaningless.

Cutting off the dialogue with Farrakhan would also have cut off the call-and-response process which, as we have seen, is fundamental to African American culture. Call and response allows all voices, however extreme or misguided, to be heard. Mistakes can be corrected through discussion, a good idea can be picked up and used even if the person who presents it is out of line on other issues. Profoundly democratic, call and response requires individuals and communities to check off ideological abstractions against concrete blues experiences. It requires that everyone stay in the game. Even when they're most clearly wrong, as Farrakhan, the Nation of Islam, and the extreme Christian right are profoundly wrong about almost everything having to do with Jewish history. This is most definitely *not* the hierarchical, top-down model shared by the Republican National Committee and, ironically enough, the Nation of Islam. By keeping the dialogue open, Jesse Jackson maintained a position that allowed him to convince desperate black folks that there were better approaches than projecting the blame onto the "white devils" or "bloodsucking Jews."

Anti-Semitism should and must be confronted and repudiated whenever it appears. The historical realities of Kristallnacht, the Holocaust, and the Warsaw Ghetto rebellion should be asserted constantly. So when Professor Griff said that Jews are responsible for "the majority of wickedness that goes on across the globe," it was proper and fitting that the statement be rejected forcefully and unambiguously. To the extent that the Nation of Islam propagates anti-Semitism, it should be confronted in open dialogue. Given the importance of dialogue, it was more disturbing when, after the original round of responses to Professor Griff's indefensible comments, Chuck D invited renewed criticism for anti-Semitism in "Welcome to the Terrordome." Announcing that "crucifixion ain't no fiction" and invoking the image of Jews as the "so-called chosen frozen," Chuck D offered a halfhearted apology while associating himself with Jesus on the cross. By that stage in the dialogue, Chuck D should have been more aware of how the words were going to be heard. It was almost impossible to respond to the renewed use of obviously provocative imagery as anything other than a cynical attempt to keep Public Enemy in the newspapers. In a context where interracial coalitions such as the one Jackson was attempting to build were already in deep trouble, the cost of Chuck D's inflammatory words was unacceptably high.

Having said that, two other points need to be made. First, the primary focus of the Nation, and of every speech by Farrakhan I have ever heard, is black empowerment, *not* anti-Semitism. It is unusual for Farrakhan to refer to Jews for more than a couple of minutes in his speeches, which typically last over two hours. Ignoring the historical and economic sources of black-Jewish tensions, the media present a very distorted image. News reports almost never observe that particular ethnic groups become ghetto merchants because they have been excluded from more desirable economic niches, a fact that casts light on the connections between historical black-Jewish tensions and those today between blacks and Chaldeans in Detroit or between blacks and Koreans in L.A. Moreover, the attacks on the Nation create the impression that blacks are responsible for most of the anti-Semitic violence in the United States. As James Ridgeway in *Prophets of Blood* and Raphael Ezekiel in *The Racist Mind* prove beyond a shadow of a doubt, almost all anti-Semitic violence is carried out by white Christian extremist groups, many of which *do* place their attacks on Jews (and blacks) in a central position. Many of these groups provide political support for conservative members of Congress, few of whom are ever called on to explicitly repudiate the extreme statements of their contributors.

It wasn't a simple situation. Chuck D was responding to a real need when he called on his audience to "refuse to lose." The problem with PE's refusal, however, was that all too often it accepted the underlying terms of the Reagan era debate. Failing to learn from the mistakes of the Black Power movement, "Who Stole the Soul?" sets up a cultural morality play in black and white; there's very little doubt about the color of the power in "Fight the Power."

But to focus on PE's acceptance of the Reagan Rules is to miss the point. Even when it was most implicated, PE's emotional power came from a blues base, a point Terminator X made explicit on the powerful cut "The Blues" from his solo album. One of PE's strongest blues statements was "911 Is a Joke," one of the few songs that featured Flav rather than Chuck D. Observing that ghetto residents calling emergency medical services might as well just "get the morgue truck" to "embalm the goner," Flav laid down a laughing-to-keep-from-crying chorus that left no room for evasion: "get up get get get down, 911 is a joke in your town." In Madison, Wisconsin, where I live, the summer the song broke, a fire dispatcher directing a unit to a black housing project "humorously" sang "Somerset is burning down, burning down, burning down" to the tune of "London Bridge." Five black children died in the blaze. They'd been left alone by their mother, who was out at a bar. In this particular Midwestern corner of the terrordome, the reality was as complicated as the blues that Reagan never sang. Moving past the us/them in the same verse of "Welcome to the Terrordome" where he claims to have been "crucified," Chuck D warned that "every brother ain't a brother," citing the murders of Malcolm X and Huey Newton by other black men as evidence. "It's weak to speak and blame somebody else," he concludes, "when you destroy yourself."

This is the heart of the blues. It's out there and it's in here. In Reagan's America it was crucial to have a voice, and a beat, that could at least start to tell the truth.

## 56
## "Know the Ledge":
## KRS-One, Rakim, and the Gangstas

Distinguishing between blues truth and media-fueled fantasy wasn't always all that easy. Ever since Daddy Rice, the original minstrel man, bought his song on the streets of Charleston, black performers who wanted to get paid found themselves in the bizarre situation of needing to "black up," to project images answering to white stereotypes of black life as primal, sexual, violent—in a (particularly unfortunate) word, "authentic." As hip-hop gained popularity, musicians who'd actually lived something resembling the life they sang about in their song faced the temptation of blacking up, catering to the fantasies of the young white men who made up the majority of gangsta rap's audience.

The careers of N.W.A. (Niggaz with Attitude) and one-time N.W.A. member Ice Cube demonstrate the difficulty of remaining true to the game. When N.W.A. released the compilation album *N.W.A. and the Posse,* it wasn't clear to an outsider who was actually in the group. Intended almost entirely for the homeboys who got the blues point, songs like "8 Ball" and "Dope Man" reflect the fast-changing realities of a West Coast street scene where crack cocaine and drive-by shootings had transformed the struggling ghettos of the seventies into out-and-out war zones. Responding to charges that N.W.A. romanticized a destructive lifestyle, Eazy E presented what was to become the standard defense of gangsta rap: "We're telling the real story of what it's like living in places like Compton. We're giving the fans reality. We give them the truth. People where we come from hear so many lies that the truth stands out like a sore thumb."

In other words, raps like "Straight Outta Compton," "Gangsta Gangsta," and "Fuck the Police" carry on the blues impulse, fingering the jagged grain of brutal street experience and helping the homeboys find the strength to carry on. Monster Kody Scott, now known as Sanyika Shakur, captured the complex relationship between the individual and the community on the streets of L.A. Speaking to journalist Leon Bing, Shakur observed that the street situation deteriorated constantly throughout the eighties. Reflecting on the changes, he said: "It's more tense now than ever before. Because back then, if you saw somebody from an enemy set, chances are you'd just fight with 'em. . . . Whereas now—it's gunplay. . . . And everything is high-tech now. Weapons, surveillance, communications, everything. Makes you wonder what would happen if some 'banger with a hate on got his hands on a nuclear device, doesn't it?"

A young man known as B-Dog, confined to a wheelchair since a bullet nicked his spine, confirmed Shakur's report. "When I was coming up," he commented matter-of-factly, "all I knew was my set and the jungle." For most members, the gang provided a source of love and loyalty in a world where the family and church had little impact on daily life. Shakur attributed the rise of gangs in part to the absence of political alternatives. "If I had been born in '53 instead of '63, I would have been a Black Panther. If I had been born in Germany in the early thirties, I would probably have joined the National Socialist Party. If I had been born Jewish, I would have joined the Jewish Defense League. Because I have the energy, the vitality to be a part of something with 'power.' Either constructive or destructive. And because there was a destructive element around me when I was growing up, I went into the Crips." Although most gang members speak of their tight bonds with their set—the gangsta phrasing of the gospel "we"—Shakur underscored the blues reality that "It's individuals who make up a gang, and it's you as individuals, who will get captured, get shot, do the time, get killed."

At its best, gangsta rap described life in the hoods with devastating precision. At its worst, it simply catered to frat row fantasies. N.W.A.'s "To Kill a Hooker" and "Appetite for Destruction" fit comfortably into a sound track along with L.A. hard rockers Guns n' Roses, who careened between the blues brilliance of "Welcome to the Jungle," the near-gospel beauties of "Paradise City," and the uncontrolled anger of "One in a Million." In fact, Axl Rose seemed to think of himself as a kind of white gangsta, frequently wearing an N.W.A. cap on stage. Setting himself up as a working-class hero dedicated to telling the unvarnished truth in "One in a Million," Rose rails against "police and niggers," "immigrants and faggots." Which put Guns n' Roses's black guitarist Slash in what can only be called a difficult position. "Everybody on the black side of the family was like, 'What's your problem?','" Slash recalled. "What am I supposed to say? Axl and I don't stop each other from doing things." Even as he emphasized that "I can't sit here with a clear conscience and say, 'It's OK that it came out,'" Slash explained Axl's determination to release the song in blues terms. "Axl is a naive white boy from Indiana who came to Hollywood, was brought up in a totally Caucasian society, and it was his way of saying how scared he was. . . . it happened and now Axl is being condemned for it, and he takes it really personally. All I can say, really, is that it's a lesson learned." It wasn't clear just what the lesson had been. Guns n' Roses's "I Used to Love Her" bears more than a little resemblance to N.W.A.'s most misogynistic raps. Generating a bizarre kind of blues humor, Rose explains that even though his girlfriend's constant whining forced him to "put her six feet under," he "can still hear her complain." Talk that N.W.A. and Guns n' Roses might tour together made a perfect kind of twisted sense.

Unlike his former bandmates and their hard-rock allies, Ice Cube rarely forgot that the blues "I" was a persona. The first rap on his debut CD, *AmeriKKKa's Most Wanted,* acknowledges the relationship between blues reality and white fantasy. While a woman's voice attacks his use of the word "bitch" and a parody gospel chorus chants "Fuck You Ice Cube," the rapper announces himself as "the nigga ya love to hate." Frequently, Ice Cube's artistic self-consciousness manifests itself through an elaborate masking strategy based on the use of samples from elders such as James Brown and George Clinton, whose music inspired West Coast rappers from N.W.A. to Dr. Dre and Digital Underground. Dre's use of "Star Child (Mothership Connection)," with its invocation of "Swing Low Sweet Chariot," adds a redemptive undertone to "Let Me Ride," while Ice Cube's "Bop Gun (One Nation)" draws on P-Funk classics "One Nation Under a Groove" and "Bop Gun" to call for an end to black-on-black violence and a renewal of unity within the community. For Ice Cube, the key to such renewal was staying, as he phrased it in what may be his most important rap, "True to the Game." Sampling the Gap Band's celebration of street style, "Outstanding," Ice Cube threatens to revoke the "ghetto pass" of a brother who has "betrayed his homeboys" for white women and the funhouse mirrors of mainstream success. After dismissing the traitor who must confront the "nigger go home" painted on his suburban house, Ice Cube walks through the ghetto where "the flavor's good."

Attacks on rap repeatedly condemned the music for glorifying violence, drugs, and the abuse of women. Beginning with the fact that few critics seemed to have bothered to actually listen to the music before they talked about it, there were a couple of dozen problems with the antirap case. Most of them stemmed from the critics' (not entirely disingenuous) reduction of "rap" to the "gangsta" subgenre. In fact, the gangsta rappers were only one set of voices in a much larger chorus of calls and responses. Hip-hop critic Toure identified two distinct approaches:

> If hip-hop were film—the metaphor isn't much of a stretch, given that many rappers are often playing tough-guy roles—there would be only two schools: one centered in Los Angeles, the other in New York. Los Angeles would produce the big-budget action dramas that rake in millions; New York would create the art films that excite critics and film students and fill Greenwich Village art houses.

Toure's geographical definition doesn't stand up under careful scrutiny; East Coast gangsta rap went back at least to Schooly D's "P.S.K. (What Does It Mean)" while San Francisco's Digital Underground ("Sex Packets") was as strange and self-reflexive as anyone in New York. But the identification of two different tendencies in hip-hop does help clarify rap's complicated attitude toward violence. Some rappers constructed "action" scenarios that ended in the death of the gangsta. Others treated similar material more analytically.

Rappers of all schools shared an awareness of the real costs of violence. On the East Coast, KRS-One took the lead in speaking to the self-destructive elements of black street life. Founder of the Stop the Violence Movement and one of hip-hop's universally recognized elders, KRS (Kris Parker) had grown up on the streets of New York. During his frequent periods of homelessness, he sometimes stayed at the Franklin Men's Shelter in the Bronx, where he met Scott LaRock, a social worker who would eventually became KRS's DJ and partner in Boogie Down Productions. The same year BDP released the enormously influential proto-gangsta album *Criminal Minded,* Scott LaRock was fatally shot while trying to smooth out an argument in the South Bronx. Dedicated to the memory of his fallen partner, KRS's next album, *By Any Means Necessary,* reflected the extensive self-education program he had been pursuing for several years. The album's cover picture echoes the famous image of Malcolm X poised at the window, gun in hand; throughout, KRS revealed a heightened political consciousness and a determination to resist the forces of self-destruction within the black community.

KRS-One's definitive antiviolence statement came on "Love's Gonna Get You (Material Love)." Where Ice Cube relied on exaggeration and masking to make his point, KRS spoke in the direct tones of an urban realist. Engaging in a call and response with the gospel impulse of Jocelyn Brown's house classic "Love's Gonna Get You," he tells the story of a B-plus junior high school student forced to watch his mother struggling to support three children in a world where gunshots ring out almost every day. Identifying himself with his character, KRS demands, "Tell me what the fuck am I supposed to do?" Determined to help his brother and sister get decent clothes and food, the young man turns to the drug trade. For over a year, things work out fine. The family eats steak, he kicks back with his brother, laughing at the "Just say no" and "This is your brain on drugs" announcements on their fifty-five-inch color TV. It doesn't last. KRS paints a stark picture of escalating violence, first limited to competing drug dealers, but eventually leading to the shooting of a policeman. When the police close in, the character's despairing cry of "Tell me what the fuck am I supposed to do?" takes on an entirely different significance. As the drama unfolds, KRS delivers a sermon that concludes with an angry condemnation of Reagan era materialism: "You fall in love with your chains, you fall in love with your car, love's gonna sneak right up and snuff you from behind." As the hypnotic beat—the exact expression of the inexorable logic that leads the character to his death—begins to fade, KRS hammers home the point: "It's all right to like or want a material item, but when you fall in love with it and start scheming and carrying on for it, remember, love's gonna get you."

Ice Cube certainly understood KRS's point. In "My Summer Vacation," the West Coast equivalent of "Love's Gonna Get You," he takes apart the gangsta myth he was accused of propagating. Set to the beat of George Clinton's "Atomic Dog," the rap tells the story of an L.A. hustler who sets out to make his fortune in the less competitive St. Louis drug market. The rap starts out in standard gangsta fairy-tale mode as the hustler takes over a corner and begins to cash in. But Ice Cube undercuts the fantasy with the shooting death of the hustler's homeboy and the sardonic comment, "My homie got shot, he's a goner, black / St. Louis niggas want their corner back." Laying down the moral of the story with absolute clarity, Ice Cube describes the turf battles as a war that benefits the police. Not even Tipper Gore would be likely to misunderstand the rap's final line: "My life is fucked."

Originally released on the sound track of the gangsta parable *Juice*, which starred Tupac Shakur, Eric B and Rakim's "Know the Ledge" echoed the messages of "My Summer Vacation" and "Love's Gonna Get You." But where Ice Cube and KRS-One work off the blues impulse, "Know the Ledge" bears a closer affinity with the jazz tradition. Eric B and Rakim had established themselves as hip-hop innovators with their breakthrough records "Eric B Is President" and "I Know You Got Soul," which redirected the music away from the sparse minimalism of Run-D.M.C. and toward the dense textures—built out of fragmentary samples that suggest more than they reveal—that would dominate the late eighties and nineties. When rap seemed to be settling into the interminable ego duels between LL Cool J and Kool Moe Dee, Eric B and Rakim's "Follow the Leader" reminded the community of rap's visionary possibilities. As Rakim put it, "The stage is a cage, the mike is a third rail."

Rakim's virtuosic vocal style, which he unveiled on "My Melody," relies on speed and a rhythmic sense as refined as Charlie Parker's. Manipulating syntax and overloading the syllable count like Chuck Berry and Bob Dylan at their best, Rakim opens "Know the Ledge" with the image of himself as ghetto warrior. Alluding to Elliot Ness and Al Capone, he situates the gangsta myth in an American tradition that celebrates outlaws as often as the police. In good Reagan era fashion, both gangsters and lawmen derive their authority from superior force. Rakim replenishes his "juice"—his power and money—by "knockin' niggers off, knockin' niggers out." As in the blues raps, the pace of events accelerates around Rakim, who takes the chorus through a series of changes. Echoing Grandmaster Flash and the Furious Five's "The Message" and commenting on the moment in the movie when Tupac Shakur plunges to his death in the alley, Rakim describes himself standing "too close to the edge" and asks himself whether he really knows the ledge. As his financial success increases, he realizes that he's moving closer to the edge and can only "hope" that he knows the ledge as well as he thinks he does. When he goes down in a hail of gunfire from black rivals out to relieve him of his juice, Rakim's character admits, "Guess I didn't know the ledge."

Eric B and Rakim's jazz impulse classic "In the Ghetto" put a different twist on the image: "Seems like I'm locked in hell / lookin' over the edge / But the R never fell." A jazzman in a blues world, Rakim refuses to surrender to the fate of the character in "Know the Ledge." Instead, he develops a ghetto-centric take on the Romantic idea of the imagination as a path out of the killing fields. The cut opens with disorienting voices—sampled from 24-Carat Black's undeservedly forgotten "The Ghetto (Misfortune's Wealth)"—echoing "Nobody smiling" and "ain't gonna be smiles in hell." Finding himself in the midst of a chaotic world, Rakim removes himself from the material plane. He determines to "Relax in my room and escape from New York / return to the womb of the world as a thought." Experiencing a kind of spiritual rebirth, he molds his father's stories and fragments of information about classical African civilization into a vision of a new world: "I take the thought around the world twice / from knowledge unformed to knowledge precise."

Adding its voice to the chorus of responses to Donny Hathaway's "The Ghetto," "In the Ghetto" has absolutely nothing in common with the cartoon gangsta rap described by the tone-deaf puritans issuing their jeremiads on the downfall of Western civilization. Rakim's vision releases him, and anyone who responds to his jazz call, from the vicious cycles that kill the characters in "My Summer Vacation," "Love's Gonna Get You," and "Know the Ledge." Freed from the Reagan era delusion that the material world is all that matters, Rakim observes: "It ain't where you're from, it's where you're at, even the ghetto." Like the great jazzmen and -women, Rakim refuses to acquiesce to the world as a given. When he tells you that where you're from doesn't limit where you can go, he's simply reiterating the basic jazz impulse point that we make the world what it is. Growing up in the ghetto—or being born white, for that matter— is only a limitation if you see it that way. Rakim isn't obsessed with leaving but he's not bound by limiting notions of authenticity. Claiming "planet Earth" as his "place of birth," he stays true to the larger game. Because, like John Coltrane and Jimi Hendrix, Miles Davis and George Clinton, he knows we can change the rules.

# 57
# "Born in the U.S.A.":
# Springsteen and Race

By the end of the eighties, a lot of the people overhearing the angry echoes of "Fuck the Police" and "Rebel Without a Pause" found themselves wondering what the hell had happened. Even as Reagan blamed welfare mothers and a mythic culture of poverty for the decay of the inner cities, white America spent most of the decade verifying, with great reluctance, the gospel truism "You can't hide from yourself." It turned out that policies that hurt blacks wound up hurting a whole lot of whites too, that violence and despair didn't stay neatly over on the other side of the tracks. If black America was less likely to suffer from hard-core delusion, it was every bit as much caught up in the maelstrom of destructive energy. While desperate young men acted out the mythology of violence and greed, lots of folks simply went into shock: black professionals reaping the benefits of "equal opportunity programs" went for the big money, just like their white colleagues; way too many black leaders followed Reagan's lead, playing race card after race card until it was clear who had the deeper deck. The hype went on and on and even though fewer and fewer people believed it, it seemed like the alternative to believing it was not believing anything at all.

When you got down to it, the question wasn't really how Reagan had put it over on us, but how we'd let our sense of community slip away and, most important, how we could start to put it back together again. In terms of black music, the challenge was to recapture the gospel vision of redemption while looking the blues realities—the devils in our heads as much as those making policy in Washington—straight in the eye. Jazz? New visions of possibility? It wasn't like anyone outside the hip-hop world was listening to Rakim. It was hard enough just to deal with what was going down.

Even though the political realities of the era precluded a clear-cut victory, no artist worked harder or more consciously to tap music's healing power than Bruce Springsteen. Whatever Ronald Reagan or the gangsta rappers who ultimately played by his rules may have thought, Springsteen knew you couldn't run from yourself. The last fair deal might have gone down, but we were stuck in the game. In a country that no longer believed it was even worth trying, Springsteen struggled heroically to link blues realism with gospel affirmation. It didn't always work, at least not the way he wanted it to. It was particularly frustrating that the vast majority of the black community never heard what he was saying. The racial divide was just too deep.

Perhaps the most insightful commentary on Springsteen's position in the tangled racial reality of mid-eighties America was provided by Amiri Baraka, the militant black artist and music critic. Frequently critical of white artists working with black traditions, Baraka praised Springsteen's "ability to translate both the form and some of the content of the blues." Placing Springsteen in the tradition of "American shouters" that includes Leadbelly, James Brown, and Wilson Pickett, Baraka honored Springsteen for

> the nature of his concerns. The often tragic poetry of the blues is packed with reflections on a brutal society in which singers are victims, lonely, broke, and hungry. Springsteen describes a visible, living America with its obvious flaws, a real world. His American blues are solid and not given to minstrelsy.

But Baraka also knew that Springsteen was to some extent a captive of the Reagan era's emphasis on image:

> What amazes is the whole "Boss" thing. It creates a false relationship to traditional blues players that even Springsteen himself doesn't desire. Springsteen knows he's not Joe Turner, the "Boss of the Blues." He has also demonstrated that he feels closer to the common people than to the "bosses." Springsteen's persona, for example—the working-class youth checking out reality—would condemn the individuality embodied by the trend-making elite who retard music lovers, as separate and unequal as we are.

But the Boss thing hung heavily over Springsteen's "Born in the U.S.A." tour, and a lot of black folks who never heard the music saw the flag behind the stage and in the hands of the white crowd in the film clips, and thought it must be the sound track for the next war.

I wish I could say that the "Born in the U.S.A." tour was about bringing people together and leave it there. But it was really about bringing *white* people together. The standing joke was that there were more black people on stage at a Springsteen show than there were in the audience. While it wasn't quite true, it wasn't really false either. During the early years of Springsteen's career, there had always been some black people in his audience; in the clubs on the Jersey shore, some black presence had simply been a given. I had no trouble convincing black friends to check out the "River" tour in Memphis and Starkville, Mississippi. But during the "Born in the U.S.A." tour, blacks were conspicuous mostly by their absence.

It wasn't a failure of Springsteen's awareness. Throughout the Reagan era, Springsteen's lyrics, song introductions, and interviews showed a clear awareness of the racial implications of the Reagan Rules: the elevation of nostalgic image over blues reality; the "gangsta" celebrations of money and violence; and, at the root of it all, the division of communities into warring groups of "us" and "them." Introducing Woody Guthrie's "This Land Is Your Land" to a Swedish audience as "the greatest song that's ever been written about America," Springsteen bore witness to how race and poverty played into the divisions:

> In America there's a promise that gets made, and over there it gets called the American Dream, which is just the right to be able to live your life with some decency and dignity. . . . But over there, and a lot of places in the world right now, that dream is only true for a very, very few people. . . . Right now in the States, there's a lot of hard times, and when that happens there's always a resurgence of groups like the Ku Klux Klan and the National Socialists, and it seems like hard times turn people against each other, people that have common interests, people that don't understand that the enemy is not the guy down the street who looks different than you.

In "My Hometown," he explored the tangled history that made it impossible to separate the nightmares of the sixties and eighties. Even at the height of America's public commitment to racial justice, violence and economic decay had begun to erode the dreams of decency and dignity. Springsteen describes a world where the fights between blacks and whites lead inexorably to shotgun blasts. Even as he mourns the "troubled times," his character shrugs and concludes, "There was nothing you could do." The fatalistic acceptance plays directly into the sense of helplessness that kills the town and drives the speaker onto the no-longer-open road in search of better opportunities. When the textile mill closes its doors, the economic reality comes straight out of Woody Guthrie. "Foreman says these jobs are going boys / And they ain't coming back to your hometown." The problem, of course, is that they ain't going anywhere else either. Springsteen hammered the point home in "Seeds," where a displaced worker leaves the Rust Belt for his place in the sun. He arrives in Houston only to be greeted by a chorus of "sorry son it's gone gone gone / It's all gone." Like his black counterparts in so many late-eighties raps, Springsteen's character winds up homeless, sleeping in the car listening to his kid's "graveyard cough." Nowhere to run.

Working to resist the growing indifference to racism in white America, Springsteen reached out, mostly without success, to black audiences. He sang a wonderful duet with Stevie Wonder on "We Are the World" and contributed to the anti-apartheid *Sun City* benefit album. Hip-hop producer Arthur Baker put together powerful dance remixes of hits from *Born in the U.S.A.* Baker's "underground mix" of "Cover Me"—a song Springsteen had written with Donna Summer in mind—featured black vocalist Jocelyn Brown. In the early nineties, Springsteen released one of the greatest blue-eyed soul albums, *Human Touch,* featuring black vocalists Sam Moore and Bobby King; "Cross My Heart," "Roll of the Dice," and "Soul Driver" are among his most mature love songs. Springsteen was aware that rap was addressing many of the issues he was concerned with: "It's the new protest music. . . . It has the same rebelliousness of 50's rock n' roll. Rap's given voice to issues and feelings that wouldn't otherwise be heard so widely. I think a lot of it is great." His remix of "57 Channels" juxtaposes chants of "No justice, no peace" with sound bites from coverage of the Rodney King riot. But black DJs ignored even the Baker remixes; by the time *Human Touch* was released, young black audiences had about as much interest in Memphis soul as they had in the Delta blues. In terms of interracial audiences, Prince, Michael, and Madonna far surpassed Springsteen. So the question remains: why?

For all of his grounding in gospel and soul vocal styles, for all that Clarence Clemons's saxophone gave the E Street Band a Memphis drive, for all the James Brown–level intensity he put into his shows, Springsteen's sound was clearly grounded in a rock and roll tradition that was increasingly being seen, heard, and marketed as a white thing. The rhythms were powerful, but they weren't syncopated. If Prince's polyrhythmic grooves let everyone find their own place in the dance, Springsteen's anthems encouraged the crowd to pump their fists in unison. For blacks, it was all on the, well, "white" side. But for whites dealing with blues realities their political leaders were encouraging them to ignore, it provided a way of at least starting to think about community.

The "Born in the U.S.A." tour provided the standard rock and roll answer to the problem of how to maintain energy in a country that, most of the time, just didn't seem to give a damn about racial divisions or much of anything else: Have a great party. But, as Springsteen said, "it ain't a party unless everyone's invited." What made the "Born in the U.S.A." shows exhilarating in ways that went beyond, even if they never quite transcended, the hype was Springsteen's ability to reaffirm the spiritual value of pure rock and roll energy. At its best, the tour gave an enormous crowd a sense of what gospel really means, a sense of participation in a living community tied together by a shared vision of what we are and what we can be.

The touchstone of the tour was the title cut of the album that catapulted the image of "the Boss"—the blue-jean-and-bandanna-wearing embodiment of ten or twelve different American myths—into megastar heaven. What was peculiar was how anti-mythic the song actually was. Far from uncritically celebrating the flag that was a constant presence at the back of the stage, "Born in the U.S.A." insists on the blues reality of Vietnam and deindustrialization. Far from Reagan's "noble cause," Vietnam was a racist war fought by kids with no other options: When he finds himself caught up in a "little hometown jam," Springsteen's persona has no choice but to go off to Vietnam where, he knows, his real purpose is to "kill the yellow man." Make no mistake, the yellow men won. The character's brother fought the Vietcong at Khe Sanh: "they're still there, he's all gone." The song hammers home the economic reality of Reagan-era America for the working-class vets returning to a world without meaningful work. When Springsteen's character goes down to the refinery, all he hears is that someone else is making the decisions. It's a scene straight out of John Steinbeck's *The Grapes of Wrath,* one of Springsteen's favorite books. Even as they watch the destruction of their homes, Steinbeck's Okies realize there's no point in shooting the tractor driver who's doing the only work he can get. There's no point in shooting the man who hired him. He's working for the local bank, which is just doing what the big banks up north tell it to. Like Steinbeck's Joads, Springsteen's vet winds up back out on the road. Only now Springsteen ends not with the mythic celebration of "Thunder Road"—"it's a town full of losers, I'm pullin' out of here to win"—but with what may be gospel's most fundamental insight: "Nowhere to run ain't got nowhere to go."

It could have been a cry of despair, but the "Born in the U.S.A." tour transformed it into a call for community. What we had to hold on to was the fact that we were in it together, which was something black communities had only recently begun to forget. When Springsteen opened the concert with "Born in the U.S.A.," it set off one of the best, most conscious parties imaginable. Part of the reason that wasn't just hype lay in the sequence of songs. Although there were variations from night to night, there were clear patterns. After setting the dominant themes with "Born in the U.S.A.," Springsteen followed up with rock and soul energizers—often "Out in the Street" and "Spirit in the Night"—that reaffirmed his roots in and commitment to the part of America that had least to gain from the Reagan Rules.

The next sequence of songs was crucial to the feel of everything that followed. Reaching back to *Nebraska* for "Atlantic City," "Johnny 99," "Reason to Believe," and "Highway Patrolman," Springsteen reminded his community of the context in which the celebration was taking place. *Nebraska* had spoken directly to "the meanness in this world," a phrase Springsteen gave to mass murderer Charlie Starkweather but clearly intended as commentary on the spiritual emptiness of Reagan's America. Painting a bleak picture of a world divided into "winners and losers" where the main point is not to "get caught on the wrong side of the line," "Atlantic City" pinpoints the gangsta values that create unsolvable moral dilemmas for his characters. Riding the highways in the middle of the night, they're no longer hoping to escape, but just to survive. As Springsteen said when the album was released, the core of *Nebraska* lies in its images of isolation: "When you lose that sense of community, there's some spiritual breakdown that occurs. You just get shot off somewhere where nothing really matters." With no sense of connection, the characters in "Johnny 99" and "Atlantic City" experience a despair that culminates in the dark ironies of "Reason to Believe." An abandoned groom stares into the darkness, a man kicks a dog's corpse as if he expects it to come back to life. Commenting on "Reason to Believe," Springsteen said "that was the bottom. I would hope not to be in that particular place ever again." If the "Born in the U.S.A." tour was something more than just another rock show, if it was about something more than making Bruce Springsteen a very rich man, it was because the celebration took place in full awareness that that place was still there. Robert Johnson, out strolling with the devil, would have understood.

Introducing "Johnny 99" in Pittsburgh, Springsteen tied the *Nebraska* sequence directly to Reagan's attempt to co-opt the "Boss" into the service of his own mythic America: "The President was mentioning my name the other day, and I kinda got to wondering what his favorite album musta been. I don't think it was the *Nebraska* album." Placed early in the evening, the *Nebraska* sequence posed the problem of life under the Reagan Rules in its starkest form. If it was all about money, about self, what was left? Forced to choose between duty and family, Springsteen's "Highway Patrolman" doesn't even pretend to have an answer. The convicted killer in "Johnny 99" doesn't claim innocence, but he also knows that his situation mirrors the corrupt world he's living in: "It was more than all this that put that gun in my hand."

The real triumph of the tour was the way it responded to the blues realities at the core of *Nebraska*. Springsteen's success centered on the powerful conclusion of the first set. In the middle of a sequence that began with "The Promised Land" and culminated in "Badlands" and "Thunder Road"—the resistance anthems that provided the spiritual center of his seventies concerts—Springsteen placed "My Hometown" and "Darkness on the Edge of Town." In addition to providing the audience with a few minutes to catch its breath, the sequence was Springsteen's way of dealing with the "Boss" hype. Acutely aware of the killing potential of fame, Springsteen understood the connection between himself and Elvis Presley. Even as he honored Elvis as a "liberator," Springsteen reflected on "how somebody who could've had so much could in the end lose so bad and how dreams don't mean nothin' unless you're strong enough to fight for 'em and make 'em come true. You've got to hold on to yourself." Springsteen knew that he wasn't "the Boss," that holding on to a deeper self required grounding in a *real* community. Throughout the "Born in the U.S.A." tour, he connected with community organizations wherever he played. Not only did Springsteen (like other rock stars) make substantial donations—typically on the order of ten thousand dollars per show—he met personally with local organizers and sought ways to make sure his audience's awareness carried over after he had moved on to the next tour stop. On the purely practical level, his efforts were strikingly successful. Bob Muller, leader of the Vietnam Veterans of America, credited Springsteen's commitment with keeping the organization alive; Chris Sprowal, the black head of the National Union of the Homeless, praised Springsteen for raising "the issue of homelessness before the whole country."

The introduction to "My Hometown" gave the clearest sense of Springsteen's growing commitment to cultural awareness, which belongs in the tradition of grassroots political activism rather than any specific ideological camp. Leading up to an appeal for support of the local organizations he had connected with, Springsteen challenged his audience to take responsibility for what was happening around them:

> It's a long walk from a government that's supposed to represent all the people to where we are today. It seems like something's wrong out there when there's a lotta stuff being taken away from a lot of people that shouldn't have it taken away. . . . And sometimes it's hard to remember that this place belongs to us—that this is our hometown.

Following "My Hometown" with "Darkness on the Edge of Town," Springsteen tied the present moment to a history of resistance and challenged us to think about what it all meant in our own lives, our own hometowns.

Then Springsteen and the E Street Band let it rip. Clarence Clemons's irrepressible horn and physical presence provided a joyous reminder that it wasn't *just* about white folks, that the door was still open. Once Springsteen established unambiguously that things had changed since the time he could play "Thunder Road" and "Rosalita" as celebrations pure and simple, he was free to let us know that it was still cool, still necessary, to straight-out rock. The second set did just that. Having gotten his audience to think, Springsteen embraced the idea that there were times when it wasn't about thinking, when you needed to get some release from the realities of closed plants and broken dreams. The blues affirmation of "Badlands" was as vital as it had been in 1978: "It ain't no sin to be glad you're alive." But it meant something different to sing it in clear response to the "meanness in this world." At its best, the "Born in the U.S.A." tour provided a place where, as a community, we could take a stand and get on with the party. Not everyone bought it. Even for some of the people in the audience, it was just another part of the decade's hype. But for those who responded fully to the calls of the *Nebraska* sequence and "My Hometown," it was the eighties' best white version of what Public Enemy had in mind in "Rightstarter (Message to a Black Man)": "Let's get this party started right." Neither Springsteen nor PE had the final answer, but they provided places where healing could begin.

# Section Five

## "Holler if Ya Hear Me": In the Nineties Mix

# 58
# Wasteland of the Free

For those who believed Bill Clinton, the nineties were a time for racial healing. Remembering Public Enemy's injunction "Don't Believe the Hype," Rage Against the Machine called the last decade of the twentieth century "Vietnow." For every positive sign, a counter-example sprang to mind. Yes, the black middle class was in good shape economically; the Census Bureau edged nervously toward a vision of race more complicated than black/white/other; greed was no longer enshrined as one of the seven deadly virtues. But then there was O. J., California Proposition 209, and Newt's Contract on America. Psychologically, things were still a mess, and there wasn't really a more precise way of saying it. Sounds of Blackness, one of the new-breed collectives that bridged the gap between R & B and gospel, summed it up best in "The Pressure." A rhythm track that sounds like a bad day on the subway when it's ninety-seven degrees and the air conditioning's out pounds away while straight-out-of-church vocalist Ann Bennett-Nesby pleads, demands, and prays for relief. It's Mahalia's burden remixed for the nineties.

In a decade of frustrated voices, Iris DeMent sounded the keynote of a conversation we've been avoiding. In her stunning anthem "Wasteland of the Free," DeMent catalogs scenes of little kids fighting "inner city wars" while the politicians "kill for oil" and "throw a party when we win." She refuses to turn away from a blues world where "the poor have now become the enemy," where we "blame our troubles on the weak ones." Spitting out a chorus that matches the fierceness of Tupac Shakur or Rage Against the Machine, she concludes "While we sit gloating in our greatness / justice is sinking to the bottom of the sea / and it feels like I'm living in the wasteland of the free."

DeMent has plenty of company in the wasteland. Much of the best music of the nineties shares her sense that the nation has simply given up, accepted a reality where, as DeMent points out, CEOs make two hundred times the average worker's pay, where blacks and whites watch the Simpsons, Bart and O. J., from separate and still not equal worlds, where a Democratic administration balances the budget by pouring in the blood of the poor. It's a world where anger distorts love, where Minister Farrakhan summons a million men to Washington, where the charred remains of black churches smolder on the back roads of the South, where neo-Nazis wave the American flag over the rubble in Oklahoma City, where AIDS ravages the children of the South Bronx. No wonder so many seem eager to flee into cyberspace and surf into a hermetically sealed world where the only sound is the clicking of the keyboard deep in the night.

Still, the music breaks the silence, calls our wandering souls back into the world. Chances are that, as you read these words, some sixteen-year-old jazz visionary—responding to the calls of DJ Shadow, and Erykah Badu, of Ani DiFranco and Wu-Tang Clan—is busy figuring out how to animate cyberspace with redemptive energies: the Orisha for Windows, version 98.6. One way or another, the conversation goes on. Some of the voices belong to musicians who have been around for a while: Curtis Mayfield, Bruce Springsteen, Rakim, Gil Scott-Heron, Madonna, Prince. Others make it clear that hip-hop—as old now as rock and roll was when Springsteen released "Born to Run"—isn't gangsta fantasy or a passing fad: A Tribe Called Quest, the Fugees, Digable Planets, and Wu-Tang Clan. Despite their radically different sounds, Rage Against the Machine, Ani DiFranco, and Dan Bern refuse to surrender rock's political intelligence to the marketing department. In stark contrast to the eighties—the worst of times for women in American music—the nineties have put an end to any lingering questions about whether girls can rock and rap. In hip-hop and R & B, rock and pop, women have emerged as the defining voices of the decade: Mary J. Blige, Liz Phair, TLC, Cassandra Wilson, Alanis Morisette, Changing Faces, Ani DiFranco, Sarah McLachlan, Me'Shell NdegeOcello, Courtney Love, En Vogue, Lauryn Hill of the Fugees, Butterfly of Digable Planets, N'dea Davenport of Brand New Heavies, Maysa Leak of Incognito, Tracy Chapman, Missy Elliott, P. J. Harvey, Toni Braxton. It's what Annie Lennox and Aretha Franklin had in mind when they got together in the dark days of the eighties on "Sisters Are Doing It for Themselves."

The question is: Will anyone outside DeMent's cult following respond to her call echoing across the wasteland? Do the voices of Wu-

Tang or the Fugees reverberate beyond the boundaries of the hip-hop nation? Does anyone outside the underground dance clubs hear the Brand New Heavies and Incognito? Do the air-guitarists at Lollapalooza care much about what the chicks are saying to each other at Lilith Fair? Have Stevie Wonder, Springsteen, and Aretha become the Sammy Davis, Jr., Frank Sinatra, and Judy Garland of the baby boomers?

The present never really makes sense when it happens, mostly because we haven't decided what we want it to mean. There are too many crosscurrents to pin down the dominant theme while we're hearing it. By the time we do, it's past. Part of Ronald Reagan's genius lay precisely in his ability to slow the process, to laminate the present as a strange kind of past. The contrast with Bill Clinton couldn't have been any stronger. Setting himself up as an alternative to Bush's halfhearted Reaganism, Clinton presented himself as a "bridge to the future." But part of the problem of making sense of the nineties was trying to establish some kind of connection between what Clinton's mouth said and what his actions said he meant.

# 59
# American Dreaming

Clinton's mouth always said the right things. At least as long as there wasn't a campaign in progress. Like Jimmy Carter, he'd grown up with black people; when he was a law student at Yale during the Black Power movement, he'd been one of the few whites to sit at the "black table" in the cafeteria. When he made his case for conscientious objector status to his draft board, he condemned Vietnam as a "war I opposed and despised with a depth of feeling I had reserved solely for racism in America." When he began his political career, Clinton sought out black audiences and was clearly at ease speaking in churches and neighborhood centers. As a centrist candidate in the 1992 Democratic primaries, he talked a good liberal game on race. Once elected, he continued to insist on the need for racial healing and spoke with unusual candor about the nation's racial history. During his 1998 trip to Africa, for example, he acknowledged that "the United States has not always done the right thing by Africa. Going back to the time before we were even a nation, European Americans received the fruits of the slave trade. And we were wrong in that." Often Clinton cast his vision of the future in images drawn from Martin Luther King's "I Have a Dream" speech, which he had once committed to memory. He told a massive crowd in Ghana that King's "dream became the dream of our nation and changed us in ways we could never imagine. We are hardly finished but we have travelled a long way on the wings of that dream. We are working for the day when all people on the entire Earth will be free and equal."

One of Clinton's strengths was his ability to distill the essence of the shared aspirations, the American dreams, of people from different backgrounds. "The American dream that we are all raised on is a simple but powerful one," Clinton said. "If you work hard and play by the rules you should be given a chance to go as far as your God-given ability will take you." In some ways, Clinton followed through on the commitment implied in his invocations of the dream. Without question, his administration was the most diverse in American history by any measure of racial, ethnic, or gender integration. Although his campaign team was almost entirely white and male, his personal confidants included African Americans, most notably Vernon Jordan. On the surface, it looked good.

But, as historian Gerald Horne wrote, "the administration's rainbow of hues is not matched by a rainbow of views." When conservative opponents launched attacks on Clinton's nominations of Johnetta Cole as secretary of education and Lani Guinier as assistant attorney general for civil rights, the administration backed away from controversies that might have raised precisely those questions that remained unaddressed by invocations of King. By the mid-nineties, everyone located slightly to the left of the White Aryan Resistance avoided openly racist statements. Newt Gingrich had a picture of Martin Luther King on his office wall and conservatives routinely cited King's vision of a "color-blind society" to bolster their attacks on affirmative action.

For the record, King strongly supported affirmative action. "Among the many vital jobs to be done," he wrote in *Why We Can't Wait*, "the nation must not only radically readjust its attitude to the Negro in the compelling present, but must incorporate in its planning some compensatory consideration for the handicaps he has inherited from the past." King's remedy was at least as radical as anything set forth in the writings of Lani Guinier: "The ancient common law has always provided a remedy for the appropriation of the labor of one human being by another. This law should be made to apply for American Negroes. The payment should be in the form of a massive program by the Government of special, compensatory measures which could be regarded as a settlement in accordance with the accepted practice of common law." You certainly didn't hear Bill Clinton quoting *that* on Martin Luther King Day every January.

There was no reason to doubt Clinton's *personal* abhorrence of white supremacy. But above all else Bill Clinton is a *political* man. Whenever a tension arose between his belief in racial justice and the needs of a campaign, there was less than no question which way he'd move. The pattern emerged when, as newly elected governor of Arkansas, Clinton attempted to "heal" the rift with the white supremacist past by inviting Orval Faubus, the man who had preferred shutting down the Little Rock school system to allowing black students to enroll at Central High, to attend his inaugural ball. The pattern continued in Clinton's 1992 presidential campaign. Aware of how Ronald Reagan and George Bush had played the race card against Walter Mondale and Michael Dukakis, Clinton set out to defuse any suggestion that he was a pawn of "special interests." The Clinton-Gore list of "31 Crucial Issues" omitted all mention of race. In the midst of the campaign, Clinton flew back to Arkansas to preside over the execution of a brain-damaged black man, Rickey Ray Rector, thereby establishing his credentials as "tough" on crime. Most crucially, Clinton aggressively distanced himself from Jesse Jackson. He chose an appearance at a meeting of Jackson's Rainbow Coalition to condemn Sistah Souljah, an inconsequential figure in the rap world, for antiwhite racism. Jackson understood it for what it was: a blatant appeal for the votes of the so-called Reagan Democrats like the Philadelphia electrician who said "the day he told that fuckin' Jackson off is the day he got mine."

Politically, Clinton's approach worked. His election deprived George Bush of the opportunity to establish a far right consensus on the Supreme Court that would have lasted deep into the next century. During the first years of Clinton's administration, it was possible to see his strategy as a variation on the one Jackson himself had used in 1988. Aggressive action on an agenda designed to address *economic* inequality would have disproportionately benefited blacks, Latins, American Indians, and women. Such a strategy would have made it more difficult to raise cries of reverse racism, and if the day ever came when women and minorities were *not* overrepresented in the ranks of the poor, that would be a good time to step back and think about what to do next. The problem was that Clinton didn't do much about poverty, either.

Especially after the Republican sweep of the 1994 congressional elections, Clinton abandoned all but rhetorical support for any sort of progressive agenda. What he *did* do was restore "economic health" to the nation in a manner that had more in common with the values of Richard Nixon than those of Lyndon Johnson. His administration cooperated with the disassembling of the last of the Great Society programs, which, thanks to Vietnam, had never really been given a chance to address the underlying sources of poverty and despair. He supported welfare "reforms" almost certain to harm those least able to protect themselves or their children. He used no political capital to resist the attacks on affirmative action. Polls soared and Clinton's job approval rating remained high even in the midst of the Monica Lewinsky sideshow. Measured by his actions, Bill Clinton may well go down in history as the greatest Republican president of the twentieth century.

So it wasn't all that big a surprise that, a decade after Ronald Reagan left office, taking the evil-demon theory of America's racial problems with him, many black Americans felt angry and confused. In her book *Facing Up to the American Dream: Race, Class, and the Soul of the Nation,* sociologist Jennifer Hochschild presents a convincing case that the most profound dissatisfaction with America in the nineties is felt not by poor residents of the inner cities, but by the members of the growing and economically secure black middle class. Citing a large array of statistical and anecdotal evidence, Hochschild concludes that middle-class blacks' belief in the American dream declined as their level of success, measured in economic terms, advanced. Surprisingly, most measures show poor blacks' belief in the dream remaining constant.

Hochschild speculates that part of the difference may come from the changing position of economically secure blacks in American society. She cites an *Ebony* magazine article which contrasted the "new middle class" consisting of "salaried workers in high-level occupations that serve the society at large" with the traditional black middle class of "ministers, educators, doctors, and small businessmen who served primarily the Black community." Noting that "rich blacks have always held a larger share of their race's income than have rich whites, and poor blacks have always held a smaller share of their race's income than have poor whites" and that "the disparities within both races are increasing," Hochschild presents evidence that supports Robert Stepto's warning that the cost of ascent, of "making it" to the symbolic North, is a sense of alienation from the black community as well as from the white mainstream.

A small avalanche of autobiographies and analytical essays published by members of the black middle class during the nineties testifies to the disturbing accuracy of Hochschild's analysis. *Washington Post* reporter Jill Nelson's *Volunteer Slavery* provides a detailed picture of the author's frustration with subtle manifestations of liberal racism and her inability to break through the "glass ceiling" limiting black advancement. Ellis Cose's *The Rage of a Privileged Class* makes it clear that Nelson's anger is by no means anomalous. Journalistic reports from the racial front written by white reporters Jonathan Coleman and David Shipler place black middle-class anger in a broader social context. Their titles express their conclusions: *Long Way to Go* (Coleman) and *A Country of Strangers* (Shipler). The papers presented at the 1997 "Race Matters" conference convened at Princeton University sound similar notes. The contributors represent a cross section of progressive intellectual perspectives: novelist Toni Morrison; historians Evelyn Brooks Higginbotham and David Roediger (*The Wages of Whiteness*); legal scholars Patricia Williams and Kimberlee Crenshaw; sociologists Howard Winant and Robin D. G. Kelley, the son of longtime Miles Davis pianist Wynton Kelley; cultural critics Stuart Hall and Cornel West. Summarizing the general consensus of the participants, West's "Afterword" concludes that American society is characterized by "the depth and breadth of racial polarization, balkanization, and de facto segregation."

Sometimes it seemed that any attempt to address the problem at a time when Bill Clinton was the *best* possibility the political system could offer was doomed to gravitate inexorably toward complaint, anger, and a sense of insurmountable isolation. As Hochschild lamented, it was a situation that cast the future of the American dream—whether Clinton's or King's—in grave doubt. But the music of the nineties told a different, more complex, and, finally, more hopeful story. It was a story based on blues realism, jazz vision, and the gospel sense of community. The story offered new ways of thinking about community, a renewed sense of connection with ancestors and elders. But that story, too, began in confusion and rage. Nowhere was that clearer than in the life and death of Tupac Shakur.

# 60
# C.R.E.A.M., or, Tupac on Death Row

The Wu-Tang Clan titled the most powerful rap of the mid-nineties "C.R.E.A.M.," and the initials passed into street currency as shorthand for the only thing the East and West Coast gangstas could agree on: "Cash Rules Everything Around Me." There's no deeper blues truth this side of "my baby left me." The amens came in from every corner of the hip-hop nation, from Houston's Scarface ("Money Makes the World Go Round"), from New York's Junior M.A.F.I.A. featuring L'il Kim and Biggie Smalls ("Get Money"), from Cleveland's Bone Thugs n Harmony ("Foe Tha Love of $"), and from Tupac's Death Row labelmate Snoop Doggy Dog, who testified in "Tha Shiznit" and "Gin and Juice" that he had his "mind on my money and my money on my mind." Even after Biggie's death, he showed up with Puff Daddy and the Family on "All About the Benjamins." Wu-Tang Clan wasn't really part of the gangsta scene, which may have contributed to its ability to pin down the reality so clearly on "C.R.E.A.M." The horn samples and gospel organ gave the cut an eerie postmodern feel, but the piano line could have come out of Chess Records or a Delta juke joint. And the blues, as Leadbelly once said, "ain't no joke." When the deal goes down, as it went down for Tupac and Biggie Smalls, Leadbelly again said all there was to say: "another man done gone."

While the gangstas' money blues would have been recognizable to classic bluesmen like Blind Willie McTell—whose "Dying Crapshooter's Ball" begs for a hip-hop remake—there was something different about the nineties version. For one thing, the violence was literal. The murders of Tupac and Biggie Smalls, probably the best rappers in their respective West and East Coast scenes, should have been mourned with the same sense of loss elicited by the murder of John Lennon. The sad fact was that anyone relying on the newspapers was likely to come away with the impression that Tupac and

Biggie had killed themselves. Still, you didn't have to be a pious moralist of the William Bennett school to believe that the increasing rhetorical violence of mid-nineties gangsta rap had something to do with the deaths. Especially after "West Coast" icon Tupac (who ironically enough was born in New York and raised in Baltimore) was shot entering a Times Square studio where Biggie and star East Coast producer Sean "Puffy" Combs were present, a feud that had been part ritual competition and part marketing ploy escalated into something deadly serious. Despite immediate and repeated denials from Biggie and Puffy, Tupac issued numerous public statements implicating them in the attack.

Tupac's move to Death Row Records, the incredibly lucrative label masterminded by Dr. Dre and Marion "Suge" Knight, intensified the conflict. A huge man (six feet four, 315 pounds) who had briefly pursued a career as a defensive lineman with the Los Angeles Rams, Knight presented himself as a nineties version of Berry Gordy, the true spirit of black capitalism. And, in a perverse but revealing sense, he was right. Like Gordy, Suge most definitely got paid; Death Row was valued at over $100 million. But if Gordy represented the mythic benevolence of capitalism, Death Row was capitalism red in tooth and claw. Knight's willingness to resort to force and intimidation assumed legendary proportions. As hip-hop journalist Ronin Ro reports in *Have Gun Will Travel: The Spectacular Rise and Violent Fall of Death Row Records,* pistol whippings and public humiliation—on several occasions Suge reportedly forced visitors to strip before sending them out onto the street—were standard operating procedure at the label's headquarters. As Scott Gordon, an Oakland DJ who had known Tupac since his days as a dancer backing Digital Underground, told cultural commentator Armond White: "Suge Knight, he a businessman to all degrees from the street to the major level. To me, 'Pac made a deal with the Devil. . . . He had everything in his hands. And to me, that's something the Devil gives you. God don't give you all of that. Especially if you sit there and worship money. Money is not what God gives you, it's what the Devil gives you." Certainly, Tupac's own rhetoric after Suge negotiated his release from Rikers Island echoed every diabolical theme of the Reagan Rules.

The son of a Black Panther mother, Tupac summed up the legacy of the Reagan Rules with ironic clarity even as he acknowledged the potential power of black unity. "When I be throwing up the W, it ain't for California, it's a W for war. When the West Coast and the middle and the East get together, we got power. You won't be seeing me throwin this when we're all together," said the man who had grown up in a household where revolutionary thinkers such as Malcolm X, George Jackson, Huey Newton, and Patrice Lumumba were part of the everyday conversation. "But we ain't there, we still all separate tribes, and I know what tribe I'm in. I'm a soldier. I'll always be true to those who are true to me." No surprise that Tupac went on to state the gangsta capitalist subtext that usually remained unsaid in the Washington of Bill Clinton and Newt Gingrich: "I tried to see if it was, like, a white thing. Everywhere I go with money, they let me in. Everywhere I go with none, they don't let you in. Trust me. That's all it is. It's all about money. When you got money, you got power." Commenting on "C.R.E.A.M.," Wu-Tang's RZA put a crucially different spin on the situation: "What we mean by that is 'Cash rules everything around me,' but cash don't rule *me*. Power borns power, but you know what the power is? Truth."

It's possible to understand Tupac's words as part of a gangsta persona he created after he moved with his mother from Baltimore, where he'd studied acting and dance at the Baltimore School for the Arts, to Northern California's Marin County projects. Reflecting on the character of Makaveli he created for his final album, Tupac revealed a deep confusion concerning the relationship between gangsta image and gangsta reality: "When you do rap albums, you got to train yourself. You got to constantly be in character. You used to see rappers talking all that hard shit, and then you see them in suits and shit at the American Music Awards. I didn't want to be that type of nigga. I wanted to keep it real, and that's what I thought I was doing."

The confusion permeated public discussions of Tupac and the gangsta scene as a whole. In a *New Yorker* article that provides evidence linking a New York City Police Department informer to Tupac's Times Square shooting, Connie Bruck claims that "Rap fans insist that performers be authentic representatives of ghetto life: that they live the life they rap about; that life conform to art, so to speak. Rap's critics, on the other hand, are terrified that life *will* conform to art, that the behavior—the drug dealing and the violence—described by rappers will seep into the mainstream culture." Acknowledging that more than half of rap's sales are to whites, Bruck continues: "It is the fear of a violent, marginalized culture's influence on susceptible young people that fuels much of the political debate, and this fear is exacerbated by the wide-spread adoption of hip-hop style." The White Citizens Council of Birmingham, Alabama, circa 1956, couldn't have said it much more clearly. The only problem is that, despite her authoritative tone, Bruck is as profoundly confused as Tupac. As the information on rap sales indicates, the demands for "authenticity" come primarily from white listeners whose knowledge of "authentic" black life derives primarily from minstrel images created specifically to attract as much of their cash as possible. On street level, the understanding of what it means to keep it real is a good deal more complicated. Suge Knight aside, very few figures in the hip-hop world live the lives of the hard-core gangstas their raps describe. As the interviews with Tupac's Marin County homeboys on the *Thug Immortal* video make clear, Tupac was at best a second-rate fighter.

It makes more sense to think of him as an uprooted intellectual artist than a thug. Certainly, no member of his generation had a more complicated array of voices in his head. By the time Tupac was old enough to follow the ideas being discussed by Panther veterans such as his stepfather, Mutulu Shakur, both the Black Power movement and his family life were in serious disarray; his mother would struggle with crack addiction throughout the eighties. After Mutulu was incarcerated early in the Reagan era, Tupac recalled, the electricity in his mother's apartment had been cut off: "I used to sit outside by the street lights and read the autobiography of Malcolm X. And it made it so real to me, that I didn't have any lights at home. . . . And it changed me, it moved me." When Tupac's career as a rapper began to take off, he frequently expressed his goals in political terms. Placing himself in the tradition of the vanquished Panther leaders, he said, "It was like their words with my voice, I just continued where they left off. I tried to add spark to it, I tried to be the new breed, the new generation."

At times, he grappled explicitly with the relationship between his music and the goals of the freedom movement: "We asked ten years ago, we were askin' with the Panthers, we were askin' in the Civil Rights movement. Now those people who were askin' are all dead or in jail so what are we gonna do? And we shouldn't be angry! And the raps that I'm rapping to my community shouldn't be filled with rage? They shouldn't be filled with the same atrocities that they gave to me? The media don't talk about it, so in my raps I have to talk about it, and it just seems foreign because there's no one else talking about it."

The albums he made before switching to Death Row provide powerful evidence that, in a different world, a world where young black men were offered serious alternatives to the Reagan Rules, he might have pulled it off. *2Pacalypse Now* and *Strictly for My N.I.G.G.A.Z.* combine gangsta attitude ("Something Wicked," "Violent") with social commentary ("Trapped," "Rebel of the Underground," "Words of Wisdom") and celebrations of black unity that mix ferocity and tenderness ("Brenda's Got a Baby" and "Keep Ya Head Up," with its beautiful samples from the Five Stairsteps' "Ooh Child" and Zapp's "Be Alright"). Like most blues-based musicians, Tupac's understanding of the big picture was sometimes just a caricature. In "Words of Wisdom," for example, he rapped: "No Malcolm X in my history text / Why's that? / Because he tried to educate and liberate all Blacks / Why is Martin Luther King in my book each week / Cuz he taught all Blacks to get slapped and turn the other cheek."

Contrast that with "Holler If Ya Hear Me," a powerful expression of street realism as political defiance. "Much love to my brothers in the pen," Tupac rapped over a frenetically speeded-up sample from Norman Whitfield's ode to paranoia "I Heard It Through the Grapevine." "I'll see ya when I free ya / if not when they shut me in." Anyone who listens closely to "Holler If Ya Hear Me" or Tupac's best-loved song, "Dear Mama," will understand that he was dead serious when he announced plans for helping his brothers use music to rise above the death waiting for them in Compton, South Central, and Marin County. He planned to call the organization "the Underground Railroad," noting that "the concept behind this is the same concept behind Harriet Tubman." Sadly, the Underground Railroad came into being as "Thug Life," the emphasis shifted back onto the internecine battles that would leave Tupac, Biggie, and hundreds of other young black men who didn't have platinum CDs dead or maimed. It was a perfect mirror of the blues confusion left by the collapse of the Black Power movement and the ascendance of hustler demagogues with no clarity about the system they were trapped in and no politics worth the name. What they did have, even in their worst moments, was a clear understanding that the game they were playing was the same game that ran the society around them. Tupac knew better than to believe anything the Clinton administration shoveled out about the need for sacrifice and altruism. Even though he named his publishing company "Ghetto Gospel," Tupac felt that he was living in a world where, as he said describing *All Eyz on Me*, the album he produced with Death Row just after his release from prison, "fear is stronger than love." The moral of the tragedy of

Tupac and Biggie Smalls was clear. Accepting the Reagan Rules, looking at success as a matter of individual financial gain, left you in deep deep trouble.

# 61
# Deeper Shades of Soul

The most conscious rappers had a sense of what had gone wrong, but it seemed that every time they tried to break it down in words, they were dancing with Tar Baby. It got so bad that KRS-One, on most days the most insightful of rap's self-taught messengers, wound up calling Frederick Douglass a "house nigger," a "fuckin' sell-out" who "tricked Africans to go fight for their freedom in the Civil War." Obviously, something was seriously amiss.

Rap's basic problem may have been precisely its reliance on *words*. As black poet Audre Lorde observed, it's hard, if not impossible, to tear down the master's house using the master's tools. The public vocabulary of the eighties had almost forced you to see the world in terms of us and them; well into Bill Clinton's second term, the problem hadn't gone away. Its most disturbing musical manifestation was not the East/West battle in hip-hop, but the split between "rap" and "R & B." "Rap" was associated with masculine virility and street authenticity, both of which often involved violence; R & B with soft feminine passivity and Uncle Tom bourgeois sellouts. Although many male rappers—most notably those associated with the Native Tongues movement (A Tribe Called Quest, the Jungle Brothers, De La Soul)—were careful to express their solidarity with the sisters, there were plenty of gangstas who responded to women's voices with contempt. It was nearly an article of faith among members of the self-identified hard-core hip-hop audience (including a large number of young white males engaged in the nineties version of white Negroism) that, when you cut away the PC bullshit, women just couldn't rap; their words didn't "flow." It wasn't difficult to imagine a connection between the refusal to listen to R & B, where women continued to play a central role, and the misogyny of raps like

Snoop Doggy Dog's reprehensible "GZ Up, Hoes Down" and Ice Cube's "Once Upon a Time in the Projects."

Just like Aretha calling for "Respect," black women in the nineties responded clearly and forcefully to those brothers who stood in need of correction. In "Step into the Projects (Where I Found Love)," Me'Shell NdegeOcello played Zora Neale Hurston to Ice Cube's Richard Wright. As June Jordan observed in her classic essay "Notes Towards a Black Balancing of Love and Hatred," a full picture of black life required both Wright's angry attack on white oppression and Hurston's eloquent insistence on black love. It was a fullness Me'Shell captured beautifully in "Dred Loc" and "I'm Diggin' You (Like an Old Soul Record)." As Jordan knew, it would have been a mistake to assign the celebrations to the women and the politics to the men, a point made explicit in Dianne Reeves's "Endangered Species," which can be heard as a response to Ice Cube's rap of the same name. Insisting on sexual violence as the blues reality beneath the gangsta fantasy—"rape isn't rape, you say I like it that way"—Reeves repudiates the image of women as passive victims: "I am an endangered species though I sing no victim's song / I am a woman, I am an artist, and I know where my voice belongs."

The most crucial part of the women's response, however, was its refusal to participate in the pissing contest. Black women were all too aware of the intense pressures faced by black men; almost all remained determined to maintain the beloved community in the face of attacks from without. As a result, some of the deepest blues of the nineties were sung by women responding to the burdens of black men. Cassandra Wilson remade Son House's "Death Letter Blues" as eulogy for the brothers lost to violence, and Rachelle Ferrell's "Too Late" painted a devastating portrait of a husband and father who had surrendered to an equally fatal silence. But there was no chance that the black women would turn away from the men in response. Ferrell's "Open Arms" and Anita Baker's "Whatever It Takes" made it clear that, whatever the tensions, they were determined to keep the community from falling apart. In fact, it was hard to find an R & B artist, or even a song, that played by the Reagan Rules. Probably because the music held closer to its roots in gospel and soul— almost every nineties star traced her roots to the choir loft of her mother's church—R & B seemed able to recognize and respond to the differences between the eighties and nineties much more rapidly than hip-hop's commercial mainstream.

There were unmistakable signs that the nineties *were* different, or at least were moving toward a different future. Almost every socio-logical survey revealed that young Americans of all races held much more fluid conceptions of race than their parents. Part of the ex-planation involved demographic changes. In most American cities and a growing number of small towns, immigration from Asia and Latin America had rendered the black/white approach to race ob-viously insufficient. Marked increases in the rate of interracial mar-riage resulted in a growing number of "mixed race" children who contemplated the boxes on the census form with a mixture of anger and bemusement.

It was a situation better expressed in tones than in words. And that was something black folk had known ever since the time cen-turies ago when "white" slavers had redefined the Yoruba and Ibo and Wolof and a hundred other groups into a "blackness" at once too simple to accept and too real to repudiate. That was what the moan was all about.

The energies worked themselves out in different ways in different places. And place was only partially a matter of geography. The best model was probably the near-underground scene that developed in London in the mid-eighties. Coming together around the multi-racial musical collective Soul II Soul, whose song "Keep On Movin' " was a clear response to the call of the freedom movements that had challenged Jim Crow and the British Empire, the "Black Britain" scene was united by its commitment to fluidity and its willingness to transcend any and all musical boundaries. Black British producer Tricky explored the jazz implications of the approach in cuts like "Aftermath," built on a haunting bass line that recalls Marvin Gaye's "The End of Our Road." His thrash rock remake of Public Enemy's "Black Steel in the Hour of Chaos" redefines rap's vision of mascu-line rebellion—the prisoners in PE's fable kill a female guard—by turning the words over to female vocalist Martine.

If there was a presiding spirit to the Black British scene, however, it belonged to Stevie Wonder. The groups that created the most powerful music—all of them interracial and all of them featuring fe-male vocalists with either biographical or spiritual roots in the Amer-ican South—shared Wonder's appreciation for the complicated energies flowing back and forth between personal experience and political life. Wonder's descendants included the Young Disciples (featuring Atlanta-born singer-songwriter Carleen Anderson), the Brand New Heavies (featuring another Atlantan, N'dea Davenport), Drizabone (featuring black British singer Kymberly Peer), and

Incognito, whose sound was shaped by the brilliant songwriter and instrumentalist Bluey Maunick. Like Wonder, the British soul groups left the door open for anyone who wanted to come in. Introduced by Davenport's sensuous tones—the moan reworked with the dance floor in mind—the Brand New Heavies' "Brother Sister" responds to the elders—"Grandma's words"—with a call for renewed commitment to the "real things that matter." Drizabone's "Real Love" and Incognito's "Keep the Fires Burning" share a gospel vision of a community flowing, dancing, moving on up.

Like their American elders, the Black British groups cautioned against confusing vision with reality. Echoing the basic gospel theme that "there's no place for me to run and hide," Incognito's "Deep Waters" immerses the beloved community in the "deep waters" where, as James Baldwin wrote in "Sonny's Blues," the threat of drowning was real. Even if you reached shore, Baldwin warned, there was no real place of safety: "it can come again." The warning carries special intensity when you remember the eventual collapse of the freedom movement in confusion and despair. Responding to the question "What have we learned from history?" the Young Disciples' "Apparently Nothing (Soul River)" urges listeners to turn away from direct "confrontation" and embrace "the struggle that thrives when we all gather / down at the bank of the soul river." The group's brilliant "Freedom Suite" gives a sense of what the gathering might be like. The first two movements of the suite express the ideals that unite the new generation of deep soul singers with their elders. In part one, Carleen Anderson envisions a world where she has the "right to live, the right to love, the right to choose." As the first movement ends, a gospel organ rises up beneath her voice and the vocal center shifts to rapper I. G. Culture. There's no hint of conflict between the R & B tones and the rap rhythms; Anderson and I. G. Culture call and respond, pass on the wisdom of the mother in Baldwin's story: "You may not be able to stop nothing from happening. But you got to let him know you's *there.*" As profoundly responsive to the gospel impulse as anything the nineties have offered, the final movement of the "Freedom Suite" weaves a constantly shifting tapestry of rhythms and tones that harkens back to the energies that filled the churches of Montgomery and Birmingham when the freedom movement was taking form.

The most powerful solo artist to emerge from the Black British scene, Seal responds to the Young Disciples' call in a series of songs that confront the crosscurrents between blues despair and gospel hope. Seal's best songs—"Fast Changes," "People Asking Why," and "Prayer for the Dying"—recall the emotional depth and social awareness of Al Green and Marvin Gaye. Intensely aware that fluidity requires openness, Seal refuses to dictate how his songs should be interpreted. "The song is always larger in the listener's mind," he wrote. "It is your perception of what I'm saying rather than what I actually say that is the key." That's a pretty good description of why the blues standards have lasted so long. We all stand at our own crossroads, stare into our own nights. Even though there's more than a touch of church in Seal's voice, "Prayer for the Dying" is a great blues because it speaks to whatever disaster has touched your life. For me, the opening image of the "fearless people" and the "careless needle" ties the song in with AIDS. But the main point of "Prayer," like all blues, is that the brutal experience isn't the end, at least not always. "Say yes while people say no," Seal moans as the song fades. "Cause life carries on / it goes on and goes on."

To which Erykah Badu lifted a loud amen. As did Maxwell in "Ascension (Don't Ever Wander)" from *Maxwell's Urban Hang Suite,* the closest thing to Marvin Gaye's *Let's Get It On* the nineties had to offer. Blurring the line between hip-hop and R & B, Badu and Maxwell brought some of Incognito's underground energy into the commercial mainstream. Sung in a voice that summons memories of Billie Holiday, Badu's breakthrough hit "On and On" plunges into a world of heartbreak and destruction but ultimately communicates a redemptive vision that responds to the calls sounding from the other side of what cultural critic Paul Gilroy called "the Black Atlantic." Addressing herself to the spiritual emptiness of a world where the intellectuals don't believe in God, Badu calls the spiritual diaspora back together, giving "mad props to the God Ja'Boom."

Badu's widespread acceptance among all but the hardest core of the hip-hop audience contributed to a reconciliation that had seemed extremely unlikely earlier in the decade. The way had been opened by Mary J. Blige, who established herself with the R & B-styled hits "You Remind Me" and "Real Love" before nailing down her place in the hip-hop nation by collaborating with Wu-Tang Clan's Method Man on the massive hit "I'll Be There for You/You're All I Need to Get By." Blige was only one of a new breed of black women soul singers who dominated both the pop and R & B charts during the mid-nineties: Aaliyah ("Back and Forth"); Toni Braxton ("Love Shoulda Brought You Home"); Monifah ("I Miss You [Come Back Home]," written and produced by soul rapper Heavy D);

Brandy ("I Wanna Be Down"), who collaborated with LL Cool J on "Sittin' up in My Room"; and Tracie Spencer ("Tender Kisses"). The solo acts were joined by female (definitely not girl) groups Brownstone ("If You Love Me"), Allure (who collaborated with rapper Nas on "Head over Heels"), and Changing Faces, whose "G.H.E.T.T.O.U.T.," written and produced by R. Kelly, voiced the blues complexities of the nineties as powerfully as Kelly's "I Believe I Can Fly" expressed the decade's gospel aspirations. Kelly's duet with Sparkle, "Be Careful," brought Harold Melvin and The Blue Notes' "If You Don't Know Me By Now" into a conversation sparked by Terry McMillan's *Waiting to Exhale*. An increasing number of brothers chimed in with Kelly to form a deep soul chorus, among them Eric Benet ("Spiritual Thang"), Ali ("Love Letter"), and the vocal group Solo, who paid tribute to the tradition by structuring their debut album as a montage of deep soul originals ("Holding On") and covers of their spiritual ancestor Sam Cooke ("Cupid," "Another Saturday Night," and the best version of "A Change Is Gonna Come" since Solomon Burke had used Cooke's anthem to sound the depths of the Reagan abyss). The most powerful expression of the underlying gospel energy of the deep soul movement may have been the version of Joi's "Freedom" used as the theme for the film *Panther*, which brought together a chorus including Aaliyah, Brownstone, Caroyn Wheeler, En Vogue, Crystal Waters, Karyn White, Mary J. Blige, Me'Shell NdegeOcello, TLC, and more than a dozen others. A rap remix featured contributions from MC Lyte, Queen Latifah, Salt-N-Pepa, and Yo Yo.

One of the most important things about the black women singers was the way they brought the values of the gospel impulse back to the popular mainstream. In his insightful essay on the new movement in R & B, critic Danny Alexander observed that as early as 1994 black women had become a dominant presence on the charts. That year half of the *Billboard* Top 20 singles were by women; six of those women were black. Noting the failure of most "serious" critics to appreciate, or even notice, this unprecedented situation, Alexander placed it in its historical context:

> Those are the voices of black women—voices of working class black women—voices this society has never listened to or particularly wanted to hear on the political mainstage. Just as nearly 300 years of slavery, 100 years without the vote, and another three decades of trying to blame blacks for their oppression characterizes a miserably

racist society, black women have borne the brunt of it all, struggling to keep families together, to keep love and hope alive. They were the silent backbone of the Civil Rights Movement, and they were neglected by the women's movement. But pop radio, perhaps because its importance is underestimated by most, is one place where black women have long had a toe-hold, and a whole new generation is building on the past to shape our cultural growth in ways that cannot be erased—whether the little boys want to understand or not.

The musical openness wasn't limited to the underground clubs of London, Tokyo, and Toronto or the direct descendants of Aretha, Stevie Wonder, and Al Green. As the decade advanced, there was strong evidence that the popular-music world as a whole might be responding to the deep soul call. For the first time since the early seventies, Top 40 radio stations were playing a fair cross section of pop styles without much concern for the racial identity of artists or audience. "Magic 104" and "Z-98"-style stations sent out an eclectic mix of hip-hop, rock, and R & B with the occasional touch of ska or the dance floor flavor of the month tossed in. The whole mix tended toward the lite side. You could hear Coolio and Puff Daddy as rap lite; Brandy as R & B lite; Hootie and the White Boys as rock lite; Boyz II Men as Temptations lite. You get my drift.

But, hey, it was Top 40, and, as always on Top 40, the best moments could be stunning. There's no question that the Spice Girls were assembled as a marketing entity in the great tradition of the Monkees, who (mostly thanks to Mike Nesmith cuts like "The Girl I Knew Somewhere") also managed to transcend their origins with fair frequency. As much a fashion statement as a musical group, the Spice Girls were a somewhat whiter pop take on the idea of Black Britain pioneered by Soul II Soul. But their massive hit "Wannabe" is *great* pop. I have no earthly idea what the "zigga zig huh" they want is, but my grade-school daughters and all their friends sure seem to know. (And, anyway, if the Spice Girls don't get their props in this book, there's no way the girls are letting me back in the house.) "Wannabe" played right alongside Hanson's "MMMbop," which was a kind of Springsteen lite, an affirmation of rock energy as the best way to deal with a world where the people who tell you they have the answers are lying. Made by three brothers from Tulsa, which is either the middle of nowhere or, judging by "MMMbop," the heartland of rock and roll, the cut sounds a little bit like every rock and roll classic you can remember and absolutely like itself. After Hanson, the

Top 40 mix might move on to "End of the Road" by Boyz II Men. The titles of the group's first single, "Motownphilly," and their first album, *Cooleyhighharmony,* let you know where they came from; "End of the Road" suggested they might earn themselves a niche in the Motown pantheon. Built around a lush arrangement that would have made Gamble and Huff smile, "End of the Road"—which stayed at number one for thirteen weeks, breaking the record set by Elvis's "Don't Be Cruel"/"Hound Dog"—provides a showcase for the group's versatility. Michael McCary lays down mellow raps in classic Barry White mode; Wanya Morris sounds like a younger, sweeter David Ruffin. After that you might hear Hootie's "I Only Want to Be with You," which includes the weirdest imaginable echo of Bob Dylan's "Idiot Wind"; TLC's "Waterfalls," Sheryl Crow's "A Change," or En Vogue's "My Loving (You're Never Gonna Get It)"; or Beck's "Where It's At," a postmodern tribute to hip-hop's "two turntables and a microphone" that bounces along on a riff that's straight out of Memphis.

The best thing about the Top 40 mix was that the kids were listening to it rather than thinking about it. It's worth remembering that both Sam Cooke and Berry Gordy embraced the politics of lite without any hint of apology. They knew it was a serious mistake to overlook the long-term implications of an audience that didn't *hear* in black and white. Top 40 circa 1998 implies calls and responses that don't seem quite as unlikely as they did five or ten or even twenty years ago. It's not quite "Everyday People," but it's definitely not 1983, when Toto's "Africa" topped the charts with singing that, as Dave Marsh observed, "wouldn't go over in a Holiday Inn cocktail lounge." And there's at least the chance that a generation that grows up listening to Puff Daddy and the Fugees alongside Sheryl Crow and Chumbawumba, to Beck and Hootie alongside TLC and En Vogue, will be attuned to some lower frequencies that haven't been heard from in quite a while. And that points us back to the elders of the tribe.

# 62
# Ancestors and Elders

When Curtis Mayfield speaks, his words resonate with the spiritual power that has allowed black folks to survive four centuries of storm without surrendering the vision of a better world. His dignity and eloquence evoke images of an urban elder, an American griot passing the gifts of the ancestors down to a community in need of sustaining wisdom. "We all have to grow," Mayfield says. "You have to stay true to yourself while recognizing and acknowledging what's going on *now*." Mayfield smiles at the image of himself as sage. "I wouldn't make the choice myself. I'm just a man. I'm certainly no saint, never have been. I've always wanted to do the right thing with living. Do unto those as you'd have them do unto you, that was more or less my church motto and that always made proper sense. It always makes me feel good to know those who might observe say, 'Hey, I can take a little something from that person.' "

Mayfield's conscious acceptance of his role as elder provides something all too rare in a nation obsessed with youth, with innovation. Yet in the nineties Mayfield was by no means the only older artist whose voice mingled with those of the younger generation. A surprising amount of the most vital music of the decade was produced by musicians who remembered the freedom movement and had lived through its long decline. Neil Young's *Ragged Glory* and *Sleeps with Angels* opened a conversation with the Seattle grunge bands who shared both his unregenerate rock and roll romanticism and his anger over a society willing to turn everything and everyone into a product. The collaboration between Young and Pearl Jam on *Mirror Ball* made both sonic and political sense. Young's contemporary George Clinton recorded with a who's who of the contemporary rappers who had sampled his work: Ice Cube, Wu-Tang Clan's Ol' Dirty Bastard, A Tribe Called Quest, Busta Rhymes, and Digital Underground. Liz Phair didn't actually go into the studio with the

Rolling Stones, but her underground debut album *Exile in Guyville* engaged in a song by song conversation with *Exile on Main Street*; songs like "Fuck and Run" and "Supernova" (from the aboveground follow-up *Whip-Smart*) made it clear that the guys hadn't cornered the market on sexual attitude or rock and roll fury. Sarah McLachlan paid homage to Tom Waits with a cover of "Ol' 55," and Waits added "The Earth Died Screaming" to a résumé that had already established him as one of the greatest white blues songwriters ("Singapore," "Clap Hands," "Cold Cold Ground," and "Telephone Call from Istanbul," which includes the most basic blues warning of them all: "Never drive a car when you're dead"). On the R & B side of town, an "All Star Choir" including Evelyn King, Will Downing, Keith Sweat, Cissy Houston, Leotis Clyburn, pretty much the whole Levert Clan, and Phyllis Hyman joined the O'Jays on the "gospel mix" of Bob Dylan's "Emotionally Yours." Passing one of Dylan's less memorable songs through the gospel flame, the group forged a soaring affirmation of love as God and God as love.

Even when the conversations were less direct, the cross-generational call and response contributed to the richness of nineties music. Madonna embraced the women rock and pop singers who'd followed in her footsteps with a mixture of humor and generosity. "I like the Spice Girls," she said, laughing. "Every time someone says something bad about them, I say, 'Hey, wait a minute, I was a Spice Girl once.' " More important, the vocal phrasing on "Swim" from Madonna's near-gospel CD *Ray of Light* made it clear she'd been listening carefully to Sarah McLachlan. At the same time, the intricate rhythms of "Frozen" reminded her younger sisters that the spirits were happiest when they could get out on the dance floor and move.

Many of the elders directly addressed what they heard as a spiritual and political malaise, a haunting uncertainty about what to do with the rage the younger generation refused to surrender. The keynote sermon from Stevie Wonder's best album since *Songs in the Key of Life*, "Conversation Peace," called for a gospel response to the violence ripping the inner cities apart. Taking on the role of Old Testament prophet, Prince called down the wrath of the Lord on the "Thieves in the Temple." Elvis Costello's "Complicated Shadows" extended the scathing investigation of what he once called "emotional fascism" begun in "Less Than Zero," "Oliver's Army," "Two Little Hitlers," "Shipbuilding," and "Brilliant Mistake." Powered by a rhythmic drive and chord structure borrowed from the Rolling Stones' "Jumpin' Jack Flash," "Complicated Shadows" arrived at the same conclusion as Ice Cube and KRS-One: "Though the fury's hot and hard / I still see a cold graveyard." More than a few politicians could have stood listening to the moral of Costello's gangsta fairy tale: "You should've never been playing with a gun in those complicated shadows." Lou Reed's "Halloween Parade" joined Diamanda Galas's harrowing "Swing Low Sweet Chariot" and "You Must Be Certain of the Devil" as the clearest reports from the heart of New York's plague years. Looking out over the annual Gay Pride celebration on Christopher Street, ground zero, Reed sees the departed—Virgin Mary, Rotten Rita, Brandy Alexander—as clearly as he sees the survivors. "It makes me mad and then it makes me sad and then I start to freeze." It's a blue that fades to black.

While "Complicated Shadows" affirmed Costello's place alongside Lennon and McCartney in the pop songwriters' Hall of Fame, Bob Dylan's *Time out of Mind* surprised almost everyone by earning Dylan a place alongside himself; that is, alongside the Bob Dylan of "My Back Pages," "Just Like a Woman," and "Tangled Up in Blue." "Cold Chains Bound," "Not Dark Yet," and the haunting "Highlands" came from the same blues-haunted terrain as Robert Johnson's "Love in Vain," Billie Holiday's "All of Me," and the Geto Boys' "My Mind's Playin' Tricks on Me." Death was most definitely about your own weary self, and the weariness was part of a world that didn't offer much response.

No one understood the importance of his ancestors, or had a deeper understanding of his own role as elder, than Bruce Springsteen. Performing at a Rock and Roll Hall of Fame concert celebrating the legacy of Woody Guthrie, Springsteen introduced his haunting ballad "Across the Border" by identifying a "spiritual center to Woody's songs next to the fun and tough optimism in the face of it all." Following Guthrie's example, Springsteen began to play a more active political role in the nineties, appearing at rallies against California's anti–affirmative action measure, Proposition 209, alongside Maxine Waters, Jesse Jackson, Dolores Huerta of the United Farm Workers, and Ellie Smeal, president of the Fund for a Feminist Majority. "Woody got you thinking about the next guy," Springsteen continued. "He got you thinking about your neighbors and the idea that salvation isn't individual, that maybe we don't rise and fall on our own."

During the mid-nineties, Springsteen refined his long-standing commitment to community. Returning to the stark acoustic style he had used for *Nebraska* at the beginning of the Reagan era, he performed in smaller venues; the increased intimacy invited audiences to respond more deeply to the new songs in his "border trilogy" ("Sinaloa Cowboys," "The Line," "Balboa Park"), which focused on the problems of Mexican immigrants in the Southwest. Springsteen was well aware that his musical choices had reduced the size of the audience that had made him a megastar in the eighties, but it was a situation he almost welcomed. "I very consciously set out to develop an audience that was about more than buying records," he reflected. "I set out to find an audience that would be a reflection of some imagined community that I had in my head, that lived according to the values in my music and shared a similar set of ideals."

Springsteen's values and ideals placed him in an American populist tradition exemplified by Walt Whitman, Langston Hughes, John Steinbeck, and Guthrie, who set the working-class hero of Steinbeck's *The Grapes of Wrath* to music in "Tom Joad," the song Springsteen sang to open his set at the Hall of Fame. The sparse, reworked versions of his standard repertoire that defined the "Ghost of Tom Joad" tour made Springsteen's spiritual kinship with Guthrie unmistakable. At different points on the tour he performed blistering versions of "The Promised Land" and "Darkness on the Edge of Town" alongside less familiar, but equally powerful songs that had never appeared on albums, among them the Guthrie-esque "This Hard Land" and his empathetic portrait of a returning Vietnam vet, "Shut Out the Light." Accompanied by Springsteen's pounding guitar, a blues version of "Born in the U.S.A." left out the anthemic chorus; not even Ronald Reagan could have missed the point.

But in case someone did miss the point, Springsteen said it straight out in the introductions to his songs, which rang with a moral clarity Bill Clinton could only dream about. Introducing his version of Guthrie's "Plane Wreck at Los Gatos (Deportees)," he addressed the sources of anti-immigrant hysteria. "As far back as the depression," Springsteen began, "Woody Guthrie understood that people comin' across the border, workin' for almost no money, doin' jobs that no one else wants to do, encouraged by American businesses, is not the problem. But somebody wants to make you think it is." Springsteen understood just how terrifying it was that so much of the music and literature of the depression sounded so current even during the "economic recovery" of the nineties.

Populism has its perils. For one thing, it's the rhetoric of choice among many right-wing groups, including the White Aryan Resistance, whose leader, Tom Metzger, hates corporate America as much as Neil Young or Public Enemy does. Only problem is, if he had his way, most of the people you've been reading about in this book would be dead, in jail, or "back in Africa where they belong." Dan Bern, a powerful young musician who traces his ancestry to both Springsteen and Guthrie, made the point with devastating clarity in "Oklahoma," a remake of "Great Duststorm Disaster" which responded to the white supremacist violence of the Oklahoma City federal building bombing. As the nation mourned the blast that "blew folks' lives apart" and "asked the dear Lord why," the "shock soon turned to anger." "They thought it was some Arab," Bern sings with a deep sadness, "and folks began to scream / First tighten up the borders / then hang 'em from a tree." The criminal of course was "a patriot government foe" who was as "white as driven snow." Bern drives home the moral: "When we build walls and borders from fear and hate and guns / the hatred turns around and strikes at everyone."

The most important part of Springsteen's development in the nineties was his conscious acceptance of his role as elder. Embracing his role as father and citizen, Springsteen made the transition with grace and dignity. He reflected on his broadening political awareness in probing interviews with the progressive magazine *Mother Jones* and the gay-lesbian monthly *The Advocate*; he reflected on the importance of reading in the highbrow *Double Take*. And through it all, he held close to the vital core of the populist vision. At the end of "The Ghost of Tom Joad," Springsteen invokes Tom's parting words to his mother in *The Grapes of Wrath*: "Wherever there's a fight against the blood and the hatred in the air / Look for me, Ma, I'll be there." Covering "The Ghost of Tom Joad" with a fury that made it clear they understood what Woody Guthrie meant when he called his guitar a "machine [that] kills fascists," Rage Against the Machine said amen.

A similar cross-generational dialogue involved the rappers and three of the men they most frequently identified as their creative inspirations: Curtis Mayfield, George Clinton, and Gil Scott-Heron. All three welcomed the energetic innovations of the hip-hop generation; all three urged the rappers to be more aware of their place in black communities. Pedro Bell's liner notes to the 1996 collection of Clinton's greatest hits that included the collaborations with the younger rappers parodied the East/West battle and reminded everyone that there was plenty of funk to go around. Presenting the conflict as a sibling rivalry between the descendants of the elder

Atomic Dog, Bell described "Two tribes of Hip Hounds . . . engaged in a conflict noted as Woof War I. The battle was being waged over the shortage of sample bytes, an essential auditory war of this sound driven planet." After a suspiciously Clintonian alien arrives "spewing boxes of Funk Munchies to the sample starved landscape," the community comes back together in a cascade of "thunderous licks, loops and bassactivity." But Bell concludes with a warning that sounds even more sobering given subsequent events: "All that was left to be said was, 'Will you still be alive after this album?' "

It was vital that the advice was not offered from the lofty heights of moral superiority, but instead with an understanding that the hip-hop generation was attempting—not always coherently and not often successfully—to revitalize the dreams of the freedom movement. Emerging from nearly a decade away from the recording studio, Gil Scott-Heron called on his creative descendants to repudiate the Reagan Rules. Calling on the sustaining wisdom of the ancestors in "The Other Side," Scott-Heron reflected on the divisions within black communities that keep the new world from coming. In an interview with *Vibe* magazine, he challenged the rappers who acknowledged his influence to take the message seriously. "If they admire what we did, then use it in the same fashion that we tried to," he said. "To say things that are positive for people and about people and get off the corner and shit. Every song ain't from the corner—and ain't nobody dancing on the corner, they're dancing in the joints." In "Message to the Messengers," he reminded the younger generation of the point he'd made in "The Revolution Will Not Be Televised":

> If you're gonna be speaking for a whole generation
> And you know enough to handle their education
> Be sure you know the real deal about past situations
> And ain't just repeating what you heard on a local TV station
> Sometimes they tell lies and put them in a truthful disguise
> But the truth is, that's why we said it wouldn't be televised

Addressing the "young rappers" directly, he offered "one more suggestion before I get out of your way." Charging his descendants to "spread that respect around" and put an end to violence against the elders, he insisted the time had come "to calm that bullshit down / 'Cause we're terrorizin' our old folks and we brought fear into our homes."

Mayfield understood Scott-Heron's point, but took a gentler approach. Reflecting on the use of his songs "People Get Ready," "Keep on Pushing," "We're a Winner," and "New World Order" in Spike Lee's film *Get on the Bus,* Mayfield expressed sympathy for the impulse behind the Million Man March: "You might sense a mass of people wanting to find some answers. That's really what a lot of young blacks and young people in poverty want. They need answers. You're not the smartest person in the world. It don't look like through schooling itself, with what's happening in the schools, you're going to be. You need answers. How do you get from here to there when you want to be a righteous person? I don't want to do crime, hey that's risky, and it takes smarts to even do that. So the young kids need something to believe and to prove and be proven that it works." The best songs from *New World Order,* "Back to Living Again," "Ms. Martha," and the soulful remake of "We People Who Are Darker Than Blue"—which incorporates a sample from "Don't Worry (If There's a Hell Below We're All Gonna Go)"—echo Springsteen's determination to maintain hope in defiance of the political and spiritual forces determined to kill those dreams. "The bigotry, the discrimination and the selfishness and the greed. All these things come from the top down," Mayfield observes. "But my philosophy hasn't changed. The concept of peace, love, get it together and maybe there'll be a new world order."

# 63
# Conversations with the Ancestors

Mayfield and Scott-Heron's words couldn't put an end to black-on-black violence. But there were encouraging signs that at least some of their calls had been heard. The most meaningful responses from the younger generation could be heard in their increasingly sophisticated use of sampling. Sampling continued to attract attacks from mainstream commentators and older musicians who saw it as a vampiric shortcut, an easy way to avoid the discipline required to master an instrument. Certainly, there were songs that used a few catchy bars of a seventies or eighties hit for a prefab hook. But to judge sampling by M.C. Hammer's use of Rick James's "Super Freak" in "U Can't Touch This" or Puff Daddy's transformation of the blues vision of "The Message" into accompaniment for the individualist ascent fantasy of "Can't Nobody Hold Me Down" would be like judging disco by the Bee Gees.

At its best, sampling encouraged a living communion between past and present that recalled the dynamics of West African cultures. The Yoruba version of the call and response between youth, elders, and ancestors is grounded in a process cultural critic Ed Pavlic calls *syndesis*. The syndetic approach allows descendants to respond to previous works of art by incorporating elements of those works into their "new" creations. In contrast with "progress"-oriented Western processes, in the Yoruba approach the latest version does not replace or correct the previous work. Rather, it adds new layers, allowing movement between new versions and earlier statements which remain intact. Their energy, which is understood as a direct response to both their immediate contexts and the ancestors, remains available at all later stages of the process.

Syndesis introduces ancestral wisdom into the current world, but does not view that wisdom as final. If subsequent events or new sources of knowledge reveal limitations or the need for adjustment, the descendant can take whatever action is necessary. Innovative responses are in no sense a betrayal of the original (Wynton Marsalis, take note). In fact, a syndetic response can increase our appreciation of the ancestors by calling attention to elements of their work that have been overlooked or insufficiently developed in previous responses. In effect, this allows the ancestor to change and grow. In a syndetic process, there is no need to repudiate Malcolm X because he was sexist, or William Faulkner because he grew up in a world where the word "nigger" was common currency. Rather, descendants can build on their insights in ways that allow the next generation of descendants to go back to the ancestors with an awareness of the paths they helped open even when they didn't walk them themselves. For the Yoruba and their creative descendants in the studios of the mid-nineties, *every* stage of the process remains available for discussion and understanding.

Whether or not they'd ever heard of the Yoruba, let alone syndesis, many musicians of the late eighties and nineties used samples in a manner consistent with its enduring democratic spirit. One of the most interesting sampled conversations with the ancestors was the one concerning women's relation to R & B and hip-hop. Some of the younger singers simply said "amen" to their female elders as in Missy Elliott's "The Rain," a bluesy response to Ann Peebles's Memphis classic. Others provided women's perspectives on "male" statements. Mary J. Blige's gospel blues "My Life" reworks Roy Ayers's lament over female infidelity "Everybody Loves the Sunshine" (which was used as a call to political consciousness in the "Sunshine remix" of Brand Nubian's "Wake Up"). Other responses were more complicated. TLC's "Switch" completed the liberating assault on the Phil Spector Memorial Ogre's Castle begun in Salt-N-Pepa's "Shoop." Sampling "Rapper's Delight," Jean Knight's proto-feminist blues joke "Mr. Big Stuff," and Earth, Wind & Fire's gospel soul classic "Devotion," "Switch" enters into what had been a mostly academic discussion of whether songs like the Shirelles' "Will You Still Love Me Tomorrow" represent patriarchal oppression or nascent feminist consciousness. With "Switch," you don't have to ask. TLC want true devotion, but if the guy acts up, their philosophy is simple: "Erase, Replace, Embrace, New Face." Any questions, guys? When it's all over, the girls have taken control of the girl groups and the liberatory potential of the ancestors is a lot clearer than it used to be.

The most powerful of the women's syndetic responses was Lauryn Hill's contribution to the Fugees' "Ready or Not." The fact that she's better known for her passable cover of Roberta Flack's "Killing Me Softly" makes about as much sense as Sam Cooke going down in history for his cover of "Ol' Man River." Fortunately, "Killing Me Softly" radically expanded the audience for "Ready or Not," which puts an end to the silly debate over whether or not women can rap. Holding her own with fellow Fugee Wycleffe Jean, whose "Gone Till November" established him in the first rank of nineties rappers, Lauryn Hill is the bomb. Her verses on "Ready or Not" release political energies that the Delfonics, whose seventies hit of the same title provides the Fugees' ancestral point of reference, never dreamed of. Responding to the gangstas' near-comic sexual personas, Hill defines her own warrior ancestry: "So while you imitating Al Capone, I be Nina Simone and defecating on your microphone." The ball's in your court, gangstas.

Another fascinating syndetic conversation investigated the historical forces shaping life in the inner cities of the nineties. One of the most striking sequences began with the Wailers' statement of political defiance, "Get Up Stand Up." The song's rhythmic riff had been used in L.A. funk band War's "Slipping into Darkness," which comments on the loss of political focus that was making the ghetto into an increasingly bleak and dangerous place. When the age of sampling arrived, New Jersey rappers Poor Righteous Teachers sampled the riff in "Rock Dis Funky Joint," which recognized the process of decay and called for a renewal of revolutionary consciousness. "Little Ghetto Boys," Wu-Tang Clan's response to Donny Hathaway's "Little Ghetto Boy," fingers the jagged grain of blues isolation while California gangsta Too Short invoked Hathaway's "The Ghetto," with its fading echo of "We Shall Overcome," to remind his brothers of the gospel politics they too often seemed to have forgotten. In "Gangsta's Paradise," Coolio traced the amnesia to a confusion of media image and blues reality. "Too much TV watching got me chasing dreams," he raps against a sample from Stevie Wonder's "Pastime Paradise." The sample's what keeps it all from sliding into generic gangsta moralizing (and no doubt what made it a monster hit). The original "Paradise" faded out with a haunting chorus of "We Shall Overcome." It's still there in Coolio's response. But just barely.

The wonderful thing about the syndetic approach is that it's true to the spirit of call and response as it was understood by the beloved community at the height of the freedom movement. We honor the ancestors and move on ahead; after all, they are always here with us. The world we're in today isn't the one faced by Martin Luther King or Mahalia Jackson, Sam Cooke or Malcolm X. But if we hear their voices clearly, they can help us imagine the paths we need to take.

# 64
# Flashes of the Spirit

If having a theory helped you go with the flow, the nineties were the best time since the mid-sixties, when John Coltrane provided a sonic orientation to Malcolm X. Not surprisingly, the most theoretically sophisticated understandings of the energies connecting the DJs, the deep soul singers, and the syndetic samplers came from the world of jazz. While the "serious jazz world bogged down in neo-musical virtuosity, Steve Coleman and an ever-changing set of musicians accociated with the Broklyn-based M-Base Collective set about imagining tomorrow. Well versed in a wide range of diasporic vocabularies, M-Base associates Coleman, Greg Osby, and Cassandra Wilson saw no reason the tradition should keep up the call and response with the brothers and sisters on the block. The spirit of Miles Davis must have smiled.

Taking their cue from Miles's seventies albums *Agharta* and *Pangaea*, which had baffled jazz critics when they were first released, a new breed of experimental DJs conjured up an ever-changing and inherently undefinable flow of styles: ambient, trip hop, acid jazz, deep house, techno, mushroom jazz, dub, jungle, drum and bass. The DJs came from more or less everywhere and few outside their immediate communities had any idea about their racial identities. In fact, jungle master Goldie, best known for his reworking of Marvin Gaye in "Inner City Life," was the son of a Scottish mother and a black Jamaican father; DJ Krush was Japanese; Aphex Twin was a white boy from the coast of Cornwall; Derrick Carter had grown up in a black working-class suburb; Carter's partner in Chicago's Red Nail Collective, G-Most, could pass for Puerto Rican but he was mixed black. DJ Spooky was white and DJ Shadow was black. Or was it the other way around? One thing was sure: no one listening to their CDs could tell.

All had embarked on the fundamental jazz quest to redefine themselves and their communities. Their willingness to use all sorts of sonic fragments identified them as members of a postmodern generation obsessed with montage. But the way they shored up the fragments against their ruins made it clear they were forging new links in the chain that stretched back to Louis Armstrong and Duke Ellington, Mahalia Jackson and Marion Williams. Red Nail's gospel house genius DJ Gant, who had a degree in Afro-American studies, frequently droppd William's "The Moan" into mixes alongside deep house and underground classics such as Blaze's "Get Up," D-Train's "Music," Robert Owens's "A.M. Blues," Pattie LaBelle's "The Spirit's in It," and "You Can Do It" by Al Hudson's One Way featuring Alicia Myers. One of the high points of DJ Gant's repertoire was Louie Vega's remix of Latin superstar La India's version of Al Green's "Love and Happiness." Her version incorporates fragments of traditional Yoruba chants. He might take it from there to Mariah Carey's "Always Be My Baby," not the version you've heard, but

David Morales's extended dance remix which makes it clear just how much Carey's suffered from "Ray Charles in the Eighties Syndrome": the delusion that *what* you sing doesn't matter. It's been said that Brother Ray could sound good singing the phone book but that doesn't explain why he thinks it's a good idea. The phone book would be a step up from most of the material Carey's handlers have saddled her with; at least it has *something* to do with reality. The Morales remix, however, makes it clear that Carey can flat-out sing and that she knows what Marion Williams was getting at. There's no reason Mariah shouldn't be making gospel soul in the tradition of Curtis Mayfield and Aretha Franklin.

DJ Shadow's "What Color Is Your Soul?" comes from a different world, but reveals an equally strong ability to jar listeners out of their complacency. It starts out with something that sounds like a Gregorian chant, but before long you're listening to sitars and a warning that your subconscious fears are about to be transformed into conscious awareness. Sure it's corny, but so was P-Funk, and the strumming guitar that follows the warning lets you know Shadow's thinking of this as "Maggot Brain" for the nineties.

Like the DJs, Cassandra Wilson traced her musical roots to Miles Davis, whom she described as "a spirit that just won't let me go. Miles is a master of spareness—one note can say volumes. The way he deals with phrasing is the essence of blackness. The phrasing is so much like our language." Wilson's Miles is the Miles of *Sketches of Spain*, who could speak flamenco as fluently as a dream. Wilson shares Miles's openness and his seductive ferocity. She's recorded Robert Johnson's "Hellhound on My Trail," Van Morrison's "Wild Nights," Hank Williams's "I'm So Lonesome I Could Cry," Neil Young's "Harvest Moon," Joni Mitchell's "Black Crow," a restlessly polyrhythmic version of Thom Bell's "Children of the Night," and, improbable as it may seem, the Monkees' "Last Train to Clarksville." Many of her best moments, however, come on her own compositions: "Memphis," "A Little Warm Death," and her response to Toni Morrison's *Song of Solomon*, "Solomon Sang."

Wilson sees African spirituality as a defining element of the tradition she and M-Base are helping to create. Her song "Sankofa" revoices the jazz impulse using the imagery of a Ghanaian legend about a "bird of redemption" which "takes you back to retrieve what is lost in the past." Like many jazz artists, Wilson has studied the historical roots of African American music. "I think everything that grows up out of the blues is jazz," she once said. "The blues is like the Mississippi River. Everything else is a tributary. Jazz is a big trib-utary, but there are other points on the river where you can go. You have to reinform jazz with other information. If you don't, it be-comes stagnant." "Recently I was reading *Blues People* by [Amiri Baraka] LeRoi Jones," she continued, "and he talks about how the blues is the form that most clearly maintains our African culture and spiritual beliefs—the belief, for example, that everything is related and there are no accidents. There's a lot of African folklore couched in the blues lyrics." Commenting on Robert Johnson, she asserted that "a lot of people miss the point about Robert Johnson. He was a contemporary of Lester Young, which is mind-boggling when you think about it. And rhythmically he's doing the same extraordinary thing, a push-me/pull-me meter all his own. He came up with all these weird harmonies between his voice and guitar, and he was a master of just hinting at something. The way he'd just sketch the outline of an idea was so intuitive, so spontaneous; it was the essence of jazz."

Wilson's M-Base associate Steve Coleman takes her eclecticism even further. As the title of his brilliant composition "Multiplicity of Approaches (An Afrikan Way of Knowing)" suggests, he under-stands radical openness as a fundamental element of African Amer-ican culture. Coleman loves the rhythmic drive of hip-hop and funk, which he uses as a foundation for jazz explorations in "Rhythm Peo-ple" and "Motherland Pulse." Seeing blackness as a launching pad rather than a turf to be defended, Coleman has reached out to Asian cultures in "The Mantra (Intonation of Power)" and "The Tao of Mad Phat," dabbled in relativistic necromancy in "The X Format (Standard Deviation)," and paid homage to Miles with a funky cover of " 'Round Midnight." There's no sign he's even partially satisfied with what he knows.

Coleman's appreciation of social and spiritual diversity runs so deep he'd probably even welcome Wynton Marsalis into the M-Base dance. And that's saying something, since Marsalis showed no inter-est at all in including the M-Base musicians, to say nothing of DJs like "mushroom jazz" innovator Mark Farina, in the programs he or-ganized at New York's Lincoln Center. But no one aware of, or even interested in, the fluid energies of the orisha or the tao of mad phat was likely to seek them out at Lincoln Center anyway. Anyone with a library card could learn a lot more from Zora Neale Hurston's *Mules and Men* or *Tell My Horse*. In his song "Zora," blues/jazzman Olu Dara paid homage to Hurston as a New World griot. The real point, as Dianne Reeves recognized in "Old Souls," was that the spirits were, literally, everywhere. "I see them in the faces of people that I know, I hear them in the voices on my radio," she sang. In live performances, she improvised in Yoruba, chanting "l'agba, l'agba," a Yoruba invocation of the old folks, the ones who possessed the past. When she sang the deep blues of "Josa Lee" or "Afro-Blue," or when Dara sang "Okra" or "Jungle," which featured a guest rap by his son Nas, you knew that the energies were flowing, and the spirits were in the house.

# 65
# Redemption Songs (The Nineties Remix)

The story I've been telling in *A Change Is Gonna Come* is a story about community, about what it takes to respond to the call James Baldwin issued in the conclusion of *The Fire Next Time*:

> And here we are, at the center of the arc, trapped in the gaudiest, most valuable, and most improbable water wheel the world has ever seen. Everything now, we must assume, is in our hands; we have no right to assume otherwise. If we—and now I mean the relatively conscious whites and the relatively conscious blacks, who must, like lovers, insist on, or create, the consciousness of the others—do not falter in our duty now, we may be able, handful that we are, to end the racial nightmare, and achieve our country, and change the history of the world.

Baldwin's call remains as central at the beginning of a new century as it was when it sounded a clarion over the freedom movement in 1962. Within a few years, the waterwheel had turned, the fires burned in Watts and Vietnam and in the hearts of people, black and white, who no longer believed in the promise of redemption, who no longer accepted Baldwin's visionary "we."

It's been a long road into and at least partway back out of the abyss. There's no evading the blues reality that, now and always, the outcome remains in doubt. Many angrily reject the idea that the warring camps of blacks and browns and whites and yellows can ever be transformed into what composer Geoff King, walking through a street festival in Brooklyn's Park Slope, called a "gorgeous mosaic." There are times when it seems that even the most powerful and conscious musical calls amount to nothing more than another packaged product. As social critic Mike Davis wrote in *The Nation,* it's a serious mistake to think modern capitalism is in any way hostile to "multiculturalism." Given half a chance, "people of color" make perfectly good consumers and, hey, they know about some really great spices and come up with sounds you just wouldn't believe. If you can't really get into dub or rai or SOCA, don't sweat it, these people cook up new stuff all the time. And *we* can sell it.

Yet, above the voices of cynicism and separation rise testimonies to the survival and renewal of the gospel vision. The spirit that lived in Bob Marley when he called on us to "emancipate ourselves from mental slavery" still reverberates. Many of the singers are too young to remember Martin Luther King or Mahalia Jackson; most have never heard of Ella Baker. But they have looked at the world they're living in, tested their blues voices, and at least begun to imagine their own beloved communities. The best music of the eighties grew out of the blues impulse, insisting on the reality of brutal experience over and against nostalgic fantasies and self-righteous lies. In the nineties, the gospel impulse has moved back to the center. Musicians working in all different styles have embraced ideals of community, often expressed in images of family. The emphasis was explicit in the names of gospel's Kirk Franklin and the Family, hip-hop's Wu-Tang Clan and Puff Daddy and the Family. But it was also present in the dynamics of the Native Tongue rappers (Jungle Brothers, De La Soul, A Tribe Called Quest) and the Austin, Texas, "cowpunk" scene, home turf for Alejandro Escovedo. Escovedo's "Gravity (Falling Down Again)" and "With These Hands" belong on the list of Latin rock classics that includes Richie Valens's "La Bamba," Santana's "Black Magic Woman" and "Samba Pa Ti," and Los Lobos' "Will the Wolf Survive?" and "One Time One Night," one of the most soulful responses to Reagan era despair.

At its best the music helped organize communities with a sense that they had a role to play in transforming the society at large. The clearest examples in rock were Rage Against the Machine and Ani DiFranco. Sounding a call to arms that matched the ferocity of the angriest rappers, Rage claimed its place on the front lines with a debut album built around searing political songs like "Bullet in the

Head"; "Township Rebellion," which envisioned a revolution extending from Johannesburg to South Central L.A.; and the cut they referred to as their "Funky Radical Bombtrack." "Take the Power Back" seconded Public Enemy's "Fight the Power," and moved ahead. Railing against the "structure of lies installed in our minds," Rage vocalist Zack de la Rocha pointed to the legacy of the Reagan years: "the holes in our spirit are causing tears and fears / One-sided stories for years and years and years." Their response on "Vietnow" from their second album, *Evil Empire*, was clear: "kill tha devil sound." While Tommy Merello's guitar screamed against the heavy-metal funk of bassist Tim Bob and drummer Brad Wilk, de la Rocha set out to "cross the white wall" in "Without a Face," a searing condemnation of California governor Pete Wilson's assault on affirmative action. Recalling Woody Guthrie and Bruce Springsteen, de la Rocha contemplated the "graves at the gate" and pledged Rage's energies to revolutionary change. In "People of the Sun," Rage dedicated itself to the renewal of the beloved community: "It's comin' back around again / this is for the people of the sun." It was an open question whether the enthusiastic crowds at Rage's concerts were responding deeply to the group's political edge, or merely accepting it because it was delivered in the most aggressive rock and roll since the glory days of the Clash.

There was little doubt that Ani DiFranco's audience, especially her core following in the lesbian-feminist community, understood exactly where she was coming from and where she wanted them to go. One of the few rock artists who kept up an active conversation with *contemporary* black music, DiFranco's sense of community was straight out of the freedom movement. For nearly a decade, she refused to enter into the musical mainstream, preferring to run a subterranean economic/musical collective out of her Buffalo home. A brilliant songwriter, DiFranco ranged from the blues realism of "Hide and Seek" to the scathing satire of "Napoleon." Her musical intelligence may have been at its strongest on *The Past Doesn't Go Anywhere*, her collaboration with legendary leftist raconteur Utah Phillips. Probably the last living progressive who described himself as a "Wobbly," after the Industrial Workers of the World ("One Big Union"), Phillips's combination of song, story, and stand-up comedy made him an even less visible white counterpart to Gil Scott-Heron. Introducing an ancestor most of her audience had never even heard of, DiFranco followed through on her theoretical commitment to extending the conversation beyond the borders of her lesbian-feminist base.

DiFranco's concerts made the strongest statement about rock as community since Bruce Springsteen was playing clubs. "Willing to Fight" challenged the members of her audience to forge themselves into a community that wouldn't dissolve when the concert ended. She was absolutely clear that community exacted a higher cost than the cover charge: "Give me a call when you're willing to fight for what you think is real and what you think is right." Her guitar—and she may be the most powerful rock guitarist since Jimi Hendrix— has been fighting all along.

It was crucial that the musicians of the nineties built their communities with an awareness of the lessons of the eighties. "If I feel a rage I won't deny it," sang Sarah McLachlan in the title song of her sonic and emotional tour de force *Fumbling Towards Ecstasy.* As Rage Against the Machine's Zack de la Rocha whispered in "Freedom," "Anger is a gift." Mobb Deep and Scarface applied the principle to the inner cities, but blues anger wasn't just a gangsta thing. DiFranco certainly fingered the jagged grain in "Untouchable," with its chorus of "Fuck you with your unforgettable face / fuck you for existing in the first place." Leaving the good girl masks of the fifties and sixties far behind, P. J. Harvey and Courtney Love matched the rappers angry beat for angry beat.

Hole couldn't play their instruments any better than the Stooges or Sex Pistols, but, in "Violet" and "Doll Parts," Love sang with the ferocity of a Janis Joplin who wouldn't even pretend to believe in peace and love. If the blues are about brutal experience, the one-time stripper knew what it meant to be "doll eyes, doll mouth, doll legs." If the blues are about frustrated desire, she spit out a working definition: "I want to be the girl with the most cake." And, if the blues are about survival, well, unlike her husband, Kurt Cobain, Courtney's still around.

Like John Fogerty, P. J. Harvey traced her musical ancestry back to the headwaters in the Mississippi Delta. "I was brought up listening to John Lee Hooker, to Howlin' Wolf, to Robert Johnson, and a lot of Hendrix and Beefheart," she said. "So I was exposed to all these very compassionate musicians at a very early age." She paid tribute to the tradition with her cover of Blind Lemon Jefferson's "Black Snake Moan," and made it clear she was acquainted with Robert Johnson's demons in "To Bring You My Love," where she sang "I've lain with the devil / cursed God above / Forsaken heaven to bring you my love." But she spoke for her generation when she made it clear in "Legs" that, at this stage of the game, women weren't going to accept a passive role: "I might as well be dead / but I could kill you instead."

Most of the women rockers understood the blues anger as a base for something more constructive. Lilith Fair, a kind of portable Woodstock organized by Sarah McLachlan in 1997, laid the foundation for a growing sense of community. Named after Adam's first wife, who was banished from Eden because she was too independent, Lilith Fair was intended not as an attack on males but, in McLachlan's words, "a family affair." Aware of the misogynist undertones of the annual Lollapalooza touring festival, which McLachlan jokingly called "testosterone crazed," many of the Lilith Fair performers understood the event as a response to both the vision and the limitations of their elders. "There was an innocence that prevailed in the sixties that was crushed with the assassinations of JFK and King," said Jewel, whose "Who Will Save Your Soul?" had more than a touch of blue-eyed soul. "Our parents have become disillusioned. It's their disillusionment we deal with in many ways; it's a kind of crust we have to break through."

Like Woodstock and Monterey, Lilith Fair presented a broad, but not inclusive, range of nineties music. The center lay with the singer-songwriters whose music critic Christopher John Farley, with a mixture of irony and admiration, labeled "Coffee House Pop." Although the lineup shifted as the Fair moved from city to city, the list of performers included McLachlan, Jewel, Fiona Apple, Meredith Brooks, Lori Carson, Mary Chapin Carpenter, Paula Cole, Sheryl Crow, Patty Griffin, Emmylou Harris, the Indigo Girls, Suzanne Vega, and Joan Osborne. A few black women performed, most notably Cassandra Wilson and Tracy Chapman. Chapman had moved on from the folk protest songs "Across the Lines" and "Behind the Walls" that had established her as a favorite on college campuses to arguably the decade's best blues hit, "Give Me One Reason." But there was no Missy Elliott to represent the new generation of women rappers; no Jody Watley to remind the audience of the singer-songwriter tradition in black women's R & B; not even Karyn White ("Superwoman") or Crystal Waters, whose dance classic "Gypsy Woman (She's Homeless)" would have fit right in with the non-ideological political agenda of a festival which collected money for various women's causes and provided kiosks for women's shelters and "voters for choice." One of the most hopeful signs of the decade came with McLachlan's announcement that Missy Elliott and Erykah Badu had accepted invitations to participate in the 1998 version of Lilith Fair.

Although the media gave a disproportionate amount of attention to the gangstas' nihilistic moments, the hip-hop nation of the nineties showed a strong commitment to rebuilding community. Even the gangsta raps that presented the most aggressively "black" fronts had gospel undertones. A responsive tenderness lay at the heart of Tupac's "I Ain't Mad at Cha" and Scarface's "Now I Feel Ya"; the gospel connection was explicit in the video of Bone Thugs n Harmony's "Crossroad," which opened with a gospel choir singing the old spiritual, later adopted by the freedom movement, "Mary Don't You Weep."

Outside the gangsta world, the gospel undertones were often dominant, as in P. M. Dawn's number one hit "Set Adrift on Memory Bliss" from its album *Of the Heart, of the Soul, and of the Cross.* Arrested Development embarked on its own spiritual quest to the homeland of their Southern ancestors in "Tennessee." Fully aware that the trees they climbed down home were the same trees their forefathers had hung from in Billie Holiday's "Strange Fruit," Arrested Development celebrated their community's survival and pledged themselves to heed its wisdom. They weren't alone. The groups associated with the Native Tongues school—A Tribe Called Quest, De La Soul, and the Jungle Brothers—wove jazz tapestries from gospel threads. A Tribe Called Quest thanked Bob Marley and nodded toward its brothers and sisters in the diaspora in "Steve Biko (Stir It Up)"; invited their audience to explore the outer reaches of consciousness in "Excursions"; sat back and grooved in "Electric Relaxation"; and convened a kind of hip-hop church in "Clap Your Hands." Tribe member Q-Tip made the group's commitment to the gospel impulse clear: "I think we—hip hop artists and the community as a whole—need to grow up. A Tribe Called Quest have always been artists who greeted a problem and never feared anyone's response—but we all need each other. I challenge every artist to be a little more aware of what's going on." Q-Tip's fellow tribesman Ali referred specifically to the need to rebuild black families: "I think hip hop has always been a reflection of whatever's going on in life. What we have now is the destruction of the family social structure. I think groups like A Tribe Called Quest or De La Soul or the Pharcyde transcend that—we're not toting guns or smoking weed—but until you have others who aren't living in a manner that's socially broken down and dysfunctional, that's going to come out in the music."

Although not formally affiliated with the Native Tongues group,

Digable Planets responded clearly to Tribe's call in "Rebirth of Slick (Cool Like Dat)" and "Where I'm From," a visionary celebration of a community that understood the openness inherent in West African philosophy. Riding a jazzy rhythm that rerouted the A train that Duke Ellington rode to the heart of Harlem to their base in Brooklyn, Digable Planets stepped off the subway platform directly onto the Mothership which delivered them safely to their corner of the gorgeous mosaic where Ahmad plays with Izzy, the brothers and sisters pass their time studying Marx and vodun, and it snows purple. Butterfly, Doodle, and Ladybug "speak in ghetto tongues cause ghetto is the life" and the "Planets pledge allegiance to the funk in all its forms." Check your stereotypes at the door and come on in.

While the redemption songs of the nineties drew inspiration from those of the freedom movement, some things had definitely changed. The most obvious shift involved the specific spiritual vocabularies of the musicians and their communities. Mahalia Jackson, Sam Cooke, and Curtis Mayfield used the tones and imagery of the black Christian church without hesitation, and their people understood. By the nineties, however, it was clear that the criticism of Christianity as a slave master's religion launched during the Black Power movement had exerted a lasting effect. With the openings created by the movement, the church did not have to fill so many functions in black communities. It became relatively less central in black life at a time churches were becoming less influential throughout American society. Although the most vocal criticism of Christianity during the eighties and nineties came from the Nation of Islam, the black community had not flocked to Louis Farrakhan's puritanical organization. For one thing, there's probably an inherent limit to the appeal of a church with the specific culinary rules of Islam. "I think the majority of black people, if you got them in a room by themselves," joked Kirk Franklin, the most important figure of nineties gospel music, "would tear up a pork chop—bacon, sausage, links, pigs feet." Amen.

Still, many African Americans did turn to orthodox Islam, which was one of the fastest-growing religions in the United States during the nineties. Others explored traditional forms of African spirituality. Many musicians followed the lead of John Coltrane, whose spiritual journey led him to every corner of the globe. The "Church of Coltrane" in San Francisco simply formalized what many already felt. Recalling Charlie Parker's identification of himself as a "devout musician," Erykah Badu's comment on her relationship to the Five

Percent Nation, an influential offshoot of the Nation of Islam which believed true spiritual insight was limited to one in twenty humans, was not at all atypical:

> I'm not a part of the organization because I don't think any one organization can define your relationship with the Creator. But I memorized and understood all the information, and I use it every day, just like I use Christian proverbs and text, Islamic proverbs and text, and Buddhist proverbs and text. Anything I can use to learn about me. I think the Creator loves that we understand to get a foundation and then to build from there. I don't stifle my creativity or my will to learn. My religion, if I have one, is probably the arts.

Without question the spiritual explorations of the younger generation shocked some of their elders. But many appreciated the impulse behind the explorations; and almost everyone understood that almost any spiritual vision was preferable to the nihilism that threatened to destroy so many communities. Kirk Franklin joined his Christian elders in his vision of Christianity as the best antidote to despair. "We've tried everything else," said Franklin. "We've tried crack; we've tried politics, this, that. But you can only drink so long, screw so long, buy so many clothes. It doesn't satisfy the total man. . . . People need to get high off something spiritual and I'm the holy dope dealer. I got this drug. I got this Jesus rock. And you can have a type of high that you've never experienced." At the same time, Franklin respected other spiritual vocabularies; he was one of the only musicians willing to appear on *The Arsenio Hall Show* the night Arsenio interviewed Farrakhan. "The Nation stands for something that's strong," he acknowledged. "And it started to stand for something strong when the church started getting weak."

Franklin's response was to do everything in his power to rekindle the church's social mission. From the time he was a youth growing up in the Greater Strangers Rest Baptist Church in a Dallas suburb, he knew that music was the key. As a teenager, Franklin began to play an active role in the church's musical life. He remembered the congregation's ambivalent reaction to the innovations that began to draw more and more young people. "I could tell, and everybody else could tell, that the way I wanted to do music was not the norm," Franklin remembered. "He's playing that piano real bluesy, and he's up in the pulpit dancing! The older people were horrified. But the majority of the younger people loved it. It gave them a chance to free themselves in worship, to cast off their cares and stand up for the first time and dance and praise."

Franklin took his approach from Dallas to the center of the gospel world, and from there reached out to audiences more at home with R & B and hip-hop. He wasn't the first gospel artist to take Sam Cooke's pioneering ideas seriously. During the sixties, the Edwin Hawkins Singers had a substantial mainstream hit with "Oh Happy Day"; the Clark Sisters' "You Brought the Sunshine" was part of the seventies disco mix; the Winans' thundering condemnation of apartheid, "Let My People Go," had gotten some airplay during the eighties; BeBe and CeCe Winans had followed the lead of Curtis Mayfield and Mavis Staples, taking their remake of "I'll Take You There" and the thinly masked gospel of "Addictive Love" and "Heaven" to the top of the R & B charts. Take 6 ("I L-O-V-E U"), Sounds of Blackness ("Optimistic"), and Soul Mission, whose "Table in the Wilderness" should have received much more attention than it did, kept up at least a quiet conversation between gospel and pop during the early nineties.

But Franklin, the guiding figure of the GospoCentric record label, made the breakthrough. Setting out to fulfill Cooke's vision of bringing real gospel to the mainstream, his groups had been getting radio play since the release of "Why We Sing" in 1993. "Stomp," released under the banner of Kirk Franklin's Nu Nation, reached out to people more at home with Puff Daddy and Babyface than the Mississippi Mass Choir and the Canton Spirituals. Powered by a sample from Funkadelic's "One Nation Under a Groove" and incorporating a guest appearance by rapper Cheryl James ("Salt" of Salt-N-Pepa), the "Stomp" video was the first gospel video to enter the heavy rotation on MTV. Franklin called it a "Holy Ghost Party" and Cooke would have approved.

Wu-Tang Clan had its own kind of party going on. Wu-Tang member Raekwon described the Clan—and the signifying on the KKK was no accident—as a group of healers, "slang doctors" who "take you on an emotional roller-coaster ride through chambers that touch parts of your mentality and make you think in certain ways. It's the way of the gods." Inspectah Deck was a bit less elevated in his style, but he made the same basic point when he attributed the group's success to its communal structure: "Nine sets of eyes and nine brains makes a big difference in this motherfucker." GZA (pronounced Jizza) described Wu-Tang's creative process as a paradoxical combination of openness and precision made possible by its collective awareness: "It's not organized with a structure. RZA [pro-nounced Rizza] will have a beat, and each individual decides whether they feel it or not. We keep it tight. The nine represent one."

There was no way to tell from the outside just how much of it was reality and how much was a conscious effort to create a Wu-Tang myth. But it may not have mattered. From their name on down to the lyrical content of songs like "Wu-Tang Revolution" and "Da Mys-tery of Chessboxin'," Wu-Tang was fully aware that the creation of community required profound acts of collective imagination. Like Kirk Franklin, Erykah Badu, the M-Base Collective, and pretty much every other black act of the nineties, they expressed their vision in spiritual terms. Like Rakim, the established rapper whose vision seemed most attuned to their own, Wu-Tang was conversant with the ideas of the Five Percent Nation, whose images echoed through songs like "Reunited" and "Older Gods." But Wu-Tang was willing and able to work jazz transformations on more or less anything that crossed their path. Taking a cue from George Clinton's manipula-tion of pop-culture images in the service of his own radical vision, Wu-Tang presented itself as a modern incarnation of the ancient masters of the Asian martial arts. Combining a near gangsta delight in images of battle with an awareness of the spiritual discipline fun-damental to the martial arts, Wu-Tang grounded the myth in a po-litical sensibility similar to that of Rage Against the Machine, with whom they toured. Hip-hop journalist Bonz Malone provided a suc-cinct summary of the Wu-Tang myth:

> In ancient times, the Shao Lin Monastery was a home for righteous monks to study Buddhism and master the martial arts for both physi-cal and mental discipline. They studied the mannerisms of reptiles and other animals, and developed superior fighting techniques. One of the deadliest of all kung fu styles was the famed Wu-Tang sword, an invincible weapon mastered only by accomplished monks. They were the guardians of humble rice farmers from the slums and villages. The monastery was a place where young kids who were tired of get-tin' beaten up in the streets could go to learn self-defense and mooch a bowl of hot soup.

Bringing the myth to life, Wu-Tang understood, required a high degree of practical knowledge, a coherent strategy for economic sur-vival in a nation whose motto—"In God We Trust"—should have been "Cash Rules Everything Around Me." Berry Gordy had known the rules of the game; Suge Knight demonstrated the cost of playing by them. Wu-Tang set out to re-create them in its own image. And, as Brer Rabbit, not to mention Berry Gordy and George Clinton, had always known, *image* was key. Getting over in Babylon required self-discipline; you could *never* make Tupac's mistake of confusing performance with authenticity. It also required the no-nonsense realism of ascent; the more you understood about the difference between the way the system described itself and the way it really worked, the better your chance of survival.

Which explains why Wu-Tang spent almost as much energy on its business enterprises as it did on its music. You could buy Wu-Wear at the Wu-Tang Boutique near Tower Records in lower Manhattan or through the Wu-Tang site on the World Wide Web. The group elevated the merchandising of its image to a minor art form. Yet their "real" faces remained relatively unknown; many hip-hop fans wouldn't have been able to pick the individual members out of a lineup, which was no doubt part of the point. The real point of Wu-Tang's economic game, however, was that it generated a jazz vision of what music journalist Mimi Valdes called "communal capitalism at its finest." According to every published report, Wu-Tang was organized along the lines of a corporate collective. While individual members were encouraged to sign distribution deals with major record companies, Wu-Tang retained full control of production. According to Valdes, proceeds from individual deals were split fifty-fifty with Wu-Tang Productions; members contributed 20 percent of all income to the collective. It amounted to a modern form of tithing, the Christian tradition of contributing 10 percent of one's crop or income to the church. Def Jam executive Russell Simmons, who'd earned his own black belt in black capitalism, praised RZA, who was generally recognized as the primary architect of Wu-Tang's music and marketing strategies, for maintaining a clear sense of the relationship between economic success and community. "[RZA's] decisions represent a positive development for a real audience," Simmons observed. "He takes risks. It shows the foundation audience you are serious about them, reminds them that they're the ones who count, who you make the music for. Creatively, he's the most important person in hip hop because he reaffirms what the culture is all about."

But if the music hadn't lived up to the myth, none of it would have amounted to more than a footnote in the ongoing story of what sociologist Robert Allen once called the *Black Awakening in Cap-*

*italist America.* Early in Wu-Tang's collective career, there had been some reasons to doubt whether it would. Following the group's debut album, *Enter the Wu-Tang: 36 Chambers,* several of the members put out solo projects (though RZA's production was a constant thread). Several of the efforts were solid and all had their moments, but none had anything approaching the power of *36 Chambers.* So it was crucial that the group's second communal album, *Wu-Tang Forever,* was a hip-hop equivalent of Stevie Wonder's *Songs in the Key of Life.*

The comparison is meant to be suggestive, not precise. The similarities rested on Wonder and Wu-Tang's shared concern with the complexity of black life, their awareness of the hopes and hardships of ordinary black people as they struggled to hold their own in a world where, as Wu-Tang rapped, "Cash Still Rules." Anyone contemplating redemption had to deal with the fact that "still don't nothin' move but the money," that, as they said in another cut, it all felt "Impossible." Both *Songs in the Key of Life* and *Wu-Tang Forever* acknowledged the crushing pressures the economic system exerted on the inner city. Taken out of context, the sequence on *Wu-Tang Forever* beginning with "Little Ghetto Boys," progressing through the harsh realism of "The City" and "The Projects," and culminating in the apocalyptic surrealism of "Hellz Wind Staff" could have been released as a gangsta nightmare on Death Row. But, like Wonder, Wu-Tang understood those moments in relation to the forces that threatened to stop the beloved community dead in its tracks. "Wu-Revolution," "Reunited," and "Triumph," a blues-gospel hybrid set to a synthesized invocation of "Wade in the Water," made it clear that Wu-Tang persisted in the redemptive spirit that kept them moving toward higher ground.

Where Wu-Tang differed most from Wonder was in its specific vision of political change. Wonder had grown up in the movement and, even in its most somber moments, his music moved with an energy that testified to his belief that, however long it took, the march would end on freedom's ground. Wu-Tang's music made it clear that the members of the Clan had come to consciousness amid the confusion and contradictions of the seventies and eighties. Their political vision was at once more aggressive and less confident; its dominant key was rage, not life.

Still, Wu-Tang avoided the nihilism and despair of its gangsta cousins, in part because of the truly communal style that marked the other major difference between *Wu-Tang Forever* and *Songs in the Key of Life*. Despite Wonder's profound love for and understanding of his people, his great albums were almost entirely individual creations. *Wu-Tang Forever* presented a more complicated, and ultimately a more realistic, model of call and response. The cost was clear. At some points, the album loses focus and seems on the verge of collapse. Some of the voices have a lot more to say than others. But that's part of the point; after all, life isn't always pretty and it often makes no sense. The whole point of call and response—its most fundamental insight into community—is that *everyone* has a voice. That includes Wu-Tang's Ol' Dirty Bastard, whose name was no mistake. (Though, tellingly, he subsequently announced that he was changing it to Big Baby Jesus.) There were times when Ol' Dirty Bastard sounded like he'd escaped from one of Ice Cube's bad dreams. But Wu-Tang's brilliance couldn't be separated from the constantly changing array of voices that entered into the conversations. Images introduced by CappaDonna, U God, or Method Man on the first disc of *Wu-Tang Forever* were likely to come back in a different key when they were reworked by GZA Raekwon, Masta Killa, or Ghostface Killah on the more tormented disc two. And while Wu-Tang continued to define itself in terms of the nine-member core, they were constantly reaching out; some of the best moments on *Wu-Tang Forever* came from "guests" Papa Wu, Uncle Pete, and Tekitha. Producer Fourth Disciple assumed RZA's role on powerful second-generation Wu albums by Killah Priest and *The Last Shall Be First* by the Sunz of Man. Yeah, there were times you could really do without another hit of Ol' Dirty Bastard, but he was part of the community, and, anyway, how the hell do you think *he* feels about *you?* There was only one way to find out, to figure out what burdens we share and what things we still needed to work through. If we didn't back off, Wu-Tang's model of the community in action implied, we just might be able to forge a plan of action that would help us find the hope to keep on pushing.

It was never more important to keep the conversation going than at the moments when it seemed to be going nowhere. As the nineties neared their end, the redemption songs continued to rise from the ghettos and the campuses; from sax players in the subway and contraltos in the cathedral; from radios on the beach and from computers downloading samples from the Web; from the elders, the ancestors, and the depths of our dreams. As the Clinton era entered its final years, the voices of the movement continued to echo, their story, against all odds, continued to be told. But its meaning was still, as always, in doubt. Reflecting on the doubt and despair and glory he heard in the black music that rings throughout this book, James Baldwin wrote: "Our history is each other. That is our only guide. One thing is absolutely certain: one can repudiate, or despise, no one's history without repudiating and despising one's own. Perhaps that is what the gospel singer is singing." Baldwin wrote those words over twenty years ago. It's been nearly three decades since Sam Cooke promised that a change was gonna come. Change came and change is coming still. Our history's still being lived. What it will be is up to us. Holler if ya hear me.

Peace.

# Notes

## GENERAL SOURCES

The best overviews of the history of American music since the fifties are Ed Ward, Geoffrey Stokes, and Ken Tucker, *Rock of Ages: The Rolling Stone History of Rock & Roll* (New York: Rolling Stone/Summit, 1986); *The Rolling Stone Illustrated History of Rock & Roll*, ed. Anthony DeCurtis and James Henke with Holly George-Warren (New York: Random House, 1992); Paul Friedlander, *Rock and Roll: A Social History* (Boulder, Colo.: Westview, 1996); Reebee Garofalo, *Rockin' Out: Popular Music in the USA* (Boston: Allyn and Bacon, 1997); Charles Gillett, *The Sound of the City: The Rise of Rock and Roll*, second edition (New York: Da Capo, 1996); and Robert Palmer, *Rock & Roll: An Unruly History* (New York: Harmony, 1995). Lucy O'Brien's *She Bop: The Definitive History of Women in Rock, Pop & Soul* (New York: Penguin, 1996) redresses earlier studies which sometimes overlooked women's contributions. Palmer's book was written as a companion to WGBH television's ten-part series *Rock & Roll*, now available in video format through the Corporation for Public Broadcasting. Another ten-part television series, Time-Life's *The History of Rock 'n' Roll*, is available through Warner Brothers video. Dafydd Rees and Luke Crampton's *Encyclopedia of Rock Stars* (New York: DK Publishing, 1996) has proven an invaluable source of factual information. The books that have had the greatest influence on my understanding of the relationships between the various currents of American music are Ralph Ellison, *Shadow and Act* (New York: Vintage, 1972); Amiri Baraka (LeRoi Jones), *Blues People: Black Music in White America* (New York: Morrow, 1963); Greil Marcus, *Mystery Train: Images of America in Rock 'n' Roll Music* (New York: Dutton, 1982); Peter Guralnick, *Sweet Soul Music: Rhythm and Blues and the Southern Dream of Freedom* (New York: Harper, 1986); and Dave Marsh, *The Heart of Rock & Soul* (New York: Plume, 1989), which, more than anything else I have read, taught me how to hear.

## SECTION ONE

## 2. Mahalia and the Movement

Basic information on the life and music of Mahalia Jackson was drawn from Jules Schwerin, *Got to Tell It: Mahalia Jackson, Queen of Gospel* (New York: Oxford UP, 1992); Laurraine Goreau, *Just Mahalia, Baby* (Waco, Tex.: Word, 1975); and Mahalia's autobiography, written with the assistance of Evan McLeod Wylie, *Movin' On Up* (New York: Hawthorn, 1966). Two useful versions of Mahalia's participation in the March on Washington can be found in *Movin' On Up,* pp. 197–200, and Taylor Branch, *Parting the Waters: America in the King Years 1954–63* (New York: Simon & Schuster, 1988), pp. 881–82. Details concerning the Nat Turner rebellion can be found in Stephen Oates, *The Fires of Jubilee: Nat Turner's Fierce Rebellion* (New York: Harper & Row, 1975).

Page 5    "I believe the blues . . .": *Movin' On Up,* p. 33.
   7    "She explained . . .": *Got to Tell It,* p. 65.
   8    "it is a guttural cry . . .": Henry Louis Gates, Jr., and Cornel West, *The Future of the Race* (New York: Knopf, 1996), pp. 81–82.

## 3. "The Soul of the Movement"

In addition to the material on Mahalia cited above, background material in this section was drawn from Jon Michael Spencer, *Protest and Praise: Sacred Music of Black Religion* (Minneapolis: Fortress Press, 1990); Bernice Johnson Reagon, "Let Your Light Shine—Historical Notes" and "Singing for My Life," both in Reagon's *We Who Believe in Freedom* (New York: Anchor, 1993), pp. 13–69 and 133–68; Pete Seeger and Bob Reiser, *Everybody Says Freedom: A History of the Civil Rights Movement in Songs and Pictures* (New York: Norton, 1989); Cornel West, "Foreword" to Richard Newman, *Go Down, Moses: Celebrating the African-American Spiritual* (New York: Clarkson Potter, 1997); Reagon's liner notes to *Voices of the Civil Rights Movement: Black American Freedom Songs 1960–1966* (Smithsonian CD SF 40084); Reagon's essay "Women as Culture Carriers in the Civil Rights Movement: Fannie Lou Hamer" in *Women in the Civil Rights Movement,* ed. Vicki L. Crawford, Jacqueline Anne Rouse, and Barbara Woods (Bloomington: Indiana UP, 1993); and Michelle Harris, *Searching for Meaning Beyond the Spiritual* (M.A. thesis, U of Wisconsin, 1993). A new movement among historians of the freedom movement has established the centrality of local communities to the freedom movement. See especially John Dittmer, *Local People: The Struggle for Civil Rights in Mississippi* (Urbana: U of Illinois Press, 1994); and Charles Payne, *I've Got the Light of Freedom: The Organizing Tradition and the Mississippi Freedom Struggle* (Berkeley: U of California P, 1995).

Page 11   "bind us together . . .": Martin Luther King, Jr., *Why We Can't Wait* (New York: Mentor, 1964), p. 61.
   12    For a thorough overview of Baker's career, including both quotations in this section, see Barbara Ransby's entry on Baker in *Black Women in America: An Historical Encyclopedia,* ed. Darlene Clark Hine (Brooklyn: Carlson, 1993), pp. 70-74.

12    "The fear down here . . .": *Protest and Praise*, p. 91.

12    "Without these songs . . .": *Protest and Praise*, p. 90.

12    "She urged us . . .": *We Who Believe*, p. 22.

13    "They sang as they were dragged . . .": *Voices of the Civil Rights Movement*, p. 6.

13    "I sat in a church . . .": *Voices of the Civil Rights Movement*, p. 2.

13    "gospel music had given . . .": *Movin' On Up*, p. 174.

13    "We don't have to sweat . . .": *Movin' On Up*, p. 175.

13    "With the need . . .": *Voices of the Civil Rights Movement*, p. 13.

14    "When Mrs. Hamer . . .": *Protest and Praise*, p. 88.

14    "It *is* the basic way . . .": *Got to Tell It*, p. 35.

## 4. Motown: Money, Magic, and the Mask

Nelson George's *Where Did Our Love Go?: The Rise and Fall of the Motown Sound* (New York: St. Martin's, 1985) remains the best introduction to the history of Berry Gordy's label. Gerri Hirshey's *Nowhere to Run: The Story of Soul Music* (New York: Penguin, 1984) includes a useful discussion of Motown. Among the many biographies and autobiographies of Motown artists that have been appearing over the past twenty years, the following provided specific information used in the discussions of Motown in this book: Berry Gordy, *To Be Loved: The Music, The Magic, The Memories of Motown* (New York: Time Warner, 1994); David Ritz, Susan Whitall, *Women of Motown: An Oral History* (New York: Avon, 1998); *Divided Soul: The Life of Marvin Gaye* (New York: Da Capo, 1991); Mary Wilson with Patricia Romanowski and Ahrgus Julliard, *Dream Girl* (New York: St. Martin's 1986); Otis Williams with Patricia Romanowski, *Temptations* (New York: Simon & Schuster, 1989); Martha Reeves with Mark Bego, *Dancing in the Street: Confessions of a Motown Diva* (New York: Hyperion, 1994); Smokey Robinson with David Ritz, *Smokey: Inside My Life* (London: Headline, 1989); and J. Randy Taraborelli's two celebrity biographies, *Call Her Miss Ross: The Unauthorized Biography of Diana Ross* (New York: Ballantine, 1989) and *Michael Jackson: The Magic and the Madness* (New York: Birch Lane, 1991). *The Motown Album* (New York: St. Martin's, 1990) is a compilation of photographs that provides a good sense of the label's "magical" feel during the early years. The material concerning Mahalia Jackson is derived from Jules Schwerin, *Got to Tell It: Mahalia Jackson, Queen of Gospel* (New York: Oxford UP, 1992). The material concerning James Brown is derived from James Brown with Bruce Tucker, *James Brown: The Godfather of Soul* (New York: Thunder's Mouth, 1990).

Page 16    The definition of *ascent* is derived from Robert Stepto, *From Behind the Veil: A Study of Afro-American Narrative* (Urbana: U of Illinois Press, 1979), p. 167.

17    "In the music business . . .": *To Be Loved*, p. 95.

17    "We didn't do right . . .": *Got to Tell It*, p. 121.

17    "James Brown is totally committed . . .": *Godfather of Soul*, p. 203.
18    "I'd rather play . . .": *Godfather of Soul*, p. 249.
18    "made too much money . . .": *Where Did Our Love Go?* p. 6.
18    "I was broke . . .": *Where Did Our Love Go?* p. 26.
19    "A producer or a singer . . .": *Temptations*, p. 157.
20    "My feel was always . . .": *Where Did Our Love Go?* p. 110.
21    "must go down . . .": *Temptations*, p. 91.
21    "These musicians were responsible . . .": *Dancing in the Street*, p. 104.
21–22  Both Martha Reeves quotes are from *Dancing in the Street*, p. 67; Otis Williams's tribute is from *Temptations*, pp. 50–51.

## 5. *The Big Chill* vs. *Cooley High*

Useful material concerning the demographics of black Chicago in the post–World War II era can be found in Nicholas Lemann, *The Promised Land: The Great Black Migration and How It Changed America* (New York: Vintage, 1992) and the introductory chapters of Daniel Wolff's *You Send Me: The Life and Times of Sam Cooke* (New York: William Morrow, 1995). LeAlan Jones and Lloyd Newman provide a sobering portrait of life in contemporary black Chicago in *Our America: Life and Death on the South Side of Chicago* (New York: Scribner, 1997), written with the assistance of David Isay. The description of the Motown Revue in Memphis is drawn from Martha Reeves's *Dancing in the Street* (pp. 77–78).

Page 26   "happy songs are happy . . .": James Baldwin, *Collected Essays* (New York: Library of America, 1997), p. 311.
27   "I saw Motown . . .": *To Be Loved*, p. 249.

### The Gospel Impulse

The standard source of information concerning gospel music is Anthony Heilbut's *The Gospel Sound: Good News and Bad Times*, revised edition (New York: Limelight, 1985). For a sense of the importance of religious music in black culture see Bessie Jones, *For the Ancestors: Autobiographical Memoirs* (Urbana: U of Illinois Press, 1983); Ralph Ellison, "When the Spirit Moves Mahalia" in *Shadow and Act*; and Leon Forrest, "Souls in Motion" in *The Furious Voice of Freedom* (New York: Moyer, Bell, 1996).

Page 28   "I have never seen . . .": James Baldwin, *The Fire Next Time* in *Baldwin: Collected Essays* (New York: Library of America, 1998), p. 306.
29   "Gospel songs are the songs . . .": Mahalia Jackson, *Movin' On Up*, p. 72.
29   "Gospel and the blues . . .": Ray Charles quoted in the liner notes to *The Birth of Soul* (Atlantic Records 82310).

30    "Music is healing . . .": Mavis Staples, personal interview with the author, March 1997.

## 6. Sam Cooke and the Voice of Change

Those interested in Sam Cooke's life and music have been blessed with Daniel Wolff's sensitive biography *You Send Me: The Life and Times of Sam Cooke* (New York: William Morrow, 1995), which incorporates almost all information previously available from other sources.

Page 31    "in trying to dodge . . .": *You Send Me*, p. 99.
33    "jammed not only with Negro fans . . .": *Parting the Waters*, p. 792.
34    "He and his boys . . .": "Sonny's Blues" in *Baldwin: Early Novels and Stories* (New York: Library of America, 1998), p. 892.
34    "Help save the youth . . .": quoted in Philip Norman, *Symphony for the Devil: The Rolling Stones Story* (New York: Linden, 1984), p. 38.
35    "When Sam took hold . . .": *You Send Me*, p. 100.

## 7. Solid Gold Coffins

Ronnie Spector tells her story in *Be My Baby* (New York: Harper, 1991). Information concerning Tina Turner is derived from Chris Welch, *The Tina Turner Experience* (London: Virgin, 1986); Turner's autobiography, *I, Tina* (New York: Avon, 1986), written with Kurt Loder; and the Time-Life *History of Rock 'n' Roll: Rock 'n' Roll Explodes* (Warner W13860). Numerous Motown memoirs touch on Tammi Terrell at least briefly. I have relied primarily on Berry Gordy's *To Be Loved*, David Ritz's *Divided Soul: The Life of Marvin Gaye*, and James Brown's *James Brown: The Godfather of Soul*.

Page 38    "how fanatical Phil was . . .": *Be My Baby*, p. 48.
38    "I'm completely prepared . . .": *Be My Baby*, p. 199.
38    "Cotton, I hated it . . .": *Rock 'n' Roll Explodes* video.
39    "a kid that people ran . . .": *Godfather of Soul*, p. 141.
39    "Tammi was the kind . . .": *Divided Soul*, p. 111.

## 8. SAR and the Ambiguity of Integration

In addition to Wolff's *You Send Me*, Peter Guralnick's liner notes to *Sam Cooke's SAR Records Story* (ABKCO 2231-2) is a crucial source of information concerning the material covered in this section. Bobby Womack confirmed material concerning Cooke's life and personal character in a personal interview with the author, August 1998.

Page 40    "greatest rock and roll . . .": *You Send Me*, p. 295.
41    "Young people like us . . .": *You Send Me*, pp. 238–39.

41    "I'll never forget . . .": *You Send Me*, p. 215.

41    "Sam was deep . . .": *You Send Me*, p. 290.

41–42  Both Womack quotes are from *Sam Cooke's SAR*, p. 57.

42    "Real gospel music . . .": *Sam Cooke's SAR*, p. 54.

42    "He said, 'Bobby . . .": *Sam Cooke's SAR*, p. 67.

42    "We knew because . . .": *Sam Cooke's SAR*, pp. 42–43.

43    "If you can understand . . .": *You Send Me*, p. 297.

43    "Oh yeah, I was a Sam Cooke fan . . .": personal interview with the author, Atlanta, Feb. 1997.

43    "Sam told me . . .": *Sam Cooke's SAR*, p. 40.

44    Cooke's conversation with Womack is reported in *Sam Cooke's SAR*, p. 63.

## 9. "The Times They Are A-Changin' "

The best history of SDS, including a complete text of the Port Huron Statement, is James Miller, *"Democracy Is in the Streets": From Port Huron to the Siege of Chicago* (New York: Simon & Schuster, 1987). Terry Anderson's *The Movement and the Sixties* (New York: Oxford UP, 1995) and Todd Gitlin's *The Sixties: Years of Hope, Days of Rage* (New York: Bantam, 1987) provide alternative perspectives on the events swirling around SDS. On Freedom Summer, see Doug McAdams, *Freedom Summer* (New York: Oxford, 1988). Among the many biographies and memoirs focusing on folk revivalists who took an active role in the movement, the most useful is Joan Baez, *And a Voice to Sing With* (New York: Summit, 1987).

Page 45  "Bringing people out . . .": *Democracy Is in the Streets*, p. 331.

45    "events too troubling . . .": *Democracy Is in the Streets*, p. 329.

45    "the tradition of civic . . .": *Democracy Is in the Streets*, p. 16.

46    "It has been said . . .": *Democracy Is in the Streets*, p. 353.

46    "looking like a strange mixture . . .": Elizabeth Sutherland, ed., *Letters from Mississippi* (New York: McGraw Hill, 1965), p. 25.

47    "They looked particularly pasty . . .": *And a Voice*, p. 110.

48    Baraka's comments on black Bohemians can be found in the "Music" chapter of *The Autobiography of LeRoi Jones/Amiri Baraka* (New York: Freundlich, 1984), pp. 48–62.

## 10. Woody and Race

The standard biography of Woody Guthrie is Joe Klein, *Woody Guthrie: A Life* (New York: Knopf, 1980). Both Woody's autobiography, *Bound for Glory* (New York: Plume, 1983; originally published 1943), and Jim Longhi's memoir *Woody, Cisco, and Me: Seamen Three in the Merchant Marine* (Urbana: U of Illinois P, 1997) present unique perspectives on Woody's racial politics.

Page 49    "You were getting along . . .": *Woody Guthrie,* p. 95.
    50    "I could see . . .": *Bound for Glory,* p. 19.
50–51    Longhi's report on the incident in the toilet of the ship can be found in *Woody, Cisco, and Me,* pp. 230–39.
    52    For information on the FBI training program, see Taylor Branch, *Parting the Waters,* p. 209.

## 11. "Blowin' in the Wind"

For information concerning the folk revival, see David Cantwell, *When We Were Good: The Folk Revival* (Cambridge, Mass.: Harvard UP, 1996), and Jerome Rodnitzky, *Minstrels of the Dawn* (Chicago: Nelson-Hall, 1976). On Dylan's relationship to the folk revival, see Bob Spitz, *Dylan: A Biography* (New York: Norton, 1989).

Page 54    "My audiences thank . . .": *When We Were Good,* pp. 336–37.
    54    "utterly pure . . .": *When We Were Good,* p. 338.
    55    "Images of the kids . . .": *And a Voice,* p. 106.

## 12. Music and the Truth

There is a particularly rich literature focusing on the Memphis music scene. Peter Guralnick's *Sweet Soul Music: Rhythm and Blues and the Southern Dream of Freedom* (New York: HarperCollins, 1986) provides an invaluable overview of Southern soul music while Robert Gordon's *It Came from Memphis* (Boston: Faber & Faber, 1995), James Dickerson's *Goin' Back to Memphis* (New York: Schirmer, 1996), Larry Nages, *Memphis Beat: The Lives and Times of America's Musical Crossroads* (New York: St. Martin's, 1998), and Rob Bowman's *Soulsville U.S.A.: The Story of Stax Records* (New York: Schirmer, 1997) focus specifically on Memphis. See also Dave Marsh, *Sam and Dave: An Oral History* (New York: Avon, 1998). Excellent sources concerning the roots of soul in rockabilly include Colin Escott with Martin Hawkins, *Good Rockin' Tonight: Sun Records and the Birth of Rock 'n' Roll* (New York: St. Martin's, 1991) and John Floyd, *Sun Records: An Oral History* (New York: Avon, 1998). The Time-Life videos *History of Rock 'n' Roll: Rock 'n' Roll Explodes* (Warner W13860) and *History of Rock 'n' Roll: Good Rockin' Tonight* (Warner W13861) include interviews with many of the shapers of the Memphis sound. Linda Martin and Kerry Segrave, *Anti-rock: The Opposition to Rock 'n' Roll* (New York: Da Capo, 1993) details the early attacks on rock and roll. For the political background against which the music developed, see Dan Carter's *The Politics of Rage: George Wallace, the Origins of the New Conservatism, and the Transformation of American Politics* (New York: Simon & Schuster, 1995).

Page 56    "Segregation now . . .": *Politics of Rage,* p. 11.
    56    "The power of white skin . . .": Timothy Tyson, *Radio Free Dixie*

(Chapel Hill: U of North Carolina P, 1999).

57    "Every channel of communication . . .": *Politics of Rage*, p. 115.
57    "Birmingham was dangerous . . .": *Sweet Soul Music*, pp. 192–93.
58    "waiting on him . . .": *Sweet Soul Music*, p. 193.
58    "to do away with this vulgar . . .": *Good Rockin' Tonight* video.
59    "I couldn't believe it . . .": *Sweet Soul Music*, p. 212.
59    "He used to sit . . .": *Good Rockin' Tonight*, p. 126.
59    "We didn't know nothing . . .": *Sweet Soul Music*, p. 199.
59    "Everybody learned it . . .": *It Came from Memphis*, p. 44.
60    "Gospel is the truth . . .": *Rock 'n' Roll Explodes* video.
60    "went to Memphis . . .": *Good Rockin' Tonight*, p. 1.
61–63  The historical background on Beale Street and Crump is derived primarily from *Goin' Back to Memphis* and personal interviews conducted with Furry Lewis in Memphis during 1980 and 1981.
64    "Nobody up to that time . . .": *Sam and Dave*, p. 47.

# 13. Down at the Crossroads

Peter Guralnick's *Searching for Robert Johnson* (New York: Dutton, 1989) played a crucial role in disentangling the historical Johnson from the many myths that had grown up around him. Stephen LaVere's liner notes to *Robert Johnson: The Complete Recordings* (Columbia C2K46222) are currently the best synthesis of what has been learned about Johnson. The best summary of Esu-Elegba, and West African worldviews, is Robert Farris Thompson's *Flash of the Spirit: African and Afro-American Art and Philosophy* (New York: Random House, 1983).

Page 66    "that you are alone . . .": Robert Penn Warren, *All the King's Men* (New York: Harcourt Brace Jovanovich, 1946), p. 19.

## The Blues Impulse

The concept of the blues impulse originates in Ralph Ellison's essay "Richard Wright's Blues" from his collection *Shadow and Act* (New York: Vintage, 1972). Albert Murray explores the implications of Ellison's approach in *The Hero and the Blues* (Columbia: U of Missouri P, 1973) and *Stomping the Blues* (New York: Vintage, 1976). Among the many sources of basic information concerning the blues, the best introductions are Robert Palmer, *Deep Blues* (New York: Viking, 1981); William Barlow, *Looking Up at Down: The Emergence of Blues Culture* (Philadelphia: Temple UP, 1989); David Evans, *Big Road Blues: Tradition and Creativity in the Folk Blues* (Berkeley: U of California P, 1982); and Samuel Charters, *The Blues Makers* (New York: Da Capo, 1991), which collects a wide range of Charters's pioneering scholarship.

Page 68   "Sad as the blues . . .": Langston Hughes, "Songs Called the Blues" in *The Langston Hughes Reader*, ed. George Braziller (New York: Braziller, 1958), p. 159.

  68   "What gives me the blues . . .": Paul Oliver, *Conversation with the Blues* (New York: Cambridge UP, 1997), p. 20.

  69   "You know, old folks say . . .": quoted in Stanley Booth, *Rhythm Oil: A Journey through the Music of the American South* (New York: Vintage, 1993), p. 31.

  69   "Singing the blues is like . . .": quoted in *Jabberock*, ed. Raymond Obstfelder and Patricia Fitzgerald (New York: Henry Holt, 1997), p. 63.

  69   "The blues is an impulse . . .": *Shadow and Act*, pp. 78–79.

  69   "No wonder Hamlet . . .": *The Hero and the Blues*, p. 38.

  70   "the most fundamental . . .": *The Hero and the Blues*, p. 38.

  70   "Perhaps I love them . . .": Gerald Early, *Daughters: On Family and Fatherhood* (Reading, Mass.: Addison-Wesley, 1994), pp. 143–44.

## 14. Soul Food

In addition to Peter Guralnick's *Sweet Soul Music*, James Brown's *James Brown: The Godfather of Soul*, David Ritz's *Divided Soul*, Gerri Hirshey's *Nowhere to Run*, and Robert Gordon's *It Came from Memphis*, information used in this section was drawn from Jerry Wexler's *Rhythm and the Blues: A Life in American Music* (New York: Knopf, 1993), written with David Ritz; Stanley Booth's *Rhythm Oil: A Journey through the Music of the American South* (New York: Vintage, 1993); and Rob Bowman's thorough liner notes to *The Complete Stax Singles 1959–1968* (Stax 782218). Nelson George's *The Death of Rhythm and Blues* (New York: Pantheon, 1988) contains a useful discussion of black radio during the postwar years.

Page 72   "It wasn't Chicago . . .": *Nowhere to Run*, p. 294.

  72   "Gospel is contentment . . .": *Godfather of Soul*, p. 42.

  72   "The word soul . . .": *Godfather of Soul*, p. 173.

  74   "There were a lot of white people . . .": *It Came from Memphis*, pp. 166–67.

  74   "where all the black bands . . .": *It Came from Memphis*, p. 61.

  74   "We worked the chitlin circuit . . .": *Sweet Soul Music*, pp. 118–19.

  75   "I must have played . . .": *Sweet Soul Music*, p. 264.

  75   "The Memphis sound . . .": *It Came from Memphis*, pp. 249–50.

  77   "Aren't you glad you recut it . . .": *Sweet Soul Music*, p. 210.

  77   "We were basically . . .": *Stax Singles 1959–1968*, p. 33.

  77   "Part of what eventually evolved . . .": *Stax Singles 1959–1968*, p. 16.

  78   "We'd play a Temptations record . . .": *Sweet Soul Music*, p. 197.

  78   "It wasn't really a rivalry . . .": Curtis Mayfield interview with the

author, Atlanta, Feb. 1997.
78   "most beautiful guitar . . .": *Stax Singles 1959–1968*, p. 17.
78   "The era was changing . . .": *Divided Soul*, p. 119.

## 15. Dylan, the Brits, and Blue-Eyed Soul

Along with Spitz's biography of Dylan, this section draws on Greil Marcus's *Invisible Republic: Bob Dylan's Basement Tapes* (New York: Henry Holt, 1997); Philip Norman's *Symphony for the Devil: The Rolling Stones Story* (New York: Linden, 1984); Stanley Booth's *The True Adventures of the Rolling Stones* (New York: Vintage, 1985); James Brown's *James Brown: Godfather of Soul;* and several videos from the *Time-Life History of Rock 'n' Roll* and the WGBH series *Rock & Roll.* Keith Richards recounts his meeting with Mick Jagger in an interview with Robert Greenfield reprinted in *The Rolling Stone Interviews 1967–1980* (New York: St. Martin's, 1981). Information concerning the position of records on the popular and black charts was provided by Joel Whitburn's *Billboard's Top Pop Singles 1955–1993* (Menominee Falls, Wis.: Record Research, Inc., 1994) and *Billboard's Top R&B Singles 1942–1995* (Menominee Falls, Wis.: Record Research, Inc., 1996). The latter volume includes a discussion of the changing name and nature of the black charts. The videos *The History of Rock 'n' Roll: The Sounds of Soul* (Warner W13864), *Rock & Roll: Shakespeares in the Alley* (WGBH video WGRRO2), and *Rock & Roll: Crossroads* (WGBH video WGRRO3) present interviews with many of those who participated in the events covered in this section.

Page 80   "twisted Jewish equivalent . . .": *Shakespeares* video.
80   "How do you know I'm not . . .": *Invisible Republic,* p. 55.
81   "If I heard John Lee Hooker . . .": *Crossroads* video.
82   "a genuine underground . . .": *Crossroads* video.
82   "I get on this train . . .": *Rolling Stone Interviews,* p. 151.
83   "helped us carry our gear . . .": *Symphony for the Devil,* p. 125.
83   "The Stones had come out . . .": *Godfather of Soul,* p. 153.
83   "had a real appreciation . . .": *Godfather of Soul,* p. 162.
84   "real black . . .": *Good Rockin' Tonight* video.
84   "One thing we're most proud of . . .": *Sounds of Soul* video.

## 16. The Minstrel Blues

The standard works on minstrelsy are Berndt Ostendorf's *Black Literature in White America* (Totowa, N.J.: Barnes and Noble, 1982), Robert Toll's *Blacking Up* (New York: Oxford UP, 1974), and Eric Lott's *Love and Theft: Blackface Minstrelsy and the American Working Class* (New York: Oxford UP, 1993). Ralph Ellison provides insightful perspectives on the minstrel dynamic in "Change the Joke and Slip the Yoke" in *Shadow and Act* (New York: Random House, 1964) and "An Extravagance of Laughter" in *Going to the Territory* (New York: Random House, 1986). Ben E. King's comments on the impact of the British Invasion on black singers are from an interview on the video *Rock & Roll: In the Groove* (WGBH video WG2201). W. T. Lhamon, Jr., *Raising Cain: Blackface Performance from Jim Crow to Hip Hop* (Cambridge, Mass.: Harvard UP, 1998) explores the links between the minstrel dynamic in different historical periods.

Page 85   "It was as though . . .": *Going to the Territory,* p. 194.
    86   "there was no separation . . .": *In the Groove* video.

## 17. Otis, Jimi, and the Summer of Love

Background information on Woodstock and Monterey can be found in *Rock of Ages.* Both Peter Guralnick's *Sweet Soul Music* and the essays by Carol Cooper, Steve Greenberg, and especially Jamie Wolf included in the liner notes to the *Otis!* box set (Rhino CD R2/R4 71439) address Otis Redding's relationship to the counterculture audience. Every Hendrix biography gives detailed attention to both Monterey and Woodstock. The most insightful treatments are in David Henderson's *'Scuse Me While I Kiss the Sky: The Life of Jimi Hendrix* (New York: Bantam, 1981) and Charles Shaar Murray's brilliant *Crosstown Traffic: Jimi Hendrix and the Rock 'n' Roll Revolution* (New York: St. Martin's, 1989).

Page 90   "This song is a song . . .": *Sweet Soul Music,* p. 320.
    91   "psychedelic Uncle Tom . . .": *Rock of Ages,* p. 376.
    93   "Hendrix knew who I was . . .": *Rock of Ages,* p. 377.
    93   "Oh yeah? I'll autograph it . . .": *Crosstown Traffic,* p. 91.
    93   "I think the difference . . .": *Crosstown Traffic,* p. 91.

## 18. Last Thoughts on the Dream

The only extended treatment of Dorothy Love Coates is in Anthony Heilbut's *The Gospel Sound.* The information on Diana Ross's childhood is derived from Ross's memoirs *Secrets of a Sparrow* (New York: Villard, 1993), J. Randy Taraborelli's *Call Her Miss Ross,* and Berry Gordy's *To Be Loved.*

Page 97   "On nights, I'd sing . . .": *The Gospel Sound,* p. 168.
    97   "Man thinks he's so grand . . .": *The Gospel Sound,* p. 169.
    98   "At that time, a bad stigma . . .": *Call Her Miss Ross,* p. 26.
    98   "Not all of us kids . . .": *Call Her Miss Ross,* pp. 25–26.

## SECTION TWO

## 19. Sly in the Smoke

For a harrowing overview of the rise and fall of Sly and the Family Stone, see Joel Selvin, *Sly and the Family Stone: An Oral History* (New York: Avon, 1998).

## 20. Death Warrants

Kenneth O'Reilly's *Nixon's Piano: Presidents and Racial Politics from Washington to Clinton* (New York: The Free Press, 1995) contains a useful overview of Lyndon Johnson's administration, as does Allen J. Matusow's *The Unraveling of America: A History of Liberalism in the 1960s* (New York: Harper, 1984). Johnson's memoirs *The Vantage Point: Perspectives of the Presidency* (New York: Holt, Rinehart, Winston, 1971) include fascinating meditations on his thoughts at the time. Dan Carter's *The Politics of Rage: George Wallace, the Origins of the New Conservatism, and the Transformation of American Politics* (New York: Simon & Schuster, 1995) chronicles the ways Johnson's opponents capitalized on his commitment to civil rights. Howard Zinn's *A People's History of the United States* (New York: Harper & Row, 1990), Harvard Sitkoff's *The Struggle for Black Equality 1954–1980*, and Richard Goodwin's *Remembering America: A Voice from the Sixties* (Boston: Little, Brown, 1988) are useful sources of information concerning the relationship between Johnson's domestic politics and the war in Vietnam. Michael R. Beschloss's *Taking Charge: The Johnson White House Tapes, 1963–1964* (New York: Simon & Schuster, 1997) is a sobering record of Johnson's private doubts concerning the war. Martin Luther King, Jr.'s speech against the war is reprinted in *A Testament of Hope: The Essential Writings and Speeches of Martin Luther King, Jr.*, edited by James M. Washington (San Francisco: HarperSan Francisco, 1986).

Page 106   For Johnson's comments on the political impact of the civil rights legislation, see Joseph Califano, *Triumph and Tragedy* (New York: Simon & Schuster, 1991), p. 55; and Nicholas Lemann, *The Promised Land*, p. 183.

106   "More and more Republicans . . .": *Vantage Point*, p. 178.

106   "the goddamnedest commitment . . .": *Nixon's Piano*, p. 254.

107   "There is no Negro problem . . .": *Nixon's Piano*, p. 254.

107   "a picture of blacks and whites . . .": *Vantage Point*, p. 165.

107   "Their cause must be . . .": *Vantage Point*, p. 165.

107   "Nigger, nigger, nigger . . .": *Nixon's Piano*, p. 243.

107   "If I hadn't left . . .": *Nixon's Piano*, p. 253.

108   "The Administration simply must choose . . .": *Remembering the Sixties*, p. 418.

108 "the bombs in Vietnam . . .": *The Struggle for Black Equality*, p. 219.

108 "I don't think it's worth fighting for . . .": *Taking Charge*, p. 370.

108 "A time comes . . .": *Testament*, p. 231.

109 "King was the person . . .": *Nixon's Piano*, p. 261.

## 21. "All Along the Watchtower"

Wallace Terry's *Bloods: An Oral History of the Vietnam War by Black Veterans* (New York: Random House, 1984) remains the best source concerning blacks in Vietnam. James Westheider, *Fighting on Two Fronts: African Americans and the Vietnam War* (New York: New York U Press, 1997) provides a more scholarly overview. Wallace Terry, "Bringing the War Home," *The Black Scholar* 2 (Nov. 1970), pp. 6–16, presents the results of Terry's extensive interviews with black servicemen during a crucial period. Colin Powell's *My American Journey* (New York: Random House, 1995) and Terry Whitmore's *Memphis Nam Sweden: The Story of a Black Deserter* ( Jackson: U of Mississippi, 1997) view the war from radically different perspectives. Roger Steffens's observations on the central role Jimi Hendrix's music played for many soldiers in Vietnam are included in "Nine Meditations on Jimi and Nam" in *The Ultimate Experience*, ed. Adrian Boot and Chris Salewicz (New York: Macmillan, 1995). Michael Herr's *Dispatches* (New York: Knopf, 1977) and Gloria Emerson's *Winners and Losers: Battles, Retreats, Gains, Losses, and Ruins from the Vietnam War* (New York: Random House, 1976) give a strong sense of how disorienting the war could be. In Stanley Karnow's *Vietnam* (New York: Viking, 1983), Zinn, Boskin, and Strauss all address the extent and nature of fragging. Nicholas Biddle's unpublished essay "Vietnam Veterans, the War, and Its Legacy" (Timothy Tyson archive, Madison, Wis., folder X 28731) is a rich source of firsthand accounts of fragging and the reception of black veterans when they returned to the United States.

Page 110 "millions of little deaths . . .": "Against the War in Vietnam," in Wendell Berry, *Collected Poems, 1957–1987* (North Point Press, 1985), p. 28.

111 "We didn't have racial incidents . . .": *Bloods*, p. 25.

111 "My first inclination . . .": *Bloods*, p. 167.

112 "Bases like Duc Pho . . .": *My American Journey*, p. 133.

112 "Both blacks and whites . . .": *My American Journey*, p. 133.

112 "Things got so bad . . .": "Vietnam Veterans, the War," p. 30.

113 "bland, censorious . . .": *Ultimate Experience*, p. 115.

113 "Unplugged the stereo . . .": *Jet* 39 (Feb. 4, 1971), p. 29.

113 "Jimi gave us the melody . . .": *Ultimate Experience*, p. 113.

113 "He represented a way . . .": *Ultimate Experience*, p. 118.

115 "I'm sure you killed babies . . .": "Vietnam Veterans, the War," p. 37.

115 "When I came home . . .": *Bloods*, p. 104.
115 "The women wouldn't talk . . .": *Bloods*, p. 122.
115 "Whenever the Ku Kluxers . . .": *Bloods*, p. 154.
115 "Rifles, guns . . .": *Bloods*, p. 261.

## 22. 'Retha, Rap, and Revolt
## and
## 23. "Spirit in the Dark"

The standard historical work on the Black Power movement is William Van Deburg's *New Day in Babylon: The Black Power Movement and American Culture, 1965–1975* (Chicago: U of Chicago P, 1992). The most inclusive collection of statements from participants in the Black Arts Movement remains *The Black Aesthetic*, ed. Addison Gayle, Jr. (Garden City, N.Y.: Anchor, 1972), which includes both Karenga's "Black Cultural Nationalism" (pp. 31–37) and Baraka's "The Changing Same (R&B and New Black Music)" (pp. 112–25). Aretha Franklin is discussed in every history of soul music, but the best sources are Peter Guralnick's *Sweet Soul Music* and Mark Bego's biography *Aretha Franklin: Queen of Soul* (London: Robert Hale, 1990). The video *Aretha Franklin: The Queen of Soul* (VPI video 50188-3) documents Aretha's dynamic performing style and includes interviews with many of her contemporaries.

Page 116 "me and the majority . . .": *Queen of Soul*, p. 145.
116 "Mrs. [Fannie Lou] Hamer . . .": Charles Payne, *I've Got the Light of Freedom*, p. 363.
118 "The three-week trek . . .": Timothy Tyson, "Civil Rights Movement" in *The Oxford Companion to African American Literature*, ed. William Andrews, Frances Smith Foster, and Trudier Harris (New York: Oxford UP, 1997), pp. 150–51.
119 *Slave Ship* is included in Baraka's collection *The Motion of History and Other Plays* (New York: William Morrow, 1978).
119 Karenga's definition of black art and his repudiation of the blues are included in his essay "Black Cultural Nationalism."
119 "as you change the time . . .": Willie Dixon with Don Snowden, *I Am the Blues: The Willie Dixon Story* (New York: Da Capo, 1989).
120 Baraka's analysis of the revolutionary potential of black music is drawn from his essay "The Changing Same (R&B and New Black Music)."
121 "You'd hear Aretha . . .": quoted in Ann Powers, "Aretha Franklin" in *The Rolling Stone Book of Women in Rock*, ed. Barbara O'Dair (New York: Random House, 1997), p. 93.
121 "People were dancing . . .": *Sweet Soul Music*, p. 345.
122 "Dr. King was a wonderful . . .": *Queen of Soul*, p. 109.

122  "this was a 'love wave' . . .": *Queen of Soul,* p. 108.
122  "I suppose the revolution . . .": *Queen of Soul,* p. 145.

## 24. Jazz Warriors .

Alan W. Barnett's lavishly illustrated *Community Murals: The People's Art* (Philadelphia: The Art Alliance Press, 1984) is the standard source of images from and analysis of the mural movement. *The Autobiography of Malcolm X,* written with Alex Haley (New York: Ballantine, 1973) remains a primary point of reference for understanding Black Power. Eric Nisenson's *Ascension: John Coltrane and His Quest* (New York: St. Martin's, 1993) introduces Coltrane's music in a manner accessible to listeners with little experience listening to jazz. Miles Davis comments at length on Coltrane's influence on his own music in *Miles: The Autobiography* (New York: Simon & Schuster, 1990), written with Quincy Troupe. *The Jazz Poetry Anthology,* edited by Sascha Feinstein and Yusef Komunyakaa (Bloomington: Indiana UP, 1991) and *Moment's Notice: Jazz in Poetry and Prose,* edited by Art Lange and Nathaniel Mackey (Minneapolis: Coffee House Press, 1993) include numerous tributes to both Coltrane and Miles. Studies that develop the approach to black music as a revolutionary force include Amiri Baraka and Amina Baraka, *The Music: Reflections on Jazz and Blues* (New York: Morrow, 1987) and Frank Kofsky, *Black Nationalism and the Revolution in Music* (New York: Pathfinder, 1970).

Page 126  "The white man . . .": *Autobiography of Malcolm X,* p. 381.
126  "The only thing I considered . . .": *Autobiography of Malcolm X,* p. 391.
127  "I'm telling it like it *is* . . .": *Autobiography of Malcolm X,* p. 273.
127  "In the past . . .": *Autobiography of Malcolm X,* p. 362.
128  "Work in conjunction . . .": *Autobiography of Malcolm X,* p. 377.
129  "Our cultural revolution . . .": Malcolm X, *By Any Means Necessary,* ed. George Breitman (New York: Pathfinder, 1970), pp. 53–54.
129  "Working with Monk . . .": *Ascension,* p. 45.
130  "represented, for many blacks . . .": *Miles,* p. 286.
130  "backward cultural nationalist . . .": *Jazz Poetry,* p. 6.
130  "a way of escape . . .": *Moment's Notice,* p. 264.

### The Jazz Impulse

Ralph Ellison provides the basic concepts behind the jazz impulse in *Shadow and Act.* Ben Sidran, *Black Talk* (New York: Da Capo, 1981) and Amiri Baraka (LeRoi Jones), *Blues People: Negro Music in White America* (New York: William Morrow, 1963) present jazz history in ways that emphasize the political implications implicit in Ellison's approach.

Page 132 "True jazz is an art . . .": *Shadow and Act*, p. 234.
   133 "[T]he slaves were only able . . .": *Black Talk*, p. 14.
   134 "Charlie Parker? . . .": Amiri Baraka, *Dutchman* in *The Norton Anthology of African-American Literature*, ed. Henry Louis Gates, Jr., and Nellie McKay (New York: Norton, 1997), p. 1897.
   135 "A percussive truthfulness . . .": Yusef Komunyakaa, "It's Always Night," *Caliban* 4 (1988), p. 52.

## 25. "Black Is an' Black Ain't"

The information in this section concerning Miles Davis is drawn from *Miles: The Autobiography*; Eric Nisenson's *'Round About Midnight: A Portrait of Miles Davis* (New York: Da Capo, 1996); Stuart Nicholson, *Jazz Rock: A History* (New York: Schirmer, 1998); and *The Miles Davis Companion*, ed. Gary Carner (New York: Schirmer, 1996). The material on Jimi Hendrix can be found in *The Ultimate Experience*, ed. Adrian Boot and Chris Salewicz; Jon Pareles, "The Jazz Generation Pays Tribute to Jimi Hendrix"; and Bill Milkowski, "Jimi Hendrix: The Jazz Connection." The latter two are reprinted in *The Jimi Hendrix Companion*, ed. Chris Potash (New York: Schirmer, 1996). Material concerning James Brown's impact on African music can be found in Chris Stapleton and Chris May's *African Rock: The Pop Music of a Continent* (New York: Dutton, 1990).

Page 137 "Black is an' black ain't . . .": Ralph Ellison, *Invisible Man* (New York: Vintage, 1990), p. 9.
   138 "When people talk . . .": *Godfather of Soul*, p. 120.
   138 "There was one sound . . .": *Godfather of Soul*, p. 119.
   138 "My whole generation . . .": *African Pop*, p. 308.
   138 "The attack was heavy . . .": *African Pop*, p. 65.
   139 "My favorite music . . .": *'Round About Midnight*, p. 232.
   139 "down into a deep African thing . . .": *Miles*, p. 329.
   139 "Everyone adds, everyone responds . . .": *'Round About Midnight*, p. 220.
   140 "I got further and further . . .": *Miles*, p. 174.
   140 "Jazz is ignored . . .": *Miles*, p. 380.
   140 "I just told them . . .": *Miles*, p. 117.
   141 "We were playing . . .": *Miles*, p. 301.
   141 "The first guitarist . . .": *Ultimate Experience*, p. 21.
   141 "It's not an act . . .": *Ultimate Experience*, p. 33.
   141 "Music is very serious . . .": *Ultimate Experience*, p. 33.
   141 "With the pyschedelics . . .": personal interview with the author, Atlanta, Feb. 1997.
   142 "Jimi was definitely . . .": *Hendrix Companion*, p. 165.
   142 "The background of our music . . .": *Ultimate Experience*, p. 234.
   142 "When I was staying in Harlem . . .": *Ultimate Experience*, p. 73.

142 "He liked the way Coltrane . . .": *Miles,* p. 292.
143 "I'd play him a record . . .": *Miles,* p. 293.
143 "playing that funky . . .": *Miles,* p. 384.
143 "When the last American tour . . .": *Hendrix Companion,* p. 97.
143 "I want a big band . . .": *Hendrix Companion,* p. 97.
144 "The main thing . . .": *Hendrix Companion,* p. 103.

## 26. Curtis Mayfield's Gospel Soul

All quotations in this section come from a series of personal interviews with Curtis Mayfield conducted by the author in Atlanta during February 1997. Additional information concerning Mayfield and the Impressions can be found in David Nathan's liner notes to *People Get Ready! The Curtis Mayfield Story* (Rhino R2 72262) and Robert Pruter's *Chicago Soul* (Urbana: U of Illinois P, 1992) and *Doowop: The Chicago Scene* (Urbana: U of Illinois P, 1996).

## 27. John Fogerty and the Mythic South

For additional information concerning Fogerty and Creedence Clearwater Revival, see Hank Bordowitz's *Bad Moon Rising: The Unauthorized History of Creedence Clearwater Revival* (New York: Simon & Schuster, 1998) and Craig Werner, *Up Around the Bend: The Oral History of Credence Clearwater Revival* (New York: Avon, 1999). All quotes from members of CCR included in this section are from the latter. Except where noted, all quotes from John Fogerty are from a personal interview with the author held in Chicago in June 1997. For information concerning Harry Smith's *Anthology of American Folk Music* see Greil Marcus, *Invisible Republic: Bob Dylan's Basement Tapes* (New York: Holt, 1997), pp. 87–126.

Page 153 "One could experience a freedom . . .": *Invisible Republic,* p. 122.
    157 "I see things . . .": "Lean, Clean and Bluesy," *Time,* 27 June 1969, p. 58.
    158 "there's this guy . . .": Dave DiMartino, "Swamp Thing," *Rolling Stone,* 26 June 1997, p. 23.

## 28. "Trouble Comin' Every Day"

Kenneth O'Reilly's *Nixon's Piano* and two books by Dan Carter—*The Politics of Rage* and *From George Wallace to Newt Gingrich: Race in the Conservative Counterrevolution 1963–1994* (Baton Rouge: Louisiana State UP, 1996)—provide a harrowing overview of the role of race in American politics of the sixties and seventies. On the 1968 Democratic Convention, see David Farber, *Chicago '68* (Chicago: U of Chicago P, 1988). Material on country musicians' responses to political issues of the time can be found in Merle Haggard's *Sing Me Back Home: My Story,* written with Peggy Russell (New York: Pocket Books,

1981) and Loretta Lynn's *Loretta Lynn: Coal Miner's Daughter*, written with George Vecsey (Chicago: Regnery, 1976). Charley Pride's *Pride: The Charley Pride Story*, written with Jim Henderson (New York: Quill, 1994), provides an interesting look at the place of black performers in country.

Page 159 "Each individual in the crowd . . .": Ed Bullins, "A Short Statement on Street Theatre," *The Drama Review* 12 (1968), pp. 11–12.
160 "move out of the dark ages . . .": *From George Wallace*, p. 25.
162 "Really, all kinds of prejudice . . .": *Loretta Lynn*, p. 173.
162 "politics and music . . .": *Loretta Lynn*, p. 174.
163 "I searched the faces . . .": *Sing Me Back Home*, p. 243.
163 "There *he* sat . . .": *Sing Me Back Home*, p. 243.
163 "hadn't hung out . . .": *Sing Me Back Home*, p. 244.
163 "The inequities of segregation . . .": *Pride*, p. 28.
163 "the color issue . . .": *Pride*, p. 155.
163 "I ain't never heard . . .": *Pride*, p. 155.
164 "an imaginary fence . . .": *Pride*, p. 155.
164 "I'm singing for my brothers . . .": *Pride*, p. 156.

## 29. Troubled Souls: Wattstax and Motown (West)

Information on the late period of Stax can be found in Rob Bowman's *Soulsville U.S.A.*, Peter Guralnick's *Sweet Soul Music*, Phyl Garland's *The Sound of Soul* (Chicago: Regnery, 1969), *California Soul: Music of African Americans in the West*, ed. by Jacqueline Cogdell DjeDje and Eddie S. Meadows (Berkeley: U of California P, 1988), and Justine Picardie and Dorothy Wade's *Atlantic and the Godfathers of Rock and Roll* (London: Fourth Estate, 1993). Berry Gordy's *To Be Loved* and David Ritz's *Divided Soul* present contrasting versions of the struggle over the release of *What's Going On*. Stevie Wonder's relationship with Motown receives attention in *To Be Loved*, Nelson George's *Where Did Our Love Go?* and John Swenson's *Stevie Wonder*. The WGBH video *Respect* and the Time-Life video *The Sounds of Soul* include interviews with most of the major participants in this period of soul music history.

Page 165 "Whose cause was it . . .": *Sweet Soul Music*, p. 388.
166 "just another record company . . .": *Where Did Our Love Go?* p. 190.
166 "too heavy for the Supremes . . .": *To Be Loved*, p. 265.
166 "we arrived at a really touching . . .": *To Be Loved*, p. 265.
167 "I'm staying at Motown . . .": *Stevie Wonder*, p. 111.
167 "There are faults . . .": *Stevie Wonder*, p. 110.
168 "Vietnam, police brutality . . .": *To Be Loved*, p. 302.
168 "Marvin, we learn from everything . . .": *To Be Loved*, p. 302.

168 "From Jump Street . . .": *Divided Soul,* p. 147.
169 "They were sayin' . . .": Mavis Staples, phone interview with the author, June 1997.
169 "Their total investment . . .": *Sweet Soul Music,* p. 357.
169 "I've got to tell you . . .": *Sweet Soul Music,* p. 357.
170 "I went blank . . .": *Sweet Soul Music,* p. 355.
170 "going to Stax . . .": *Respect* video.
171 "You don't stick a gun . . .": *Atlantic and the Godfathers,* p. 182.
171 "The people who came to the fore . . .": *Atlantic and the Godfathers,* p. 166.

## 30. "Where Is the Love?"

Nina Simone's reflections on the changing currents of the freedom movement can be found in *I Put a Spell on You: The Autobiography of Nina Simone,* written in collaboration with Stephen Cleary (New York: Da Capo, 1993).

Page 173 "true singer of the civil rights movement . . .": *I Put a Spell,* p. 98.

### SECTION THREE

## 32. Reverend Green

Robert Gordon has been an invaluable source of information about and insight into Al Green. In addition to the material on Green in *It Came from Memphis,* see Gordon's liner notes to *Hi Times: Hi Records: The R&B Years* (Right Stuff T2-30548) and the *Al Green Anthology* (Right Stuff 72438-53033-2-6), which also includes a moving tribute to Green by Robert Christgau. See also the chapters on Green in Guralnick's *Sweet Soul Music* and Marc Taylor, *A Touch of Classic Soul: Soul Singers of the Early 1970s* (Jamaica, N.Y.: Aloiv, 1996).

Page 179 "Love between man and God . . .": Karen Schoemer, "Praise Be to Al Green," *Newsweek,* 13 November 1995, p. 83.
180 "He was like a black Elvis . . .": *Hi Times,* p. 35.
180 "The miracle is . . .": *Al Green anthology,* p. 54.
181 "We were born . . .": *Hi Times,* pp. 9–10.
181 "I used half-jazz . . .": *Al Green Anthology,* p. 24.
183 "He was doing it so simple . . .": *Al Green Anthology,* p. 28.

## 33. Demographics 101

*A Common Destiny: Blacks and American Society,* ed. Gerald Jaynes and Robin Williams (Washington: National Academy Press, 1989) and William Julius

Wilson's *The Truly Disadvantaged: The Inner City, the Underclass, and Public Policy* (Chicago: U of Chicago P, 1987) chart the demographic shifts of the seventies. Focusing primarily on Chicago, Wilson provides an incisive analysis of their social impact. Ze'ev Chafets's *Devil's Night and Other True Tales of Detroit* (New York: Vintage, 1990) sounds many of the same themes as Wilson in relation to Detroit.

Page 184 "The same people . . .": *Devil's Night*, p. 168.
   184 "It starts with economic pressure . . .": *Devil's Night*, p. 167.
   186 "[T]he less frequent . . .": *Truly Disadvantaged*, p. 261.
   186 "the key theoretical concept . . .": *Truly Disadvantaged*, p. 261.

## 34. Black Love in the Key of Life

Several of the anecdotes concerning Stevie Wonder can be found in Nelson George's *Where Did Our Love Go?* and Berry Gordy's *To Be Loved*. The best overview of Wonder's life is John Swenson's *Stevie Wonder* (New York: Perennial, 1986).

Page 187 "Dr. King left . . .": *Stevie Wonder*, p. 127.
   187 "I'd like to thank . . .": 1976 Grammy Awards telecast.
   188 "Some of that psychedelic music . . .": *Stevie Wonder*, p. 57.
   188 "a combination of R&B . . .": *Stevie Wonder*, p. 67.
   189 "A girl who was born . . .": *Stevie Wonder*, p. 9.
   189 "To a poor person . . .": *Stevie Wonder*, p. 15.
   189 "I hadn't really taken it . . .": *Stevie Wonder*, p. 22.
   190 "Black people have . . .": *Stevie Wonder*, p. 89.
   190 "If I can do anything . . .": *Stevie Wonder*, p. 89.
   190 "I hate to sound pessimistic . . .": *Stevie Wonder*, p. 89.
   190 "Their hearts were recalling . . .": liner notes to *In Square Circle* (Tamla 6134).

## 35. Jimmy Carter

Kenneth O'Reilly's *Nixon's Piano* includes a useful chapter on the role of race in the Carter administration. James Baldwin's eloquent public statements regarding Carter are included in *The Price of the Ticket: Collected Nonfiction 1948–1985* (New York: St. Martin's/Marek, 1985). Derrick Bell's *Faces at the Bottom of the Well* (New York: Basic Books, 1992), Amy Gutman's essay in *Color Consciousness: The Political Morality of Race* (Princeton, N.J.: Princeton UP, 1996), which she wrote with K. Anthony Appiah, and Patricia Williams's *The Alchemy of Race and Rights: Diary of a Law Professor* (Cambridge, Mass.: Harvard, 1991) defend affirmative action in ways that illuminate the limitations of the Carter approach.

Page 192  "John Kennedy read about . . .": *Nixon's Piano*, p. 337.
192  "I must add, in honor . . .": *Price of the Ticket*, p. 640.
193  "Black access . . .": *Nixon's Piano*, p. 341.
193  "Young and his 'Manson family' . . .": *Nixon's Piano*, p. 348.
193  "My friend, Mr. Andrew Young . . .": *Price of the Ticket*, p. 656.
194  "The Justice Department's *Bakke* brief . . .": *Nixon's Piano*, pp. 345–46.
194  "We are going to suffer . . .": *Nixon's Piano*, p. 346.

## 36. Roots

Background information on Philly International can be found in Tony Cummings, *The Sound of Philadelphia* (London: Methuen, 1975); Marc Taylor, *A Touch of Classic Soul*; and "The Philly Sound: Kenny Gamble, Leon Huff & the Story of Brotherly Love (1966–1976)," published as the liner notes to the compilation *The Philly Sound* (Epic Legacy Z3K 64647). Robert Stepto introduces the concept of "immersion" in *From Behind the Veil*, pp. 164–67. The WGBH video *Rock & Roll: Make It Funky* (WGRRO4) places Philly in the context of seventies funk.

Page 197  "the joy of love . . .": *Philly Sound*, p. 48.
197  "They walked a tight line . . .": *Philly Sound*, p. 33.
197  "that's when in some wild . . .": *Philly Sound*, p. 1.
198  "I'm still thrilled . . .": *The Sound of Philadelphia*, p. 76.
199  "funk with a bow tie . . .": *Make It Funky* video.
199  "The MFSB band is something special . . .": *The Sound of Philadelphia*, p. 132.
200  "Being of truth and understanding . . .": liner notes to *Family Reunion* (Philly International 33807).
201  "voyage through death . . .": Robert Hayden, "Middle Passage" in *Collected Poems* (New York: Liveright, 1985), p. 54.

## 37. God Love Sex

There is no good overall history of disco, but useful sources include Iain Chambers, *Urban Rhythms: Pop Music and Popular Culture* (New York: St. Martin's, 1985), the relevant sections of *Rock of Ages*, and Ricky Vincent's *Funk*. Anthony Haden-Guest's *The Last Party: Studio 54, Disco, and the Culture of the Night* (New York: Morrow, 1997) examines the relationship between disco music and the New York club scene. Anthony Goldman's *Disco* (New York: Hawthorn, 1978) includes numerous photographs that give a sense of the club scene's feel. Gloria Gaynor's *I Will Survive* (New York: St. Martin's, 1997) looks back on the era from a highly critical perspective. Martin Duberman's *Stonewall* (New York: Plume, 1994) includes interesting information on the role of music in the gay culture that provided the background for the disco scene.

Page 203 *"En leur regle . . ."*: *Last Party*, pp. 123–24.
    204 "We resorted to using music . . .": *Last Party*, p. 82.
    205 "the definitive disco manifesto . . .": Ken Barnes, liner notes to *The Disco Years, Volume 2, On the Beat (1978–1982)* (Rhino Records R2 70985).
    205 "As a guitarist, I was . . .": Michael A. Gonzalez, "Chic!" *Vibe* 5, no. 6 (August 1997), p. 160.
    206 "We wear no underwear . . .": *Stonewall*, p. 201.
    207 "I think it was kind of hard . . .": *Have a Nice Decade* video.
    207 "In disco the musical pulse . . .": *Urban Rhythms*, p. 147.
    207 "My grandmother was very religious . . .": *Last Party*, p. 151.
    208 "It was definitely R&B . . .": *Last Party*, p. xxi.

## 38. Disco Sucks

For interviews clearly stating the antidisco tendencies in rock music, see the Time-Life video *The History of Rock 'n' Roll: The '70s: Have a Nice Decade* (Warner video W13867). Jesse Jackson's statements on disco are quoted in Ricky Vincent, *Funk*. For additional material on the attacks, see Lindal Martin and Kerry Segrave, *Anti-rock*.

Page 210 "garbage and pollution . . .": *Funk*, p. 207.
    210 "Nothing get on your nerves . . .": *Have a Nice Decade* video.
    211 "Our goal in the seventies . . .": *Have a Nice Decade* video.
    211 "The machine age . . .": *Have a Nice Decade* video.

## 39. Punks and Pretenders

The punk scene has received extensive attention from first-rate music critics including Jon Savage, *England's Dreaming: Anarchy, Sex Pistols, Punk Rock, and Beyond* (New York: St. Martin's, 1992); Lester Bangs's brilliantly deranged *Psychotic Reactions and Carburetor Dung*, ed. Greil Marcus (New York: Knopf, 1987); and Greil Marcus, *Ranters and Crowd Pleasers: Punk in Pop Music, 1977–1992* (New York: Anchor, 1993). Peter Doggett, *Lou Reed: Growing Up in Public* (London: Omnibus, 1992) and Victor Bockris, *Transformer: The Lou Reed Story* (New York: Da Capo, 1994) discuss Reed's changing relationship to the scene. Richard Marshall's *Jean-Michel Basquiat* (New York: Whitney Museum of American Art, 1992) includes wonderful plates of Basquiat's art along with insightful essays by Dick Hebdige, Robert Farris Thompson, and Greg Tate.

Page 214   "The scene downtown . . .": *Jean-Michel Basquiat,* p. 236.
   214   "There's not enough black people . . .": *Jean-Michel Basquiat,* p. 236.
   215   "the general atmosphere . . .": *Psychotic Reactions,* p. 230.
   215   "secret yes the punk no . . .": *Ranters and Crowd Pleasers,* pp. 5–6.
   215   "You see, dear reader . . .": *Psychotic Reactions,* pp. 225–26.
   216   "It's not about getting the bloody . . .": *Psychotic Reactions,* p. 245.

## 40. Rebellion or Revolution

Information in this section was derived primarily from Marcus Gray's *Last Gang in Town: The Story and Myth of the Clash* (New York: Holt, 1997); Lester Bangs's chapter on the Clash in *Psychotic Reactions and Carburetor Dung,* pp. 224–59; and Dave Marsh's *Born to Run: The Bruce Springsteen Story,* volume 1 (New York: Thunder's Mouth, 1996).

Page 220   "There was racial tension . . .": Kelly-Jane Cotter, "To His 6-Year-Old, Bruce Springsteen is 'Barney for Adults,' " *Asbury Park Press,* 27 November 1996, p. 1.
   220   "should be spoken in reverence . . .": *Born to Run,* p. 31.
   221   "I write a lot about action moments . . .": *Born to Run,* pp. 50–51.
   222   "Look, the situation . . .": *Last Gang,* p. 180.
   222   "If you wanna fuckin' enjoy . . .": *Last Gang,* p. 180.
   223   "We were like a plantation . . .": *Last Gang,* p. 12.
   223   "If Sixties punk rock . . .": *Last Gang,* p. 186.
   224   "We know the blacks've got . . .": *Last Gang,* p. 186.
   224   "black sticksmen were running . . .": *Last Gang,* p. 319.
   225   "Somewhere in their assimilation . . .": *Psychotic Reactions,* p. 238.
225–226   "Listen, punk love reggae . . .": Stephen Davis, *Bob Marley* (Rochester, Vt.: Schenkman, 1990), p. 184.

## 41. P-Funkentelechy

The best sources of information concerning P-Funk and funk in general are Ricky Vincent's *Funk: The Music, the People, and the Rhythm of the One* (New York: St. Martin's, 1995) and *George Clinton and P-Funk: An Oral History* (New York: Avon, 1998), compiled by David Mills, Larry Alexander, Thomas Stanley, and Aris Wilson. Useful sources based on interviews with Clinton include Greg Tate's *Flyboy in the Buttermilk* (New York: Simon & Schuster, 1992); Chip Stern, "The Serious Metafoolishness of Father Funkadelic, George Clinton" in *The Rock Musician: 15 Years of Interviews from Musician Magazine,* ed. Tony Scherman (New York: St. Martin's, 1994); John Corbett, *Extended Play: Sounding Off from John Cage to Dr. Funkenstein* (Durham, N.C.: Duke UP, 1994); and Vernon Reid, "Brother from Another Planet," *Vibe,* September 1994, pp. 45–48. The WGBH video *Rock & Roll:*

*Make It Funky* (WGBH video WGRRO4) captures the feel and look of the era beautifully.

Page 226 "Jazz is the teacher . . .": *Funk,* p. 147.
227 "The rhythm is so hip . . .": "Serious Metafoolishness," p. 12.
227 "Everybody got somethin' . . .": "Serious Metafoolishness," p. 12.
227 "we became the loudest . . .": *Extended Play,* p. 149.
227 "a populist black poststructuralism . . .": *Flyboy,* p. 208.
227 "war and peacetime use . . .": *Flyboy,* p. 156.
228 "See, you're a damn fool . . .": "Brother from Another," p. 48.
229 "This is the type of thing . . .": "Brother from Another," p. 46.

## 42. Redemption Songs

Basic information on Bob Marley can be found in Adrian Boot and Chris Salewicz, *Bob Marley: Songs of Freedom* (New York: Penguin Studio, 1995); Timothy White, *Catch a Fire: The Life of Bob Marley* (New York: Holt, 1989); Stephen Davis, *Bob Marley,* rev. ed. (Rochester, Vt.: Schenkman, 1990); and *Bob Marley In His Own Words,* ed. Ian McCann (London: Omnibus, 1993). For more general information concerning reggae and its relationship to Rastafarianism, see Stephen Davis and Peter Simon, *Reggae Bloodlines* (New York: Da Capo, 1992) and Chris Potash's *Reggae, Rasta, Revolution: Jamaican Music from Ska to Dub* (New York: Schirmer, 1997). Background material on the Rastafarians can be found in Leonard Barrett, *The Rastafarians* (Boston: Beacon, 1977). For a clear discussion of Garvey's importance in the African American political tradition, see Lawrence Levine, "Marcus Garvey and the Politics of Revitalization" in *Black Leaders of the Twentieth Century,* ed. John Hope Franklin and August Meier (Urbana: U of Illinois P, 1982). The concepts of dispersion and recuperation were introduced by Judylyn Ryan in her Ph.D. dissertation "Water from an Ancient Well: The Recuperation of Double Consciousness" (U of Wisconsin, 1990).

Page 230 "Music is music . . .": *In His Own Words,* p. 25.
230 "The god who mek . . .": *In His Own Words,* p. 54.
232 "The world has made being black . . .": *Black Leaders,* p. 105.
233 "Name Wailers come from . . .": Davis, *Bob Marley,* p. 61.
234 "Like Jah say, the West . . .": *In His Own Words,* p. 40.
235 "Reggae can't do anything . . .": *In His Own Words,* p. 27.
235 "Ya cyaan return . . .": *In His Own Words,* p. 16.

## 43. The Message

A surprisingly rich literature concerning hip-hop has developed in a reasonably short time. Among the most useful books concerning the early days are Steven Hager's *Hip Hop: The Illustrated History of Break Dancing, Rap*

*Music, and Graffiti* (New York: St. Martin's, 1984); David Toop's *Rap Attack 2: African Rap to Global Hip Hop* (London: Serpent's Tail, 1991); S. H. Fernando's *The New Beats: Exploring the Music, Culture, and Attitudes of Hip-Hop* (New York: Anchor, 1994); and Tricia Rose's *Black Noise: Rap Music and Black Culture in Contemporary America* (Hanover, N.H.: Wesleyan UP, 1994). Useful background information on the Jamaican sound systems can be found in Stephen Davis's *Reggae Bloodlines.* Paul Gilroy's *Small Acts: Thoughts on the Politics of Black Culture* (London: Serpent's Tail, 1993) and Dick Hebdige's *Cut 'n' Mix: Culture, Identity and Caribbean Music* (New York: Routledge, 1987) include insightful discussions of hip-hop in the context of diasporic culture.

Page 237  Afrika Bambaata's list of rap influences is printed in Michael Small, *Break It Down: The Inside Story from the New Leaders of Rap* (New York: Citadel, 1992), p. 12.

238  "A man named George . . .": *New Beats,* p. 4.
238  "You had to be entertaining . . .": *Hip Hop,* pp. 35–36.
239  "The Bronx wasn't really . . .": *Rap Attack,* p. 65.
239  "Hip-hop is all kinds . . .": *New Beats,* p. 6.
239  "I used to like to catch . . .": *Rap Attack,* p. 66.
240  "It's like if Greg Louganis . . .": *New Beats,* p. 13.

## SECTION FOUR

# 45. Springsteen and the Reagan Rules

Kenneth O'Reilly's *Nixon's Piano* provides an incisive overview of the role of race in the Reagan and Bush administrations. For information concerning the economic realities of the period, see Kevin Phillips, *The Politics of Rich and Poor: Wealth and the American Electorate in the Reagan Aftermath* (New York: Random House, 1990); Edward N. Wolff, *Top Heavy: A Study of the Increasing Inequality of Wealth in America* (New York: Twentieth Century Fund Press, 1995); and William Julius Wilson, *When Work Disappears: The World of the New Urban Poor* (New York: Knopf, 1996). Randy Shilts's *And the Band Played On* (New York: Penguin, 1995) remains the best overview of the development of the AIDS crisis. Alinor Burkett's *The Gravest Show on Earth: America in the Age of AIDS* (Boston: Houghton Mifflin, 1995) brings the story closer to the present. Dave Marsh's *Glory Days: Bruce Springsteen in the 1980s* (New York: Pantheon, 1987) picks up Springsteen's story where *Born to Run* left off. Jim Cullen's *Born in the U.S.A.: Bruce Springsteen and the American Tradition* (New York: HarperCollins, 1997) is a cogent analysis of Springsteen's work. *Springsteen: The Rolling Stone Files* (New York: Hyperion, 1996) reprints every significant article on Springsteen from 1973 to 1995.

Page 246 "America's future rests . . .": *Glory Days*, p. 260.
247 "I don't know what you thought . . .": *Glory Days*, p. 29.
247 "I think what's happening . . .": *Glory Days*, p. 285.

## 47. The View from Black America

The best sources of information concerning the growing split between black and white social realities since the eighties are Andrew Hacker, *Two Nations: Black and White, Separate, Hostile, Unequal*, expanded edition (New York: Ballantine, 1995) and Douglas Massey and Nancy Denton, *American Apartheid: Segregation and the Making of the Underclass* (Cambridge, Mass.: Harvard UP, 1993). For Reagan's responses, see Kenneth O'Reilly, *Nixon's Piano* and Kevin Phillips, *The Politics of Rich and Poor.* Tricia Rose's *Black Noise*, S. H. Fernando's *The New Beats*, and Brian Cross's *It's Not About a Salary: Rap, Race and Resistance in Los Angeles* (New York: Verso, 1993) tie the changing economic circumstances to the rise of hip-hop.

Page 248 "The 1980s were the triumph . . .": *Politics of Rich and Poor*, xvii.
250 "A lot of lies are told . . .": *Nixon's Piano*, p. 355.
254 "You, your spouse . . .": *Nixon's Piano*, p. 385.
254 "I looked like a zombie . . .": *Nixon's Piano*, p. 384.
255 "You needed that job . . .": *Nixon's Piano*, p. 393.
256 "When we was doin' the shit . . .": *The New Beats*, p. 94.

## 50. Run-D.M.C. Negotiates the Mainstream

Every history of hip-hop gives extended attention to Run-D.M.C. For a good overview of their career see the section devoted to them in Havelock Nelson and Michael Gonzales, *Bring the Noise: A Guide to Rap Music and Hip-Hop Culture* (New York: Harmony, 1991).

Page 263 "the sound you hear . . .": *Bring the Noise*, p. 212.

## 51. "A Hero to Most"

The chapter on Elvis in Greil Marcus's *Mystery Train* is crucial to anyone seriously interested in either Elvis's presence in American culture or the dilemmas faced by megastars of any era. Peter Guralnick's biography of Elvis will certainly become the definitive source of information. The first volume, *Last Train to Memphis: The Rise of Elvis Presley* (Boston: Little, Brown, 1994) was the source of most of the material concerning Elvis's relationship to black culture during the fifties. B. B. King's comments on Elvis are from *Blues All Around Me: The Autobiography of B. B. King*, written with David Ritz (New York: Avon, 1996). Additional information on Elvis's early career can be found in Martin Hawkins's *Good Rockin' Tonight*, John Floyd's *Sun*

*Records: An Oral History*, and the Time-Life video *The History of Rock 'n' Roll: Good Rockin' Tonight.*

Page 263   "got white folks . . .": *Good Rockin' Tonight* video.
   264   "I liked Elvis . . .": *Blues All Around Me*, p. 188.
   264   "frankly, I'd heard . . .": *Last Train*, p. 426.
   264   "He is very spiritually minded . . .": *Last Train*, p. 425.
   264   Quotations concerning the controversy over Elvis's alleged racism are drawn from *Last Train*, p. 426.
   264   "Negro artists in the South . . .": *Last Train*, p. 5.
   265   "I wasn't looking for no tall stumps . . .": *Good Rockin' Tonight* video.
   265   "There was no [segregation] . . .": *Good Rockin' Tonight* video.
   266   "you cannot fail to recognize . . .": LeRoi Jones, *Home* (New York: William Morrow, 1966), p. 191.
   266   "Elvis has dissolved . . .": *Mystery Train*, p. 123.

## 52. Megastardom and Its Discontents

Benjamin DeMott presents his provocative approach to race in contemporary America in *The Trouble with Friendship: Why Americans Can't Think Straight About Race* (New York: Atlantic Monthly Press, 1995), which is an extended version of his essay "Put on a Happy Face: Masking the Difference Between Blacks and Whites," *Harper's*, September 1995, pp. 31–38. While both Michael Jackson's autobiography *Moon Walk* (New York: Doubleday, 1988) and J. Randy Taraborelli's *Michael Jackson: The Magic and the Madness* (New York: Birch Lane, 1991) present interesting angles on Jackson's career, by far the most insightful book on his rise to megastardom is Dave Marsh, *Trapped: Michael Jackson and the Crossover Dream* (New York: Bantam, 1985). Information on Madonna in this section was derived primarily from *Madonna: The Rolling Stone Files* (New York: Hyperion, 1997); *Madonna: In Her Own Words* (London: Omnibus, 1990); and *Desperately Seeking Madonna*, ed. Adam Sexton (New York: Delta, 1993). The best overviews of women in rock are Lucy O'Brien, *She Bop* (New York: Penguin, 1995), Gillian G. Gaar, *She's a Rebel: The History of Women in Rock & Roll* (Seattle: Seal Press, 1992), and *The Rolling Stone Book of Women in Rock*, ed. Barbara O'Dair (New York: Random House, 1997). The Madonna videos discussed in this section are available on *Madonna: The Immaculate Collection* (Warner Reprise video W38195-3); the Michael Jackson videos can be found on *Michael Jackson: History: Video Greatest Hits* (Epic Music video 19V 50123).

Page 271   "What's dreamed of and gained . . .": *Trouble with Friendship*, p. 15.
   271   "Yesterday white people . . .": "Put on a Happy Face," p. 33.
   272   "the most famous woman . . .": *Madonna: Rolling Stone Files*, p. 1.

273  "To me, your real victory . . .": *Trapped,* p. 205.
274  "In this sense, if *Thriller* . . .": *Trapped,* p. 205.
275  "Madonna kicked a huge . . .": Amy Raphael, *Grrrls: Viva Rock Divas* (New York: St. Martin's, 1996), p. 220.

## 53. Duke Ellington for Our Time

Miles Davis's comments on Prince are from *Miles: The Autobiography.* Dave Hill, *Prince: A Pop Life* (New York: Harmony, 1989), Liz Jones, *Purple Reign: The Artist Formerly Known as Prince* (Secaucus, N.J.: Birch Lane, 1998), and John Duffy's *Prince: The First Illustrated Biography* (London: Omnibus) include quotes from Prince drawn from a number of interviews. Eric Nisenson, *Blue: The Murder of Jazz* (New York: St. Martin's, 1997) includes an insightful discussion of Wynton Marsalis's place in contemporary music.

Page 277  "he can be the new Duke . . .": *Miles,* p. 385.
277  "I really love Prince . . .": *Miles,* p. 384.
278  "a black thing . . .": *Miles,* p. 385.
279  "Who's interested to go on? . . .": *Prince,* pp. 91–92.

## 54. West Africa Is in the House

House music has received little attention from music historians, but David Toop's *Ocean of Sound: Aether Talk, Ambient Sound and Imaginary Worlds* (London: Serpent's Tail, 1995) and Sarah Thornton's *Club Cultures: Music, Media and Subcultural Capital* (Middletown, Conn: Wesleyan UP, 1996) deal with issues related to the club scene. The best sources of information concerning house are magazine articles and unpublished research including Carol Cooper, "Check Yo'Self at the Door: Cryptoheterosexuality and the Black Music Underground," *Vibe,* September 1996, pp. 55–59; "An ABC of House," *Village Voice Rock & Roll Quarterly* (summer 1989), pp. 28–30; Frank Owen, "Paradise Lost," *Vibe,* September 1996, pp. 62–66; Glenn Berry's M.A. thesis, "House Music's Development and the East Coast Underground Scene" (U of Wisconsin, 1992); and Ed Pavlic's Ph.D. dissertation, "Crossroads and Consciousness: Communal Underground Space and Diasporic Modernism in African-American Literature" (U of Indiana, 1997).

Page 282  "I grew up with blacks . . .": "ABC of House," p. 29.
282  "House music surely speaks . . .": Brian Chin, liner notes to *House Music: All Night Long: The Best of House Music, Volume 3* (Profile PCD 1286, 1990).

## 55. "Bring the Noise"

Public Enemy receives extensive attention in every history of hip-hop including S. H. Fernando's *The New Beats*, Tricia Rose's *Black Noise*, and Havelock Nelson and Michael Gonzales's *Bring the Noise*. Chuck D defends his own positions in *Fight the Power: Rap, Race and Reality* (New York: Delacorte, 1997), written with Yusuf Jah. For information concerning the controversy involving Farrakhan and Jesse Jackson, see Marshall Frady, *Jesse: The Life and Pilgrimage of Jesse Jackson* (New York: Random House, 1996). The realities of right-wing involvement in anti-Semitic violence are documented in James Ridgeway, *Blood in the Face: The Ku Klux Klan, Aryan Nations, Nazi Skinheads, and the Rise of a New White Culture* (New York: Thunder's Mouth, 1990) and Raphael Ezekiel, *The Racist Mind: Portraits of American Neo-Nazis and Klansmen* (New York: Viking, 1995).

Page 288  "the majority of wickedness . . .": *New Beats,* p. 138.

## 56. "Know the Ledge"

Brian Cross's *It's Not About a Salary* and S. H. Fernando's *The New Beats* are the best overviews of the rise of West Coast rap. Ice T's *The Ice Opinion,* as told to Heidi Siegmund (New York: St. Martin's, 1994) provides an insider's analysis of the issues dealt with in the raps. For information on the human realities behind media stereotypes of gangs, see Leon Bing, *Do or Die* (New York: HarperCollins, 1991) and Sanyika Shakur, a.k.a. Monster Kody Scott, *Monster: The Autobiography of an L.A. Gang Member* (New York: Atlantic Monthly Press, 1993). Mike Davis's *City of Quartz* ties the growth of gangs to larger patterns in the social and economic context of Los Angeles. Ricky Vincent discusses George Clinton's importance in West Coast rap in *Funk*.

Page 290  "We're telling the real story . . .": *It's Not About a Salary,* p. 37.
    291  "It's more tense now . . .": *Do or Die,* p. 257.
    291  "When I was coming up . . .": *Do or Die,* p. 217.
    291  "If I had been born in '53 . . .": *Do or Die,* p. 237.
    291  "It's individuals . . .": *Do or Die,* p. 263.
    292  "Everybody on the black side . . .": Mark Putterford, *Guns n' Roses: In Their Own Words* (London: Omnibus Press, 1993), pp. 16–17.
    293  "If hip-hop were film . . .": Toure, "Only One Star in the Two Schools of Rap," *New York Times,* August 14, 1994, p. H-26.

## 57. "Born in the U.S.A."

Information for this section was drawn from Dave Marsh's *Glory Days* and *Springsteen: The Rolling Stone Files.* Baraka's comments on Springsteen were published in a colloquium on "The Meaning of Bruce," *Spin,* September 1985, pp. 45–51, 80.

Page 298 "the nature of his concerns . . .": "The Meaning of Bruce," p. 51.
    298 "What amazes is . . .": "The Meaning of Bruce," p. 51.
    299 "In America there's a promise . . .": *Glory Days,* p. 101.
    300 "It's the new protest music . . .": David Corn, "Bruce Springsteen Tells the Story of the Secret America," *Mother Jones* (March/April 1996), p. 26.
    302 "When you lose that sense . . .": *Glory Days,* p. 148.
    302 "that was the bottom . . .": *Glory Days,* p. 43.
    303 "The President was mentioning . . .": *Glory Days,* p. 263.
    303 "how somebody who could've . . .": *Glory Days,* p. 40.
    304 "It's a long walk . . .": *Glory Days,* p. 263.

## SECTION FIVE

## 59. American Dreaming

Background information on Clinton's racial attitudes was derived from Kenneth O'Reilly, *Nixon's Piano.* Among the most useful sociological and journalistic overviews of race in the nineties are Jennifer Hochschild, *Facing Up to the American Dream: Race, Class, and the Soul of the Nation* (Princeton, N.J.: Princeton UP, 1998); David K. Shipler's *A Country of Strangers: Blacks and Whites in America* (New York: Knopf, 1997); and Jonathan Coleman's *A Long Way to Go* (New York: Atlantic Monthly Press, 1997). For specific information on black middle-class perspectives, see Jill Nelson, *Volunteer Slavery: My Authentic Negro Experience* (New York: Penguin, 1994) and Ellis Cose's *The Rage of a Privileged Class* (New York: Perennial, 1995). The essays collected in *The House That Race Built,* ed. Wahneema Lubiano (New York: Vintage, 1998), present a broad range of personal and analytical perspectives on the nature of white supremacy in the nineties.

Page 310 "the United States has not always . . .": Mimi Hall, "Clinton: We Were Wrong on Slavery," *USA Today,* 25 March 1988, p. 1.
    310 "dream became the dream . . .": Roger Simon, "Shared Past, Future," *Wisconsin State Journal,* 24 March 1998, p. 1.
    310 "If you work hard . . .": *Facing Up to the American Dream,* p. 18.
    310 "the administration's rainbow . . .": *Nixon's Piano,* p. 417.
    310 "Among the many vital jobs . . .": Martin Luther King, Jr., *Why We Can't Wait* (New York: Signet, 1964), p. 134.
    311 "The ancient common law . . .": *Why We Can't Wait,* p. 137.
    311 "the day he told . . .": *Nixon's Piano,* p. 415.

312  The material from the *Ebony* article is presented in *Facing Up to the American Dream*, p. 43.

312  "rich blacks have always . . .": *Facing Up to the American Dream*, p. 48.

313  "the depth and breadth of racial polarization . . .": *The House That Race Built*, p. 301.

## 60. C.R.E.A.M.

The best sources of information on Tupac Shakur are Armond White, *Rebel for the Hell of It: The Life of Tupac Shakur* (New York: Thunder's Mouth, 1997) and *Tupac Shakur, 1971–1996* (New York: Crown, 1997), a collection of articles originally published in *Vibe*. For economic details concerning Death Row Records, see Ronin Ro, *Have Gun Will Travel: The Spectacular Rise and Violent Fall of Death Row Records* (New York: Doubleday, 1998). Although it perpetuates serious misconceptions concerning the meaning of "authenticity" in hip-hop, Connie Bruck's article "The Takedown of Tupac," *New Yorker*, 7 July 1997, pp. 46–64, presents factual information concerning Tupac's first shooting.

Page 315  "Suge Knight, he a businessman . . .": *Rebel for the Hell of It*, p. 165.

315  "When I be throwing . . .": *Tupac Shakur*, p. 126.

316  "I tried to see . . .": *Tupac Shakur*, p. 126.

316  "What we mean by that . . .": Chairman Mao, "Next Chamber," *Vibe*, September 1996, p. 114.

316  "When you do rap albums . . .": "Takedown of Tupac," p. 48.

316  "Rap fans insist . . .": "Takedown of Tupac," p. 48.

317  "I used to sit outside . . .": "Takedown of Tupac," p. 48.

317  "It was like their words . . .": "Takedown of Tupac," p. 48.

317  "We asked ten years ago . . .": *Rebel for the Hell of It*, p. 168.

318  "the concept behind this . . .": *Rebel for the Hell of It*, p. 81.

318  "fear is stronger . . .": *Tupac Shakur*, p. 98.

## 61. Deeper Shades of Soul

Background information on the diasporic cultures that contributed to the Black British scene may be found in Dick Hebdige, *Cut 'n' Mix: Culture, Identity and Caribbean Music* (London: Routledge, 1987); Charles Keil and Steve Feld, *Music Grooves* (Chicago: U of Chicago P, 1994); and George Lipsitz, *Dangerous Crossroads: Popular Music, Postmodernism and the Poetics of Place* (New York: Verso, 1994). Paul Gilroy applies the theoretical insights into diasporic culture he developed in *The Black Atlantic: Modernity and Double Consciousness* (Cambridge, Mass.: Harvard UP, 1995) to popular music in *Small Acts: Thoughts on the Politics of Black Culture* (London: Serpent's Tail, 1994). My approach to the Black British scene has been heavily influenced by Ed Pavlic's dissertation, "Crossroads and Consciousness" (Indiana U, 1997). Danny Alexander's review of albums by Mary J. Blige, TLC, and others published in *New Times* (Kansas City), 4 January 1995, and reprinted in shorter form in *Rock & Rap Confidential*, no. 221, had an equally strong impact on my understanding of the importance of black women's R & B.

Page 319 KRS-One's comments on Frederick Douglass can be found in Joe Wood, "KRS-One: Act Like Ya Know," *Vibe*, November 1995, p. 71.

322 The quotations from "Sonny's Blues" are from James Baldwin, *Early Novels and Stories* (New York: Library of America, 1998), pp. 845, 859.

323 "It is your perception . . .": liner notes to *Seal* (Sire Records 9 45415-2), 1994.

324 "Those are the voices of black women . . .": Alexander review, p. 9.

326 "wouldn't go over in a Holiday Inn . . .": Fred Bronson, *The Billboard Book of Number One Hits*, 3rd ed. (New York: Billboard Books, 1992), p. 567.

## 62. Ancestors and Elders

All quotations from Curtis Mayfield are from a personal interview with the author, Atlanta, February 1997. Bruce Springsteen's comments on Woody Guthrie were delivered at a concert sponsored by the Rock and Roll Hall of Fame in Cleveland during October 1996. For a sense of Springsteen's development during the nineties, see Nicholas Dawidoff, "Steinbeck in Leather," *New York Times Magazine*, 26 January 1997, pp. 27–33, 64, 69, 72, 77; Will Percy, "Rock and Read," *Double Take*, spring 1998), pp. 36–43; David Corn, "Bruce Springsteen Tells the Story of the Secret America," *Mother Jones*, March/April 1996, pp. 25–27; and Judy Weider, "Bruce Springsteen: The Advocate Interview," *The Advocate*, 2 April 1996, pp. 47–52. Pedro Bell's mythic history of hip-hop comes from the liner notes of George Clinton, *Greatest Funkin' Hits* (Capitol CDP 7243 8).

Page 330 "I very consciously set out . . .": "Steinbeck in Leather," p. 30.

332 "If they admire what we did . . .": James Ledbetter, "The Message," *Vibe*, August 1994, p. 70.

## 64. Flashes of the Spirit

Material on Cassandra Wilson is drawn from Rob Tannenbaum, "A Diva's Progress," *GQ*, July 1994, pp. 47–49; Rick Mitchell, "Southern Comfort," *Replay*, July 1996, pp. 10–11; and Geoffrey Himes, "Cassandra Wilson: Bridging the Gap Between the Urban World of Jazz and the Pastoral Heritage of Mississippi Blues," *Replay*, July 1994, pp. 2–5.

Page 338    "a spirit that just won't let me . . .": "Diva's Progress," p. 48.

338    Wilson's description of the Ghanaian legend is from "Diva's Progress," p. 49.

338    "I think everything that grows up out of the blues . . .": "Southern Comfort," p. 11.

339    "Recently I was reading . . .": "Bridging the Gap," p. 2.

339    "a lot of people miss the point . . .": "Bridging the Gap," p. 3.

## 65. Redemption Songs (The Nineties Remix)

For information on the white women rockers of the nineties, see Judith Fitzgerald, *Building a Mystery: The Story of Sarah McLachlan and Lilith Fair* (Kingston, Ontario: Quarry Music Books, 1997); Lucy O'Brien, *She Bop: The Definitive History of Women in Rock, Pop, and Soul* (New York: Penguin, 1995); and *The Rolling Stone Book of Women in Rock*, ed. Barbara O'Dair (New York: Random House, 1997). The information and quotes from Kirk Franklin are from Alan Light, "Say Amen, Somebody," *Vibe*, October 1997, pp. 90–96. Information on Wu-Tang Clan is drawn primarily from Mimi Valdes, "Right and Exact," *Vibe*, September 1997; Bonz Malone, "Deep Space Nine," *Vibe*, June/July 1995; and Chairman Mao, "Next Chamber," *Vibe*, September 1996.

Page 340    "And here we are . . .": James Baldwin, *Collected Essays* (New York: Library of America, 1998), pp. 346–47.

343    "I was brought up listening . . .": *Women in Rock*, p. 544.

344    For McLachlan's comments on Lilith Fair, see *Building a Mystery*, pp. 196–98.

344    "There was an innocence . . .": *Building a Mystery*, p. 200.

345    "I think we—hip hop artists . . .": Joan Morgan, "Tongues Untied," *Vibe*, August 1996, p. 85.

345    "I think hip hop has always been . . .": "Tongues Untied," p. 84.

346    "I think the majority . . .": "Say Amen," p. 96.

347    "I'm not a part . . .": Greg Tate, "Soul Sister Number One," *Vibe*, August 1997, p. 86.

347    "We've tried everything else . . .": "Say Amen," p. 92.

347    "The Nation stands for something . . .": "Say Amen," p. 96.

347    "I could tell . . .": "Say Amen," p. 94.

348    "slang doctors take you . . .": "Right and Exact," p. 118.

348    "Nine sets of eyes . . .": "Right and Exact," p. 116.

349    "It's not organized . . .": "Right and Exact," p. 117.

349 "In ancient times . . .": "Deep Space Nine," p. 72.

350 "[RZA's] decisions represent . . .": "Right and Exact," p. 117.

353 "Our history is each other . . .": James Baldwin, *Just Above My Head* (New York: Dial Press, 1979), p. 428.

# Playlist

Songs or albums are listed only on their first occurrence in the text. On a few occasions when the major discussion of a song follows its first mention, the song is placed with its second occurrence. See the index for additional information. For songs that made the *Billboard* charts, the year listed refers to the year of peak popularity. For other songs, the year refers either to its first appearance on an album or the year of its recording. In the case of a few underground dance records (which are notoriously hard to document), the years provided are based on the memories of DJ G-Most (Glenn Berry) and DJ Gant (Gant Johnson). For additional listening suggestions, see the Gospel Top 40 (p. 28), the Blues Top 40 (p. 68), and the Jazz Top 40 (p. 132).

## SECTION ONE

Marvin Gaye, *What's Going On*, 1971
Charles Wright and the Watts 103rd Street Rhythm Band, "Express Yourself," 1970
Charles Mingus, "Haitian Fight Song," 1957
———, "Meditations on Integration," 1964
Mahalia Jackson, "Keep Your Hand on the Plow," 1954
Staple Singers, "Freedom Highway," 1965

Ray Charles, "I Got a Woman," 1955
Traditional, "There's a Man Going Round Taking Names"
———, "I'm So Glad Jesus Lifted Me Up"
Mahalia Jackson, "I've Heard of a City Called Heaven," 1965
———, "Move on Up a Little Higher," 1947
———, "Walk in Jerusalem," 1963
Traditional, "Swing Low Sweet Chariot"
———, "Wade in the Water"
———, "Steal Away to Jesus"
Mahalia Jackson, "I'm on My Way," 1958
———, "Walk All Over God's Heaven," 1954
Marian Anderson, "He's Got the Whole World in His Hands," 1962

Mahalia Jackson, "Take My Hand, Precious Lord," 1956
———, "I've Been 'Buked and I've Been Scorned," 1958
———, "How I Got Over," 1951
Swan Silvertones, "How I Got Over," 1959

Charles Mingus, "Wednesday Night Prayer Meeting," 1960
———, "Three or Four Shades of Blue," 1977
Traditional, "Oh Freedom"
———, "We Shall Not Be Moved"
Fannie Lou Hamer, "This Little Light of Mine," 1964

Barrett Strong, "Money," 1960
Jackie Wilson, "Lonely Teardrops," 1958
———, "To Be Loved," 1958
Martha and the Vandellas, "Dancing in the Street," 1964
———, "Nowhere to Run," 1965
Supremes, "Stop! In the Name of Love," 1965
Stevie Wonder, "I Was Made to Love Her," 1967
Temptations, "Ain't Too Proud to Beg," 1966
Marvin Gaye, "I Heard It Through the Grapevine," 1968
Smokey Robinson and the Miracles, "The Tracks of My Tears," 1965
———, "I Second that Emotion," 1967
Supremes, "Baby Love," 1964
Little Stevie Wonder, "Fingertips, Part 2," 1963
Four Tops, "I Can't Help Myself," 1965
Marvelettes, "Beachwood 4-5789," 1962
Smokey Robinson and the Miracles, "Ooo Baby Baby," 1965
Temptations, "My Girl," 1965
Four Tops, "Standing in the Shadows of Love," 1966
Marvin Gaye and Kim Weston, "It Takes Two," 1967

Soul Stirrers, "Jesus Gave Me Water," 1951
Sam Cooke, "Wonderful World," 1960
———, "Cupid," 1961
———, "You Send Me," 1957
———, "Soothe Me," 1962
———, "A Change Is Gonna Come," 1965
Soul Stirrers, "Come Go with Me to that Land," 1954
———, "Pilgrim of Sorrow," 1957
———, "Touch the Hem of His Garment," 1956
Ray Charles, "What'd I Say," 1959
Howlin' Wolf, "Back Door Man" (written by Willie Dixon), 1960
Drifters (featuring Clyde McPhatter), "Such a Night," 1954
Elvis Presley, "Such a Night," 1964

Drifters (featuring Clyde McPhatter), "Honey Love," 1954
Sam Cooke, "Only Sixteen," 1959
Jerry Butler and the Impressions, "For Your Precious Love," 1958
Ben E. King, "Stand by Me," 1961
Traditional, "Stand by Me, Father"
Herman's Hermits, "Wonderful World," 1965
Art Garfunkel with James Taylor and Paul Simon, "Wonderful World," 1978

Ronettes, "Walking in the Rain" (produced by Phil Spector), 1964
———, "Baby, I Love You" (produced by Phil Spector), 1963
———, "Be My Baby" (produced by Phil Spector), 1963
Ike and Tina Turner, "A Fool in Love," 1960
Marvin Gaye and Tammi Terrell, "If I Could Build My Whole World Around You," 1967
———, "You're All I Need to Get By," 1968
———, "Ain't Nothing Like the Real Thing," 1968
Crystals, "He Hit Me (It Felt Like a Kiss)" (produced by Phil Spector), 1962
Hole, "He Hit Me (It Felt Like a Kiss)," 1994
Tina Turner, "River Deep Mountain High" (produced by Phil Spector), 1966

Sam Cooke, "Bill Bailey," 1964
———, "Tennessee Waltz," 1964
———, "If I Had a Hammer," 1964
———, "This Little Light of Mine," 1964
Soul Stirrers, "Wade in the Water," 1959
———, "Stand by Me Father," 1959
———, "Mary, Don't You Weep," 1964
———, "Free at Last," 1963
Sam Cooke, "Just for You," 1961
Smokey Robinson and the Miracles, "You Really Got a Hold on Me," 1962
Sam Cooke, "Bring It on Home to Me," 1962
Beatles, "Don't Let Me Down," 1969
Simms Twins, "Soothe Me," 1961
Sam and Dave, "Soothe Me," 1967
Soul Stirrers, "Lead Me Jesus," 1961
Valentinos, "It's All Over Now," 1964
Rolling Stones, "It's All Over Now," 1964

Bob Dylan, "Blowin' in the Wind," 1963
———, "The Times They Are A-Changin'," 1964
———, "Masters of War," 1963
———, "A Hard Rain's A-Gonna Fall," 1963

——, "Oxford Town," 1963
——, "Only a Pawn in Their Game," 1964
——, "The Ballad of Emmett Till," 1962
——, "Talkin' John Birch Paranoid Blues," released 1991
Phil Ochs, "Talking Birmingham Jam," 1965
——, "Too Many Martyrs (The Ballad of Medgar Evers)," 1964
——, "Love Me, I'm a Liberal," 1966
Peter, Paul & Mary, "Very Last Day," 1963
——, "If I Had a Hammer," 1962
——, "Blowin' in the Wind," 1963

Woody Guthrie, "This Land Is Your Land," 1944
Traditional, "This Train"
Woody Guthrie, "Hang Knot," 1946
——, "Plane Wreck at Los Gatos (Deportees)," 1948
——, "John Henry," 1938
Leadbelly, "The Midnight Special," 1934
——, "The Bourgeois Blues," 1934
Kingston Trio, "Tom Dooley," 1958
Weavers, "Goodnight Irene," 1955
——, "So Long, It's Been Good to Know You," 1955

Traditional, "We Shall Overcome"
Stevie Wonder, "Blowin' in the Wind," 1966
Joan Baez, "We Are Crossing Jordan's River," 1961
——, "Oh Freedom," 1962
——, "We Shall Overcome," 1963
——, "With God on Our Side," 1963
——, "A Hard Rain's A-Gonna Fall," 1965
Barry McGuire, "Eve of Destruction," 1965
Rolling Stones, "Get Off of My Cloud," 1965
Beatles, "Help," 1965

Robert Johnson, *King of the Delta Blues,* 1936–37
Bob Dylan, *Bringing It All Back Home,* 1965
Wilson Pickett, "Land of 1000 Dances," 1966
——, "Mustang Sally," 1966
——, "Funky Broadway," 1967
Solomon Burke, "Just Out of Reach (Of My Two Open Arms)," 1961
Ray Charles, *Modern Sounds in Country and Western Music,* 1962
Hank Williams, "Six More Miles (To the Graveyard)," 1948
——, "A Mansion on the Hill," 1948
Jimmie Rodgers, "Waiting for a Train," 1929
——, "In the Jailhouse Now," 1928

————, "T for Texas," 1928
Wilson Pickett, "In the Midnight Hour," 1965

Robert Johnson, "Stones in My Passway," 1937
————, "If I Had Possession over Judgement Day," 1936
————, "Hellhound on My Trail," 1937
————, "Crossroads Blues," 1936
Cream, "Crossroads," 1968
Bob Dylan, "Just Like Tom Thumb's Blues," 1965

Muddy Waters, "I'm Your Hoochie Coochie Man" (written by Willie
    Dixon), 1954

King Curtis, "Memphis Soul Stew," 1967
Carla Thomas, "Gee Whiz," 1961
James Carr, "Dark End of the Street," 1967
Aretha Franklin, "Do Right Woman," 1967
Box Tops, "Cry Like a Baby," 1968
Sweet Inspirations, "Sweet Inspiration," 1968
Aretha Franklin, "Natural Woman," 1967
Neil Diamond, "Holly Holy," 1969
Box Tops, "Soul Deep," 1969
Dusty Springfield, "Son of a Preacher Man," 1968
Elvis Presley, "Suspicious Minds," 1969
————, "Kentucky Rain," 1970
————, "In the Ghetto," 1969
————, "True Love Travels on a Gravel Road," 1969
————, "Only the Strong Survive," 1969
————, "Stranger in My Own Home Town," 1969
Mar-Keys, "Last Night," 1961
Booker T. and the MGs, "Green Onions," 1962
Sam and Dave, "Hold On, I'm Comin'," 1966
Percy Sledge, "When a Man Loves a Woman," 1966
Temptations, "Don't Look Back," 1965
Otis Redding, "I've Been Loving You Too Long," 1965
————, "For Your Precious Love," 1965
————, "Chain Gang," 1966
Sam Cooke, "Chain Gang," 1960
Otis Redding, "Wonderful World," 1965
————, "A Change Is Gonna Come," 1965
————, "My Girl," 1965
Temptations, "It's Growing," 1965
Otis Redding, "It's Growing," 1966

Johnnie Taylor, "Who's Making Love (to Your Old Lady)," 1968
———, "I Believe in You (Believe in Me)," 1973

Muddy Waters, "Rolling Stone," 1950
Rolling Stones, "Satisfaction," 1965
———, "Paint It Black," 1966
Animals, "It's My Life," 1965
Bob Dylan, "Like a Rolling Stone," 1965
———, "Ballad of a Thin Man," 1965
———, "Subterranean Homesick Blues," 1965
Chuck Berry, "Too Much Monkey Business," 1956
———, "Nadine," 1964
———, "Brown Eyed Handsome Man," 1956
Bob Dylan, "Outlaw Blues," 1965
———, "Tombstone Blues," 1965
———, "Stuck Inside of Mobile with the Memphis Blues Again," 1966
Van Morrison, *Astral Weeks*, 1968
———, *Moondance*, 1970
———, *A Period of Transition*, 1977
Herman's Hermits, "Silhouettes," 1965
Rays, "Silhouettes," 1957
Rufus Thomas, "Walking the Dog," 1963
Rolling Stones, "Walking the Dog," 1964
Chuck Berry, "Carol," 1958
Rolling Stones, "Carol," 1964
Muddy Waters, "I Just Want to Make Love to You," 1954
Rolling Stones, "I Just Want to Make Love to You," 1964
Chris Kenner, "I Like It Like That," 1961
Dave Clark 5, "I Like It Like That," 1965
Bobby Day, "Over and Over," 1958
Dave Clark 5, "Over and Over," 1965
Marv Johnson, "You Got What It Takes," 1959
Dave Clark 5, "You Got What It Takes," 1967
Clovers, "Love Potion Number Nine," 1959
Searchers, "Love Potion Number Nine," 1964
John Mayall's Bluesbreakers, *John Mayall's Bluesbreakers with Eric Clapton*, 1966
Marvelettes, "Please Mr. Postman," 1961
Beatles, "Please Mr. Postman," 1964
Beatles, "You Really Got a Hold on Me," 1964
Arthur Alexander, "Anna," 1962
Beatles, "Anna," 1964
———, "Money," 1964
James Brown, "Please Please Please," 1964

Who, "Please Please Please," 1965
James Brown, "I Don't Mind," 1961
Who, "I Don't Mind," 1965
Surfaris, "Wipe Out," 1963
Kingsmen, "Louie Louie," 1963
Otis Redding, "Pain in My Heart," 1963
Rolling Stones, "Pain in My Heart," 1965
Penguins, "Earth Angel," 1954
Five Satins, "In the Still of the Night," 1956
Mystics, "Hushabye," 1959
Dion and the Belmonts, "I Wonder Why," 1958
Dell Vikings, "Come Go with Me," 1957
Crests, "Sixteen Candles," 1958
Four Seasons, "Let's Hang On," 1965
———, "Sherry," 1962
———, "Big Girls Don't Cry," 1962
Righteous Brothers, "You've Lost that Lovin' Feeling," 1964
———, "Soul and Inspiration," 1966
Rascals, "Groovin'," 1967
———, "People Got to Be Free," 1968

Fats Domino, "Ain't That a Shame," 1955
Pat Boone, "Ain't That a Shame," 1955
Charms, "Two Hearts," 1955
Pat Boone, "Two Hearts," 1955
Flamingos, "I'll Be Home," 1956
Pat Boone, "I'll Be Home," 1956
Little Richard, "Long Tall Sally," 1956
Pat Boone, "Long Tall Sally," 1956
Little Richard, "Tutti Frutti," 1956
Pat Boone, "Tutti Frutti," 1956
Beach Boys, "Surfer Girl," 1963
———, "Surfin' USA," 1963
Chuck Berry, "Sweet Little Sixteen," 1958
Arthur Alexander, "You Better Move On," 1962
Rolling Stones, "You Better Move On," 1965
———, "Can I Get a Witness," 1964
Marvin Gaye, "Can I Get a Witness," 1963
John Lee Hooker, "Boom Boom," 1962
Animals, "Boom Boom," 1965
Jimmy Reed, "Bright Lights, Big City," 1961
Animals, "Bright Lights, Big City," 1965
Animals, "We Gotta Get Out of This Place," 1965
Bruce Springsteen, "It's My Life" (live in Memphis), 1976

Rolling Stones, "19th Nervous Breakdown," 1966
———, "Sympathy for the Devil," 1968
———, "Gimme Shelter," 1969
Muddy Waters, "I Can't Be Satisfied," 1948
Otis Redding, "Satisfaction," 1966
Aretha Franklin, "Satisfaction," 1967

Otis Redding, "I've Been Loving You Too Long" (live at Monterey), 1967
Mamas and Papas, "California Dreamin'," 1966
Scott McKenzie, "San Francisco (Be Sure to Wear Some Flowers in Your Hair)," 1967
Byrds, "Chimes of Freedom," 1965
Lou Rawls, "Love Is a Hurtin' Thing," 1966
———, "Dead End Street," 1967
———, "Tobacco Road," 1976
Who, "My Generation" (live at Monterey), 1967
Eric Burdon and the Animals, "Monterey," 1967
Jimi Hendrix, "Killing Floor" (live at Monterey), 1967
———, "Like a Rolling Stone" (live at Monterey), 1967
———, "Wild Thing" (live at Monterey), 1967
———, "Fire" (live at Monterey), 1967
———, "Purple Haze" (live at Monterey), 1967
Buffalo Springfield, "For What It's Worth," 1967
Janis Joplin, "Down on Me," 1967
———, "Ball and Chain," 1967
Jimi Hendrix, "The Star-Spangled Banner" (live at Woodstock), 1969
Sly and the Family Stone, "I Want to Take You Higher" (live at Woodstock), 1969
Beatles, *Sgt. Pepper's Lonely Hearts Club Band*, 1967
Otis Redding, "Dock of the Bay," 1968
———, "Try a Little Tenderness," 1966
———, "Ton of Joy," 1966

Dorothy Love Coates and the Original Gospel Harmonettes, "You Better Run to the City of Refuge," 1955
———, "That's Enough," 1956
Ray Charles, "That's Enough," 1959
Johnny Cash, "That's Enough," 1958
Dorothy Love Coates and the Original Gospel Harmonettes, "I Wouldn't Mind Dying," 1954
———, "99 1/2 Won't Do," 1955
Traditional, "Nobody Knows the Trouble I've Seen"
———, "Go Down Moses"

Dorothy Love Coates and the Original Gospel Harmonettes, "Get Away Jordan" medley, 1955
Supremes, "Where Did Our Love Go?" 1964
———, "Nothing but Heartaches," 1965
Ray Charles, "I Can't Stop Loving You," 1962
———, "A Worried Mind," 1962
Mahalia Jackson, "I'm Gonna Live the Life I Sing About in My Song," 1958
Sly and the Family Stone, "I Want to Take You Higher," 1969


## SECTION TWO

Sly and the Family Stone, "Stand," 1969
———, "Don't Call Me Nigger, Whitey," 1969
———, "Everyday People," 1968
———, "Family Affair," 1971


Jimi Hendrix, "All Along the Watchtower," 1968
———, "Machine Gun," 1970
———, "Love or Confusion," 1967
Sgt. Barry Sadler, "Ballad of the Green Berets," 1966
Pete Seeger, "Waist Deep in the Big Muddy," 1967
Tim Buckley, "No Man Can Find the War," 1967
Tom Paxton, "Lyndon Johnson Told the Nation," 1968
———, "Talking Vietnam Potluck Blues," 1969
Byrds, "Draft Morning," 1968
Creedence Clearwater Revival, "Run Through the Jungle," 1970
———, "Who'll Stop the Rain," 1970
John Lennon and Yoko Ono, "Give Peace a Chance," 1969
Country Joe and the Fish, "I Feel Like I'm Fixin' to Die," 1967
Doors, "Five to One," 1968
———, "The Unknown Soldier," 1968
Turtles, "It Ain't Me Babe," 1965
Tommy James and the Shondells, "Sweet Cherry Wine," 1969
Edwin Starr, "War," 1970
Eddie Harris and Les McCann, "Compared to What?" 1970
Fifth Dimension, "Let the Sun Shine In/The Age of Aquarius," 1969
Freda Payne, "Bring the Boys Home," 1971
Jimmy Cliff, "Vietnam," 1970
Funkadelic, "Wars of Armageddon," 1971
———, "Maggot Brain," 1971
Little Feat, "Mercenary Territory," 1975
Radiators, "Zigzagging Through Ghostland," 1989
Funkadelic, "March to the Witch's Castle," 1973
Curtis Mayfield, Back to the World, 1973

*      *      *

Aretha Franklin, "Respect," 1967
Archie Shepp, "Attica Blues," 1972
————, "The Cry of My People," 1973
————, "Money Blues," 1971
John Coltrane, "Meditations," 1966
Albert Ayler, "Spiritual Unity," 1964


Aretha Franklin, "I Never Loved a Man," 1967
————, "Think," 1968
————, "Rock Steady," 1971
————, "Spanish Harlem," 1971
————, "Chain of Fools," 1967
Rev. C. L. Franklin, "The Eagle Stirreth in His Nest," c. 1960
Aretha Franklin, *Aretha Live at Fillmore West*, 1971
————, *Amazing Grace*, 1972
————, "The Thrill Is Gone," 1970
B. B. King, "The Thrill Is Gone," 1969
Aretha Franklin, "Young, Gifted and Black," 1972
————, "Spirit in the Dark," 1970
————, "Border Song (Holy Moses)," 1970


Miles Davis (with John Coltrane), "So What," 1959
————, "Bye Bye Blackbird," 1955
Thelonious Monk (with John Coltrane), "Trinkle, Trinkle," 1957
————, "Ruby, My Dear," 1957
John Coltrane, "Alabama," 1963
————, "Spiritual," 1961
————, "Song of the Underground Railroad," 1961
————, "Wise One," 1964
————, "Africa," 1961
————, "Ascension," 1965
————, *A Love Supreme*, 1964
Beethoven, "Ode to Joy" (from the Ninth Symphony)


Bobby Timmons, "This Here," 1960
————, "Dat Dere," 1960
Thelonious Monk, "Misterioso," 1951
Duke Ellington, "Satin Doll," 1958


James Brown, "Cold Sweat," 1967
————, "Papa's Got a Brand New Bag," 1965
————, "I'll Go Crazy" (live at the Apollo), 1963
————, "Please Please Please" (live at the Apollo), 1963

Byrds, "Eight Miles High," 1966
John Coltrane, "India," 1961
Miles Davis, "Miles Runs the Voodoo Down," 1970
Karlheinz Stockhausen, *Hymnen,* 1967
———, "Pharaoh's Dance," 1970
Jimi Hendrix, "Foxy Lady," 1967
———, "Angel," 1970
———, "Hey Baby (New Rising Sun)," 1970
John Coltrane, *Interstellar Space,* 1967
Miles Davis, "Right Off," 1970
Sonny Sharrock, *Seize the Rainbow,* 1987
———, *Guitar,* 1986
Jimi Hendrix with Larry Young, *Nine to the Universe,* 1969 (released 1980)

Curtis Mayfield, "(Don't Worry) If There's a Hell Below We're All Gonna
    Go," 1970
Jimi Hendrix, "Little Wing," 1968
———, "Message to Love," 1970
Impressions, "People Get Ready," 1965
———, "I'm So Proud," 1964
Roscoe Mitchell, "Spiritual," c. 1970
Muhal Richard Abrams, "Blues Forever," 1982
Little Walter, "Dead Presidents," 1963
KoKo Taylor, "Insane Asylum," 1967
Bo Diddley, "You Can't Judge a Book by Its Cover," 1962
Herbie Hancock, "Watermelon Man," 1962
———, "Maiden Voyage," 1965
———, "Riot," 1968
Ramsey Lewis, "The In Crowd," 1965
———, "Wade in the Water," 1966
Impressions, "Keep on Pushing," 1964
———, "We're a Winner," 1967
———, "This Is My Country," 1968
———, "Choice of Colors," 1969
Curtis Mayfield, "Superfly," 1972
———, "Stone Junkie," 1971
———, "I Plan to Stay a Believer," 1971
———, "The Other Side of Town," 1970
———, "Mighty, Mighty (Spade & Whitey)" (live version), 1971
———, "We Gotta Have Peace," 1972
———, "Beautiful Brother of Mine," 1972
Isaac Hayes, "Shaft," 1971
Bobby Womack, "Across 110th Street," 1973
Marvin Gaye, "Trouble Man," 1972

Curtis Mayfield, "Pusherman," 1972

———, "Freddie's Dead," 1972

———, "New World Order," 1996

———, "Doo Doo Wop Is Strong in Here," 1997

———, "It's Alright," 1979

———, "Never Say You Can't Survive," 1977

———, "Something to Believe In," 1980


Creedence Clearwater Revival, "Green River," 1969

———, "Wrote a Song for Everyone," 1969

Ike and Tina Turner, "Proud Mary," 1971

Creedence Clearwater Revival, "Down on the Corner," 1969

———, "Don't Look Now," 1969

———, "Cotton Fields," 1969

Clarence Ashley, "The Coo Coo Bird," 1929

Dock Boggs, "Sugar Baby," 1928

Furry Lewis, "Kassie Jones," 1928

Mississippi John Hurt, "Frankie," 1928

Blind Lemon Jefferson, "See that My Grave Is Kept Clean," 1928

Blind Willie Johnson, "John the Revelator," 1930

Skip James, "Devil Got My Woman," 1931

Tommy Johnson, "Big Road Blues," 1928

Ralph Stanley, "Rank Stranger," 1954

Hank Williams, "Lost Highway," 1949

Creedence Clearwater Revival, "Wrote a Song for Everyone," 1969

———, "Proud Mary," 1969

———, "Born on the Bayou," 1969

———, "Bootleg," 1969

———, "Bad Moon Rising," 1969

———, "Sinister Purpose," 1969

Bob Dylan, "Desolation Row," 1965

Bessie Smith, "Downhearted Blues," 1923

Howlin' Wolf, "Killing Floor," 1964

Creedence Clearwater Revival, "Fortunate Son," 1969

———, "Midnight Special," 1969

John Fogerty, "Old Man Down the Road," 1984


Gil Scott-Heron, "The Revolution Will Not Be Televised," 1970

Mothers of Invention, "Trouble Comin' Every Day," 1967

Last Poets, *This Is Madness,* 1969

Watts Prophets, *Rappin' Black in a White World,* c. 1970

Gil Scott-Heron, "Whitey's on the Moon," 1970

Loretta Lynn, "Coal Miner's Daughter," 1970

———, "One's on the Way," 1972

Merle Haggard, "Okie from Muskogee," 1969

———, "Working Man's Blues," 1969
———, "Hungry Eyes," 1969
———, "Mama Tried," 1970
———, "California Blues," 1969
Charley Pride, "Kiss an Angel Good Morning," 1971
———, "Is There Anybody Going to San Antone," 1970
———, "The Snakes Crawl Out at Night," 1969
Waylon Jennings, "Black Rose," 1973
Neil Young, "Southern Man," 1970
———, "Alabama," 1972
Lynyrd Skynyrd, "Sweet Home Alabama," 1974
———, "Gimme Three Steps," 1973
———, "That Smell," 1977

"Lift Every Voice and Sing"
Supremes, "Love Child," 1968
Temptations, "Ain't Too Proud to Beg," 1966
———, "Beauty Is Only Skin Deep," 1966
———, "I'm Losing You," 1966
———, "I Wish It Would Rain," 1968
Gladys Knight and the Pips, "I Heard It Through the Grapevine," 1967
Temptations, "Cloud Nine," 1968
———, "Papa Was a Rollin' Stone," 1972
Stevie Wonder, "Superstition," 1972
———, "Maybe Your Baby," 1972
———, "I Believe (When I Fall in Love It Will Be Forever)," 1972
———, "For Once in My Life," 1968
Supremes and Temptations, "I'm Going to Make You Love Me," 1968
Jackson Five, "I Want You Back," 1969
Isaac Hayes, "By the Time I Get to Phoenix," 1969
———, "One Woman," 1969
———, "Walk on By," 1969
Soul Children, "I'll Be the Other Woman," 1974
Frederick Knight, "I've Been Lonely for Too Long," 1972
Dramatics, "Whatcha See Is Whatcha Get," 1971
———, "In the Rain," 1972
Staple Singers, "Respect Yourself," 1971
———, "If You're Ready," 1973
———, "City in the Sky," 1974
———, "Touch a Hand, Make a Friend," 1974
———, "I'll Take You There," 1972

James Brown, "Say It Loud (I'm Black and I'm Proud)," 1968
O'Jays, "Back Stabbers," 1972

Undisputed Truth, "Smiling Faces Sometimes," 1971
Gladys Knight and the Pips, "I've Got to Use My Imagination," 1973
Chi-Lites, "(For God's Sake) Give More Power to the People," 1971
———, "Have You Seen Her?" 1971
Donny Hathaway, "The Ghetto," 1970
———, "Giving Up," 1971
———, "Someday We'll All Be Free," 1973
Nina Simone, "I Loves You Porgy," 1959
———, "Sinnerman," 1965
———, "I Put a Spell on You," 1965
———, "I Shall Be Released," 1970
———, "Mississippi Goddam," 1964
———, "Young, Gifted and Black," 1969
———, "Four Women," 1966
———, "Why (The King of Love Is Dead)," 1970
Roberta Flack, "Go Up Moses," 1971
Donny Hathaway and Roberta Flack, "Where Is the Love?" 1972


**SECTION THREE**
Al Green, "Love and Happiness," 1977
———, "Let's Stay Together," 1971
———, "I'm Still in Love with You," 1972
Syl Johnson, "Take Me to the River," 1975
Temptations, "I Can't Get Next to You," 1969
Al Green, "I Can't Get Next to You," 1970
———, "Back Up Train," 1967
Traditional, "Ain't No Chains Strong Enough to Bind Me"
Al Green, "Tired of Being Alone," 1971
Ann Peebles, "I Can't Stand the Rain," 1973
———, "Breaking Up Somebody's Home," 1972
———, "I'm Gonna Tear Your Playhouse Down," 1973
Traditional, "Samson and Delilah"
Al Green, "Call Me," 1973
———, "Here I Am," 1973
———, "Take Me to the River," 1974
———, "Belle," 1978
——— with Shirley Caeser, "Sailing (On the Sea of His Love)," 1987

Parliament, "Chocolate City," 1975
Earth, Wind & Fire, "Devotion," 1974

Stevie Wonder, "Heaven Help Us All," 1970
———, "Higher Ground," 1973

————, "Love's in Need of Love Today," 1976
————, "Black Man," 1976
Beach Boys, "Good Vibrations," 1966
Walter Carlos, *Switched-On Bach*, 1969
Cream, "Strange Brew," 1967
————, "Tales of Brave Ulysses," 1967
Beatles, "We Can Work It Out," 1965
Stevie Wonder, "We Can Work It Out," 1971
————, "Living for the City," 1973
————, "Easy Goin' Evening (My Mama's Call)," 1976
————, "Village Ghetto Land," 1976
————, "Ordinary Pain," 1976
————, "Joy Inside My Tears," 1976
————, "As," 1976
————, "Sir Duke," 1976
————, "Isn't She Lovely," 1976
————, "Golden Lady," 1973
————, "Dark 'n Lovely," 1987
————, "Big Brother," 1972
————, "You Haven't Done Nothin'," 1974
————, *Journey Through the Secret Life of Plants*, 1979
————, "Happy Birthday Martin," 1980
————, "Apartheid (It's Wrong)," 1985
————, "Front Line," 1982

MFSB, "TSOP," 1974
Delfonics, "La La Means I Love You," 1968
————, "I'm Sorry," 1968
————, "Didn't I (Blow Your Mind This Time)," 1970
Intruders, "Cowboys to Girls," 1968
Wilson Pickett, "Don't Let the Green Grass Fool You," 1971
Jerry Butler, "Only the Strong Survive," 1969
Harold Melvin and the Blue Notes, "Wake Up Everybody," 1975
————, "Bad Luck," 1975
O'Jays, "Put Your Hands Together," 1973
————, "Don't Call Me Brother," 1973
Lou Rawls, "You'll Never Find Another Love Like Mine," 1976
Three Degrees, "When Will I See You Again?" 1974
Commodores, "Sail On," 1979
Spinners, "I'll Be Around," 1972
————, "Ghetto Child," 1973
————, "Could It Be I'm Falling in Love," 1973
Manhattans, "Kiss and Say Goodbye," 1976
Chi-Lites, "Oh Girl," 1972

Hall and Oates, "She's Gone," 1976
Fleetwood Mac, "Rhiannon," 1976
Eagles, "Take It to the Limit," 1975
Harold Melvin and the Blue Notes, "If You Don't Know Me By Now," 1972
McFadden and Whitehead, "Ain't No Stoppin' Us Now," 1979
Luther Vandross, "Never Too Much," 1981
Anita Baker, "Angel," 1983
Phyllis Hyman, "Living All Alone," 1986
Frankie Beverly and Maze, "Joy and Pain," 1980
O'Jays, "For the Love of Money," 1974
————, "Love Train," 1973
————, "Ship Ahoy," 1973
Harold Melvin and the Blue Notes, "I Miss You," 1972
————, "Don't Leave Me This Way," 1975

Chic, "Dance Dance Dance," 1977
————, "Everybody's Dancing," 1978
————, "Le Freak," 1978
Sister Sledge, "He's the Greatest Dancer," 1979
————, "Lost in Music," 1979
————, "We Are Family," 1979
Chic, "Good Times," 1979
Queen, "Another One Bites the Dust," 1980
Platters, "Smoke Gets in Your Eyes," 1959
Eddie Kendricks, "Keep On Truckin'," 1973
————, "Boogie Down," 1974
Jacksons, "Dancing Machine," 1974
Chaka Khan and Rufus, "You Got the Love," 1974
————, "Sweet Thing," 1976
James Brown, "Doing It to Death," 1973
Lyn Collins, "Think," 1972
Kool and the Gang, "Jungle Boogie," 1973
————, "Higher Plane," 1974
————, "Spirit of the Boogie," 1975
Donna Summer, "Love to Love You Baby," 1975
————, "Hot Stuff," 1979
————, "Bad Girls," 1979
————, "She Works Hard for the Money," 1983
Gloria Gaynor, "I Will Survive," 1978
Marvin Gaye, "Let's Get It On," 1973
————, "Keep Gettin' It On," 1973
————, "Sanctified Lady," released 1985
Sylvester, "Dance (Disco Heat)," 1978
————, "Power of Love," c. 1979

————, "You Make Me Feel (Mighty Real)," 1979
————, "Trouble in Paradise," c. 1979
————, "Cry Me a River," 1980
Teddy Pendergrass, "You Can't Hide from Yourself," 1977
Sylvester, "Sell My Soul," 1980

*Saturday Night Fever* soundtrack, 1977
Rolling Stones, "Miss You," 1978
Ohio Players, "I Want to Be Free," 1975
————, "Fire," 1974
Isley Brothers, "It's Your Thing," 1969
————, "Harvest for the World," 1976
Bar-Kays, "Cozy," 1976
————, "Holy Ghost," 1978
Slave, "Slide," 1977
Brass Construction, "Movin'," 1976
War, "Cinco de Mayo," 1981
————, "The World Is a Ghetto," 1972
————, "Low Rider," 1975
Isley Brothers, "Fight the Power," 1975
Earth, Wind & Fire, "Africano/Power," 1975
————, "Sun Goddess," 1975
————, "Gratitude," 1975
————, "Celebrate," 1975
————, "New World Symphony," 1975
————, "Reasons," 1975

Lou Reed, "I Wanna Be Black," 1978
————, "Walk on the Wild Side," 1973
Patti Smith, "Rock 'n' Roll Nigger," 1978
————, "Radio Ethiopia Medley," 1976
Talking Heads, *Remain in Light,* 1980
Brian Eno and David Byrne, *My Life in the Bush of Ghosts,* 1981
Blondie, "Rapture," 1981
————, "The Tide Is High," 1980
————, "Heart of Glass," 1979
Simon and Garfunkel, "Go Tell It on the Mountain," 1966
————, "The Times They Are A-Changin'," 1966
Paul Simon, "Me and Julio down by the Schoolyard," 1972
————, "Mother and Child Reunion," 1972
———— with the Dixie Hummingbirds, "Love Me Like a Rock," 1973
Simon and Garfunkel, "Bridge over Troubled Water," 1970
Aretha Franklin, "Bridge over Troubled Water," 1971
Paul Simon with the Jessy Dixon Singers, "Bridge over Troubled Water," 1974

The Band with the Staple Singers, "The Weight," 1978
The Band, "This Wheel's on Fire," 1968
———, "I Shall Be Released," 1968
Jackson Browne, "The Pretender," 1977

Bruce Springsteen, "Rosalita," 1975
———, "Born to Run," 1975
———, "Backstreets," 1975
———, "Incident on 57th Street," 1975
———, "Jungleland," 1977
Chuck Berry, "Around and Around," 1964
Bruce Springsteen, "Around and Around" (live)
Buddy Holly, "Rave On," 1958
Bruce Springsteen, "Rave On" (live)
Elvis Presley, "I Can't Help Falling in Love with You," 1961
Bruce Springsteen, "I Can't Help Falling in Love with You" (live)
Little Richard, "Good Golly Miss Molly," 1958
———, "Jenny Jenny," 1957
Mitch Ryder and the Detroit Wheels, "Devil with a Blue Dress," 1966
———, "Jenny Take a Ride," 1965
Bruce Springsteen, "Detroit Medley" (live)
Manfred Mann, "Pretty Flamingo," 1966
Bruce Springsteen, "Pretty Flamingo" (live)
Yardbirds, "Heart Full of Soul," 1965
Bruce Springsteen, "Heart Full of Soul" (live)
Searchers, "Needles and Pins," 1964
Bruce Springsteen, "Needles and Pins" (live)
Sam Cooke, "Shake," 1965
Bruce Springsteen, "Shake" (live)
Jackie Wilson, "Higher and Higher," 1967
Bruce Springsteen, "Higher and Higher" (live)
Solomon Burke, "Cry to Me," 1962
Bruce Springsteen, "Cry to Me" (live)
Eddie Floyd, "Raise Your Hand," 1967
———, "Knock on Wood," 1966
Bruce Springsteen with Eddie Floyd, "Raise Your Hand" (live)
———, "Knock on Wood" (live)
Crystals, "Then He Kissed Me," 1963
Bruce Springsteen, "Then She Kissed Me" (live)
Darlene Love, "Fine Fine Boy," 1963
Bruce Springsteen, "Fine Fine Girl" (live)
James Brown, "Prisoner of Love," 1963
Bruce Springsteen, "Prisoner of Rock 'n' Roll" (live in New Jersey), 1979
Clash, "Washington Bullets," 1981

Culture, *Two Sevens Clash,* 1977
Clash, "White Riot," 1979
———, "White Man in Hammersmith Palais," 1979
Toots and the Maytals, "Pressure Drop," 1970
Clash, "Pressure Drop," 1980
Rulers, "Wrong 'em Boyo," c. 1976
Clash, "Wrong 'em Boyo," 1980
Junior Murvin, "Police and Thieves," 1977
Clash, "Police and Thieves," 1979
———, "Rudie Can't Fail," 1980
———, "Lost in the Supermarket," 1980
———, "Clampdown," 1980
———, "The Guns of Brixton," 1980
———, "Death or Glory," 1980
———, "Revolution Rock," 1980
Bob Marley, "Punky Reggae Party," 1978

James Blood Ulmer, "Jazz Is the Teacher (Funk Is the Preacher)," 1994
Funkadelic, *Free Your Mind and Your Ass Will Follow,* 1970
Parliament, "Up for the Downstroke," 1974
———, "Standing on the Verge of Gettin' It On," 1974
———, "P-Funk," 1976
———, "Tear the Roof off the Sucker (Give Up the Funk)," 1976
———, "Flash Light," 1978
Funkadelic, "Cosmic Slop," 1973
George Clinton, "Doo Doo Chasers," 1983
Parliament, "Aqua Boogie (A Psychoalphadiscobetabioaquadoloop)," 1979
George Clinton, "Loopzilla," 1982

Bob Marley and the Wailers, "One Love," 1977
Burning Spear, "Marcus Garvey," 1976
Steel Pulse, "Worth His Weight in Gold (Rally Round)," 1982
Jimmy Cliff, "You Can Get It If You Really Want," 1975
———, "Sitting in Limbo," 1975
———, "The Harder They Come," 1975
Melodians, "Rivers of Babylon," 1975
X Clan, *To the East, Blackwards,* 1990
Bob Marley and the Wailers, "Exodus," 1977
———, "Concrete Jungle," 1975
———, "Slave Driver," 1975
———, "400 Years," 1975
———, *Kaya,* 1978
———, "No Woman No Cry," 1975
Toots and the Maytals, "Spiritual Healing," 1983

Marvin Gaye, "Sexual Healing," 1982
Bob Marley and the Wailers, "Them Belly Full," 1975
———, "Rebel Music (3 O'clock Roadblock)," 1975
———, "Natty Dread," 1975
———, "Redemption Song," 1980

Cab Calloway, "Minnie the Moocher," 1932
Shirley Ellis, "The Name Game," 1964
Monkees, "Mary, Mary," 1967
Sugar Hill Gang, "Rapper's Delight," 1979
Mickey and Sylvia, "Love Is Strange," 1957
Shirley and Company, "Shame Shame Shame," 1975
Grandmaster Flash and the Furious Five, "The Message," 1982

## SECTION FOUR

Public Enemy, "Welcome to the Terrordome," 1990
N.W.A., "Fuck the Police," 1989
Bruce Springsteen, "Badlands" (live), recorded 1980
———, "War" (live), 1986
Robert Johnson, "Me and the Devil Blues," 1937
Public Enemy, "Night of the Living Baseheads," 1988

WC and MAAD Circle, "Ain't a Damn Thing Changed," 1991
Paris, "Bush Killa," 1992
Tone Loc, "Wild Thing," 1988

Ice T, "Squeeze the Trigger," 1987
Gil Scott-Heron, "Re-Ron," 1984
———, "B Movie," 1981
Run-D.M.C., "It's Like That," 1983
Grandmaster Flash and the Furious Five, "White Lines," 1983
Sinead O'Connor and M.C. Lyte, "I Want Your Hands on Me," 1988
Talking Heads, *Stop Making Sense,* 1984
Suzanne Vega, "Tom's Diner," 1987
Time Zone, "World Destruction," 1984
Run-D.M.C., "Hard Times," 1984
———, "Rock Box," 1984
———, "Rock the House," 1985
———, "Can You Rock It Like This?" 1985
—— with Aerosmith, "Walk This Way," 1986

Carl Perkins, "Blue Suede Shoes," 1956
Fats Domino, "Blueberry Hill," 1956

Elvis Presley, "Mystery Train," 1954
———, "Good Rockin' Tonight," 1954
———, "Milkcow Blues Boogie," 1954
Chuck Berry, "Johnny B. Goode," 1958
———, "Roll Over Beethoven," 1956
———, "Maybellene," 1955
Little Richard, "Rip It Up," 1956
———, "Slippin' and Slidin' (Peepin' and Hidin')," 1956
Da Lench Mob, "You and Your Heroes," 1992
U2, "Elvis Presley and America," 1984
Nick Cave, "Tupelo," 1985
Paul Simon, "Graceland," 1986
Public Enemy, "Fight the Power," 1989
Living Colour, "Cult of Personality," 1989
———, "Elvis Is Dead," 1990
John Trudell, "Baby Boom Che," 1992
Elvis Presley, "Don't Be Cruel," 1956
———, "I Want You, I Need You, I Love You," 1956
———, "Jailhouse Rock," 1957
Passengers, "Elvis Ate America," 1995
Elvis Presley, "American Trilogy," 1972
Mojo Nixon and Skid Roper, "Elvis Is Everywhere," 1987

Michael Jackson, "Rock with You," 1979
———, "Don't Stop Til You Get Enough," 1979
———, "Billie Jean," 1983
———, "Beat It," 1983
———, "Black or White," 1991
Madonna, "Lucky Star," 1984
———, "Like a Virgin," 1984
———, "Material Girl," 1985
———, "Live to Tell," 1986
———, "Papa Don't Preach," 1986
Patti Smith, "Gloria," 1975
Pretenders, "Stop Your Sobbing," 1980
———, "Brass in Pocket (I'm Special)," 1980
Liz Phair, "Whip-Smart," 1994
Alanis Morisette, "Hand in My Pocket," 1995
———, "All I Really Want," 1995
Ruth Brown, "Mama, He Treats Your Daughter Mean," 1962
KoKo Taylor, "Wang Dang Doodle," 1966
Jan Bradley, "Mama Didn't Lie," 1963
LaBelle, "Lady Marmalade," 1975

Tina Turner, "What's Love Got to Do with It?" 1984
Madonna, "Like a Prayer," 1989

Prince, "Head," 1980
———, "Do Me, Baby," 1981
———, "Purple Rain," 1984
Beatles, *Magical Mystery Tour,* 1967
Prince, "The Ladder," 1985
———, "Temptation," 1985
———, "Housequake," 1987
———, "The Most Beautiful Girl in the World," 1994
———, "Sign of the Times," 1987
———, "When Doves Cry," 1984
———, "1999," 1982
———, "The Cross," 1987
———, "I Wish U Heaven," 1988
———, "Kiss," 1986
———, "God," 1984
Wynton Marsalis, *Blood on the Fields,* 1996

Kraftwerk, "Trans-Europe Express," 1978
Jamie Principle, "We Dance to Political Destruction," c. 1985
Adeva, "Respect," 1989
Loletta Holloway, "Hit and Run," 1977
Liz Torres, "Can't Get Enough," 1986
MFSB, "Love Is the Message," 1974
Blaze, "We Must All Live Together," 1988
CeCe Rodgers, "Someday," 1984
First Choice, "Let No Man Put Asunder," c. 1977
Inner Life, "Ain't No Mountain High Enough," c. 1980
Fingers, "Our House," 1985

Public Enemy, "Don't Believe the Hype," 1988
Eric B and Rakim, "Eric B Is President," 1986
———, "I Know You Got Soul," 1987
———, "Follow the Leader," 1988
Public Enemy, "Bring the Noise," 1988
———, "Contract on the World Love Jam," 1990
———, "Rebel Without a Pause," 1988
EPMD, "Strictly Business," 1988
Bob Marley, "I Shot the Sheriff," 1974
Eric Clapton, "I Shot the Sheriff," 1974
Public Enemy, "Bring the Noise," 1988
———, "Who Stole the Soul?" 1990

————, "911 Is a Joke," 1990
Terminator X, "The Blues," 1991

N.W.A., "Eight Ball," 1988
————, "Dope Man," 1989
————, "Straight Outta Compton," 1989
————, "Gangsta Gangsta," 1989
————, "To Kill a Hooker," 1991
————, "Appetite for Destruction," 1991
Guns n' Roses, "Welcome to the Jungle," 1988
————, "Paradise City," 1988
————, "One in a Million," 1988
————, "I Used to Love Her," 1988
Ice Cube, "The Nigga Ya Love to Hate," 1990
Parliament, "Star Child (Mothership Connection)," 1976
Dr. Dre, "Let Me Ride," 1993
Ice Cube, "Bop Gun (One Nation)," 1993
Parliament, "Bop Gun (Endangered Species)," 1977
Funkadelic, "One Nation Under a Groove," 1978
Ice Cube, "True to the Game," 1991
Gap Band, "Outstanding," 1982
Schooly D, "P.S.K. (What Does It Mean?)," 1985
Digital Underground, "Sex Packets," 1990
Boogie Down Productions, *Criminal Minded,* 1987
————, *By Any Means Necessary,* 1988
————, "Love's Gonna Get You (Material Love)," 1990
Jocelyn Brown, "Love's Gonna Get You," 1986
Ice Cube, "My Summer Vacation," 1991
George Clinton, "Atomic Dog," 1983
Eric B and Rakim, "Know the Ledge," 1992
————, "My Melody," 1987
————, "In the Ghetto," 1990
24-Carat Black, "The Ghetto (Misfortune's Wealth)," 1973

Bruce Springsteen, "This Land Is Your Land," 1986
————, "My Hometown," 1984
————, "Seeds," 1986
Various artists, "We Are the World," 1985
————, "Sun City," 1985
Bruce Springsteen, "Cover Me" (Arthur Baker remix), 1984
————, "Cross My Heart," 1992
————, "Roll of the Dice," 1992
————, "Soul Driver," 1992
————, "57 Channels and Nothing On" (remix), 1992

————, "Born in the U.S.A.," 1984
————, "Out in the Street," 1980
————, "Spirit in the Night," 1975
————, "Atlantic City," 1982
————, "Johnny 99," 1982
————, "Reason to Believe," 1982
————, "Highway Patrolman," 1982
————, "The Promised Land," 1978
————, "Thunder Road," 1975
————, "Darkness on the Edge of Town," 1978
————, "Rosalita" (live), 1975
————, "Badlands," 1978
Public Enemy, "Rightstarter (Message to a Black Man)," 1987


## SECTION FIVE

Rage Against the Machine, "Vietnow," 1996
Sounds of Blackness, "The Pressure, Part One," 1991
Iris DeMent, "Wasteland of the Free," 1996
Eurythmics with Aretha Franklin, "Sisters Are Doing It for Themselves," 1985


Wu-Tang Clan, "C.R.E.A.M.," 1994
Scarface, "Money Makes the World Go Round," 1997
Junior M.A.F.I.A., "Get Money," 1995
Bone Thugs n Harmony, "Foe Tha Love of $," 1994
Snoop Doggy Dog, "Tha Shiznit," 1993
————, "Gin and Juice," 1993
Puff Daddy and the Family, "All About the Benjamins," 1997
Leadbelly, "Another Man Done Gone," 1934
Blind Willie McTell, "Dying Crapshooter's Ball," 1949
Tupac Shakur, "Something Wicked," 1991
————, "Violent," 1991
————, "Trapped," 1991
————, "Rebel of the Underground," 1991
————, "Brenda's Got a Baby," 1991
————, "Keep Ya Head Up," 1993
Five Stairsteps, "Ooh Child," 1970
Zapp, "Be Alright," 1980
Tupac Shakur, "Words of Wisdom," 1992
————, "Holler If Ya Hear Me," 1993
————, "Dear Mama," 1995


Snoop Doggy Dog, "Gz Up, Hoes Down," 1993

Ice Cube, "Once upon a Time in the Projects," 1990
Me'Shell NdegeOcello, "Step into the Projects (Where I Found Love),"
    1993
———, "Dred Loc," 1993
———, "I'm Diggin' You (Like an Old Soul Record)," 1993
Dianne Reeves, "Endangered Species," 1994
Ice Cube, "Endangered Species," 1990
Cassandra Wilson, "Death Letter," 1995
Son House, "Death Letter Blues," 1942
Rachelle Ferrell, "Too Late," 1992
———, "Open Arms," 1992
Anita Baker, "Whatever It Takes," 1990
Soul II Soul, "Keep on Movin'," 1989
Tricky, "Aftermath," 1994
Marvin Gaye, "The End of Our Road," 1970
Public Enemy, "Black Steel in the Hour of Chaos," 1988
Tricky, "Black Steel in the Hour of Chaos," 1994
Brand New Heavies, "Brother Sister," 1994
Drizabone, "Real Love," 1994
Incognito, "Keep the Fires Burning," 1994
———, "Deep Waters," 1994
Young Disciples, "Apparently Nothing (Soul River)," 1993
———, "Freedom Suite," 1993
Seal, "Fast Changes," 1994
———, "People Asking Why," 1994
———, "Prayer for the Dying," 1994
Erykah Badu, "On and On," 1997
Maxwell, "Ascension (Don't Ever Wander)," 1996
Mary J. Blige, "You Remind Me," 1992
———, "Real Love," 1992
Method Man with Mary J. Blige, "I'll Be There for You/You're All I Need
    to Get By," 1995
Aaliyah, "Back and Forth," 1994
Toni Braxton, "Love Shoulda Brought You Home," 1992
Monifah, "I Miss You (Come Back Home)," 1995
Brandy, "I Wanna Be Down," 1994
——— with LL Cool J, "Sittin' up in My Room," 1995
Tracie Spencer, "Tender Kisses," 1991
Brownstone, "If You Love Me," 1994
Allure with Nas, "Head over Heels," 1997
Changing Faces, "G.H.E.T.T.O.U.T.," 1997
R. Kelly, "I Believe I Can Fly," 1996
Sparkle, "Be Careful," 1998
Eric Benet, "Spiritual Thang," 1996

Ali, "Love Letter," 1998
Solo, "Holding On," 1995
———, "Cupid," 1995
Sam Cooke, "Another Saturday Night," 1963
Solo, "Another Saturday Night," 1995
———, "A Change Is Gonna Come," 1995
Solomon Burke, "A Change Is Gonna Come," 1986
Joi, "Freedom," 1994
*Panther* All-Star Choir, "Freedom," 1995
*Panther* All-Star Choir, "Freedom" (rap version), 1995
Monkees, "Girl I Knew Somewhere," 1967
Spice Girls, "Wannabe," 1996
Hanson, "MMMbop," 1997
Boyz II Men, "Motownphilly," 1991
———, "End of the Road," 1992
Elvis Presley, "Hound Dog," 1956
Hootie and the Blowfish, "I Only Wanna Be with You," 1994
Bob Dylan, "Idiot Wind," 1975
TLC, "Waterfalls," 1994
Sheryl Crow, "A Change," 1997
En Vogue, "My Loving (You're Never Gonna Get It)," 1992
Beck, "Where It's At," 1996
Toto, "Africa," 1983

Neil Young, *Sleeps with Angels*, 1990
—— with Pearl Jam, *Mirror Ball*, 1995
Liz Phair, "Fuck and Run," 1994
Rolling Stones, *Exile on Main Street*, 1972
Liz Phair, "Supernova," 1994
O'Jays, "Emotionally Yours" (gospel mix), 1991
Madonna, "Swim," 1998
———, "Frozen," 1998
Stevie Wonder, "Conversation Peace," 1995
Rolling Stones, "Jumping Jack Flash," 1968
Elvis Costello, "Complicated Shadows," 1996
Prince, "Thieves in the Temple," 1990
Lou Reed, "Halloween Parade," 1989
Diamanda Galas, "Swing Low Sweet Chariot/Balm in Gilead," 1992
———, "You Must Be Certain of the Devil," 1992
Bob Dylan, "My Back Pages," 1964
———, "Just Like a Woman," 1966
———, "Tangled Up in Blue," 1975
———, "Cold Chains Bound," 1997
———, "Not Dark Yet," 1997

————, "Highlands," 1997
Robert Johnson, "Love in Vain," 1936
Billie Holiday, "All of Me," 1941
Geto Boys, "My Mind's Playin' Tricks on Me," 1991
Bruce Springsteen, "Across the Border," 1995
————, "Sinaloa Cowboys," 1995
————, "The Line," 1995
————, "Balboa Park," 1995
Woody Guthrie, "Tom Joad," 1942
Bruce Springsteen, "Tom Joad," 1996
Bruce Springsteen, "The Promised Land" (live acoustic version), 1996
————, "Born in the U.S.A." (live acoustic version), 1996
————, "This Hard Land" (live acoustic version), 1996
————, "Shut Out the Light" (live acoustic version), 1996
————, "Plane Wreck at Los Gatos (Deportees)" (live in Cleveland), 1996
Woody Guthrie, "Great Duststorm Disaster," 1935
Dan Bern, "Oklahoma," 1996
Bruce Springsteen, "The Ghost of Tom Joad," 1995
Rage Against the Machine, "The Ghost of Tom Joad," 1997
Gil Scott-Heron, "The Other Side," 1994
————, "Message to the Messengers," 1994
Curtis Mayfield, "Back to Living Again," 1996
————, "Ms. Martha," 1996
————, "We People Who Are Darker Than Blue," 1996

M.C. Hammer, "U Can't Touch This," 1990
Rick James, "Super Freak," 1981
Puff Daddy and the Family, "Can't Nobody Hold Me Down," 1996
Missy Elliott, "The Rain," 1997
Mary J. Blige, "My Life," 1994
Roy Ayers, "Everybody Loves the Sunshine," 1976
Brand Nubian, "Wake Up (Sunshine Remix)," 1991
TLC, "Switch," 1994
Jean Knight, "Mr. Big Stuff," 1971
Salt-N-Pepa, "Shoop," 1993
Shirelles, "Will You Still Love Me Tomorrow?" 1960
Fugees, "Ready or Not," 1996
Delfonics, "Ready or Not," 1968
Fugees, "Killing Me Softly," 1996
Roberta Flack, "Killing Me Softly," 1973
Wycleffe Jean, "Gone Till November," 1997
Wailers, "Get Up Stand Up," released in U.S. 1975
War, "Slipping into Darkness," 1971
Poor Righteous Teachers, "Rock This Funky Joint," 1990

Donny Hathaway, "Little Ghetto Boy," 1972
Wu-Tang Clan, "Little Ghetto Boys," 1997
Too Short, "The Ghetto," 1990
Coolio, "Gangsta's Paradise," 1995
Stevie Wonder, "Pastime Paradise," 1976


Miles Davis, *Agharta*, 1975
———, *Pangaea*, 1975
Goldie, "Inner City Life," 1996
Marion Williams, "The Moan," c. 1965
Blaze, "Get Up," 1988
D Train, "Music," 1983
Robert Owens, "A.M. Blues," 1990
Patti LaBelle, "The Spirit's in It," 1981
Al Hudson and One Way featuring Alicia Myers, "You Can Do It," 1979
La India, "Love and Happiness" (Louie Vega remix), 1996
Mariah Carey, "Always Be My Baby" (David Morales remix), 1996
DJ Shadow, "What Color Is Your Soul?" 1996
Miles Davis, *Sketches of Spain*, 1959
Cassandra Wilson, "Hellhound on My Trail," 1993
Van Morrison, "Wild Night," 1971
Cassandra Wilson, "Wild Night," 1993
Hank Williams, "I'm So Lonesome I Could Cry," 1949
Cassandra Wilson, "I'm So Lonesome I Could Cry," 1995
Neil Young, "Harvest Moon," 1992
Cassandra Wilson, "Harvest Moon," 1995
Joni Mitchell, "Black Crow," 1976
Cassandra Wilson, "Black Crow," 1993
———, "Children of the Night," 1993
Monkees, "Last Train to Clarksville," 1966
Cassandra Wilson, "Last Train to Clarksville," 1995
———, "Memphis," 1995
———, "A Little Warm Death," 1995
———, "Solomon Sang," 1995
Steve Coleman and the Five Elements, "Multiplicity of Approaches (An Afrikan Way of Knowing)," 1995
———, "Rhythm People," 1990
———, "Motherland Pulse," 1987
———, "The Mantra (Intonation of Power)," 1995
———, "The Tao of Mad Phat," 1996
———, "The X Format (Standard Deviation)," 1991
———, " 'Round Midnight," 1995
DJ Mark Farina, *Mushroom Jazz*, 1998
Olu Dara, "Zora," 1998

Dianne Reeves, "Old Souls," 1994
———, "Josa Lee," 1994
———, "Afro-Blue," 1991
Olu Dara, "Okra," 1998
—— with Nas, "Jungle," 1998

Alejandro Escovedo, "Gravity/Falling Down," 1992
———, "With These Hands," 1996
Richie Valens, "La Bamba," 1958
Santana, "Black Magic Woman," 1969
———, "Samba Pa Ti," 1970
Los Lobos, "Will the Wolf Survive?" 1984
———, "One Time One Night," 1987
Rage Against the Machine, "Bullet in the Head," 1992
———, "Township Rebellion," 1992
———, "Bombtrack," 1992
———, "Take the Power Back," 1992
———, "Without a Face," 1996
———, "People of the Sun," 1996
Ani DiFranco, "Hide and Seek," 1997
———, "Napoleon," 1996
—— with Utah Phillips, *The Past Doesn't Go Anywhere*, 1996
———, "Willing to Fight," 1997
Sarah McLachlan, "Fumbling Towards Ecstasy," 1994
Rage Against the Machine, "Freedom," 1992
Ani DiFranco, "Untouchable," 1996
Hole, "Violet," 1994
———, "Doll Parts," 1994
P. J. Harvey, "Black Snake Moan," 1995
Blind Lemon Jefferson, "Black Snake Moan," 1926
P. J. Harvey, "To Bring You My Love," 1995
———, "Legs," 1993
Jewel, "Who Will Save Your Soul?" 1994
Tracy Chapman, "Across the Lines," 1988
———, "Behind the Wall," 1988
———, "Give Me One Reason," 1995
Crystal Waters, "Gypsy Woman (She's Homeless)," 1991
Tupac Shakur, "I Ain't Mad at Cha," 1996
Scarface, "Now I Feel Ya," 1993
Bone Thugs n Harmony, "Crossroad," 1995
P. M. Dawn, "Set Adrift on Memory Bliss," 1991
Arrested Development, "Tennessee," 1992
Billie Holiday, "Strange Fruit," 1947
A Tribe Called Quest, "Steve Biko (Stir It Up)," 1993

————, "Excursions," 1991
————, "Electric Relaxation," 1993
————, "Clap Your Hands," 1993
Digable Planets, "Rebirth of Slick (Cool Like Dat)," 1993
————, "Where I'm From," 1993
Edwin Hawkins Singers, "Oh Happy Day," 1969
Clark Sisters, "You Brought the Sunshine," 1983
Winans, "Let My People Go," 1985
BeBe and CeCe Winans, "I'll Take You There," 1991
————, "Addictive Love," 1991
————, "Heaven," 1988
Take 6, "I L-O-V-E U," 1990
Sounds of Blackness, "Optimistic," 1991
Soul Mission, "Table in the Wilderness," 1993
Kirk Franklin and the Family, "Why We Sing," 1994
Kirk Franklin's Nu Nation, "Stomp," 1996
Wu-Tang Clan, "Wu-Revolution," 1997
————, "Da Mystery of Chessboxin'," 1997
————, "Cash Still Rules," 1997
————, "The City," 1997
————, "The Projects," 1997
————, "Hellz Wind Staff," 1997
————, "Reunited," 1997
————, "Triumph," 1997
Sunz of Man, *The Last Shall Be First*, 1998

# Index